LITHUANIA

Independent Again

LITHUANIA
Independent Again

The Autobiography of
VYTAUTAS LANDSBERGIS

Prepared for an English-speaking audience by
Anthony Packer and Eimutis Šova

UNIVERSITY OF WALES PRESS
CARDIFF
2000

English-language version, edited by Anthony Packer, first published in 2000 by University of Wales Press and University of Washington Press

British Library Cataloguing-in-Publication Data.
A catalogue record for this book is available from the British Library.

ISBN 0–7083–1454–6

T

Typeset at Action Publishing Technology, Gloucester
Printed in Great Britain by The Cromwell Press, Trowbridge, Wiltshire

610038

Contents

List of illustrations

Editor's preface

Vytautas Landsbergis's story tells us how Lithuania 'returned to the map of Europe, and how she was allowed to re-enter Western society'. It is a compelling account which is likely to give its readers a new understanding of events of enormous significance both for Europe and the wider world.

The task of preparing this book for an English-speaking audience was shared with Eimutis Šova. His name is not to be found in its text, but Vytautas Landsbergis's words will often be found to reflect the emotions which he, and the many others who spent their lives in exile, felt during the long years when their homeland lay imprisoned. His family had fled Lithuania in 1944, but their story reflects the experience of many who found refuge in the west. They kept faith with the ancient language of their country, and were passionately committed to the hope that Lithuania would eventually become independent again. If their suffering was less extreme than that of the hundreds of thousands who were exiled eastwards under Stalin's oppression, they also experienced a kind of martyrdom.

The international community again acknowledged Lithuania's right to be a free and independent country only after the failed Moscow *putsch* of August 1991. Soon after this it was suggested that Eimutis's experience as a leading member of the Lithuanian community in Britain would be useful in the nation's Parliament. However, he concluded that it was now too late in his lifetime to serve in that way and remained in Wales, his adopted country, but continued making national and international links to benefit the Lithuanian economy. He made repeated visits to his native land, where he enjoyed privileged access to almost every corridor of influence until his death in 1999.

The English translation reflects a close co-operation between Eimutis and myself, and it is a profound sadness that he did not live to see its publication. We first met in March 1991 at the inaugural meeting of the Wales Baltic Society, itself a response to the events of 12–13 January 1991, described in these pages. My family had watched those bloody scenes on the television news as they were happening, in the company of Rimantas Zelvys, then director of the Vilnius Pedagogical Institute, who was staying with us. Some months earlier I had invited a number of Lithuanian academics and politicians to the University at Cardiff for an educational conference in the Welsh capital which seemed likely to provide useful ideas as they began to de-sovietize their schools. Several had planned to come, but the Soviet squeeze on their country which began in December 1990 was extreme, and Rimantas was the only person who managed to escape the restrictions.

As we watched the news bulletins our visitor drew attention to the faces of his friends, who were prepared to face death in that courageous Vilnius crowd. Before he left us we discussed how the democratic cause could be assisted in the aftermath of these horrors. Shortly afterward I received an invitation to arrange a delegation of educationists to visit Vilnius and advise on the reconstruction of the school curriculum. There was also a request, in the name of the government of Lithuania, asking 'intellectuals and people of goodwill around the world', to form 'committees to work for the liberties of the Baltic countries', which led to the foundation of the Baltic Society in Cardiff some weeks later. It gathered together members of the exiled Lithuanian, Latvian and Estonian communities in Wales, and a handful of Welsh people, some of whom felt that developments in the Baltic countries reflected arguments which affected their own national identity, though in extremer form.

In March 1991 the society saw its task as one of prompting the conscience of the community and the government, perhaps for a period of years. However, events moved rapidly. Only four months later its members gathered to celebrate the Baltic countries' independence! During that August meeting I told them how our educational delegation had arrived in Vilnius, only six weeks before, in July 1991, as visitors in a city under occupation, where the KGB was accommodated more luxuriously than the nation's Parliament. Aware of these facts, I had judged it best that my companions were not informed that I had a mission beyond our common purpose, and had gone privately to the headquarters of Sąjūdis with a message from the general secretary of the Welsh political party Plaid Cymru. It was a simple note of democratic regard, and support for the movement's objectives, but was the first such message to come from any British political party.[1] When I reached Sąjūdis's offices its general secretary and spokesmen for economic and external affairs received me. The atmosphere was, at first, very formal, and after introduction, I was asked three questions before I could put my own. The first was: 'What is your movement's attitude to the violence in Ireland?' There was a notable relaxation when I asserted: 'We abhor violence.' The second enquiry was about Lithuania's chance of admission into the European Community. I responded, in the context of the time, by noting the historical links between nations around the Baltic shores, suggesting that EFTA with its Scandinavian interests might be more favourable to early admission. The third question was: 'When will Wales be free?' I parried by asking, somewhat forcibly: 'When will Lithuania be free?!'

We had all laughed! No date for Lithuania's freedom could possibly have been set that July afternoon, and there was the obvious and dreadful possibility that the real answer was 'maybe never', but now, *scarcely six weeks later*, we were celebrating its accomplishment! The Baltic Society members talked into that summer evening, rejoicing not just at what had been achieved, but for *what it symbolized for the future of the global community*. Estonian, Latvian, Lithuanian, Welsh and English people together, we were celebrating the return of three national states to the map of Europe. To recall Matthew Arnold's words, 'It was good on that day to be alive!', but it is also important to say that this was no celebration of murky nationalism, but rather happiness that a gentle dream had been realized, and that the weak had overcome the strong. The Baltic lands were rejoicing at the failure of a prolonged attempt to end their distinctiveness. Their communal identities are a product (like those of the nations of Britain) of long centuries of community life. Although a part of the glorious variety of human cultural accomplishment which is Europe, they had suffered an attempt, driven with consistent determination over fifty years, to push families from the land and to alienate communities from their identity. During that time nothing of their achievement – neither culture, nor language, nor religion, nor the memorials of history – was regarded as anything but an obstacle to be removed. The enveloping utilitarianism of the communist state had dissembled this empty brutalism, claiming a lofty universalism for its goals. It successfully deceived not a few in the western world as a result.

As we rejoiced on that August evening many issues left unfinished at the end of the Second World War seemed to be moving toward resolution. Many lives had been ended in its course, and many more wasted or violently remade in its aftermath. These things were dramatically true for many in our party, whose older members had passed their lives in its long shadow, which had lingered even after the death of the two great bullies of Moscow and Berlin, whose para-noiac need to control was a common factor in the separate socialisms they espoused. Stalin, the longer-surviving of these evil Titans, had spawned the Cold War, which had poisoned the collective psyche of the entire world, its malignant stalemate infecting attitudes everywhere. We were thankful that this dreadful phase of history had reached its end, and being in Cardiff, the capital city of a nation which presents one of its central cultural forms to the wider world at the Llangollen International Eisteddfod, many of us hoped that what had now been achieved might encourage other small historic communities to explore the politics of harmonization and peaceful diversity. We hoped that this success would encourage the politicians of larger states, who can influence the future of smaller countries for good or for ill, to respond to such legitimate communal aspirations with civilized magnanimity.

This book gives a privileged glimpse of the mind of one of the makers of modern Europe. Sajūdis's objective of reinstating the sovereignty and indepen-dence of Lithuania must have seemed virtually unattainable when first announced. Its leader, Landsbergis, was required to tread a dangerous path knowingly, and he reached its end only because his actions were in considered harmony with events. He took risks as the confrontation neared its climax, placing his life, and that of others, on the line. Yet as one reads this account one is more likely to be impressed with the economy of his risk-taking than to criti-cize him for impetuosity. He directed situations with a careful calculus. His precise insistence on the legality of Lithuania's case and the total illegality of the Soviet occupation, together with his stubborn refusal to compromise the restora-tion of the Lithuanian state, ensured that this goal was achieved. Yet while his determination to reinstate that embodiment of what the Welsh writer D. J. Williams has referred to as *y bod cenhedlig* (the national being) was pursued with extraordinary restraint, the implied passion was remarkable. It is probable that the source of the formidable gifts of interpretation apparent throughout his political career is best located by reference to the intellectual inheritance of his family, and particularly to his grandparents' participation in that luminary circle whose brilliance and tenacity enabled the reconstruction of the Lithuanian linguistic inheritance. Their success made a modern Lithuanian state possible in defiance of the Tsarist autocracy, which consistently suppressed all attempts to promote education in the native tongue or constitutional reform throughout its two centuries of occupation. We also note Landsbergis's devotion to the work of the great Lithuanian composer Čiurlionis. His identification with the lofty universalism of that many-sided, artistic and mythopoetic genius of which he is the leading interpreter is the key to our comprehension of his own vision. As for other influences, I recall a conversation when he referred to the older literature and music of Wales. This memory allows me to observe that survivals from the primordial level of the national tradition are much more extensive in Lithuania than in Wales, and that the enjoyment of this profound folkloric and vernacular musical tradition is as fundamental to Landsbergis's outlook as it was to Čiurlionis's. This affection was integral to his family's devotion to the nation's cause in earlier generations. The nation's song has always been a vehicle which allowed its people to hint at their real aspirations in the darkest times, and to give full voice to them at others.

Landsbergis's triumph emerged from the tense manœuvring of the last decade of Communist influence. Four events are selected to suggest the momentum of those years, and to illustrate how the Lithuanian experience contributed to the global outcome. We first recall the strikes organized in the Polish shipyards by Lech Walesa in the early 1980s; then the scenes in 1989 when the people of Berlin ripped down the Wall which had divided their city, with bare hands and hammers. The Vilnius nightmare of January 1991 follows, but the last scene is that of Boris Yeltsin, standing on a tank near White House (the parliamentary home of the infant Russian democracy) in Moscow in August of the same year. Defiant, and inviting the people to dismiss the *putschist* threat to reinstate Stalinism, he said: 'Remember the people of Vilnius. They showed us the way!' Such recollections, and particularly this last, will help the reader take measure of the account rendered in this book. It relates the attempted *coup* in Moscow to the earlier events in Vilnius in a way which raises profound questions about the real relationship between Gorbachev and the conspirators. Yeltsin's choice of words at that revolutionary moment helps us recall the state of public awareness at that time, to recognize just how awful were the forces which confronted Vytautas Landsbergis, and to understand just how finely balanced the outcome actually was.

Just before Easter 1993, in a meeting in the Lithuanian Seimas between Professor Landsbergis and a University of Wales delegation visiting the Lithuanian universities, I mentioned that he had arranged to visit Cardiff in 1991, but had changed course when the deepening crisis of that autumn made it necessary for him to travel to Washington instead, and said that he 'might be pleased to visit the capital city of Wales at some time in the future'. The reader will be amused to learn of my dismay when he turned without further thought to name a date – as I was entirely without authority to arrange the civic visit appropriate for someone of his standing! The outcome, however, was his visit to Cardiff, by courtesy of its lord mayor, in April 1994 when Eimutis Šova and I arranged his programme. It was during that visit that I asked Professor Landsbergis if he had considered writing his memoirs, volunteering our services to translate them into English if he should! This work is the outcome of that discussion, and while it was essentially translated by Eimutis, I take responsibility for the present text, as each phrase and sentence has needed to reflect the finely honed expression and razor-edged nuancing of Professor Landsbergis's style in the English idiom. The reader will perceive a laconic humour at work, which provides some measure of his restless intelligence in application both to the affairs of state and their narration.

I record my thanks to Professor Vytautas Landsbergis for allowing our involvement in so interesting a task. Engagement with his text was an opportunity to observe closely a political strategy conducted with scrupulous regard for the need to sustain human dignity, and with profound respect for the deep ties which unite human beings beneath the necessary carapaces of culture, locality and opinion. These values are what make us human, for we are less than that when they are absent. Their reflection here is the more striking for their having been pursued when the all-encompassing Soviet state did not promote them unconditionally in the public realm. Landsbergis's insistence that these matters were respected when others had lost sight of them underwrites the moral force of the revolution for which he worked. The spiritual kernel of this work is found in its description of truth, justice and human rights as 'the most precious gifts of humanity', and the author's consequent announcement that these gifts 'are to be proclaimed to the far corners of the world as the essence of the human love for freedom'. Here is the true message of his book, and it is my hope that our translation will give that message wings.

Appreciation is due to Dr Alan Kemp, Professor Desmond Hayes, Professor John Hines and John Rowe for extensive observations on the script and other encouragement, and to Cerian and Tomos Packer for typing many corrections as the manuscript was pulled into shape. I am indebted to Councillor Peter Perkins; the late Councillor Malcolm Thomas; Councillor Chris Franks; Dick Regan of Premiere Books; Professor David Reynolds; Professor Rimantas Zelvys; Virginia Zjukienė; Dr Irena-Egle Laumenskaitė; Dr Laima Andrikienė; and the late Antanas Nesavas, former Lithuanian ambassador in London, for help at various stages of our Lithuanian project. I should like to record my thanks to Ned Thomas and Susan Jenkins, former and present directors of the University of Wales Press for their enthusiasm, and to other members of the Press staff for help with the preparation of the manuscript, particularly Janet Davies; to Mary Madden for preparing the index; and especially to Ceinwen Jones, editorial manager at the Press, for consistent cheerfulness and firm professionalism in guiding the manuscript through the final stages. Darius Furmonavicius of the University of Bradford has ensured correct accentuation of Lithuanian names and taken great care that my final interpretation rings true to the original intentions of the author, while Dr Thomas Lane and Professor Vejas Liulevicius provided helpful comment on our joint work in the Appendix, which should be read if a longer perspective on Professor Landsbergis's achievement is needed.

I return finally to the memory of my partner in this task, Eimutis Šova, who also worked indefatigably for the ideals for which Sąjūdis struggled. *Pie Jesu Domine, dona ei requiem*, and my deepest appreciation to Ruta his wife, who has also shared in the work.

Anthony Packer, Cardiff: St David's Day, 2000

Note
[1] Plaid Cymru – the Party of Wales, is the political group which has traditionally held the concepts of self-government and full national status before the electorate in Wales. When I met Professor Landsbergis for the second time two years later (the first meeting was with the educational delegation, and took place at a time when the Lithuanian Parliament was heavily guarded by Lithuanian volunteers and carried disturbingly obvious scars of recent conflict) I told him about this discussion with the Sąjūdis officials and he told me that it was 'not forgotten' that Dafydd Wigley of Plaid Cymru had been the first politician to request full diplomatic recognition for independent Lithuania in the House of Commons.

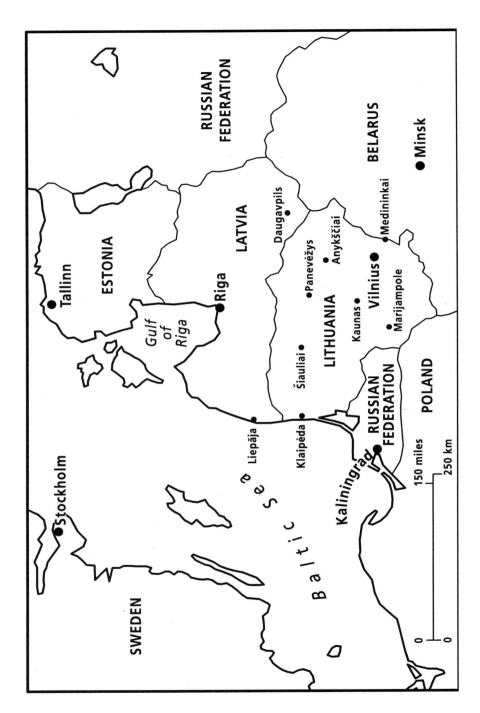

CHAPTER 1

Introductory

Wherever one may live in this world, truth, justice and human rights are ideals which must be fought for. Our country, Lithuania, was occupied by the Soviet Union during the years when the Soviet system was at its most oppressive, yet those ideals were always close to the hearts of our people, who kept alive with fierce determination the hope that our land would become an independent nation once again. They were dark times, and it was depressing to realize that our very determination had become something of an embarrassment to the western powers whom we had regarded as natural allies in our cause. When we learned to our dismay that our attitudes had come to be viewed as unrealistic with the passage of time, we clung to them the more closely, believing that even if the world of *realpolitik* viewed us with amused tolerance it would find it hard to disregard our small nation entirely. Our patience was sorely tried and there were times when both sides in the Cold War seemed obviously irritated by our persistence, but neither the communist bloc nor the western powers ever treated us with complete indifference, and when we eventually found that we were in a position to make a serious bid to regain our freedom we discovered that the weakening Soviet system treated us with considerably more caution than it had shown in the earlier cases of Hungary and Czechoslovakia.

Lithuania is a small country on the Baltic Sea which has common borders now with Poland, Belarus, Latvia and Russia. In 1940 it was occupied by, and then incorporated into, the Soviet Union. This occupation ended within a year when the German army marched in to subjugate us, but was renewed in 1944 and continued after the war with Germany came to an end in 1945. The Soviet army re-entered our country with renewed violence, and the second occupation which began then continued until 11 March 1990, when, after free elections (the first to take place for over fifty years), our Parliament declared our country 'independent again'. These events took place at a time when the Soviet Union was undergoing a process of reform (*perestroika*), and those of us who spoke for our country in that period were attempting to take advantage of the new attitudes at the heart of that process. Recalling the injustices which had accompanied the Soviet invasion, and all that had happened in the years which had passed, we asked for negotiations which would lead to the withdrawal of the Soviet army from our country. Naturally we hoped this would bring both sides to a real reconciliation, but our proposals for intergovernmental negotiation were briskly rejected by the Soviets with the argument that Lithuania was a 'part of the Soviet Union' and the assertion that any change in Lithuania's position 'could only be discussed within the constitution of the Soviet Union'. These diktats implied that independence would come (if ever) only on terms which had been fully agreed by Moscow, and it was only too evident that the authorities there were wholly unsympathetic to our cause. It was natural in these circumstances that our reply should be blunt. We had already made what we believed were the necessary decisions about our country's future, and therefore responded by pointing out that the Soviet constitution was *not* ours because it had been imposed on Lithuania without consent. We announced that we did not recognize the authority of a constitution which was imposed on our people only by the fact that Soviet forces had occupied, and continued to occupy, our territory, and affirmed: 'We have our own constitution. As no foreign constitution can have legal standing in another sovereign state, the decrees which are issued under your authority can have no validity in Lithuania.' It was a defiant stand, and it was taken in the belief that those western countries which had never recognized Lithuania's incorporation into the Soviet Union in 1940 would support us. Sadly, however, such support did not come, and it quickly became apparent that western attitudes towards us were ambivalent at best. They said: 'We recognize your *right* to independence', but they also modified and trimmed their position by saying: 'We cannot give diplomatic recognition until you have control of your country's borders', asking us in the mean time 'not to rock the boat for Gorbachev'.

The concern of the western powers for Gorbachev's success was apparent to us at every turn. They took this position without regard for the justice of our case, which seemed to be of small importance to them at that time. From our point of view, however, they were in fact supporting the continuing illegal occupation of Lithuania and reinforcing the Soviet view that the mere act of retaining a military force in Lithuania, and controlling its borders, would be sufficient to ensure the acquiescence of the West in our continued subjugation. While the West proclaimed in principle our people's right to control its future through the democratic process, and claimed that they did not recognize the legality of the original annexation of our country, in practice they were not prepared to apply these principles by supporting our demand that the control of our country's borders should be placed in the hands of its legally elected government. In this situation we were forced to be realistic, recognizing the West's difficulty, while maintaining our own position staunchly. We formulated demands which were not inflexible, advancing our proposals with considerable caution even though our opponents insisted in portraying us as demanding, undiplomatic and impolite. The propaganda war against us was systematic, and for a while it had the effect of making our policies unpopular with many Western politicians, though events eventually carried us through these difficulties. In the end it was our actions which touched Europe's conscience rather more than our arguments, and though the path we followed turned out to be a difficult one, it was probably the only one we could have taken. Events proved that we were right, but the cost was high. Our cause survived only because it was supported at every point by countless private individuals who contributed through their beliefs and their deeds to our nation's struggle for freedom. Their selflessness and their sacrifices were huge, and were certainly equal to those of the martyrs and heroes of other times, being particularly evident during the days and nights between 11 and 15 January 1991, when the whole world saw the awful casualties we suffered as we came face to face with the brutal and absolutely unrelenting forces of a totalitarian regime which had oppressed us for so long, and showed no shame in trying to crush us in the full glare of the world's television cameras.

Our national suffering came to a head on that night of 12–13 January 1991 when demonstrators took their own lives in their hands. Journalists and camera crews relayed the people's determination and bravery to the free world. We can truly say that this was the night when Lithuania was reborn, to become a nation again; when our nationhood, so brutally abrogated by the aggressors of the Second World War and trampled upon during the fifty years of Soviet subjugation, was truly restored; when our people, standing in unarmed crowds and singing as they faced the menace of the Red Army's tanks, reclaimed their country's birthright and its future for themselves. Though they were shot at, and in many cases were crushed by the tanks, they refused to give way. Though they were taunted bitterly, and insulted in the language of the Cold War as 'extremists' and 'nationalists', they stood their ground and in doing so discovered a new freedom which would triumph over those who had planned to be their murderers. It is difficult to express in words the moral force of the occasion; it was as if the crowd, as it sang, became invincible. People became fearless, their spirits soared, and the threats, the insults and the violence hurled at them seemed, by some strange contradiction, to strengthen their resolve.

Of course, the crowd was neither extremist nor fascist. The extremists were the men they were facing, who were prepared to kill unarmed people because they had orders from Moscow to do so. As I think back to the events, I recall only too painfully how little attention was paid by the civilians who turned up that evening to the personal danger which they faced. They thought of nothing but the independence and honour of their country; and had no hesitation in claiming it for their own. Many people have asked me since whether I experienced any doubts that Sunday night as the tanks came roaring into Vilnius in anger, with their guns blazing, ready to spill blood. I have been asked whether, with the whole future of Lithuania in the balance, it did not occur to me and my associates that our stand was not justified and that we might be precipitating a tragedy. Was I, at any time during that awful night, in the thick of what must have seemed a quite desperate attempt to revive the Lithuanian state and liberate our country, uncertain of our stand? Did I consider that we might be fighting for a lost cause, or that we would perish, together with the nation?

My answer to these questions is an emphatic 'No!' It did not enter our minds even for a moment to consider that ours might be a lost cause. It was not in our hearts, either as leaders or as the ordinary people, to contemplate defeat. 'They may *kill* us', I told a journalist, 'but they cannot do worse than that!' Those who were guilty of the murders and the other atrocities of that awful night were *outsiders* who had *come* to Lithuania to commit their evil deeds. Whenever in history the occupying armies of foreign conquerors have been confronted by an oppressed people which has taken its own stand, on its own ground, and in its own cause, there is always an attempt to blame the resistance for the casualties. We understood these tricks of propaganda, not least because that dreadful night was not the first time in its history that our people had felt forced to offer lives in sacrifice on the altar of liberty. It was well understood by everyone present that the outcome of this struggle depended simply on the preparedness of the few to sacrifice themselves for the many. Time and again, both outside and inside Parliament, in the centre of Vilnius, outside the television centre and elsewhere in the city, our civilian soldiers of freedom had vowed, sometimes aloud, sometimes in the quietness of their hearts, a simple vow of 'No retreat!' No one who was there could ever reproach our people for their insistence that our country should stand equal with other nations. We all knew the risk of casualties, and we all knew that our lives were on the line, but our hearts told us clearly that the struggle was a noble one which we must face with dignity, without ever contemplating the possibility of abandoning our principles. If I regret anything of that night, it is that if lives had to be lost, mine was not one of them, and I still ask myself from time to time why the Soviet system, so long practised in studied brutality, did not adopt the simpler course of sending a trained assassin to take me out.

The events of those days in Vilnius soon became known throughout the world and have had a much greater effect on the world than the war which began in the Persian Gulf at around the same time, because they started a chain of events which resulted in the eventual failure of Gorbachev's attempt to restructure communism. Our actions and his response to them demonstrated that what some western journalists termed Gorbachev's 'prison reform' was wholly inadequate. What happened that night in Vilnius made it clear that true independence for the nations inside the Soviet Union could be achieved only through such sacrifices, and revealed the new dangers which would follow as that 'prison of nations' began to crumble and fall. My small, brave country was at the forefront of this change. Our unwavering belief in truth, justice, human rights and freedom, and some fifty years of waiting, had enabled us, at last, to promote the transformation which had been hoped for by so many for so long, in both East and West.

This book is my testimony to startling events which remain vivid in the minds of many people in Lithuania, and I hope that it will introduce Lithuania and the quality of its national spirit to people around the world. But I must also emphasize that while my country's spiritual victory was achieved by the struggle of its own people, the recovery of our national independence is not an achievement for Lithuania alone. I say this because we all knew during our hour of crisis that our hope was shared with other human communities throughout the world. We were sustained in that dark hour by *ties of humanity*, and we knew with certainty that the spirit which sustained us, both before and during the hour of victory, was a common bond with many others, both inside and beyond our own land, who also longed for what we hoped to achieve. This bond, the common concern for truth, justice and human rights, is the most precious of gifts, and this book is an attempt to celebrate their importance and to proclaim to the far corners of the world that fundamental love for freedom whose realization is an absolute condition for retaining our humanity in the modern world. What we have achieved in Lithuania is something which we must share urgently with all humankind. It was the recognition of the need for such fundamental values to be expressed in the fabric of our social and political life which sustained us all through the unforgettable experiences which are discussed in this book, which recalls a time when the struggle to achieve freedom for our nation was at its most difficult.

CHAPTER 2

The night that stirred the world's conscience

We approached that night in January 1991 in a political gloom which deepened through the cold, dark nights of December. In October 1990 Soviet officials of the highest rank had abandoned negotiations with us, making it plain that they had no interest in further discussion. They had decreed that Lithuania must stay inside the Soviet central planning system with no control of its own production, and that its finances were to remain under the supervision of the State Bank of the USSR. However, as we were already moving towards complete independence we rejected their conditions, and proposed further negotiations to establish an *international* trade agreement. This brought on fierce Soviet scorn and anger and a threat that our economy would be brought to its knees during the winter of 1990–1. When I mentioned these threats to the British prime minister, Margaret Thatcher, during a visit to London in November 1990, she was astounded, and asked: 'Why should they want to crush you when you are manufacturing for them?' However, it soon became clear that the aim was not economic but political. The Soviets had no wish to allow a controlled colony to become an independent partner.

It is probable that the failure of their attempt at economic blockade, together with our determined but passive resistance to the campaign of terror which had been conducted by their military authorities against Lithuania during the spring of 1990, was what provoked the Soviet government to consider further measures to crush Lithuania's spirit. They were already determined not to give the country away under any circumstances, and the drastic and brutal action which followed was planned in total secrecy. Though we had no information about what was afoot, we could sense that something was coming, and so were able to brace ourselves for what followed.

Gorbachev was encouraged by the French to demand the expulsion of the Lithuanian, Latvian and Estonian foreign ministers from the December meeting of the newly constituted CSCE (Conference for Security and Co-operation in Europe), which they had been invited to attend as official observers. It is possible that he had come to the conclusion that the West would not object to the Soviet Union taking more stringent and imperialistic measures. In Paris, the president of Finland, eager to ingratiate himself with the Soviet leader, argued relentlessly that the 'troublesome' Baltic states were responsible for the increasing tension. The Kremlin also intended that the Baltic states should take the blame for the Soviet policy of repression.

Subversive organizations had already been established by Moscow, and they were now activated. Military operations were then set in motion and the announcement made that young men throughout Lithuania were to be conscripted into the Soviet army, by force if necessary. Various tactics of psychological warfare were used to undermine us, including attempts by groups planted within our movement to persuade the supporters of independence to capitulate.

Official Soviet propaganda at this time was humming with reports which represented Lithuania and the neighbouring Baltic countries as unstable. The implication was that supporters of the Soviet regime were increasingly in need of some kind of protection, and it was openly suggested that it might soon be necessary to disarm the 'illegal armed forces' of our sovereign states by direct action from Moscow and to take over our defence establishments in order to eliminate the 'local criminal elements' who were alleged to have taken charge of them. The purpose was clear, and orders were issued authorizing the Soviet army to patrol the streets of Lithuania and the other Baltic states, and 'to use its legal right' to break into people's homes. As such decrees were in fact in blatant disregard of the Soviet constitution which was supposedly being 'defended', we arranged for a joint session of the Parliaments of the three Baltic states in Vilnius, held on 1 December 1990, to discuss these problems and to formulate a common response. It declared that our countries would not sign any 'federation treaty' dictated by the Kremlin, and demanded the withdrawal of Soviet troops from our territories. We were, however, careful to guarantee their safety and the legal rights of their families throughout the process of withdrawal.

On 10 December I was in Washington, where I asked George Bush, the president of the United States, to extend his government's political support and protection to Lithuania. I would have been satisfied with a simple statement acknowledging that our constitutional independence was being established and should not be interfered with by anyone. As Lithuania already had its own constitution by then, I believed that such an acknowledgement by the USA would be sufficient to check Gorbachev and to limit the Soviet threat to Lithuania. The president, however, felt that Gorbachev would be reluctant to risk damaging Soviet relations with the West, and so failed to recognize the danger to us as significant. Today with the wisdom of hindsight we know better, and we also suspect that a tacit agreement existed between the two capitals that Moscow was not to shed blood in Lithuania, while Washington would not openly recognize our independence by appointing a diplomatic representative. Gorbachev broke that agreement in January, but sadly Bush did not change his position until the following September.

On 11 December 1990, an international organization called Tradition–Family–Property presented Gorbachev with a petition in support of Lithuanian independence: it contained 5,218,020 signatures collected in some twenty-six countries and found a place in the *Guinness Book of Records*. Its political efficacy, however, depended on how much heed the rulers of the USSR were prepared to pay to the expressed opinion of ordinary people. Unfortunately but unsurprisingly, the opinion of the common people once again carried no weight.

I summed up the position at a conference speech in Oslo at the beginning of January 1991, when I said that European cohabitation with the Soviet communist dictatorship had produced a convoluted pragmatism, and a consensus which seemed to lack any will to recognize the independence of the Baltic states. I added that Europe was 'welcoming a monster, sick in body and mind – a terrorist state' by embracing the Soviet Union. Later that evening I had cause to reflect bitterly on these words when the news came that the son of Romualdas Ozolas, our deputy prime minister, had been brutally murdered in Vilnius.

Events in Lithuania were now moving at great speed. The pro-Soviet factions began to rally mobs, engage *provocateurs* and float rumours – of an imminent price rise for example – in an attempt to create a situation which would allow the potential leaders of the *coup d'état*, who were already gathering in Moscow, to intervene when it was convenient. A body called Future Forum emerged around this time. Ostensibly offering a 'third road' in the political difficulties which faced Lithuania, it had in fact been created by the KGB. It offered nothing for our country's future, proposing ideas which implied only a return to the past with renewed dependence on Moscow. At around the same time Lithuania's 'separated' Communist party, clearly hoping to retain some chance of being elected, changed its name, though it showed its true colours simultaneously by declaring its opposition to our policy of restoring properties which had been confiscated under the Soviet system to their original owners. Some of its leaders added to the growing tension by threatening to take over our state-owned television service for their own purposes 'by any means necessary'. It was increasingly clear that a crisis was looming, and it was precipitated soon enough when the government announced a general and very steep increase in food prices, without either warning or explanation, despite the fact that Parliament had already refused to agree any increase, because it recognized that serious destabilization of the country could follow.

The sequence of events which now unfolded was too threatening to be seen as accidental. The government took advantage of the parliamentary New Year recess to issue the fateful price increase order. On Sunday 6 January, I stayed up until the small hours of the morning expecting Mrs Kazimiera Prunskienė, the prime minister, to come to an appointment at which I hoped to persuade her to rescind the order implementing price rises. Significantly, she failed to turn up. A meeting of the Presidium of the Supreme Council had been arranged for the following morning in order to discuss the Soviet Union's actions with regard to Lithuanian conscripts. The meeting issued a protest against this aggression, declaring it to be an 'abduction of our citizens'. Just before I went into the meeting, I sent a telegram to President Gorbachev, which offered to meet him 'at any time, at any place' to negotiate on this and other matters. As it was Christmas Day according to the calendar of the Russian Orthodox Church, I added seasonal greetings to him. Though he did not reply to me, I then heard that my prime minister had arranged her own meeting with him. On learning this, we quickly decided to authorize her to speak on our behalf about negotiations with the Soviet Union, and she flew to Moscow almost at once. We had plenty to think about on that front, but I wanted to calm the general fears about price increases, so I decided to broadcast to the nation that evening to tell the people that the Supreme Council planned to debate the country's food prices fully on the following day, and used the opportunity to plead against over-reaction, which might cause confusion at home at a time when we faced this overwhelming threat from abroad.

As we were preparing for this debate on the question of food prices on the morning of 8 January, a crowd gathered outside the Lithuanian Parliament. It included a mixture of Soviet *provocateurs* – Russian soldiers in civilian clothes – and Vilnius residents who were shouting and cursing in Russian. The *provocateurs* in the crowd were encouraging its members to storm the Parliament building, either to ransack it or to force the guards to use arms. Those of us who were inside the building were not intimidated by this display and stood firm despite the threat. There was no intent of having recourse to armed force, but this disturbance made us aware of the extreme threat which our democracy was now facing. For this reason I decided to address the people of Vilnius on television once again before the debate began, and appealed to everyone who supported national independence to come at once to stand outside the Parliament buildings 'to defend the government, because otherwise a foreign one will be installed'. After this I went straight to the debating chamber, where the session was beginning, attended by all members of the government (with the exception of the prime minister who was now in Moscow). Members of the Supreme Council[1] then decided to repeal the government's decision to raise food prices after a very short debate. The situation was an extraordinary one, and the deputy prime minister, Algirdas Brazauskas, demonstrated his frustration at this unprecedented scene in which members of Parliament were combining to rescind an important government decision by urging his ministerial colleagues to leave the Chamber. This was an obvious attempt to set the government against Parliament and I immediately intervened, reminding members of their oath to the Republic of Lithuania, and of the crisis we were facing. It was a successful move, and the ministers remained in the chamber to see the defeat of their policy. When the debate ended, I went immediately to a window at the front of the Parliament building, where I announced a return to the old prices to the crowd below.

People everywhere had now become fully aware of the momentous character of the events going on in Parliament, and many of them had assembled outside the building, some carrying the Lithuanian tricolour. This huge crowd peacefully brushed aside the remnants of the earlier hostile demonstration. Those people were now outnumbered and confused, so they kept quiet, but everyone was aware that their threat remained. The tension subsided, though there was anger in many minds at what had just happened, and at the fact that the Soviet military were still threatening over 9,400 young Lithuanian men who had refused conscription into the armed forces of a foreign state with forcible abduction. As president I had already written urgent letters to the leaders of the democratic nations, and to the president of the European Parliament, indicating Gorbachev's responsibility for any casualties which might result from this policy. Though we can now see that the threat was probably a tactic designed to divert attention from even larger issues, it created a great deal of tension at the time.

Political events were moving apace, one shock following another. The prime minister returned from her discussion with Gorbachev on the afternoon of 8 January, her visit having achieved nothing. She resigned her position immediately, and the government fell with her, as the constitution required. The resignation was, of course, a gesture against us. Mrs Prunskienė put on a brave face in the debating chamber, but her subsequent explanations were clumsy and conflicting because she went about accusing members of Parliament of accelerating the crisis. With or without her help, the tensions inside Parliament were now reflected everywhere, and the supporters of the Soviet regime decided to call a general strike. Their efforts brought Vilnius railway station and the airport to an immediate stop, but on the other side of the argument members of the Sąjūdis independence movement supplied food to stranded travellers, and began a civic vigil outside Parliament. The next development came when Soviet forces appeared suddenly in armoured vehicles and surrounded the television and radio broadcasting installations in several places in the city. People were quick to recognize this provocation and responded by coming out in large numbers to surround these buildings with a human chain. On 9 January, as I began to discuss the appointment of a new prime minister with various parliamentary groups, two huge demonstrations formed. One of them, consisting mainly of Russians, was opposed to independence. The other was larger, as the supporters of independence gathered together. Many of those in this crowd were ready to lay down their lives.

On 10 January, Gorbachev sent a message to our Parliament which stated that unless we accepted and recognized 'the continuing validity of the Soviet constitution in Lithuania' he would institute 'presidential rule to prevent the rebirth of the bourgeois system'. It was an ultimatum which reflected exactly what the local communist groups had been demanding, and as it was increasingly obvious that Soviet armed forces were planning brutal action to implement the threat which this message carried, trouble seemed to be inevitable when we rejected the ultimatum. However, what was hard to predict was the timing and the type of action being considered. It seemed likely that the Kremlin's response would be timed to coincide with the Gulf War, which everybody knew was about to begin, because events in the Middle East would distract attention from its actions. It seemed we might have only a few days to wait, and in fact Soviet military action began without warning on 11 January, when troops began to occupy the government administrative buildings, beginning with the Press Centre. Their subsequent actions were brutal in the extreme, and many civilians were wounded. The situation was confusing, and became further confused when the Soviet Union's supporters in Lithuania seized the opportunity to announce the formation of a 'National Salvation Committee' with the purpose of 'taking the government into its own hands'.

While all this was going on, the KGB was rushing Vytautas Sakalauskas (a member of the Soviet diplomatic corps, and a former prime minister of the Lithuanian Soviet Socialist Republic) back from a posting in Mozambique to Moscow. It was intended that he should become head of a puppet government. This was not known to us at the time, but I did have some insight into the political dangers which lurked in the governmental vacuum. The tactics of the Soviet leadership were to undermine and harass us on every front, and Moscow was now busy broadcasting 'that the crisis in the Lithuanian government' could be resolved only by supporting the National Salvation Committee. The pressures being put on us were constant and extreme, and the intention was to push us into a position where we would move in panic. We had been hard at work, and most of us had not left the Parliament building for days. For myself, I was engaged in almost constant discussion as we did our best to make sense of the situation. On the night of 10 January Parliament assented to my appointment of Albertas Šimėnas as the new prime minister, and we threw open the front windows on the second floor of the Parliament building to allow me to present him to the patriotic crowd which filled the square and the streets outside, as 'the son of poor peasants, a people's elected deputy, and the new prime minister of Lithuania'. The crowd responded with thunderous approval, and on the following day the Council confirmed the new government. Except for the new prime minister and the appointment of a few temporary ministers, there were few changes and we did not appoint new deputy prime ministers at this point. It was a relief to know that Lithuania had a working government again, and we were pleased to have re-established a semblance of normality. None of us anticipated that this government was destined to hold office for less than two days. We were part of a larger drama, which was being prepared without reference to ourselves. While there is still a mystery about what exactly our opponents were planning at that time, I now believe that an assault on our Parliament building was scheduled for the night of 11 January, and that it was deferred because something had gone wrong between the political leaders of the USSR, the KGB headquarters in Moscow, the Soviet military intelligence staff and their conspiring supporters in Vilnius. This is conjecture, but it has come to light that the idea of enticing Albertas Šimėnas, our new prime minister, to Moscow under the pretext of new negotiations, was actually considered, but for some reason the move was abandoned.

On 12 January the Lithuanian Supreme Council made the highly significant declaration that the Soviet Union's actions constituted 'an act of open war against Lithuania', and ordered that a Temporary Council for National Defence should be established. An instruction was also issued for documents to be prepared to authorize the legal establishment of a Lithuanian government-in-exile, if the elected government in Lithuania should be prevented from carrying out its responsibilities. The crisis was deepening, and our foreign minister was given authority to implement this plan if circumstances should so dictate. On the evening of the 11th, he was actually instructed to leave for Poland. We devised these plans knowing the Soviet capacity for psychological warfare. Had we been overthrown, a puppet government would have been installed immediately, and we would have been blackmailed: 'give in to our demands or be responsible for the casualties'. A puppet structure under Soviet control would then have assumed the title and authority of a 'Supreme Council', so we stated that the lawful government would relinquish its legal right to govern rather than collaborate under duress with Soviet policy. Not everyone (even among our ministers) comprehended the full importance of the decisions which were taken so urgently that night, and some even felt insulted when they did. However, some of us remembered the events which had overtaken our country in 1940 only too well, and knew that we were working against time.

Our contingency plans were an attempt to ensure that something would be rescued from the crisis which was threatening to engulf us: they were also a response to what was happening in other places. The Soviet leaders held their own sessions in Moscow, some of them in secret, some in public. On 12 January, the Supreme Soviet decided to send a delegation to Vilnius, to analyse the situation and supposedly to mediate. That evening I spoke on the telephone with Nikolai Dementey, chairman of the Supreme Soviet in Belarus, who was designated as leader of that delegation, attempting to persuade him to come at once, with his colleagues, to Vilnius. I really implored him to do this, but he replied stolidly that they would stay overnight in Minsk and proceed to Vilnius by car the next morning. I noticed that his explanation was laboured, and I was filled with foreboding, and kept thinking of the Tbilisi massacre of 1989 when it had seemed more than mere coincidence that Eduard Shevardnadze (the Soviet foreign minster of the time) had also found excuses to delay his departure from Moscow 'until the following morning'. While he slept the military had gone on a killing spree. I telephoned Nikolai Dementey repeatedly, trying to persuade him to change his mind, but to no avail. He and his colleagues stayed in Minsk overnight.

My anxiety was justified: the Soviets had decided to act without delay, and a terrible slaughter took place on the streets of Vilnius that very night. The disturbance began just after midnight when Soviet tanks and armoured troop carriers loaded with special KGB riot troops came roaring through our streets. They drove straight to predetermined destinations: their orders were to seize the radio and television studios and offices in the town, and the television tower which stands on the outskirts of the city of Vilnius. But as they followed their instructions, the people responded to their manœuvres, and a sequence of events ensued which stirred the conscience of the world. Some people had already kept vigil at the television facilities for several days and nights, and now others hurried through darkened streets, often passing the cumbersome tanks as they lurched slowly forward. When they reached the threatened buildings they linked hands, and began to sing the old folk-songs of Lithuania, or shouted slogans, such as: 'Lithuania will be free!' and 'We know exactly what you fascists are up to!' Soon they heard bullets passing over their heads as automatic rifles and machine guns swung into action. The noise was deafening, and bright tracer bullets flew in all directions. According to standard Soviet calculations the crowd should have scattered under this onslaught, but they did not move, and so the strategy was changed, with shots being directed at people's legs, then at their bodies. Next, an attack was mounted by men with metal rods, followed by a charge into the crowd with rifle butts. A young woman, Loreta Asanavičiūtė, fell victim under the tracks of a tank. Back at the Supreme Council I learned what was going on, and immediately summoned the deputies to a rally in Parliament. Most responded without delay, and as they assembled they witnessed the volunteer defenders inside the building gathering together to take the oath of allegiance afresh. Indeed, many of them went on to make their confessions, in grim recognition of what we might all soon be facing. A small group of defence establishment and parliamentary security officers also came to help protect the building. Our defenders had no other weapons than a few pistols and rifles, sticks and petrol bombs.

As the tension mounted I tried to ring Gorbachev and found myself begging his personal assistant, in the firmest voice that I could command, to inform the president of the Soviet Union of what his forces were doing in Vilnius. I said that, since everyone knew he was the only person who could stop what was happening, he would be incriminated if he did not. I then rang both Boris Yeltsin and Yuri Afanasyev, asking them to relay the same message to Gorbachev. After this, I turned my attentions to the West, where I was successful in contacting Leon Bodd, Lithuania's representative in Oslo, who immediately briefed the foreign ministers of Norway and Iceland. They responded immediately and Boris Yeltsin was also resolute. He told me at a later meeting that he had demanded that Gorbachev should *'perekratit eto bezobraziye'* ('stop this barbarism'), and on that same day, 13 January, with fine disregard for the advice of his friends, and indeed for his own safety, he flew to Tallinn to sign a four-part declaration announcing that Estonia, Latvia, Lithuania and Russia recognized 'each other's sovereign statehood and relationships according to the principles of international law'. It was a historic meeting which also sent a message to the secretary-general of the United Nations protesting at what was happening in Vilnius.

The most difficult hours still lay ahead of us as I tried to set these wheels in motion. Long before dawn on 13 January, the local hospitals had begun to overflow with the dead and injured. Because Vilnius TV was now in Soviet hands the Kaunas station replaced it as our chief means of disseminating information, and as the new day broke we realized that our new prime minister had disappeared.

We remained in Parliament awaiting an onslaught. I asked the women to leave us, but they all refused. I then addressed the crowd surrounding the Parliament buildings in some agitation, imploring them to move away to avoid casualties, but received the same response. Everyone there knew exactly what to expect, but they refused to move. Their heroism was unflinching, and later I was told that some had even been angry that I had urged them to leave. I had prepared a videoed speech which could be transmitted if we were killed. In it I gave careful directions for a campaign of passive resistance and suggestions about how life could be made difficult for our enemy under a new occupation. Fortunately this did not come about, because the assault ended at daybreak, and though the threat was not over, it was never repeated on that scale. It was a people's victory in the best sense. Indeed a cynical KGB officer was later overheard to say: 'we did not attack the Parliament because of the excess flesh surrounding it.'

Invaluable work was done by journalists and the media that night and in the days which followed. Many of them were foreign, and they photographed, filmed, wrote and delivered the truth of what was happening, seemingly without consideration for their own lives. Their testimony rocked a world which had until then been reluctant to abandon its mesmerized expectation of what Gorbachev might still achieve. The Western ambassadors, having called on 13 January on the Soviet leader to ask questions about what had really happened, heard him claim that he had known nothing of what was really going on in Vilnius, and simply took it for granted that the perpetrators of the outrage would be punished. In fact, none of them received any punishment and Gorbachev was not even questioned during the subsequent judicial investigation. On the morning of 13 January we dismissed the absent prime minister Albertas Šimėnas, and installed Gediminas Vagnorius in his place, with Zigmas Vaišvila as deputy prime minister. Gediminas and I then sat down immediately to compose a letter of thanks from the whole government, which generously commended the bravery of the journalists. Next I used the radio to tell the nation something of the huge wave of protest which was sweeping western countries in indignation at what happened. I said that we hoped that the USA, Britain or France would help us by raising questions about the events in the Security Council of the United Nations and concluded: 'While this is perhaps the way the world goes about its business, it is very unfortunate that our people have had to pay such a high price for moving our problems onto the international agenda.' I also used that speech to express sympathy to the relatives of the victims of that night's violence: 'Please believe that their sacrifice was not in vain. The world has begun to change. The path which has brought us to this moment has been painful and difficult but we are fully on the way at last.'

Time has passed quickly since 13 January 1991, and I know this account will be read by many who could not share those experiences. To all those who trouble to read my account I must explain that this book tells the story of how Lithuania returned to the map of Europe, and how she was allowed to re-enter western society. One outcome of the events of that terrible night is that foreigners no longer ask, 'Where is Lithuania?' They now enquire instead, 'Where did the people come from, who sang the songs of freedom; who, unarmed, were ready to lay down their lives for their country's independence; and who, though undefended, were victorious against a nuclear empire?' We shall reply: 'Those people were Lithuanians, and they were Lithuania's best people. They were nurtured by the memory of her long resistance to oppression and to the foreign occupation of their country throughout its history, and were inspired by an unbroken and enduring hope for their people's freedom.'

CHAPTER 3

My parents

My father outlived my mother by thirty-six years, but my mind's eye still sees them standing together, just as they did when they were photographed in front of our garage at Kačerginė in the autumn of 1940 or 1941. I also think of an earlier picture, which hung in one of our rooms in Kaunas, an enlargement of a holiday snapshot taken at Capri, when they went to Italy. When he graduated from the Royal School of Architecture in Rome in 1925, my father returned to his young wife who was waiting patiently at home and went back to Italy with her so that she too could see that beautiful country. As they were not rich, they stayed at the cheapest places, though it did not matter to them, and as a child I used to stare at the photograph, thinking: 'Daddy and Mummy in Italy!', though it took me a long time really to understand what it must have meant to them as a memento of the precious and joyful days of a belated honeymoon.

Mamutė

I shall barely skim the surface of what I could write about my mother. She was an ophthalmic surgeon by profession, and had graduated in medicine at St Petersburg soon after the Russian Revolution. She had then returned to Lithuania to work at the Kaunas University Clinics as a senior assistant, and after that she went into private practice, although she continued to work at the Kaunas City Clinic for a medical insurance scheme. She was heavily involved in the fight against trachoma, the eye disease which was then one of the cruellest enemies of country people in Lithuania. This became her specialism, to which she contributed a lot of research although her interests were actually much wider, embracing all the human eye afflictions. She gave several papers on the causes of blindness in Lithuania at medical conferences, and these were published as transactions by the Medical Faculty of the Vytautas Magnus University in Kaunas. She later republished them in a book of her own in 1934, in which she wrote:

Many of those whom we examine and diagnose as blind would not have succumbed if the right treatment had been available at the right time. My main interest has been to explain the causes of blindness in cases where it need not have occurred if treatment had been offered under different conditions.

That comment seems to me to sum up her commitment.

'Mamutė',[2] as I called her, would perform operations at her clinics and in her surgery at our home. Her patients were mostly sufferers from infectious trachoma who came for plastic surgery on eyelids eaten away by the disease. She kept a photograph album to show their faces before and after treatment. Sadly, the album is now lost, but one could see the improvement, and I can remember her vivid descriptions of how the various operations were performed. She once took a splinter, the relic of an accident during the First World War which had irritated the patient for many years, from a former soldier's eye. He returned to his farm, and later became a firm friend of the family. Two world wars had come and gone and had left many splinters behind, in hearts as well as in maimed human eyes. As a child I would often go into Mamutė's surgery to see her working, and sometimes she would tell me cautionary tales about boys who had found ammunition lying around and suffered burnt or punctured eyes after playing with it. After all the fighting in Lithuania, there had been many such incidents, and this was a mother's protective strategy. It was frequently repeated, obviously in the hope that her son would use his brain before he took risks in life. When she caught me playing with a sling one day she did not confiscate it. This took me by surprise, but soon she told me in a loud voice, that I must destroy that nasty weapon myself. She was acutely aware that someone might be maimed, and that I could regret the incident for the rest of my life, and one day she called me to see the victim of a stupid street gang war who had an ugly slingshot wound to his eyeball. As the country was littered with all kinds of war debris, much of it capable of exploding, her warnings had a good chance of being unsuccessful, and one day I actually found some gunpowder. It looked like flour, but I suspected that it might behave differently and started experimenting. The experiment was over almost as soon as it began, and the result was that my face and fingers were quite seriously scorched by the explosion. My face hurt badly and was covered with red patches and burns, though fortunately there was nothing worse, and I ran into the house with my face buried in my hands, not so much to seek a doctor as to ask for my mother's attention. I was not a pretty picture, being covered in soot, and she was entertaining guests. The visitors panicked when they saw me, but Mother was unperturbed, and calmly led me into her surgery where she inspected the damage and then pronounced: 'But the eyes are safe!' Only when you are older do you appreciate fully what a mother goes through at moments like that.

It is evident that my mother had the wit to sum up a complicated situation in a short time, and determine precisely the action which needed to be taken. In the spring of 1944, during the German occupation, a Dr Fruma Gurvičienė came from the Kaunas ghetto to visit her surgery. Though she scarcely knew us, she was desperate. She knew what fate threatened the children of the ghetto, and had come to beg shelter for her own daughter. 'Let her come!' Mamutė replied. From then on Bela (whom we called Barbutė), who was a few years older than me, shared our home. Though I remember her being warned that she must cover her distinctive black hair with a scarf, I was quite ignorant both of the danger and of the fact that other people had been too afraid to give her shelter. Nor did I have any idea of the terrible repercussions which could have followed from Mamutė's generosity had it been revealed to the authorities.

Awareness of the fate of the Jews was a recurrent theme, a consciousness of tragedy and crime on a massive scale. Some citizens of the Lithuanian state assisted in the implementation of the doctrines of the occupying power. Others resisted and were instrumental in saving the lives of Lithuanian Jews. Raging inhumanity existed side by side with a passionate concern for humanity. It was the Bolshevik–Nazi alliance that opened up the way for the perpetration of inhuman acts in Lithuania. Later, the participants in the conferences held at Teheran, Yalta and Potsdam put their seal on further injustices which determined the fate of families and whole nations.

As the youngest in the family I was alone with Mother at home at the end of the war. In May 1944 the Gestapo arrested Gabrielius, my fifteen-year-old brother, just before the German retreat. He was already a resistance fighter, and was accused of 'treason against the Third Reich', for which the penalty was death. It was rumoured at first that he had been taken to the Ninth Fort at Kaunas, which was a place of fearful executions, but in fact he had been deported to Germany along with many other prisoners. For several years afterwards Mamutė did not know where he was, or indeed whether he had survived at all. In July 1944, she had implored my father to go in search of him, which resulted in his being lost to us as well. His whereabouts were unknown because he had followed his son westwards into the confusion of the collapsing German Reich, in the hope of finding him and somehow bringing him back. It was not our only tragedy, as we also lost track of Alena, the eldest child of our family, at this terrible time. She and her husband were members of the Čiurlionis Folk Ensemble (named after the famous Lithuanian composer M. K. Čiurlionis), which had found itself in

Austria during the final days of the war. There she too was swallowed in the general confusion of the collapsing Reich. Mamutė's sorrow was intense, and I now understand her long vigils into the night at this time. She would often sit alone, knitting or playing patience. It was her way of finding some peace, and of coming to terms with her loss. Sometimes, though, she would be waiting up for me, the unheeding and useless boy who contributed so little. Her knitting improved as a result of much practice, and she often supplied our relatives with lovely woollen blankets, in wonderful unfamiliar modern patterns.

Mamutė was strong-willed. She was one of those people on whom the world depends. Women of her kind have always sustained the spirit of Lithuania during our country's darkest periods. During the First World War she had volunteered to be at the front as a nursing sister, not to support the Russian war effort, but because people were suffering. At one point she was working in a field hospital near a town which was under siege by the Austrians, when the Russian army was forced to retreat. The generals had decided it was not possible to move the wounded, and they were left to their fate, along with a nurse to attend and console them. Ward Sister Ona Jablonskytė was then left behind with them, to pursue her duties. Fortunately events took an unexpected course, and the worst did not take place. The Austrians did not capture the nearby town, and also failed to take the hospital. In due course the brave young nursing sister was decorated with the Imperial Order of the Georgian Cross for her courage, and it is still a family treasure. Mamutė, however, never said much about this bravery, and I learned about these things from my father, or from my Aunt Jadvyga, who had also worked as a nursing sister on the same front. However, Mamutė would sometimes talk about the similarity of the Slavonic languages, telling us how she had been able to converse with Russians, Serbs and Bulgarians in the field hospital. She had been at ease with them all.

A generation had scarcely passed before another terrible war came, and Mamutė was once again prepared to make sacrifices, this time by sharing her home with those who were persecuted or in need. She did this both during the German occupation and after the war, and was not prepared to discriminate between those who needed her help. During the German occupation she helped Jews, and in the case of Juozas Vitas and his family, a communist. Later, under the communist regime, she helped those who were trying to avoid the massive deportations or worse fates. She would give her assistance wherever it was needed. It was her way of expressing opposition, and though hers was a silent testimony, she would act without hesitation whenever someone needed help. Nothing she did in this way was ever discussed. Whether it was a matter of sending parcels to the prisoners in the Siberian gulags, or sheltering those who had come back, she just carried on, saying nothing about it. I have vivid recollections of her baking bread for food parcels, and cutting it into finger-length strips, which were then dried and soaked in lard. The result was not appetising, but it was very nourishing, and was intended for my uncle, Tadas Petkevičius, her brother-in-law. It was not until more than a decade after her death that I learned from a foreign obituary how close Mamutė's involvement had been in the humanitarian and political work of the Lithuanian women's movement, and the story brought to my mind how, around 1949, my class at school had conceived the idea of sending a parcel to help one of our classmates who had been imprisoned and deported. We spent a long time debating and discussing our options on what to send and how to send it. I then discovered that Mamutė had simply taken his address and sent a parcel out in my name while all this had been going on. It was another lesson from her, and it was taught without a word being spoken.

We lived rather poorly, though I scarcely noticed it until after I started work, which did not happen until I was twenty years old. Mamutė never seemed to buy new clothes for herself. Once I was rummaging in our loft, and came across a silver fox fur. I took it down to her, and asked why she had not worn it during the winter. She replied: 'These are not the times for wearing such things', and in the end the moths enjoyed it. Shortly after the German occupation started she began to suffer from the heart condition which eventually cut short her life (1894–1957). However, she did not complain about the difficulty it caused her, and if the subject of her health ever came up, she would turn the conversation in a different direction. Just once, however, she mentioned an angina attack which had occurred as she was walking home from work. Feeling severe chest pains, dizzy and unable to speak, she had leaned unsteadily against a wall. While this was happening a gang of workmen had passed by, and she told me, laughing at herself, how they had misinterpreted her problem. Their contribution to the situation was to insult her by shouting 'Drunkard!' A long time afterwards I realized that she had really been giving me another lesson – that I should never behave in this way.

When I was sixteen I myself developed an inflammation of my heart muscle. It took a long while to cure, and I almost needed to learn to walk again. For a while Mamutė took me for walks along the street, gripping me under the arm. I was still growing then, but for the first time I noticed how small and fragile she was. Yet, tiny as she was, she was strong in her profession, and keen to pass her experience on. The university at Kaunas was not, however, prepared to allow her to teach. Rumour suggested that this was for 'ideological reasons'. This is very likely, as after all her husband was abroad, so he might have been involved in some kind of politics, or might become involved! However, the university eventually relented, and invited her to teach auxiliary medical staff, perhaps because no one else was interested. Another person of her capabilities might have felt insulted, but Mamutė taught with enthusiasm and her preparation was painstaking and filled many exercise books. She must have found the teaching rewarding because it gave her some recognition. It was a moral compensation, of the kind which never came in her long struggle to reclaim her home. The house, which had been built and furnished for our family's needs, had been nationalized by the communist authorities, and was then filled up with other people, leaving only two rooms for our use. Her efforts to reclaim the rest of the house met with consistent disappointment, even after Stalin's death.

Around 1952–3, Mamutė seriously considered moving to Vilnius, where I was studying, to get away from it all. However, having weighed up the issue she decided that she was not going to give up quite so easily, and determined to stay put. All her friends and close acquaintances were in Kaunas, which was where her professional status was most recognized and admired. For similar reasons she had chosen to retain our family name of Landsbergis despite its German origin, even though my father decided to adopt the Lithuanian name of Zemkalnis after German aggression in Poland had begun in 1940. This determination to stay loyal to the past ran deep in her character in spite of the insulting situation in which she found herself, so despite the fact that the house in Kaunas had been nationalized, she continued to live there and to cherish and care for every corner of it. There were of course many other things to anchor her there. Her mother and sister, my Aunt Julija Petkevičienė, also lived in Kaunas, and her father, the linguist Jonas Jablonskis, was buried in the city cemetery near Vytautas Prospect. She must also have remembered how, when many others had chosen to flee westwards in the summer of 1944, it had been her decision to stay in Lithuania. Her resolve to remain reflected her perseverance and the related virtues of enduring patience and charity. I remember these qualities as those most characteristic of her way of life. When I grew older I came across some simple lines in Jonas Mekas's poetry:

> *Mano vaikai toli, toli*
> *mano linai balti, balti . . .*

> (Though my children are far distant from me
> my linen is kept white, pure white . . .)

and his calm description of a mother's painful longing:

> *Pažiūrèt ar žmonès*
> *nesugrįzta*
> *iš kelionès*

> (Watching in hope,
> waiting for travellers
> to return from their journey.)

They are lines which release treasured memories for me when I pause to consider them.

Tėtė

I still think of my father often. He left home in 1944 in his attempt to find my elder brother Gabrielius. Only a few scattered, but often wonderful, impressions of him remain with me from early childhood, for my adolescence passed without him. When the war ended he was in Western Germany. It was impossible for him to come back, so he went on to Australia where he stayed until he was finally able to return home in 1959. Only when this happened could I begin to appreciate him, admire his outlook, and share his humanity and his understanding of the world. 'Tėtė' was a determined and active man, who was given neither to brooding resentment nor to prevarication. His main attribute was a sense of duty, and his honour was of a kind which was rarely to be found in the Soviet years. He had many friends, loved companionship and had a great interest in the affairs of our large Landsbergis-Jablonskis-Petkevičius clan. He was always ready to share his experiences with me, so his opinion rapidly became the measure of my own principles. After his return to Lithuania he chose to use his considerable experience to fight against society's evils and set about this task very openly and with real determination, entering into flurries of controversy about planning and conservation whenever he felt it was necessary, and as time went by I found myself more and more drawn into his concerns. He increasingly made me his adviser on these public issues, and his influence took me beyond my own involvement in music and teaching.

I have now begun to understand how Tėtė's personality, and his closeness to me, shaped my own character and enabled me to avoid conformism. We became friends, and like-minded friends at that, and even when I was past sixty years of age I still sought his advice, and could sometimes find myself being told off. The Almighty was gracious to him, and he was allowed to see his hundredth birthday in full possession of his faculties (he lived from 1893 to 1993), retaining a sensitive perception and a real love for life to the end of his days. He always stood erect, holding his head high in the military manner, a habit which must have been acquired when he entered the officer training school of the Tsar's army at the outbreak of the First World War. When he came back from Russia at the end of 1918, he retained his commission by volunteering for the army of the reborn Lithuania, and fought in the Lithuanian Wars of Independence between 1918 and 1920. He had a strong affection for Bėris, the horse which he was riding during the battle of Seinai when it was shot beneath him, and the unnerving news reached the family in Kaunas, that Captain Landsbergis had been killed in action. Mercifully, the tale was mistaken, but his interest in horses was replaced after the war by a passionate love of motor cars, and he even took up flying for a while. However, despite his military background, I saw him in his officer's uniform only once, when he took part in a march one day in the autumn of 1939, when the Soviet Union returned the City of Vilnius to Lithuania, to become our capital again. Captain Vytautas Landsbergis took part in the event as a member of the Reserve Artillery. He raced ahead of his unit in a car, and so became the first soldier to enter the keep of Gediminas Castle, which stands high above the city. There must have been some element of competition in the achievement, and this would have appealed to him greatly.

My father's upright bearing reflected his character. He found it important to establish a position and to select his objectives, and would then act without wasting time. He was intolerant of any kind of hypocrisy, and of ingratiating or caddish behaviour. If he had something to say, he would go straight to the point, and he would reply to others in the same fashion. I think he was a little more tolerant with me than with most others, and we could discuss matters very freely. Nevertheless he liked to listen to my advice and would sometimes come round to my opinion and accept a new viewpoint, or occasionally consider a more flexible approach! Around 1978 he faced one of the more critical episodes of his later life when he fell out completely with the Soviet authorities. A proposal had been submitted (and been accepted by my father's fellow architects) to build major underground car parks and a motorway connection between Basanavičius Street and the Cathedral Square in the medieval part of Vilnius. This plan meant the large-scale destruction of historic Gothic buildings, and Tėtė protested vigorously to the Ministry of Culture and to the Architects' Society on hearing of it. When he did not get the results that he wanted in those places, he threatened a public protest. Despite the difficulties of censorship he pressed on with his arguments. Near to despair, he told me that he would resign from the Architects' Society, surrender his Soviet passport and return to Australia if the scheme went through!

This behaviour was totally without precedent under the Soviet system and I felt that I had to calm him down. I suggested that other routes could be explored before resorting to such a measure. The board of the Architects' Society had certainly not responded to his concerns, but he had uncovered the fact that the minutes of the meeting in which he had raised the question had been falsified. When he told me this I advised him: 'Then that's not the end of this matter. You must now go to the Architects' Society of Lithuania as a whole', and added that he must try to ensure that the branches of the Society in other cities around the country would also discuss the problem. I promised to prepare and distribute leaflets to inform other people of the issues, and said that he should resign from the Society of Architects only if the whole profession remained wholly indifferent to this campaign. If it turned out to be successful, he would have no need to resign, because no one would consider him a freak! These arguments changed his mind, and we made copies of the correspondence, and the Vilnius Architects' Society's minutes, and forwarded them to around a hundred addresses, a move which produced swift and highly gratifying results. Positive replies came back from every direction, not only from the architects but also from artists and writers to whom we had also directed letters. The Writers' Society, which had special publishing privileges, was a force to be reckoned with because its members could manipulate the censorship more easily than we could, and their help enabled the protest to gather momentum. In the end we won, and both the underground garages project and the plan to construct a motorway through the Old Town were abandoned.

One might well wonder about the significance of my father's threat to return to Australia. The answer is simple: having spent some years there, he was no longer afraid of the Soviets. While the act of demanding a permit to leave the Soviet Union to go to a country in the West might have placed a 'normal Soviet citizen' in an unpredictable, even a potentially fatal situation, Tėtė was in a different position. Because he had lived elsewhere and was a free man in himself, he was not intimidated by the clumsiness of the system and as a result he was able to deal with the Soviet authorities as if he were in a normal country, with a chance to enjoy freedom of expression. So his stand was constructive rather than naïve, and having made it he became very popular with the younger generation. He had always enjoyed turning on his charm, especially to women. Now his gallantry became an encouragement to those who were oppressed by the Soviet system. Soon his contribution became, in the best medical sense, a real tonic for a people who had been living in constant fear. He himself thrived on this response and his optimism was unbounded. When we were discussing the Soviet government and its methods, he would often say: 'They will have to go in the end. I won't ever see them clicking their heels, and setting out on the road home – but you will.' As things actually turned out, Tėtė's life was just long enough for him to witness that moment of happiness too!

My father's story is worth a novel, or more. He had fought as a soldier in his youth in battles on a number of fronts. After this he studied architecture, and graduated in Rome. When he returned to Lithuania he designed many hospitals, schools, churches, offices and dwellings, and was active in social life, and in the Architects', Civil Engineering, and Rotary Societies, as well as the Flying Club. At a critical moment after the 1940 occupation he took up politics in order to work for the restoration of Lithuanian independence. When the anti-Soviet resistance organized an uprising against the invaders in 1941, he became minister for communal welfare in the provisional government. Unfortunately that government did not last long and was suppressed after a brief interval because the German occupation refused to recognize it. After the Gestapo arrested my brother Gabrielius, Tėtė followed him to Germany. He wanted to help him avoid the death sentence which he almost certainly faced for his clandestine anti-Nazi activity, which was described as 'high treason against the Reich', and eventually made contact with the prisoners. He too had by then risked his own life by using falsified documents and becoming a member of the resistance. Gabrielius was eventually liberated at Bayreuth in Bavaria by the Americans, and both managed to survive, though they could not return to Lithuania which had now been occupied by the Soviet Union, and would have been too dangerous for them. To have returned home would have led, at the very least, to the gulags of Siberia. For a while Tėtė and Gabrielius stayed in Germany, and my brother finished his secondary education at a refugee school. Tėtė taught art history at this same school until he was invited to become a deputy professor at the International University for Displaced Persons established in Munich by the Allies under the auspices of UNRRA (United Nations Relief and Rehabilitation Administration). Later he received an invitation to teach at the University of Nebraska in the United States, but Gabrielius had married by then, and was leaving for Australia to start a new life there, following Alena, my eldest sister, who had already settled there with her husband. Father decided to follow his son and his daughter to Australia.

Meanwhile, my mother and I remained in Lithuania. Eventually we were able to exchange letters with the family in Australia, at first indirectly through third parties, and later more openly. Tėtė had already begun serious planning to return home before Mamutė died in 1957, and after her death the thought obsessed him totally. He finally decided to return after hearing of a misfortune in my personal life, my divorce, and eventually came back to Lithuania in the spring of 1959. I went out to meet him, joining him on the train from Belarus at the little town of Beniakainiai, and we travelled to Vilnius together. It had been fifteen years since I had last seen him, and though he looked older and his hair had greyed, he was as vibrant and full of energy as before. I was able to arrange for him to live in the two rooms in our nationalized home which I had been allowed to retain after Mamutė's death. Though the authorities had promised to return the whole house to us if Tėtė returned, they did not keep their word. They had also indicated that he would be allowed to work, but then they refused to let him teach because they did not want any 'ideological contamination' of the students. However, they did keep their promise not to persecute him politically, and they did not arrest him, although the KGB visited him twice, asking for information about Lithuanian activists abroad. He refused to collaborate, and asked them to leave. His reward for this was to be told that he had 'forfeited his right to own his home'. Yet, despite this unwelcome episode, he was eventually given work at the Institute for Planning and Construction, as a consulting architect. After a while he married a widow, a doctor whose first husband had been imprisoned with Gabrielius but had died in the Nazi gaol. He then embarked afresh on his independent and varied lifestyle, retaining an intense concern for his large and scattered family, and enjoying his personal contacts and correspondence with all kinds of people to the full.

Having returned home as if he were preparing for the end of his days, Tėtė paid little further attention to the business of ageing, and went on enjoying his work, and the fight for Lithuania's ecological and cultural heritage and the rights of the human mind, which came to preoccupy him. Thirty years after his return to Soviet Lithuania, he saw his country's rebirth, and having lived to see Lithuania become an independent nation once again, he saw his youngest son taking responsibility in its government. From that time on, it was often hard for me to find time to see him, but Tėtė did not grumble, saying only that he 'believed and prayed'. He was confident in himself. When he celebrated his eightieth year he jokingly invited his guests to his hundredth birthday party, and while he had shown some signs of worry that something might go wrong as his ninetieth birthday approached, his fortune held and the celebration of that event was beautiful. His hundredth birthday approached slowly, and Tėtė began to look very serious indeed, as if he was quite determined to reach this great jubilee, if only to prove something to himself! His legs were failing, and so were his eyes, and he eventually stopped reading newspapers, but he continued to watch television, to discuss politics and life, and to write letters in his orderly and stylish script and with a wonderfully steady hand. The centenary came in 1993, and was celebrated twice, as he had always done: on 26 February, according to the old calendar of tsarist times, and again according to the new calendar, on 10 March. He was obviously very happy to have all his three children by his side, his daughters-in-law, his grandchildren, great-grandchildren, and his many, many friends, and he delivered his own speech at the celebrations, a meaningful examination of his life's achievements. Thereafter his health deteriorated fast.

Tėtė passed his last weeks in hospital, a situation which he had done much to avoid. As he weakened, he distanced himself, and died as a small and tired old man. This was a sad end, but I shall never forget how different he seemed to us when we came to collect him in his coffin. He was now on the way to eternity and seemed so profound, noble and dignified as he lay there in his black suit with his white head raised. As I bent to place the badge of the Lithuanian Volunteers, which had always been his favourite association, in his lapel, his face seemed very proud. We laid him in state in St Mikalojus's Church in Vilnius, with which his association was long and special, since he had served as an altar boy there. Then we took him on his last journey, to Kaunas to lie in state again, this time at his home. Finally, we took him on to Petrašiūnai cemetery, to join Mamutė. As the cortège passed the Statue of Liberty, the crowds who had come to say their final farewell grew and grew. We lowered him to his eternal resting place, and poured down our handfuls of earth. Then we stood still. Our hearts quivered as a guard of honour from the Lithuanian Volunteers fired three salvos. It was a farewell salute to an old Lithuanian soldier, a retired colonel, who had carried out his duties to the end. *Requiescat in pace*.

CHAPTER 4

When my grandparents were young

Inever knew my grandparents on my father's side, but they are both buried in Vilnius, where my grandmother Česlava Landsbergienė died in 1907. Grandfather Gabrielius Landsbergis lived on in the city until 1916, when he died alone in a nursing home after being separated from the rest of the family by the misfortunes of the First World War. Because they died before I was born, the only visual impression I have of them derives from their portraits, which hung in our house in Donelaitis Street in Kaunas throughout my childhood. There was another portrait which I also recall hanging there, of my mother's father Jonas Jablonskis, who had died in the bosom of his family in Kaunas in 1930. His wife, Konstancija Jablonskienė, who was 'Bobutė' (Grandmother) to me, survived until 1948, living with her daughter, my aunt Julija and her husband Tadas Petkevičius in the part of Kaunas called Ąžuolynas (Oak Wood), and I remember how all her grandchildren of different ages would descend on her every year on her birthday, and work together to present her with a family newspaper, 'The Grandchildren's Voice'.

Some impressions of my grandparents were reflected back to me by other people, and many of those tales went far back into the past. Among the photographs in our house in Kaunas was one of both my grandfathers. Gabrielius and Jonas were standing together in the middle of a group of men, most of whom sported beards, and to my eyes as a child they all looked very old indeed, though I realize now that most of them were around forty years of age, and full of life and determination. Mamutė told me that the picture had been taken at her christening. Her godfather Vincas Kudirka was there, and grandfather Jablonskis's brother-in-law, Motiejus Čepas. There was another Motiejus, and a lawyer called Lozoraitis, who was later the father and the grandfather of two well-known Lithuanian diplomats. Also in the picture was a rather young-looking priest, Juozas Tumas-Vaižgantas. They were all very prominent in their time, and I learned later that the event was much more than a christening party, as everyone in the photograph belonged to the important Lithuanian renaissance movement Varpininkai, so called from their newspaper *Varpas* (The Bell), which was edited by Dr Vincas Kudirka. They had gathered at Mintauja for a meeting, my mother's baptism providing convenient cover for this clandestine event. They had immortalized themselves in the photograph, but had not included their womenfolk, and had then returned to work for their beloved country with new enthusiasm.

After my father returned from Australia in the summer of 1959 he showed me a copy of a lecture which he had published there on Kudirkos Sąjūdis (Dr Kudirka's Independence Movement). He was very fond of it, and once in a while he would bring it out to talk about it, saying: 'It is important to remind young people of these things, so that the nation will remember.' There was a portrait on the cover of Vincas Kudirka by the artist Viktoras Simankevičius which took the form of a collage of newsprint columns pulled together by a few deft strokes. Its style was one which was quite unimaginable in Soviet-occupied Lithuania, and he would show it to his visitors with a pride which I came to share. Thirty years after I first saw it, at the time when our own Sąjūdis[3] movement was beginning to gather its strength, I would sometimes take this pamphlet to our meetings to talk about it, and to show its cover to our people because I wanted to commemorate Vincas Kudirka and his movement, and to suggest that we were on the same road again. One day a journalist asked me out of the blue how the ideology of Sąjūdis reflected Lithuanian culture, and I found myself responding immediately by tracing the sources of our movement back to Vincas Kudirka. It was an inspired answer. The question had not been discussed in the movement before then, but I knew instinctively that it rang true to what people were feeling.

In that summer of his homecoming in 1959, my father took me to visit Motiejus Čepas. I had not previously registered that this ancient relative was still in the land of the living, and when we met him I was overawed by the impression of a patriarch who had stepped straight out of the pages of the works of Vincas Krėvė, whose novels about Lithuania's ancient past had awakened me and many others of my generation. This venerable old man told us about a Varpininkai meeting which had taken place long ago at the family home of Kazys Grinius, who later became president of Lithuania. A man with a black beard was there, who spoke a somewhat fractured Lithuanian, and Motiejus had suspected him of being a Russian infiltrator. He reported his suspicions rather nervously to Grinius who heard him sympathetically, but then laughed heartily after exclaiming: 'There's no need to worry about him at all, that's our Landsbergis.' He was of course talking about my grandfather!

It is sometimes interesting to reflect on how fleeting moments of our lives are retained in the memory, and how such incidents can continue to influence us. I recall a meeting at the Lithuanian Academy of Sciences in which Vanda Zaborskaitė,[4] who had often experienced the political displeasure of our rulers, gave a lecture on the life of the Lithuanian poet Maironis. She observed that the Aušrininkai, the members of the 'Lithuanian Dawn' movement of Dr Jonas Basanavičius, with which the young Maironis had been associated, and the Varpininkai, of which my grandfather was a member, were 'movements of the younger generation, which consisted mostly of students and young people'. It was a remark which lodged firmly in my mind, because I realized in a flash that they had actually been younger than we were!

My grandfathers Gabrielius and Jonas had worked together on the staff of the same Lithuanian newspaper, *Vilniaus Žinios* (The Vilnius News), which was at that time the only legal publication of its kind in our language. They lived near each other during 1904 and 1905, and became firm friends. At other times differences of temperament, profession and background might have kept them apart, but the circumstances of history, and their common aims placed them shoulder to shoulder. Their characters were very different. Gabrielius was a great lover of the theatre, quick-tempered, and excitable, while Jonas was a scientist with an orderly and methodical nature, but their interests complemented each other. The Jablonskis family was of peasant descent, Jonas coming from a family of freemen farmers. Gabrielius Landsbergis was a descendant of the *bajorai*, the landed gentry (a class which corresponds roughly with the squirearchy), and had a pedigree which was explained to me with a reference to a tale from the fourteenth-century Chronicles of Livonia. It was the story of a crusading monk of the Livonian Order,[5] whose family name was Landsberg, who had stolen horses which belonged to the Grand Master of the order and escaped to live among the pagans of Lithuania. It would not take much to write a romantic novel based on this legend, which tells how the gaze of a beautiful Lithuanian maiden had led him to abandon his vows. While the accusation that he was a criminal rather than a political refugee was all too reminiscent of what was happening in Soviet times, this fable may explain how the name of Landsbergis first came to the Baltic territories, though my ancestors are much more certainly traceable to the central districts of Lithuania during the seventeenth and eighteenth centuries.

Grandfather Gabrielius's family was impoverished, and had been polonized. Indeed, he began to learn Lithuanian only after entering the high school at Šiauliai, where his interest had been encouraged by the youthful Petras Vileišis, who later became a minister in the first Lithuanian government. The Tsar's regime, intent on its policy of russification, had strictly banned the use of the Latin alphabet in Lithuanian publications. This policy was maintained between 1864 and 1904, and during those years our people resorted to printing books and journals abroad, usually in Prussia, and smuggling them over the border. Grandfather's interest in the Lithuanian movement was first captured when he came across copies of the newspaper *Aušra*, which had been smuggled in by the *knygnešiai*, the heroic book-carriers who defied persecution by the Tsarist police in order to satisfy the demand for works printed in our language. The books which he purchased from these men, and their example, had a lasting influence on him, and in later life he described the admiration which came across him when he first met 'these serious and educated people who were striving so earnestly for the re-establishment of Lithuanian culture, and were prepared to risk so much in order to write and publish in our Latin-based Lithuanian alphabet'. The young man was deeply affected, and concluded that these people were worthy of his respect and trust. His life changed as he mastered Lithuanian and became a prolific writer in the language. Firm and enthusiastic in his belief that he was a Lithuanian, he consciously embraced the culture of his forebears at a time when this required much daring and determination. His renunciation of the Polishness which was then dominant in urban communities throughout the country ran counter to the predominant thinking of his class, and when he was arrested for his Lithuanian propaganda his wife and sister went to Moscow to seek the help of some Russified relatives in obtaining his release, only to be told that 'people like Gabrielius deserve to be hanged!'

Despite these convictions Gabrielius married Česlava, a Polish girl, who became my grandmother. He did not insist that she spoke only Lithuanian, and the women at home often worshipped in Polish, yet every one of his five children spoke perfect Lithuanian, and he considered it the greatest compliment he ever received, when Stasė, his eldest daughter, taught Vytukas (the diminutive for Vytautas), her little brother and my father-to-be, to read in Lithuanian. Many of his contemporaries and relatives considered this process of reclaiming the Lithuanian language to be an affectation which bordered on eccentricity, but Gabrielius ignored these pressures and ensured that his family became entirely Lithuanian with the support of his wife, who was a kind-hearted, wise, subtle and understanding woman. She was patient of his exceedingly broad social and public involvement in the national movement, and tolerated the meagre financial support for his family which was its consequence, because the Lithuanian activities which took up his time never earned money. It must often have been difficult for her to feed the family, which consisted of five children, together with his sister and his mother, and it was especially hard for her when his activities resulted in periods of imprisonment or deportation to Russia. Eventually, grandmother was forced to take in lodgers and cook their meals in order to bring in enough income to feed the family. She died in 1907; he lived on until 1916, dying just before the coming of Lithuanian independence, which was achieved in 1918. Both of them lie in the Rasos cemetery in Vilnius.

The young men of my grandfathers' generation faced certain problems when contemplating marriage. Most of the leading scholars of that early phase of the Lithuanian renaissance were born on farms but faced the dilemma of either marrying a farmer's daughter with little or no education, or else a more educated Russian or Polish woman who might then refuse to adopt the Lithuanian culture and language. If this happened, complications could follow, and the children would be brought up contrary to the father's intentions. Gabrielius, however, seems to have paid relatively little attention to this problem, and clearly married my grandmother simply because he loved her. While he was fortunate and never regretted his decision, this was not always the case when the bride was from another nationality. This delicate matter of 'Lithuanian brides' really worried many of his contemporaries, and was even discussed in print by Vincas Kudirka. Clearly my other grandfather, Jonas, was concerned to select his wife according to these patriotic principles because he asked his friends to help him find a suitably educated Lithuanian wife. It was not at all an easy quest, and when he eventually met Konstancija Sketerytė he found that there were other complications, because he was a Catholic and she was a Protestant, albeit with liberal attitudes to religion. Before taking their marriage vows they agreed that their boys would be christened as Catholics, and the girls as Protestants. Gabrielius seems to have taken a real interest in Jonas's predicament, because when the time was ripe, he made a list of ten Lithuanian maidens for the attention of his son, my father. The name of Ona Jablonskytė, my future mother, was on that list!

Theatre was Gabrielius Landsbergis's greatest passion. The first Lithuanian amateur drama was performed in 1899 at Palanga, a town on the Baltic coast which was then administered as a part of the province of Kurland by the governor of Riga, whose permission had to be sought before a play written in Lithuanian could be staged. The necessary authority was not sought, and when the populace greeted the play with huge enthusiasm, the joy was short-lived because the actors had all been rounded up by the police before the next morning. After their arrest they were fined, and a wave of persecution of Lithuanian intellectuals followed. These events naturally involved my grandfather, who was flung into Liepoja prison before being deported, first to Moscow and then to Smolensk. After this he did not get back to Vilnius until 1904, but he was unabashed when he arrived and full of energy and new ideas.

At first he worked as administrator in the offices of the newspaper, the *Vilniaus Žinios*, then moved to a bank. Later he worked in insurance offices, and then in a lawyer's office, but he would always dive into his theatrical activities immediately after work. He had noticed how the public reaction to the events at Palanga had resulted in lively support for the amateur theatre, and he now pioneered the first professional theatre company to work in Lithuanian. This was established in 1905 with the foundation of the Vilniaus Kanklės Drama and Music Society which performed plays, many of which were written, translated or directed, and sometimes even acted in, by Gabrielius. Soon he discovered another interest, and founded a choir which he then employed in his staging of Mikas Petrauskas's *Birutė*, the very first Lithuanian opera, in 1906. Its libretto, which was something of a melodrama, was written and produced by Gabrielius, who had a fine voice and also took part in the acting and singing. He had the gift of being able to draw almost everyone into his enthusiasms, and hugely enjoyed singing. The first night of that opera saw my father, then thirteen years old, recruited to a part in which he led a blind druid around the stage. Gabrielius is considered to be the father of the Lithuanian theatre, and is remembered there under his pen name, Žemkalnis (which is the Lithuanian for Landsbergis), which he always used when writing and for his theatrical work. It is sad to think that, at the end of so full a life, he was to die alone in a nursing home for the poor in Vilnius. Having been separated from his children by the turn of events in the First World War, he was put there for want of anything better.

My other grandfather, Jonas Jablonskis, was born in the south-western region of Lithuania, on the banks of the Šešupė, which was then on the border between Prussia and Russia. Though the Tsarist government repressed the trade with some savagery, Lithuanian books and newspapers were regularly smuggled across the river there by daring couriers, who were watched for relentlessly by the Russian border police. Anyone discovered carrying even a Lithuanian prayer book would be sure to end up serving time in the Siberian Katorga, the hard-labour camps of the Tsar's regime. Grandfather spent his adolescence at the Marijampolė Gimnazija (gymnasium or high school), and he recalled the majority of the students there as using Polish and thinking of their province of Suvalkija as a part of Poland. Lithuanian was spoken, but was only treated as appropriate outside the towns, and these able young men felt that their future lay with the Polish language. However, this viewpoint was being actively challenged by the illegal, but nevertheless popular patriotic Lithuanian newspapers, *Aušra* and *Varpas*. It was an anomaly, but the Tsarist policy of russification was not applied to prevent the teaching of the Lithuanian language at the gymnasium, and Jonas was able to attend an additional voluntary lesson after school hours once a week. He attended this class eagerly, and its teacher, Petras Kriaučiūnas, taught Lithuanian songs and inspired pupils with lectures on the noble history of their nation and its past independence. Here was a man who understood only too well how a hundred years of foreign propaganda had instilled the idea that Lithuania was inferior to other countries, and that to use its language was to turn against progress. Having grasped this idea he had dedicated himself to resisting the unremitting process of absorption into Slavdom which his people faced. This dedicated aware-ness, and the progressive development of facilities for intensive study of the Lithuanian language at that time, created many more patriots ready to defend our Lithuanian identity and the rights of our people.

Grandfather Jonas graduated from the gymnasium with excellent grades and went on to further studies in Moscow, where he promptly joined an illegal Lithuanian students' organization. After this he dedi-cated his life to study of the Lithuanian language, regardless of the difficulties which inevitably arose from acting on these opinions while working as a teacher employed by the government. Inevitably he was sent to teach outside Lithuania, but continued to be involved in publish-ing in Lithuanian. This was illegal, but he used a series of false names, and is still renowned under one of these *noms de plume* – Rygiškių Jonas (Jonas of Rygiškiai, the village where he was brought up) – as the author of the first standardized Lithuanian grammar and syntax. It was an accomplishment of the first rank, and it fulfilled his great ambition to rationalize the language, drawing on the work of other linguists. As a result of this publication, and his other achievements, he is considered to be the creator of the common literary language of Lithuania and, because of this, can be held to be the teacher of us all. Before his standardizing work was generally accepted, and in the absence of the unifying effect of a common educational system, people would write in the diverse dialects of Lithuanian. Those who had been educated in foreign schools and universities were also prone to use barbarisms and foreign words, often importing Slavic clichés to the point where Polish propagandists were busy proclaiming that Lithuanian did not exist, but was a mixture of languages, a kind of pidgin. It was extremely fortunate that German, French and other scholars had by this time begun to assert the great antiquity of Lithuanian, describing it as the cross-over point between Sanskrit and the European languages. They even stated that anyone who wished to hear how our first European ancestors had spoken should listen to the language of our Lithuanian peasants, which still carries much of the vocabulary and many of the forms of the ancient Indo-

European parent language from which most of the languages of Europe are descended.

The peasant language of nineteenth-century Lithuania had lacked modern terminology, and Jonas was particularly inventive in coining new Lithuanian words to meet modern needs. His diligence was directed towards purging the language of inaccuracies, and he adapted some verb forms, like *degti* (to burn) and *piešti* (to draw), to create some necessary new proper nouns such as *degtukas* (match) and *pieštukas* (pencil), which we all use today without realizing that he coined them. Naturally gifted with words, he was quick to adapt them to new uses as the opportunity arose. For example, our Lithuanian word *mokinys* (a learner), used to describe a student of any age, was adopted after he heard ploughmen use it to describe a young horse which was as yet not broken in to the plough, and was therefore unable to drive a straight furrow! Even in advanced old age when he was confined to an invalid chair, Grandfather Jonas continued to review books, write articles, proof-read and lecture at the linguistics faculty at Kaunas University as its professor! His knowledge of Lithuanian was vast, but he regularly told students whose language he considered to be incorrect: 'If you don't know how to say something correctly in Lithuanian, think hard about how your mother would express it in her own village.' After his death in 1930, his collected works were published, and a close colleague who wrote the introduction concluded: 'He brought up five children. All of them have made their own way in life. He left no riches.'

Neither of my grandfathers belonged to a political party, but both leaned towards liberal opinions. They first met as members of the same Varpininkai section of Kudirkos Sąjūdis, and the links between them became wider and deeper as the years went by. Their children were natural friends, and eventually his son Konstantinas married Sofija Landsbergytė, while his daughter Ona married Vytautas Landsbergis. After this, both families were in a double blood relationship, and there were many other links – for example, Vytautas and Ona's wedding was conducted by Father Juozas Tumas-Vaižgantas, the young priest whose features were so prominent in the photograph of that covert gathering of Varpininkai members who had met on the excuse of attending Ona's christening! Their movement contributed hugely to the rebirth of our nation and the re-establishment of the Lithuanian state, but it is worth remembering that it does not stand alone in Lithuania's history, because even at the beginning of the nineteenth century a strong revival movement had begun among Lithuanian intellectuals. It was dispersed by Tsarist repression, but it reflected a sentiment which again surfaced when the authorities closed Vilnius University in reaction to the uprising of 1831. In the mid-twentieth century, under the rule of communist Russia, Lithuanian freedom fighters took up the armed struggle against Soviet occupation. This was bloodily repressed, and was followed by repressive deportations, but their ideals remained. They emerged again almost forty years later in the Lithuanian Sajūdis reform movement, and having participated in this movement I take great pride in its achievements. I recognize the analogies between its experience and the struggles of generations of Lithuanian patriots in our earlier history with a sense of exhilaration. Their example stands and is an inspiration for us all.

CHAPTER 5

Debussy and despair

When I was a secondary school student maths and physics were among my best subjects. Though I liked literature and found that writing came easily to me, I received no encouragement to go in that direction, and perhaps this was just as well, because any kind of literary career at that time required conformity to the communist system. When the time came for advice about further study, my teachers proposed that I should take technical subjects, and they suggested that I went to Kaunas Polytechnic to read architecture. It seems to me that these suggestions were not well thought through, as only a moment's reflection would have confirmed that I was not likely to gain entry to a place where the graduates often went on to key positions, and were required to join the Communist party, which was known to be particularly careful about the selection there, making sure that places did not go to students with suspect political inclinations. Our family history in these matters, especially my father's record, would have been an insurmountable barrier.

Students going on to higher education were required to fill in forms which put questions about their parents and grandparents in order to allow positive discrimination in favour of candidates from working-class and peasant families. Knowing that my parents would be identified as 'members of the bourgeois intelligentsia', I always answered the question which asked for details about father by saying that I knew nothing of him. This was a half-truth, of course, but it would have been unwise, to say the least, to declare that we knew he was living abroad, as it was known that he had been a member of the provisional government which declared independence when the uprising of June 1941 ended the first Soviet occupation. It was because they knew just how perilous this connection could be for us that my father, and my brother and sister, did not attempt to contact us when they were in Germany, and even for some years after they arrived in Australia. However, it is doubtful whether my dissimulation in answering the question really made any difference to my prospects, because the communist system always had a long memory. The fact that I was my father's son ensured that my application to enter higher education would be carefully scrutinized whatever I said.

I was taking piano lessons, which I thoroughly enjoyed, and had been successful in the examinations at all the intermediate musical grades when I was at school, so there were no objections when I came up with the idea that I might go on to study music after finishing high school. Going to the Vilnius Conservatoire seemed to offer the best prospect of avoiding being politically compromised. Because music was not considered a key profession, a place there was less likely to be withheld. Of course, I had to pass the entrance examination, and I knew that the staff would still look at the socialist credentials of every prospective student as a matter of routine. Questions about my father were bound to come up, but my music teacher and the rector colluded to avoid them. The rector, who was a keen chess player and a highly accomplished pianist, opened the discussion about me by announcing loudly, before anyone had time to think, that 'Landsbergis's chess skills were just what the conservatoire's chess team needed'! The manœuvre sufficed to displace interest in my family history, which was passed over, so the discussion of my application was soon finished. Though this took place behind the closed doors of the Council Chamber at the conservatoire, I know what went on, and that it was the chess which got me in, because I had crept up under the open windows to eavesdrop on the deliberations inside in the company of all the other candidates. We heard every word.

Some of my contemporaries at school had joined the Komsomol (the Soviet Young Communist League). I was not pressed into membership and had come to believe that I had had a happy escape, but it was different at the conservatoire where there was continual pressure on us to join. Stalin died during my third year there, and it was soon after that one of the heads of department, a woman with a great deal of influence, summoned me for a conversation in which she asked about my father. I told her that we had no links with him, and that we were not even sure where he was. She made approving sounds at this, and then pushed me straight out to join Komsomol: 'there is no reason why you should not be a member', she said, 'and we think you ought to join as soon as you can.' My wits came into sharp focus, and I noticed that she mentioned twice that she was 'pleased that no one had objected to my application to become a member', a turn of phrase which alerted me to the fact that the question of my membership had already been discussed. This meant, all too obviously, that it might be serious for me if I refused. The manœuvre was not subtle, and it was quite clear what she was driving at. I was being reminded that anyone deemed to be unsuitable for membership of the Komsomol could be prevented from continuing as a student. Whether I might really want to become a Young Communist or not was no part of this discussion. I felt tongue-tied and deeply uncomfortable. Feeling frustration, I began to explain the situation with regard to my father, but she was ready for this and calmed me down, insisting that this would not debar me, as my application had *already* been accepted. While the game being played now seems a silly one, I was worried at the time because it had come home to me that they were actually pretending that I had *applied* to join their movement! I was being faced with a stark alternative. If I pointed out that I had *not* applied, I would be rejecting their 'offer'; otherwise I had simply to comply with what had been decided. I thought about it and talked it over with my mother, then shrugged the problem off, because it was not of my making. So I spent the last two years of my course at the conservatoire as a member of the Komsomol, despite the fact that one of my closest friends, then and now, was brave enough to refuse membership. He was ill with tuberculosis and needed regular treatment, and he explained that his strength was wholly taken up just in continuing with his education. Despite this, the party continued to pester him.

Marxist philosophy was a compulsory subject at the conservatoire, just as it was in other places. We were required to learn its dogma in order to explain aesthetics and cultural developments in terms which reflected the teachings of Marx and Engels and their current interpretation by Comrade Stalin. It was of course necessary to learn these formulae by rote just as one learns a catechism, and the subject was in general exceedingly boring. However, we were expected to write essays which were critical of what was called 'bourgeois philosophy', the inclusive term which was used to describe all non-Marxist teachings, and this exercise sometimes allowed us brief glimpses of other views of the world. While our official reading was firmly confined to approved Soviet books, a handful of the texts set for this course criticized twentieth-century bourgeois philosophy in a way which allowed us to broaden our horizons. For example, in the year when Stalin died I was expected to write an essay on existentialism using a book by a Russian author. The writer was obviously no fool, and he proved it to us by the way he quoted rather long passages from western authors in his criticism. This book, like others of its kind, was much sought after and we read it avidly, digesting these passages eagerly, because they gave access to the intellectual world which we knew lay beyond the narrow confines which officialdom permitted to us. Even the recognition that these were secondary sources did not reduce our excitement, because we were able in this way to read something about sources to which it seemed we might never gain direct access. When we wrote our essays we often attempted to present new and interesting angles, which drew on what we had learned from these extracts. Our interest may have been disapproved of by those who followed the Marxist line, but our young minds eagerly retained everything that was fresh.

The spiritual crisis which faced us at that time was profound, and it is extremely difficult for young people now, especially those from the West, to understand the atmosphere we lived in. Some of my generation had taken up arms, and had left the rest of us behind when they went to join the national resistance deep in the forests. Many of those who did not follow them took to alcohol to subdue their anger and despair. While my small circle certainly did not abstain from strong drink, we imbibed little in comparison with many of those around us. We did not become alcoholics; we knew more than enough of the bleak depression which dragged so many others down. Perhaps my immediate colleagues and I avoided the worst of all this because we spent so much of our time talking about the arts, a subject which gave hope though it did not work for all of us. I still have a handwritten score of Debussy's *Preludes*, which was meticulously copied out by a fellow student who was also a composer who later committed suicide. It was shortly after the death of Stalin and such music could not be purchased because Debussy's work was viewed as the starting-point of the decadence of western music, and therefore deemed quite unsuitable for public performance. It was of course inevitable in this climate that we found such works irresistibly attractive, and the rigidity of official attitudes enabled us to interpret our sympathies as a symbolic resistance to the existing order. We were able to exploit this situation as the discovery of our interest in such music would not in itself have caused dismissal from the Conservatoire, and students were allowed to play any composer's music for personal enjoyment or with friends. So we transcribed and circulated such pieces among ourselves, seeing it as a means of preserving personal values and the greatness of European culture. As a result, our recitals and concerts often included pieces which were not openly recommended. Personally, I greatly enjoyed Wagner, and my friends loved to hear me perform his work. It had not been forbidden, though it was not approved of, and I performed Isolde's 'Liebestod' publicly on several occasions. Professor Balys Dvarionas, who was widely known both as pianist and conductor, introduced the 'Ride of the Valkyries' into a public concert one evening, and the result was a musical and political sensation, simply because Wagner had been performed! His works had not been heard anywhere in the Soviet Union for a long time because he had been admired by the Nazis. Interestingly, we discovered that Lenin had preferred Wagner above all other composers. This was not then generally known, and was kept secret deliberately because in that extraordinary climate awareness of Lenin's pleasure in listening, for example, to Beethoven's *Appassionata* might actually be used as a political argument for supporting the cultural standards set by western music!

I am still indebted to my parents for the large private library they had collected at home. There were books on architecture, medical journals and also many works of literature and of cultural importance. When we were young my friends often came to borrow books about musketeers and Indians, and later to read the works of the Lithuanian poets and imprisoned authors who had angrily condemned the atrocities of the Soviets during their first occupation of Lithuania. Many of the writers of these books had been forced to flee when their names were entered on Soviet blacklists, and many had gone to the West as displaced persons. Some of those books, especially those printed during the German occupation, were dangerous to have in the house. Some had been written by survivors of the Soviet atrocities of 1940–1 and named those who had suffered arrest and torture, been shot, murdered in the prison camps, or banished to Siberia. Other volumes contained photographs of official documents of the NKVD (forerunner of the KGB) which they had failed to destroy when they were forced to leave in 1940, and one included a crucial transcript of the details of General Serov's plan to deport 300,000 Lithuanians during the first year of the annexation.

Our library contained some rare literary treasures; in particular we possessed a number of autographed volumes, some of them translations, which had been given as presents to my sister, my brother and myself, by Pranas Mašiotas, the famous Lithuanian educationist. They were written in the exquisite literary language which was his hallmark, and had a considerable influence on me. In later years I remember reciting his translation of *Dr Dolittle,* which I had learned by heart, to my eldest daughter. Such 'bourgeois' books could not of course be published when she was a child, but eventually Vaga, the main publisher of children's books in Lithuania, was brave enough to reprint one of his works, and when there were no repercussions, other publications which I remembered from my childhood gradually reappeared in the bookshops. Slowly, and sometimes reluctantly, the henchmen of the governing ideology began to allow books to be published in response to demand even when they did not conform exactly to the preferences of the party. Mašiotas's books were republished because of their intrinsic merit, and were refreshing to read because they were not prefaced by boring eulogies to the Komsomol, exhortations to struggle against the bourgeoisie, or tributes to the way the Soviet army had triumphed over the Germans!

Jazz was not acceptable publicly, and almost unknown privately when we were younger. It was something which I learned to appreciate slowly. While we would listen eagerly to the pre-war records that friends had managed to preserve, there was a time when I simply did not understand jazz, and took no interest in it. Later, when we had the opportunity to listen to the real thing, it began to grow on me and then the improvisations of the best jazz musicians gave me endless pleasure. I can now listen to this music for hours, enjoying every moment. While jazz first put down roots during the reign of Nikita Khrushchev, it was not of course officially approved, though it caught on in Lithuania rather rapidly just as it did in Russia. When I recently met Vladimir Tarasov, our distinguished percussionist, he reminded me of a well-known propaganda poster of the time. Today, enthusiasts would give their back teeth for an original copy! It depicted a repugnant-looking musician and bore the caption: 'Today you're playing jazz: tomorrow you'll be selling your country.' Jazz was defined in this way because it was bourgeois, a sentiment which was intensified *because it was American*, and this prejudice ran very deep. I recall chatting with an elderly lady who was an aristocrat and a singer when I was leaving the conservatoire one day. She was a Russian, but had lived in Kaunas since between the wars. She voiced her disgust at the current trend in men's hairstyles, reserving special venom for what she called 'slicked-down American haircuts'. While I had never really admired film stars with hair smothered in brilliantine, it was astonishing to hear her waste so much energy in running them down. Of course I was familiar with hearing the Young Communists saying that they 'could not bear anything American', but it was different coming from an old woman, and I have since wondered how she might have reacted to the long-haired youths with baggy trousers and flowery shirts who came later, and the liberated girls with short skirts and exposed flesh who followed them! These fashions caused conflict because Soviet officialdom was trained in intolerance, but they soon caught on everywhere in the Soviet Union. The response in Lithuania was more accepting, probably because we had always been rather closer to western Europe.

Lithuanian folk culture was well established on the syllabus of the Vilnius Conservatoire when I was a student. Jadvyga Čiurlionytė, sister of Mikalojus Konstantinas Čiurlionis, the internationally renowned artist and composer, was chiefly responsible for this. She had studied the piano in Berlin, but when she returned to Lithuania she became intensely interested in popular folklore. Later, she began to lecture on folk music at the Conservatoire, eventually establishing a department of Lithuanian folk music there by her own efforts. Soon students vied with one another to accompany her on expeditions into the country, to record Lithuanian songs among the people. The numbers of those interested in our ancient national culture grew as a result, and many of the best of them stayed on to become professional folklorists. There were two or three women who worked closely with her, and the department assembled a valuable collection of traditional musical instruments, and compiled a priceless catalogue of tunes. She and her assistants transmitted their rich understanding with real passion and managed to bring others to an appreciation of the cultural importance of this tradition. A very conscientious person, she worked without favouritism and lectured without political propaganda and certainly without Soviet ideology. Her contribution was exemplary, and the students who followed her courses for a term or two gained an inspired understanding of our national music.

It was through Jadvyga Čiurlionytė's teaching that I developed a close feeling for the creative work of Mikalojus Konstantinas Čiurlionis. He is probably the greatest Lithuanian composer and painter, but his work did not conform to the 'socialist realism' which was the canon of Soviet aesthetics at that time. According to its theorists, this so-called 'realism' was a naturalism which reflected the Soviet system and its leaders accurately. It usually portrayed the citizens of the Soviet Union as happy collective farm workers or victorious soldiers, with an avuncular Stalin or Lenin standing in their midst. One of the best of our established Lithuanian landscape painters once presented a picture of a forested river bank. It was a scene in which logs were being floated downstream, and he had dubbed it *The Forest is for the State*. He had calculated well. His story is characteristic of the way in which Sovietization affected our culture. This same daft process affected all the arts. I remember Balys Dvarionas writing a lyric about 'a little star in the sky guiding our way'. It can still sometimes be heard, but then it was officially categorized as 'bourgeois art'. It was sent back to him for revision because it was not ideologically acceptable, and there was some discussion about it. It was finally agreed that it could be accepted but only when mention of God was deleted and when the words *vargstančio žmogaus,* 'for the poor', were altered to read *darbui ir keliams žmogaus*, 'to glorify the people's work and progress'! Once Dvarionas had agreed to adapt his wording in order to fit in with this politically correct advice, permission was given for the song to be performed at public concerts, though in reality the changed wording added nothing to people's respect for the Soviet system.

Because of the prejudice against him, Čiurlionis's paintings were never exhibited during the time that I was a student, although we were aware of his music for the piano, which some of us performed. My friends and I valued these compositions greatly, and a circle of student musicians and writers formed in which they were frequently played. This group often gathered in my rented room, which became known as the 'music room', because of the piano which I had brought from our home in Kaunas. Sometimes Mamutė came with food for me, and I would call my friends together to share a bottle of wine between five or six persons. We would chatter and joke about almost everything, and I would play Čiurlionis's preludes on my piano, followed by something by Debussy. It was a small enclosed world which seemed to have a life of its own. There were no spies amongst us and we could relax in enjoyable companionship, but we all knew that outside there were restrictions which we had to accept because the creative arts were required to fit in with all the prescriptions of the ruling ideology. The resulting atmosphere was stifling, and I knew poets who could share their writing with almost no one because it was not of the 'approved type'. Had their work been discovered they would have faced problems, and there was of course absolutely no chance of publication. All this did not deter our natural curiosity, and when we discovered the significance of the literature which was being forbidden in this way we were keen to read it. One day I went out hiking in the country with a friend, having stuffed a book of 'anti-Soviet' poems which had been published by Bernardas Brazdžionis in 1943 (after the first Soviet occupation) into my backpack along with our sandwiches. We were out walking in the forest where we accidentally entered a military zone and were promptly arrested by soldiers despite our explanations that we had neither climbed fences, nor seen any barbed wire. The fact that we were in that area without passes made us suspects, so we had to be interrogated. Guns were pointed and we were marched off to Vilnius. We were in a farcical but dangerous situation. My awareness of the forbidden book sent shivers down my spine as we reflected on our predicament. I wondered whether I should lose it before our pockets were turned out, and struggled with the thought that it would be a shame to part with so valuable an item. So, with some temerity in the face of the unknown (and we would have been dismissed from the Conservatoire at the very least if the book had been discovered), I took the risk of keeping it. When we reached the militia station we were dumped in the waiting-room along with a few thieves and drunks. The rest of the story was something of an anticlimax. Later in the evening we were asked to sign a report of the incident, and then we were released. We were not searched, and I can only think that Providence had taken great care of us.

Of course, many people at that time, some of them young, really believed in the Soviet ideology. This became very obvious when Stalin died. Many people in Moscow saw his demise as an absolute tragedy; and there were traces of grief in Lithuania among members of the Komsomol and the like. Perhaps this was not surprising: it had been instilled into us all that Stalin was the one human being upon whom everything depended, and perhaps a small section of the people were really slow to grasp that life could go on without Big Brother. I remember a meeting for students and lecturers at the Conservatoire to help us all face the fact of Stalin's death. It took on a therapeutic character, and there were maudlin speeches. I saw women party members weeping openly and inconsolably. Needless to say, other people responded quite differently, and our neighbour in Kačerginė told us about an old woman who was in her kitchen garden when the death was announced. A party activist passed by a little afterward and stopped to ask why she was not flying the traditional mourning flag from her house. She had retorted 'Death is death: whether it's a dead Stalin or a dead stallion there's no difference, it's all the same to me!' As a reward for her cheek she was sentenced to ten years in prison, in exile. When a few years later, Comrade Khrushchev exposed Stalin's criminal character, this woman was released and rehabilitated, but in the year that Stalin died everything continued in the old way. Even a misplaced word might make one an 'enemy of the people' overnight, and though our instinct was to feel some contempt for those who wept for the tyrant, it would have been dangerous to laugh at them.

Our generation had a high toll of suicides. Specific explanations might be offered case by case, but whether the story was one of unrequited love, mental or physical illness, alcoholism, or promiscuity, they could all in the end be attributed to a single factor – namely that we lived under a forced and crushing conformity, which oppressed the human spirit relentlessly. During my first year at the Conservatoire, a fellow student, the elder sister of my girl-friend, took her own life. Because of this, the officials would not allow her body to lie in state as was the usual custom, and even advised students not to attend her funeral. Those of us who mourned her death openly displayed an unusual maturity and resilience in ignoring this insensitive instruction. The country was defined as 'living happily under socialism', so suicide was regarded as a sort of treason. It was heavily disapproved of, and news about suicides tended to be suppressed. In this case there were rumours that the girl had led an unconventional life after falling in love with another student a year before. He was an older man, who boasted his conquest among his friends in a way which hurt her pride. Though still in love, she had stopped seeing him, and then his cronies played a dirty trick on her by getting her drunk. They then engineered an ambiguous situation which was followed up with nasty gossip, and she had been unable to cope with this defamation. A deep disillusion with everything in this world had swept over her, and finally she had ended her despair. She was not alone in her misery, and many others shared this awful experience of blank depression, which they expressed by being drawn to suicide. Between

1952 and 1955 I lived on a new estate which had a scarcely used railway line running through it. One New Year's Eve a close friend of mine was suffering from such a depression; he emptied a bottle of vodka and left us to go and lie down on the tracks. We knew what he was up to, but we were also more aware than he was that no train was due. At worst he would catch a cold, but this kind of black humour reflected a blackness which also filled our own minds.

Our existence was dominated by a well-established communist routine, which seemed to offer no prospects for the future. This feeling of being enclosed, of having no choice, was the main cause of the many suicides which affected our generation. Often the only inspiration to which a despairing young person might cling was a belief that the future might bring hope, even when the present seemed to offer little or nothing. I have to admit that this dismal mood also overcame me at times. It is easy when things are better to forget the past and its darker feelings, but we need to remember how much the dreadful threat of nuclear war hung over us at that time. The idea that the world could soon succumb to atomic annihilation was very strong in those years. It pervaded everything and made us seem entirely powerless. The paranoia shared by both the superpowers was overwhelming, and we felt paralysed by the oppressive system which had engulfed our nation, a system intended – consciously and callously – to keep us helpless. A certain pessimism touched us all as a result. Despite our profound frustrations, however, I believe my contemporaries tried very hard throughout this terrible period to retain a humanitarian perspective and disposition. Every one of us was of course attempting to save himself, but we also wanted to help each other, and wanted to survive. Even in the circle of friendship each of us had to learn how to do this in his or her own way, and the costs were often very high.

We rationalized our predicament as best we could. While our aspirations were not greatly different from those of the rest of our generation, the angry challenge which youth often addresses to its elders was not open to us. We were students who did not believe in the prevailing socialist ideology, nor in the state which embodied it. While we were acutely aware of the oppression and hypocrisy prevailing in the Soviet Union, we were forced to associate daily with people who did believe in the system, and it was absolutely necessary to hold back our opinions and to go along with things which we did not like. Once one's support for 'the way things were done' was known to be anything other than immediate, open and public, one would be marked out as holding an alternative ideology and after that the door to jobs controlled by the state would be barred. We lived in a world in which the private sector in the job market simply did not exist. This placed us all in an uncomfortable psychological position. One was dependent on being approved. It was difficult to sustain oneself morally in such conditions. One had to find some way of developing one's inner resources. To be able to continue, even to survive, some alternative way of justifying one's ideas had to be found if one was to hold on to one's integrity, even one's sanity. In this situation our moral and cultural ideas were strengthened by the little resistance which we could offer, symbolic though it may have been, because we had seen that those who failed to acknowledge their discomfort under the oppression, and therefore offered no resistance to it, often succumbed to deep moral conflict as the system entrapped them, often in subtle ways. For instance it was compulsory, during our examinations, to answer questions 'in a way the system expected'. This often forced us to depart from the truth, and we would knowingly mimic some awful lecture to produce the answer which was required. Obviously, it was possible to keep these discomforts to a minimum, but it was wise to make this effort sparingly and only when the circumstances allowed. We were therefore forced to pay our tax to the devil. One's position was comparable with that of the writer who composed an ideological poem 'in praise of the Party' simply in order to ensure that his more creative work would also receive permission to be published. Yet there were others who went much further, by trying to show that they were 'of the system and for the system'. If they were poets, they would write 'suitable' verses, and though the results were frequently scarcely more than parody, the effort might be rewarded by the Komsomol with the chance to have a holiday, improved accommodation or a better job. The pressure of such bribes encouraged dissimulation, and some young people, once 'hooked', were then exploited by the system. The intention was to create a permanent dependency, and if the victims came to recognize their hypocrisy later, they would find that their new insight could not easily be acted upon. The system would habitually react to the individual's doubts by enforcing public assent to what was not believed privately. Profound inner conflict would often result when private beliefs were repressed in the attempt to escape conscious conflicts. It was a diabolical system which could take away a person's self-respect, replacing it with indoctrination and self-delusion, and which could turn repugnant lies around until they were believed as the truth.

While the system under which we lived demanded 'high communist morality' from us all, this was a transparent hypocrisy and it was evident that what was really being asked for was conformity. Those who operated the system were in fact Pharisees, who actually had no morality because the 'socialist ethic' which they taught was defined officially by the fearsome formula which Lenin had himself enunciated to the Komsomol, that *everything is good if it serves the communist interest.* We could examine the value of this dictum as a measure of good and evil by asking the question: 'would it then be a good deed to betray one's own father in the name of communism?' The answer to this simple question was of course already prescribed for us. Our entire generation had been required to learn the sad story of Pavlik Morozov. It was a tale known to everyone as it was printed in official textbooks and studied in all schools. During the revolution, the boy Pavlik had informed the Cheka (the political police, forerunner of the KGB) that his father, a peasant farmer, had hidden some of the grain which the family had harvested to protect themselves from famine and to prevent its being commandeered by the Soviet government. His father was then arrested and executed by a firing squad. The grandfather then killed the boy to revenge this act. And that is how it was: Pavlik was presented as a revolutionary martyr, a hero, and indeed granted the accolade of revolutionary ennoblement. All this for betraying his family!

We often saw such denunciations and betrayals at first hand. We also experienced the pressure of recruitment drives which were meant to make informants of us all. The only safety lay with the small group of trusted friends in whom one's open thoughts could be confided. Beyond such little islands of trust normal conversation extended only to the practical matters of everyday life. Not much was discussed of any importance – and never any matter which related to the system. Such a regimented existence, torn between conformity and discontent, and filled with resentment at not being allowed to function as an individual, was the main cause of our personal depressions. Yet, we would often joke at the system, using subterfuge and black humour to cope with our desperation. It was therefore natural for us to go about collecting the countless political jokes about the system . . . about Stalin and socialism, and we found that some of these anecdotes came close to describing the reality in which we had to live. One story was about a competition which 'had been announced by the Soviet Union itself', for the best political anecdote of the year. The first prize was to be ten years in Siberia! Later, under Khrushchev's rule when this 'prize' was largely withdrawn, a flood of new jokes came in to match the new atmosphere. Such stories obviously afforded individuals a kind of moral compensation for the reality of their lives, and the change in the spirit of those stories must have helped many to find a new courage in dealing with the system. Sadly, however, the opportunity to change the wider situation which was there in Khrushchev's time was missed. Along came the Brezhnev era with its new cynicism. We can now see that a definite rot had set in among the Soviet supremos by this time as the greatest preoccupation of the cabal in the Kremlin was the question of whose turn it would be to die next. Revolutionary mythology was by then less convincing than ever as a cover for oppression, as was proved finally when they spared neither force nor brutality in their vicious determination to subdue the Prague Spring and every similar development. Their terrible actions at that time replanted despair in a soil which was already fertile with despondency, and it survived for another generation. There were protests as hope turned to disappointment, and perhaps the sharpest and the most painful memory for the people of Lithuania is that of the young student Romas Kalanta, who set fire to himself in public, in front of the Kaunas opera house.

I married when I was twenty-two years of age, while I was still a student in the fourth year of the Conservatoire. I remember the day very well, because it was exactly a year after Stalin's death. Many of us took our marriage vows early in our lives, some of my friends even marrying in the first year of their studies. There were many reasons for this. In the first place it was quite impossible to enjoy courting visits because none of us was allocated a flat or other suitable accommodation. If a student did manage to get a bed in a student hostel, he or she was likely to be surrounded by hard-drinking and promiscuous neighbours, and these were hardly the best circumstances for true love to flourish. A young married couple could, however, acquire a room for themselves more easily, even if it was only in a student hostel. Some of us, being averse to promiscuity and constant changes of partner, felt it was better to get married and to struggle on even if it was in an attic somewhere. My wife and I spent that year in an old timber house which had no plumbing. All through that winter we had to go outside to break the ice in a bucket with a hammer to obtain water for our morning ablutions!

Our nation, like all others, has its own literary giants, but as young people we had the special misfortune of having little easy access to international literature. Under the communist system, only well established western authors, such as Shakespeare, Cervantes and Victor Hugo, were allowed into secondary schools. When I was at the high school just after the war, the European literature course was distinct from the compulsory Russian literature course, but later everything was deliberately swamped by Russian and Soviet publications. This meant that even the greatest of the classical western authors were relegated to a supplementary 'foreign writers' course. My circle had the rare good fortune to have its own sources of reading because of the books which had been accumulated by our parents' generation. We certainly made good use of these reserves. My uncle's library provided me with a book of poems by his favourite

Russian poet, Sergei Yesenin, which I borrowed 'for keeps', though fortune eventually played the same trick on me when someone 'borrowed' it from me. During Stalin's time Yesenin was regarded as a bad influence, so his books were not reprinted, with the exception of some of his lyrical verse which remained popular. When I read this old book for the first time, I noticed verses praising figures in the Soviet regime like Trotsky, Zinoviev and Bukharin, who had all been heroes once. They had fallen from grace, and much later, when his works were eventually reprinted, I made a point of checking on these verses. They had of course been censored!

I was also the proud owner of a pre-war Lithuanian translation of Nietzsche's *Thus Spake Zarathustra*. It fascinated me, and made me re-evaluate many things in my life, but it was also one of those books which were regarded as ideologically harmful. Even in Khrushchev's time I dared lend it only to my closer friends. When some other students heard about it, they asked to borrow it but I had to feign ignorance as it was very dangerous, especially in a student hostel, to gain a reputation as the lender of books which were not approved of. My uncle, who had provided Yesenin's book, was a historian, and a lawyer by profession, and had been a great reader from an early age. He encouraged me to read his many old books in Russian, and in the end I read them all. There was a complete set of Ibsen's works, which was a revelation as the *Doll's House* was the only play of his which was then allowed to be staged. His work meant a great deal to my generation, and gave us much food for thought. His *Enemy of the People* probably made the biggest impact and remained, for me, unforgettable. The story revolves around a Dr Stockman who fought for the health of a whole town by trying to protect a clean spring-fed well for the people against the interest of unscrupulous developers whose only concern was for profit. This hero struck me as a man who knew his priorities. He had a practical objective, and was not dominated by an abstract idea. His observation that a 'human being is strongest when he is left standing alone' stuck in my mind, like Nietszche's deprecatory comments about the 'human herd', which were also contrary to the teachings of the prevailing Soviet collective ideology which taught that the individual is innately self-interested and essentially inconsiderate of the needs of the multitude. To develop the individual was therefore held to be harmful to the interests of the collective, and it followed, at least in the Soviet interpretation, that to hold fast to a belief and certainly to fight for it, must be regarded as wrong if the majority should think differently. Ibsen's book clearly contradicted this collectivist doctrine because it maintained that the hero keeps his integrity by retaining his original vision of truth and justice, even when he is forced to stand alone. Moreover, I was impressed by the scene in the mountains in *Peer Gynt* where the hero seemed to be struggling for something dark and intangible. Apart from this, I felt that Ibsen's symbolic and moral motifs applied easily to life in the Soviet Union, and found that our reading of him enabled us to form critical opinions. His influence was also useful because it enabled us to consider idealistic evaluations of people and their achievements. In the prevailing cynicism this was attractive. It helped us preserve our ideals.

As young people we adored the works of Erich Maria Remarque, especially the novel *The Three Comrades,* which describes a post-war generation, not dissimilar to our own, in which peace and love were found only within the confines of a small group. During my Conservatoire years I also became acquainted with the works of Rabindranath Tagore, whose poems were translated into Lithuanian before the war. I read *Gitanjali* many times, and liked its simplicity and its deep spiritual meaning. I borrowed this book from our city library and kept it far too long. I received a reminder that it was overdue, and took it back. I then learned that it had been put on a list for destruction, and managed to persuade a young lady librarian to agree to record that I had lost it. I am still the proud possessor of that volume. When Adolf Hitler sponsored his rampage of book-burning, he did it all in one sweep. The Soviets were more efficient because they continued to destroy books which they found unacceptable throughout the years of their rule, and until very recently, though not in public and not on bonfires. When they occupied Lithuania for the first time in 1940, they immediately removed what they considered to be 'bad books' from the library shelves for paper recycling. Not satisfied with that, they went on to destroy our cultural archives on the pretext that they contained 'bourgeois material', a mealy-mouthed formula for describing unwelcome, and so unwanted, documents. When I became a historian of music and culture, I missed these lost treasures very much. As the case of *Gitanjali* discloses, our libraries were 'purified' on a regular basis, until the party's censors had left no books unchecked except those published under the Soviet occupation, while nothing from our entire heritage of poetry and literature which contained references to religious feelings or Lithuanian patriotism was ever considered fit for publication.

The ultimate paradox of the whole Soviet effort at indoctrination, in the schools and in the armed forces, was that it had virtually no result. Our younger generation never embraced Soviet patriotism, and finally turned down the demand that they should be 'proud of our motherland which stretches to beyond Kamchatka' as a Soviet ballad put it. Military service was compulsory, but few ever entered the Soviet forces willingly. Students did not enter the forces on leaving their secondary schools but were exempted until they had completed higher education, but as luck had it I was able to avoid military service entirely. As a student I was subject to delayed call-up, but the myocardial illness I suffered when a pupil at the high school had left a heart murmur, and in addition my eyes were weak, and when I had completed my studies I was summoned to the recruitment commission on several occasions and eventually received a 'white ticket' which released me from the immediate obligation of military service. The certificate was issued by a doctor who had known my mother and the family, probably at some risk to himself, but this was not the end of the story. I knew that this exemption was no final protection, if only because the medical specifications for military service could be varied, so an alteration in the regulations could bring the question of service up again at almost any time. The recruitment commission persisted in calling me in over a period of many years, but I followed a policy of ignoring its letters, pretending that I had received nothing until eventually a message would be delivered by hand. I would then have no option but to attend an interview, and this happened on a number of occasions. Curiously, however, I never received another medical examination, nor was I ever asked to provide further proof of my vision or my health. This meant that I was never called up, though I was nearly fifty when I received my last summons to the recruitment office. I was then written off because of my age. A decade earlier I was among a group attending the office which was told: 'The government is fighting for peace, but we must also prepare for war.' Though I was acknowledged to be 'unsuitable for service during peacetime', we must all have been assigned to a reserve list because the white tickets we had carried were taken away and never reissued. None of us, however, received papers confirming our final release from the threat of military duties. We just carried on with our lives in the knowledge that if a war should start, we would all start marching!

Though I do not overlook the fact that some of my contemporaries succumbed to despair along the way, I believe that most of my generation never wholly lost hope for our own and our country's future despite all our difficulties. We knew about the Lithuanian partisans and of their sacrifice, and people of my generation still remember with bitterness how the West abandoned them and their cause, along with that of other Baltic countries. However, the West was rewarded for its perfidy and the betrayal of its own principles by the long-extended threat of the Cold War and the terrible stalemate which it brought. In Lithuania we lived in the shadow of military service and – like the rest of the human race – under the grim and perpetual threat of atomic war, always aware that the Soviet Union might call on us one day to fight against the West. It was a thought which was hard to bear, but we would joke that this might be the 'only way we would ever get to see Paris'. Yet as we laughed we knew in our hearts that if history had taken that grim turn, we would probably have perished in the conflict along with a whole generation. Such a catastrophe sometimes seemed to be the only way in which the absurd nightmare which had enveloped our lives would be brought to an end. I have no idea whether western politicians ever had any inkling of the responsibility their countries bore, nor do I know whether the West has begun to understand, even now, the enormity of the crime its democracies committed by leaving the Baltic countries in the wilderness and without succour for forty years after what they had announced as the end of the Second World War. I continue to ask, 'What purpose did all the suffering serve?', and 'Of what crimes were our partisans, and those of our young people who were driven to suicide, ever guilty?' As long as such questions remain unanswered, the case remains open.

There is a danger for us all whenever we fail to face up to questions such as these which relate to wider unresolved questions for humanity as a whole. At times of great moral conflict, human beings sometimes express themselves absurdly, preferring 'being nothing' to 'being something'. At such times the race itself engages in worthless, and even suicidal behaviour, rather than taking the difficult decision to be free. The choices facing us at these times are great. The human spirit is complex and hard to understand. Sometimes it appears to be enlightened, and at such moments it is prepared to stand up against the forces of evil. It is ennobled by such experiences and soars as the eagle soars. At other times it capitulates. At such times the world seems to tire of itself.

CHAPTER 6

The power of music

When my time as a student at the Conservatoire ended in 1955, I was appointed to work there as a piano accompanist, and I also taught at the Children's Music School. Most of my work was with the opera class, though I sometimes accompanied the lecturer who trained future actors to sing, or worked with the violin class. In the second year of my employment the council of the Conservatoire asked me to work in its department of Marxism-Leninism. They had noticed that some articles which I had published on Čiurlionis had been followed up in a series of four radio programmes. My appearances at student conferences must also have come to their attention, as I had been fairly active, and they had been informed that I had become interested in aesthetics. This appointment meant that I had been given a research post. These positions were usually tenable at one of the universities in Moscow or Leningrad, but in my case it was to be held at the Conservatoire and it meant that I would have sooner or later to prepare and defend a dissertation for a higher degree. The successful completion of my doctorate would double my salary and obviously improve my social and employment prospects.

The idea of working in the field of aesthetics was of great interest to me. Of course I knew that there were constraints under the Soviet regime on those who worked in this field, and that my interpretation would have to be adapted to concepts such as the dictatorship of the proletariat and theories of class struggle. However, I remembered Lenin's assertion, made fairly early in his career, that though nothing of real worth could be achieved without establishing a 'proletarian culture', the bourgeoisie could 'make valuable contributions'. It had, of course, been decreed early on that all art must conform to communist theory, so everything was to be branded either as 'bourgeois' or 'proletarian' art as a result. However, though these classifications were said to be 'common to humanity', it was also taught that it was necessary to differentiate between 'worthy' and 'unworthy' contributions! Taking all these things into consideration allowed aesthetics to have a certain complexity as a science that studied art, and this made the post attractive to me. My work would offer possibilities in a field which included all the arts, not just music, so discussion and argument on the wider aspects of aesthetics, including the Russian literature of the day, would be possible.

Despite the dead dogmas with which we were surrounded, I would be able to find fresh things to consider, and also to prepare for intellectual battles to come. Indeed, I felt that such work might allow one to introduce worthwhile concepts into the discussion. Although I would have to work within the prevailing perspectives of the Soviet system, I felt there might even be the chance, when the time was ripe, to defend and even to reinstate Čiurlionis's reputation. It would be impossible for me to ignore the system of Marxist dialectics, but I might well circumvent it by proposing new interpretations, and that was precisely what I set about doing.

With these motivations I accepted this offer of work at the Conservatoire. The curriculum of the department of Marxism-Leninism required first-year students to take a course on the history of the Communist party, which was followed by instruction in political economy. These topics provided the groundwork of the curriculum, and I was expected to conduct seminars in philosophy for fourth-year students who were studying dialectical materialism, a course which embraced the history of European philosophy, showing how it had evolved through Kant, Feuerbach and, of course, Karl Marx, to become 'the highest type of outlook', or 'true philosophy'. I had no previous qualification in philosophy, and little comprehension of its content or how to present it, but I was comforted by the knowledge that most of my colleagues in the department were no better off. From my own experience of their teaching, I knew that they lectured from a stated position, and demanded instant dogmatic responses. They were wholly dependent on Lenin's teachings, and I am still doubtful whether any of them had ever read a book by either Kant or Hegel. While my colleagues presented their viewpoint in lectures, my duty was to talk with the students about a specific text, and I determined from the start that I would find interesting and thought-provoking passages, and then ask students to elaborate their own thoughts, for example by discussing Engels's formula that 'every nation deserves the government it gets'. Of course, it was inevitable that sooner or later someone would complain that I was not discussing the issues which were regarded as essential, and when this happened, I was called up for appraisal, and my seminars were discussed in several interviews. Eventually, I was asked to join the Communist party, and at this point I attempted to clarify whether this was a condition of my continuing employment. This straightforward question obviously did not go down well, but I received an affirmative answer, together with a reminder that the salary paid in this department was twice that paid elsewhere! Armed with this information I then declined the offer to join the 'most glorious party in the world', and so the discussion ended abruptly. My career in the Marxism–Leninism department was over before the beginning of the second term.

Perhaps the fact that student riots had taken place that year had contributed to my dismissal. It was a period when exiles were beginning to return home, and Antanas Kučingis, a prominent singer who had just returned from a long exile in the Siberian mines, had been invited to take the role of Mephistopheles in a production of *Faust* by the Vilnius Opera. Huge crowds of his admirers, including many of our students, turned out to welcome this famous deportee with bouquets of flowers. Their welcome was so effusive that the government panicked at its warmth, and ordered that the opera programme should be changed at the last minute. The decision upset our students badly and they made an immediate protest, demanding that *Faust*, and *Faust* only, should be performed. The situation boiled over when the students ignored the authorities who tried to calm them down, and things then deteriorated very quickly as the students began to threaten the KGB officers and other officials who were standing around and seemed likely to inform on them. Even some of the Young Communists got caught up in the emotion. They were naturally hauled quickly before a party disciplinary board, and the drastic measure was taken of dismissing them from the Komsomol. Worse was to follow, as they were dismissed from the Conservatoire to be conscripted into the forces. As I was on the teaching staff, the party members expected me to condemn my friends. A Komsomol meeting was called to discuss the situation. I was clearly expected to support the measures taken, but after being silent for a while, I felt forced to speak out, reminding them that Khrushchev had recently revealed and condemned Stalin's crimes, and adding that possibly our students had merely wanted to honour one of Stalin's victims. I said that I hoped my colleagues might also show public support for the party's new policy of rehabilitating those who had suffered injustice. They were disappointed in me, however, and the officials noted my comments for future reference.

In the following year, which was 1957, the Pedagogical Institute in Vilnius opened a new department to train music teachers for secondary schools, and I was asked to teach the piano there. Even though I had been dismissed from tutoring philosophy, I was allowed to continue teaching the piano to vocalists and wind instrument players at the Conservatoire, though my post was now only a supplementary position and I was not well paid. This new offer meant that I would at last be working full-time, not as an accompanist, but as a lecturer, a real teacher, and what is more, I knew that by moving to the Institute I would be working closely with friends. I knew them well, for as far back as the time of the Hungarian Rising, and during the years of the Soviet thaw, we had often discussed how to find ways of saving our

Lithuanian culture, our human values and our schools. We realized that the school curriculum had been adapted to communism, and how the younger generation was being alienated by policies which relentlessly propagated communist and atheist ideas, and refused pupils the freedom to develop independent thought. During the Khrushchev era the party had issued a decree which emphasized the need to teach the arts to young people. The document argued that there had been a deterioration in young people's morals and had proposed that an understanding of the arts might persuade them to become more honest. This new policy seemed to open a door which might allow music to be restored to its pre-war position as an important curriculum subject, although that position could not be considered entirely safe because other instructions also came down the line thick and fast – to increase time for chemistry, mathematics, the Russian language, and so on and so on. Amid this welter of more recent pressure on the curriculum, music lessons were again in danger of being neglected. There was now a feeling in some quarters that music teaching was relatively unimportant, and even that this lesson was an hour which could be 'saved' on the weekly timetable, to be given to the other subjects. Of course, we felt that such attitudes needed to be fought, and when we arrived at the Pedagogical Institute we acknowledged among ourselves that we had a lot to achieve and that time was short. As time passed we learned from experience, and discovered that we had been naïve, and that the real situation we faced was complicated. Of course, the little time that was given to music in the schools could never even begin to 'reverse the moral degeneration' of our society, but as we faced up to what we could achieve, I recalled Jadvyga Čiurlionytė's portentous words from my earlier years that 'many things can be achieved through music'. It was this thought which helped me and my colleagues to recognize that music can be an instrument of purposes which were both more general and more important than those which had been proposed by our political masters.

When we arrived at the Institute we were a group of eight (or ten including the part-timers), and we found that our new department had been allocated four rooms, with a single chair to be shared between us all! Only fifteen students had been enrolled, and so during the first and the second years of the course we all got on particularly well. With so small a group many students became personal friends. We were still young ourselves, often the same age as the students, some of whom came after completing military service, while others had already been working as schoolteachers. Most of them came from the provinces, and they were a very different crowd from the students I had known at the Conservatoire. The experience at the Institute was very interesting, and I ended up spending seventeen years working there. Should anyone ask me if the work was difficult, I would answer that it was not. There were, of course, the usual problems that teachers face, and the need to spend extra time and energy on ensuring that the occasional less talented student came face to face with the basic issues, but my overall memories are of a wonderful conviviality. This is because music offers great rewards to teacher and student alike. There were plenty of opportunities for discussing our work, the arts and our attitudes to life and experience of life in general. The experience was endlessly rewarding and the atmosphere did the students a great deal of good, because many of them had real aptitude. Though they often arrived with lower standards of instrumental achievement than those at the Conservatoire, the three or four years which they spent in this dedicated environment made quite serious performers of them.

Our conversation with these students was prolonged and close. It expanded naturally to other subjects, such as the relationships between people and the events which were taking place around us, springing up and flowing naturally from the power of music. When one plays a piano the sound responds subtly to one's mood. As the keys are depressed, they can be manipulated in many ways. As I taught these students I needed to demonstrate, again and again, just how this is done, until each had learned how to discriminate, knew how to discern the individual colour and tone of notes on the music sheet, and had learned that it is more than a simple increase or decrease in volume which exploits their potential quality and range. While it is vital for musicians to know how sound is generated, it is equally necessary for them to recognize the role which the mind plays in achieving the desired result. It is also vital to understand that the human hand relates to the mind and that the mind responds to what radiates from the soul itself. If a musical instrument is ever to produce the sound one is seeking, the hand must be wholly obedient to one's intentions. When the soul is angry the hand will reflect dissatisfaction, and the sound which results will not match what was intended. Much can be learned from a single note, and much more can be discovered when the notes blend together to become a phrase. This is the moment in which art is created, born as if out of nothing. All my piano lessons were given individually, and I was of the opinion that our conversation about music was every bit as important as the students' playing of the piano, because we were training teachers who would in turn be enabling their pupils to appreciate music. They needed to be able to express, in simple words, what they felt about music, and this was what I did myself, because I enjoy participating in music and engaging through music with people. Whenever I was working with a student, perhaps on Beethoven's sonatas or on one of Bach's variations, I would find myself discovering new details in the composition, and sharing those discoveries inside our partnership. As the students listened, I could feel myself responding to their reflections and excitement, sharing the understanding (and sometimes the misunderstanding) which they felt. Every music teacher is familiar with this phenomenon, and knows how the brain is stimulated at these times, to the point where the effort being made and even the passage of time is wholly disregarded. It is twice as hard to achieve a level of musical performance in another person as it is to achieve it for oneself, but when one succeeds in this way one is doubly rewarded, because the participants resound to each other as much as to the music.

I spent seventeen years at the Pedagogical Institute, and put a lot of energy into my musical work there. Yet when I look back on that period, the achievement can seem very small. Though children somewhere may still be receiving the benefits of what I passed on, that thought is mere speculation on my part, and I sometimes feel there were no long-term results at all. The thought is discomforting: I imagine one might feel the same if one had given that amount of time to writing and then discovered that almost no one had bothered to read any of one's books! Time just seems to have flown while I was at the Institute, though some political problems occurred from time to time and marked its passing. Most of these occurred simply because the communist system created differences of opinion about relatively small matters, which would then suddenly blow up out of all proportion to their true importance because they had acquired a political dimension. A case in point was the cultural festival at the Institute, in which each of the faculties was expected to participate each year. The real interest of the organizers of the event was political rather than artistic, but the music department would be asked to judge many of the competitions. Having been asked to do this, we would apply our own professional criteria to the task, and did this unchallenged until it dawned on the managers of the event that our application of cultural and artistic standards completely ignored the blunt political criteria which they expected us to operate. A storm broke when a performance by students in the faculty of Russian language and literature became a point of contention. The show which they had devised was full of stereotyped atheistic slogans and propaganda of the kind so keenly promoted by the Komsomol. There was so little regard for taste or artistic presentation, that we, the judges, placed them last. Immediately they appealed, claiming that the 'most important factor of their performance', namely its political content, had not been recognized and certainly had not been taken into account, and in the rumpus which followed we were denounced as 'nationalists who had set out to wrong-foot them because they were Russians'. There it stood. The Board of the Institute listened to them, and then advised us to 'think again and to improve the result achieved'. However, we did not comply, and stood our ground, insisting that judges must apply the criterion of *artistic achievement*, which implied something quite different from what was intended by *socialist ideology*. If ideology was to be reflected in a performance, then, we recommended, it was important to preserve artistic form, the absence of which would inevitably compromise the political ideas being presented. Such clumsiness, we said, would be harmful to the cultural festival and to socialism, which was why we could not allow it. The Institute's principal seemed convinced by this argument, but the Russian students, and their faculty, continued to be aggrieved, and their grumbles continued for a long time.

Such tensions continued right through the 1960s, and often preoccupied us in the period before the national movement was launched. We spent a lot of time during those years encouraging interest in our national folk music. We knew its endearing and enduring qualities, and saw it as true art, but we also recognized that when people are in a depressed mood they are often disposed to listen passively to weak pop songs. Even in the countryside, peasant people were increasingly shy of singing the traditional songs, feeling that to do so was old-fashioned, 'because people just don't sing them any more', and were turning to popular new songs, many of them in Russian style, and with poor and often incomprehensible lyrics. Naturally we deplored this trend, and encouraged a group of our students to take an interest in collecting and promoting traditional music and defending its value to the nation. The members of the group charged themselves with learning about Lithuania's history and discussing its future course. With this interest at heart, it was perhaps inevitable that they would come to the notice of the authorities after a while. They were then singled out as enemies of the Soviet system, and expelled from their studies. Yet times had already begun to change, and information about young people in other parts of the world singing 'country' ballads to the sound of a guitar was by now beginning to creep even into the Soviet press. The trends were perplexing to us too, and we were somewhat apprehensive of the growing interest in 'beat' music which was also associated with the change in values, but we encouraged an interest in 'country and western' music as a way of promoting interest in our own folk music. This was carefully debated, but we were firmly assured by our students that this relaxed attitude was of great value because our Lithuanian folk-songs were still widely known. People might feel them to be old-fashioned because there was no popular means of promoting them, but the introduction of 'country' music would help to change attitudes because it could be beneficially associated with our own national music. They were absolutely correct, and if this association had not taken place one of the greatest gifts from our Lithuanian past might have been in danger of being lost for ever, or perhaps confined to the folk museum, as an object of mere antiquarian interest.

The time was clearly ripe for us to arrange a competition at the institute to promote wider interest in our national folk music. When we did this, it proved to be a wonderfully fresh and enlightening experience, and a real success. There was widespread support from lecturers and students alike, though as usual there were those who frowned on the idea, because it did not toe the line of official ideology. Some of our detractors even went so far as to try to obstruct the event, asking us to explain why we wished folk-songs to be performed, instead of Soviet patriotic songs. Our answer was that as such patriotic songs were now commonplace, we needed to reconsider how folk-songs should be presented. The grumblers were not satisfied with this, and their questions continued: 'Why *Lithuanian* folk-songs only?', we were asked, and we replied, 'It does not *have* to be Lithuanian music only, but we need to assess who sings best, and for that we need a single genre; it is quite acceptable for Russians to participate in singing the Lithuanian folk-songs if they wish to.' The outcome of this exchange was a positive one, as both the Russian and the Polish faculties at the Institute entered choirs in the competition, and they all sang with real pleasure and from their hearts. We felt that everything had gone well, but our detractors then began to make further politics of our success and started putting it about that the competition was unnecessary, and that its repertoire was unsuitable for student performance. We took no notice of this carping, but some people at the Institute went along with the attitude that it was always best to avoid anything which our superiors might not like. Theirs was a reflex response which had remained ingrained from the Stalinist era, reflecting the submissive spirit and the self-censorship which his bullying had imposed throughout the whole Soviet Union. It had resulted in a set disposition which now just carried on without anyone really thinking about it. Anton Chekhov neatly described this phenomenon when he wrote: 'The most dreadful thing in Russia is its submissive spirit.' It was this dispiritedness which had spread in Lithuania so far that it was apparent everywhere, even in the syllabus provided for music lessons in the schools and in the response of children. Officialdom had always prescribed Russian and Soviet composers for class performance, clearly preferring them above all others. Western classical music was

mentioned only as an afterthought, and presented as having little importance. The work of contemporary western composers had never figured
in the syllabus. Praise had been reserved for teachers whose lessons
were mainly filled with Russian music, and teachers knew well that if
their students had ever begun singing or playing western compositions,
the idea would soon spread that something subversive was going on. The
whole scenario was a formula for an enveloping dullness. Even the
programmes for school concerts had to be scrutinized by people with this
attitude, and it had gone on throughout the entire post-war period. It had
now resulted in a situation in which political questions came up everywhere in life. This twisted mentality was a constant drain on everybody
and a real pollutant. Everyone had to submit before 'big brother', and
the more profound the submission, the better it satisfied the government.

In 1961, the Society of Composers asked me to prepare a programme
of public lectures on 'The Popularization of Music', which I was to
introduce with a lecture of my own. I therefore delivered a public
address and when I had finished speaking those party members who were
most prominent in the Society's Council began the discussion, appraising
my address in terms of their politics. Although I discussed classical
works, mentioning Beethoven, Bach and Wagner, I was criticized for
'speaking too long on the subject of western music'. They were, of
course, telling me that I should have concentrated on Russian music and
Soviet composers, and it was not enough that I had referred to a
Shostakovich symphony. These critics were certainly not amused when I
replied, drawing on my experience of teaching Marxist-Leninist dialectics, by quoting Lenin as having said: 'A communist is a person who has
adopted the culture of the whole world.' I added: 'This is the Leninist
attitude, and whatever you think of Beethoven, he was certainly not a
reactionary westerner.' At another point I said: 'I disagree with you, and
believe that your attitudes are somewhat Stalinist. This is the real
problem.' At this juncture, the chairman cut across me saying that the
discussion must end. Looking back I realize how fortunate I was that the
matter ended there; the outcome could have been more drastic.

My lecture had referred to Shostakovich's Seventh Symphony, which he
wrote during the siege of Leningrad. I described the heroic dimension of the
work, portraying the starving composer writing his music in a starving city,
with people dying around him everywhere. He had written with magnificent
disregard for the immediate circumstances, and had arranged a concert in
defiance of the terror which surrounded him. I described the work as
heroic, even awesome in its spiritual strength, given the dreadful conditions
in which the composer worked, and the horrors of the siege of his native
city. My elaboration made some of those present uncomfortable. I pointed

out how the German forces had driven deep into Soviet territory in 1942. It could have seemed that the war was all but over for the people of Leningrad and I suggested that it was the agony of this realization which had led the composer to set his example of endurance and spiritual courage. My aim was to draw out the meaning of the symphony, but the critics saw it differently and told me I had implied that some of the people in the city had not believed that the victory of the Soviet Union would come about. It was obvious that this was not at all what I was saying but my views had evidently clashed with the dogmatic mythology known as 'socialist realism in the arts', a doctrine which defined clearly how everything should be and how everything should be perceived and interpreted. According to this teaching everything had to be 'just so', fitting in with this established view of reality. Its logic was static and circular, and no deviation from its canons of political correctness could possibly be tolerated. It was a complete view of the world, and if ever they were faced by a different interpretation or new evidence, they would repeat their formula with renewed conviction. Anything said to the contrary, the slightest challenge, was to be regarded as an attempt to subvert the socialist truth, and the person who was rash enough to make such a statement was to be viewed as being on the way to becoming an enemy of the state. The Soviet leaders were also caught up in this miserable circularity, and they would nit-pick at every level, scrutinizing the smallest shortcoming in those who failed to repeat the holy mantras of their mythology over and over again. Of course, we did not expose ourselves by attacking this mythology openly as the dissidents did, but we dared to refrain from repeating its incantations. This, too, was a defiance, and it meant that our 'management' knew very well that we were unbelievers, heretics who were pursuing other values.

I can vouch for the fact that a large part of the Lithuanian intelligentsia in the generation which grew up during the Soviet years had never really identified itself as Soviet. This attitude was not declared in public, either by individuals or by groups, and few of us took part in illegal activities. However, if our communist 'big brothers' had been able to make windows into our minds they would have discovered us to be 'anti-Soviet', and certainly have denounced us. The largely silent struggle for freedom of expression in the arts was a battlefield to which we were attracted. Earlier, during Stalin's lifetime it would certainly have been quite impossible to go as far as we did, but we learned to conduct ourselves without yielding an inch of moral ground, even though some of us suffered severe stress. It was because we had offered this private resistance, and had learned how to discern the truth rather than fitting in with the Soviet mythology, that a small free space was opened up which we could extend later.

The result of our efforts in the field of musical expression was that new textbooks for piano practice arrived in the schools. They were still of the 'Soviet' kind, but were much less conservative than those which had previously been in use, and most importantly they allowed Lithuanian folk-songs back into the schools' repertoire. I asked one of my students to carry out a social analysis of the attitudes of students at our institutes of higher education, and his questionnaire asked how many folk-songs they knew, how much they were liked, and how frequently they were sung. It also enquired if they had been learned from their parents, at school or from friends, and we were surprised by the discovery that they were widely known and that while a few had learned them at school and a small number from their parents, most had picked them up from friends. It is also interesting to recall the regrettable fact that the authorities at the Vilnius Conservatoire did not allow the questions to be put to *their* students. They were of course following instructions from Moscow which disapproved of 'uncontrolled sociology'!

Slowly the scene changed, and organized folk groups began to come forward to sing genuine unadapted folk-songs openly in public places. In the mean time the University of Vilnius and the Conservatoire continued with the work of gathering songs from old people, and the many students who participated in these expeditions learned to love and admire the beauty of the songs, often memorizing them for themselves as they were collected. Eventually a few graduate students formed an ensemble, which later turned professional, and the village people who flocked to hear them perform as they toured the countryside often could not help weeping openly as they heard the exquisite songs of their youth being performed by these sophisticated young townspeople. Initially the group called itself the Ethnographic Ensemble, but it later became better known as the Lithuanian Folk Theatre. I wrote a small book supporting their work and the growing interest in folklore which it reflected. This small contribution was of course out of line with official thinking, which continued to declare that this folk art was 'not relevant to modern conditions' because 'it reflected ancient times' and that our ancient folk arts would 'soon die a natural death and fade away'. The attitude of the ideologists was pragmatic and utilitarian – they viewed the ending of this beautiful and age-old legacy with equanimity; the fact that people continued to sing these songs was something best ignored. 'Such activities will gain no official support' was their constant stance. Obviously we were working against the grain when we argued that art is timeless, and that if something which was created many centuries ago remains beautiful, it is not to be rejected 'because it has had its day'.

The Pedagogical Institute and our department were both busy expanding throughout the time that I was associated with them. Eventually the department became the Institute's faculty of music, and this status brought new opportunities, allowing us to arrange major concerts and influence cultural life. We took bold initiatives and within a few years had the pleasure of seeing our choir successfully performing works that others would rarely contemplate. The choir was widely appreciated, and toured the German Democratic Republic (East Germany) and Czechoslovakia. Yet though we dispatched well-prepared graduates back to the educational system each year, the schools of Lithuania still seemed to remain in a cultural vacuum. The unpalatable truth about our situation was that conditions were *not* favourable, as the state considered music useful only as decoration at ceremonies commemorating the Revolution. This knowledge did not, however, stop our efforts. We recalled that passage in the New Testament which tells how a master gave a silver talent to each of his servants before leaving them when he went on a journey. Two of them worked and made a profit, but the third was afraid to take risks, so he buried the money to keep it safe. When the master returned and asked all three servants to give an account of themselves, he dug it up and returned it. When he presented it to the master he was able to say that he had at least lost nothing, but he was then *condemned because he had attempted nothing*. We knew that it was far better to have tried and failed than to have done nothing.

Again and again in my life I have had good reason to recall and ponder something which Jadvyga Čiurlionytė used to repeat quite often. When I first heard her saying, 'Many things can be achieved through music', her words seemed to be some kind of truism, but I now perceive their wisdom. They embody a useful truth which has often guided my dealings with the world.

CHAPTER 7

Čiurlionis

Much of my working life has been dedicated to the study of the work of the Lithuanian composer and painter Mikalojus Konstantinas Čiurlionis.[6] He was a man of extraordinary intellect and powerful vision, who opened new horizons in the world of art and music, and his works express deep secrets of human uniqueness, and of the power of the human spirit in general. My interest in the man and his work took off during my years at the Conservatoire, but it had begun much earlier with an old and rather rare copy of a painting called *Auka* (The Sacrifice) which hung in my parents' house and which depicted the smoke of a sacrifice reaching to high heaven. This painting had affected me deeply even before I learned that the original had been painted by Čiurlionis, and as there were books about him in the house, I set out to discover more. That reproduction had played powerful tricks on my childish imagination and I realized later that I had believed that it depicted the time in which Čiurlionis lived!

My grandfather, Gabrielius Landsbergis, had been introduced to Čiurlionis at the first Lithuanian art exhibition in Vilnius in 1906. Gabrielius, as the leader of Vilniaus Kanklės, had immediately invited Čiurlionis to conduct its choir. It was the period just after the repeal of the Tsar's more restrictive laws, and new Lithuanian organizations, societies, publishing houses, political parties and so on were springing up everywhere. Choirs and theatres followed, and Gabrielius was already planning to turn his amateur theatrical association into a professional company. He had begun printing posters in the name of Vilniaus Kanklių Teatras. Čiurlionis undertook the artwork for him, including the illustrations for his play *Blinda*, with a frontispiece showing the symbolic representation of a great bird flying through clouds before the rising sun. It was not published because the publisher feared political repercussions. Even though Čiurlionis had not put his name to the artwork, its provenance would have been immediately recognized by any of the book's prospective purchasers. The illustration stayed in my aunt's hands for many years before she eventually gave it to a museum.

In 1908 Gabrielius was directing *Mindaugas*, a play by Juliuz Slovacki about the first Lithuanian king. He gave the main female part to Čiurlionis's fiancée, Sofia, and Čiurlionis would sit admiringly in the auditorium during rehearsals, becoming agitated when one of the actors needed to kiss her while playing his part! He first met her in the autumn of 1907 at a concert held in Vilnius to commemorate Dr Vincas Kudirka, when she read one of the presentations. The organizer had asked Čiurlionis to play the piano that evening, and when he had finished he walked straight over to sit down next to her, and said: 'You spoke so beautifully. I shall have to ask you to teach me how to speak Lithuanian!' Čiurlionis's father was Lithuanian, but his mother was of German descent and, though born in Lithuania, spoke Polish at home. However, she knew many Lithuanian songs and adored singing them, and the boy learned Lithuanian to some degree from his father's sisters. After graduating at the Warsaw Conservatoire he had conducted a Lithuanian choir there, and learned to paint while he was there. Meanwhile he had continued to struggle with Lithuanian, though his grasp of the spoken language was comparatively weak until he met his future wife. Needless to say Sofia took up his challenge and began to teach him, using the grammar written by my grandfather, Jonas Jablonskis.

I have already mentioned that I came to know Jadvyga Čiurlionytė, who was a professor of music at the Vilnius Conservatoire when I was a student there. I had already begun playing Čiurlionis's preludes when I was a junior at the music school in Kaunas, and my interest in his work grew under the quiet influence of his sister. Her presence at the Conservatoire served to remind the students of this great Lithuanian artist, and she was a gentle influence on the patriotic atmosphere which grew up among us. Elsewhere, his reputation was badly neglected because it was forbidden to exhibit his works. The ban had been imposed after the war, probably when officialdom noticed that our intellectuals and artists continued to value our own culture and were refusing to become sovietized. They saw him as a pillar of those values which they felt must be destroyed, and clamped down with particular vigour during the years 1952–4. Though many painters at that time valued his work and defended his name, their views gained them nothing but displeasure. However, for some reason it was easier for musicians to perform his music and so propagate the values associated with his work. I began to concentrate seriously on it during my fourth term at the Conservatoire after a friend encouraged me to read and copy Čiurlionis's unpublished manuscripts. Jadvyga supported the idea because she was anxious to preserve the manuscripts for posterity and had confided that she was afraid that an 'accident' might befall them. A little while later I followed up this line of enquiry and played some of the unpublished, and previously unperformed, works in concerts, eventually presenting five of them for my diploma examinations in 1955. Stalin had been dead for two years, Čiurlionis would have been eighty in that year and my efforts contributed to the first favourable comments on his work appearing in print for many years. I was naturally proud of this as it served to remind people of his contribution, and to confirm my view that he had created something of real value even though his works were far from receiving official approval.

I often visited the Čiurlionis Museum in Kaunas where another of his sisters worked, and she showed me more of his manuscripts. As I examined them closely I noticed that many were written in pencil and had become blurred, and that there were definite differences between these manuscripts and the scores which I had seen previously which had all been published before the war. I had already noticed that there were many strange-sounding sequences in these editions, so it was not hard now to work out where the errors lay, and how they had crept in. Most of the problems were not typographical but editorial, and had arisen because of the poor legibility of the manuscripts. This discovery excited me, and helped me to appreciate his work even more, and I began to work in earnest, treasuring the thought that while others were playing his works, I was playing them *correctly*! I took enormous pleasure in researching scores which had barely been touched by anyone other than the composer, and became very excited when I came across pieces which were previously unknown and details which others had missed entirely. It was a rare opportunity, and this excitement enabled me to work that much harder. As a result it was less than a year after my graduation from the Conservatoire that I was able to publish the first article from this treasure trove, which I then presented at a student conference, where I pleaded that it was high time that all Čiurlionis's works were published. The response was highly gratifying and I was invited to follow this up with a series of radio broadcasts. An extremely important event followed when the first public concert of his work to be held in the post-war era was permitted to take place. This was planned for 1955 as a commemoration of the eightieth anniversary of his birth, but had to be delayed until early in 1956 because of unforeseen difficulties. Musicians wanted his symphonic poem *Jūra* (The Sea) to be performed, but the bureaucratic situation demanded that a special concert should be arranged by the Society of Composers before a decision about its public performance could be taken. While this was not hard to arrange, and the necessary permission was not withheld, the discussion resulted in the verdict that the score needed editing. Eduardas Balsys, then a promising young composer at the Leningrad Conservatoire, was nominated to undertake the work.

Despite the delay, the Čiurlionis concert was without any doubt a major event. Two of his symphonic poems were performed, *Jūra* (The Sea), and *Miške* (Down in the Forest), and the audience was so excited by the first that it demanded an encore. The programme was also planned to include choral performances of his harmonized folk-songs, and I played his preludes on the grand piano. Thereby hangs an interesting story. Though I had completed my studies, and was the guiding spirit of the occasion I was regarded as a young and more or less unknown pianist. This was now an official concert at which representatives of the government might appear, and it was clearly doubtful whether I could be considered a suitable performer in such an august context! Well, that might have been the end of the tale, had not my old tutor, Aldona Dvarionienė, conspired to create the opportunity for me to display my talents in the evening's programme. She used her influence to arrange for the prominent pianist Balys Dvarionas, who was her husband, to play at the concert, asking me to be his understudy. Then at the last moment, when it was far too late to find anyone else, Professor Dvarionas simply bowed out, leaving me to take his place. It was their way of ensuring the young pianist, whose repertoire now contained dozens more of Čiurlionis's works than the few which had been chosen for that evening's performance, was given a chance to play. Their kindness then and afterwards allowed me to demonstrate that there were many more Čiurlionis compositions which were worthy of a public hearing. Interest in his work grew steadily as a result, and in 1962 I was in a position to produce a long-playing record of his music. This was the first time his work had been recorded in his own country, or in the whole Soviet Union for that matter, although the pianist Andrius Kuprevičius had done so in the USA. Just before the record was released, Dorothy Oldham, the Australian pianist, produced another Čiurlionis record. Several more years passed before we could make another record in Lithuania. I was not then a sufficiently accomplished pianist to make a great impression in an official recital, but I continued to play Čiurlionis's compositions at every opportunity. I always found a profound value in his work, even when it was being played at home and for my own pleasure. As I urgently wanted it to be interpreted correctly and popularized, I began to edit his works myself in 1975. Until then the printed notation of his work had always bothered me because of the errors which had crept into the scores.

When the ninetieth anniversary of Čiurlionis's birth occurred in 1965, the climate was more receptive and an exhibition was planned. The state recording studio co-operated in the production of a commemorative album of records which included his orchestral works, together with his string quartets, and piano and choral works. I wrote the companion volume and advised on which of his designs should be used in illustration. Several other articles of mine about Čiurlionis were published around this time, a success which itself indicated changing attitudes. A decade earlier, in 1959, I had written a long article arguing against the destructive Soviet criticism directed against his art, which had been peremptorily rejected by the *Literatūra ir menas* (Vilnius Literary Gazette). I discovered the background to this rejection when I happened to visit the editor's office there not long after it had been submitted, and was allowed to see the referees' reports on it. There were by then a set of additional notes in several hands written into the margins of my own text. I was even able to copy them down. They were most interesting to read: one scribble said, 'These words might give rise to problematic thoughts', while the art editor had added: 'He probably lives on the moon', no doubt because I had cheekily suggested that the Vilnius Art School should be renamed in honour of Čiurlionis. That idea may have seemed preposterous to many at the time, but I can record here, with great delight, that the school was indeed renamed after him only six years later. However, when this incident occurred, I was reduced to going around a whole series of editors, with very little real hope of the article ever being published. It was read by the editors and their secretaries, and they circulated it among their friends. However, as I felt that it was eminently suitable for circulation among ordinary mortals too, I set myself the target of writing and distributing articles which *would be read*, if only by a few. During the following year I gained more experience, and then wrote another article on Čiurlionis which discussed the themes of his *Jūra*, and made a comparative analysis of his music, illustrations and poetry – the three expressive forms which he used. This script was both more condensed and less controversial than the previous one. It was published, and this success gave me clues as to how to proceed with future work. I then began to write more directly about his music, or to discuss his paintings and his music in conjunction, deliberately giving the authorities fewer opportunities to pick on me. My approach was justified by my own wish to propagate knowledge of his work, and also by his own unique style in composition. Čiurlionis was above all a man who intimately understood what he described as 'the parallelism of the branches of Art', and made purposeful use of this understanding, which was the conscious source from which his greatest works poured out. His paintings were intended to echo the structure of sonata and fugue, though since they were at one and the same time symbolic and phantasmagorical, they recalled also his finely structured style in musical composition. This singular purposefulness, which permeated Čiurlionis's entire art, had a profound effect on me. The essence of his vision was the unity of all art, expressed in, and through, all its diverse forms.

My first book, which was also about Čiurlionis, came out in 1965. It was first planned as a collection of commissioned articles, though it eventually turned out to be more of a monograph. I had prepared a biographical essay and studies of his music and art, which were circulated in manuscript among colleagues, some of whom responded by writing to the publishers on their own initiative to say that the book should be abandoned! Fortunately there were others who thought differently, and my work was finally accepted, probably because the commemoration of the ninetieth anniversary of Mikalojus Konstantinas Čiurlionis's birth had already been officially announced. It was published without alteration, and its success led to another offer when one of my friends who was working in the film studios read it and encouraged me to write a script about Čiurlionis in the hope that he could obtain permission to turn it into a film. The gamble came off, and we found a director, cameramen and other consultants, and together formed a working group. My script had consciously used only Čiurlionis's own words, which I had selected with enormous care from his poems and letters, but I soon discovered that I was still working against the grain of official prejudices when the management of the state cinema studio made this an excuse for announcing their unwillingness to pay for my work, 'because of the absence of my own words'! I had also arranged the musical score for the film with the same care, using fragments of the symphonic poems and relating these to a presentation of the pictures, indicating the precise order in which these sequences were to be presented. Although I say it myself, the work was well crafted, and I had done my very best. We now realized that Čiurlionis's art was still unfamiliar to officialdom, and were apprehensive as to whether permission to show the film would be forthcoming. The doubts lingered even longer than usual, and we guessed that the bureaucrats needed a device to protect them from criticism in case they had to justify themselves to their superiors. We were therefore not surprised that they eventually told us to put a 'safe' evaluation of Čiurlionis *into* the film. In fact I was even told that I must incorporate Maxim Gorky's praise of Čiurlionis into our commentary. If we wanted the film passed for viewing there was nothing to be done but to comply, even though it seemed unacceptable to obtrude an outsider's words into Čiurlionis's text. However, I realized that this 'approval' would at least be a defence against party criticism, which we might well have to face. In the end, we agreed to do what was required of us, and found a way around the problem by making a trailer using Gorky's text. I then took care to add comments by Romain Rolland, the French musical critic and author whose opposition to Nazism also made him 'acceptable'. We said that this would be used as an *introduction* to the main film but, in fact, we managed to lose the addendum at the first opportunity, and nobody noticed.

Shortly after the film had been completed the authorities had the idea of showing it at the Writers' House in Moscow and began to plan a Čiurlionis evening to be held there, but then we learned that the Ministry of Culture of Soviet Lithuania and the Communist party's Central Committee for Culture considered the film to be risky. They now feared it might cause offence, and that it might be dangerous to show it publicly. A special viewing was therefore arranged in Vilnius, to which the managers of the film industry and other officials of the Ministry of Culture, together with representatives of the Central Committee of the Communist party, were invited. Among those present was Eduardas Mieželaitis, a prominent writer who had been a member of the Komsomol before the war, before serving in the Lithuanian Division of the Soviet army. We were well aware of his potential influence within the Central Committee. He was a poet whose work had caused a few brushes with officialdom in Khrushchev's time as he wrote in a modern style. Since then one of his books of poetry had been awarded a state literary prize by the Soviet Union, and had been translated into Russian and other languages. Having received this accolade Mieželaitis was famous, and therefore well placed in the political structure. As nobody now doubted his commitment to communism he was quite free to indulge his interest in modern art forms.

When these officials came to the preview, they were probably expecting a simple documentary explaining who Čiurlionis was, and when and where he lived, with some discussion of his progressive (or perhaps even revolutionary!) attitudes, and how his achievements could be interpreted in socialist terms. Had it met these expectations, our film would have been accepted without difficulty, but it disappointed all of them. Indeed it had a quite different character because there was no biography and no explanation, only Čiurlionis's own words and his music, used either in harmony with, or in counterpoint to, the commentary on his paintings, as the camera moved from one image to another in a measured progression which carefully echoed the cycles of his own themes, connecting motifs found in works such as the *Sun*, the *Road,* and other compositions, with his canvases. The major visual theme had been selected from one of his short stories, whose subject had taken a walk through a grey, stone-built town, with no green trees or grass, which was quietly decaying under a merciless sun. The traveller wants to escape the maze of streets, and is desperate to find a field or meadow, even a single blade of grass to relieve the urban scene, but as he wanders, he meets a very old man, whose clothes are covered with a multitude of small crosses, who becomes his companion on the journey. As they tread through these dreary and endless streets, the ancient tells his own story, how he too had wandered into just such a grey town when he had been young, to find other people also 'wandering there, with no thoughts, as if in a dream'. All he had wanted in the many long years which had since passed, was to find a shaded place where he might take rest and find cool shade from the intense heat of the sun. So the story went on, beginning afresh, only to repeat itself from the beginning, its theme of recurrence providing a metaphor for the history of mankind. Later in the tale, the old man feels tired, and finding a bench which has been set aside for messengers, decides to rest awhile. However, before parting from the younger man who must continue on his way, he urges him 'to climb every high tower and scan every horizon, in the quest for a road which may lead away from this place'.

We chose Vilnius Old Town as the location for the film. Its almost empty, almost silent cobbled streets and windowless walls were filmed in black and white with a conscious play on their symbolic realism. Scenes of iron-bound doors solidly bolted, with shadows thrown here and there and silhouetted barbed wire in a jungle of high brick walls, added a political undertone to this part of the film. The effect was deliberately enhanced by the sound-track, which consciously played with brooding echoes and keening cadences in order to emphasize the monochrome character and threatening atmosphere of the opening scenes. A tension was created which gave an impression that the traveller had stumbled into something unexpected. This depressing scene was then transformed, and the viewer was suddenly thrust into a world of vivid fantasy, with Čiurlionis's pictures presented in full colour, while his words were spoken to the accompaniment of his music. All this symbolism was carefully balanced, and the music was hauntingly employed to deliver an emotional response to the pictures. We used a stop-watch to measure every take of the production, and to achieve the best effects we made sure that every sequence was cut precisely to reflect the developing mood of the music. The score of Čiurlionis's great symphonic poem *Jūra* was used to great effect in the sound-track, and the images complementing it were carefully arranged to ensure that every phase of the music would have a precise relationship with the visual presentation. The camera dwelled on his pictures and then moved rapidly back to a distant shot of the long, empty pavements and bricked-up windows of Vilnius Old Town, as if to emphasize the musical refrain. We planned that the film would have a positive ending so as to leave the viewer with a feeling of hope and a 'way out of the dilemma'. To this end we had used a special angle in filming the steeple of the Russian Orthodox monastery, which is close to the heart of the Old City. The camera then focused on this feature more and more closely, making its image seem strangely larger than life. Finally, it led the eye down across the roofs of the Old Town, and swept across the sky before presenting a distant view of 'the way out' – a street which ran between the houses before opening out on to a main road. These ultimate shots were in black and white once more, but the music was softer now to make the most of the low murmuring, almost whispering, sounds of *Miške* from his symphonic poem, played to bring back a gentle suggestion of hope.

The film is a mere twenty minutes long and its viewing by the 'bosses' was followed by a complete silence before they began to voice their opinions. At first progress was unsteady, and they were uncertain whether a film without captions or subtitles could be released at all, let alone be shown in Moscow. As the doubts began to grow the tension for us was extreme. Then the poet Mieželaitis interrupted. He said simply and firmly: 'This film *has* to be shown in Moscow.' At once the atmosphere changed, with the officials responding to his authority and abandoning their misgivings. They announced that the film was 'not bad', and gave permission for it to be screened, though with conditions and we later realized that we would not be allowed to show it in any film festival abroad! This might have made me despondent, as I knew that a film dies if it is not seen. However, I was determined that this one should be seen, so once the initial showings were over I took it on myself to pack it into my suitcase whenever I travelled so that I could show it to small groups of enthusiasts. It was seen in this way in Poland, by a group of art historians, and elsewhere, but within three years I faced another problem because the colours had begun to fade. Fortunately, the negatives were good enough to allow a few more copies to be made, and the work was saved in the nick of time by the arrival of the new video technology, which enabled me to continue to provide copies to interested parties abroad. Of course, we would have liked everyone to see it when it was first made, so that Čiurlionis could be talked about openly and positively in a context which left no room for the usual clichéd accusations. But it undoubtedly reflected another view of life, another mode of Lithuanian being, and showed that there were *other dimensions* in our world, which was why the system could not allow it to be made widely available. Such a perspective, such an understanding, was wholly foreign to Soviet ideology, which makes the film an especially valuable representation of non-Soviet Lithuania to the wider world. Our struggle in the years between 1955 and 1975 'to give Čiurlionis a reputation' was a long-drawn-out process, and though the struggle to 'rehabilitate' him was a dedicated one, the progress we made seemed almost imperceptible. Nevertheless the Soviet *nomenklatura* was beginning to adjust to events. They were of course not above using any passing opportunity for their own benefit, and we noticed towards the end of their tenure that they had begun to claim Čiurlionis as their own 'Soviet' treasure! At first, however, progress in that direction was gradual in the extreme. Even in 1975, his centenary year, the Lithuanian Communist authorities firmly refused a proposal to honour their country's most able and creative artist by erecting a monument in our capital city. Even the members of the Čiurlionis centenary celebration committee accepted the advice of the Lithuanian Communist party's Central Committee 'that Moscow might be angry if all these plans go ahead'. I was not alone in feeling ashamed, and a number of the country's most prominent artists protested strongly. These pleas got us nowhere and more time was needed.

I have now published eight books about Čiurlionis. One of them contains his letters to Sofia as his fiancée and later as his wife, together with other documents. Much of his correspondence was published in the 1960s, but few of the letters to his wife were included at that time, and I discovered that he had written to her almost every day while he was in St Petersburg, and that while her side of the correspondence had been destroyed, she had kept his letters, which were still safe in the hands of their daughter. I therefore determined to fill the gaps in the published record, and with the daughter's agreement the book, *Laiškai Sofijai* (Letters to Sofia), was published. In preparing it I collected the letters, put them in order and supplemented them with additional material and a detailed commentary, before writing an introduction. I can still feel quite aggrieved when I remember how the publisher then deleted something like three-quarters of the original intro-duction as being 'politically unacceptable', but despite this surgery the book remains one of my favourites. Čiurlionis's life was full of nostalgia. His love story has a poignant quality, and at one stage I tried to interest publish-ers in Russia, Poland and the West in it, suggesting that it would also be enjoyed by non-Lithuanians. I had little luck but I kept on trying to publish a monograph in western Europe, and eventually my English-language monograph, *M. K. Čiurlionis: Time and Content*, was accepted and published in Vilnius in 1992. Earlier, my co-operation with one friendly publisher enabled me to publish five selected portfolios of his paintings, each with my introduction. In 1965 an annual Čiurlionis piano competition was established, and I have since taken part in its adjudication. During the Soviet era Moscow would not allow us to hold open international piano and organ competitions, although the authorities permitted Lithuanian, Latvian and Estonian musicians to compete on the same stage in Lithuania. Before our independence these restrictions allowed us to involve only two among the Soviet republics in such an event, and so young musicians from Belarus and Moldova sometimes participated. These limitations always rankled, and once the barriers had been lifted in the autumn of 1991 I was overjoyed to be able to use my influence to promote a festival for pianists and organists from around the world, and to welcome their representatives, together with our Baltic neighbours, to share fully in an open, and truly international, competition.

My interest in research on Čiurlionis started in my early youth and has met with some success. For a number of years this task absorbed my main efforts, and the results were very pleasing. As a result, I published a major volume *Čiurlionio dailė* (Čiurlionis's Art), in 1976, which was followed ten years later in 1986 by *Čiurlionio muzika*, a second volume on his music. Both included a complete list of his works and full bibliographies. These volumes should have been complemented by a third, dedicated to his collected poems, as I had already fully researched this field and published articles on his poetry in a literary magazine. Extracts from the poetry began to appear elsewhere from time to time, once even in an almanac published in Belarus, but the publishers were reluctant to allow me to dedicate yet another volume to this third sphere of Čiurlionis's genius. At the end of 1997, I finally satisfied a long-held ambition with regard to Čiurlionis. I was eager to edit a full collection of his piano compositions, music which I had played over so many years. Because no invitation had come to do this, I decided to begin the task for myself in 1975, and was eventually successful in having five separate collections of his music printed in Leningrad, Cracow, Kaunas and Vilnius before the end of 1991.

In 1983 I had edited some of Čiurlionis's choral compositions, which were then published in Leningrad, and went on to prepare the academic catalogue of his entire output to accompany this text. It was while I was busy with this task that the Sajūdis movement began its work, which allows me to make a point about the contribution which the spirit of Mikalojus Konstantinas Čiurlionis has made to this movement. His artistic genius has captured, and still conveys, the essence and irrepressible strength of the Lithuanian character, and his works challenge all those who engage with them to join in that permanent struggle which is necessary to ensure that a humane spirit is central to public life, whether inside the nation or between nations. What is more, he demands a bold commitment, and a passionate imagination from each of his hearers when he challenges them to fulfil their humanity to the utmost. His independence and creativity of mind constituted a call to individuals, and to the nation as a whole.

CHAPTER 8

Gražina and the deportees

Gražina Ručytė came into my life at a most difficult time. My first marriage had taken place when I was still a student at the Conservatoire. When I finished my studies there in 1955, we already had a daughter, but, unfortunately, my wife was not happy with the marriage and fell in love with another man. So I left the flat which we shared with my mother-in-law, and moved back to the two rooms in Kaunas which the council had allocated to my mother when her house was nationalized and which, since her death, were available to me. However, I continued to rent a room in Vilnius, where I worked in the Pedagogical Institute. In fact Vilnius was my real home, as it would have been too arduous to travel the hundred kilometres between the two cities by train on a daily basis.

In 1959 my wife and I divorced amicably to allow her to legitimize her new family, and that same year my father, whom I had not seen for fifteen years, came back from Australia and moved into the rooms in Kaunas. We had hoped that the whole house would be returned to him, as the authorities had agreed in correspondence before he came back from exile, but the promise was not kept.

I continued to live and work in Vilnius, where I met Gražina. She had returned from a period in Siberia and was completing her piano studies at the Conservatoire. We married in the spring of 1960, in the registry office; in December we had a baby daughter, and eighteen months later a son. Our professional lives were demanding, but we shared the burdens of family life, taking turns at staying at home with the children when they were small, juggling my lectures with her rehearsals at the theatre. Our home was a council flat shared with other families, a semi-basement room with rising damp and rot in one corner. It had a single window, half sunk below a backyard which was often busy with traffic coming and going to the garages which were the only view from our window. There was a small space to hang washing in the yard, and both the kitchen and the bathroom were shared with a number of other neighbours. In all our room was about eighteen metres square, and we had to make the best we could of it. Here we lived, all four of us, and sometimes we were five, because we helped Gražina's younger brother, who was a student. He would often baby-sit for us, but occasionally we had to pay a woman to look after our children. The difficulties of this situation forced me to train myself to write at night, when everybody else was asleep, and in this way I produced a number of articles for publication, including my first book on Čiurlionis. We did not regard ourselves as particularly poor or unfortunate, because many people lived in these conditions, but when we eventually managed to acquire a separate flat with three rooms a few years later, we felt we were the luckiest family on earth!

Then, as now, Gražina carried the triple burden of her work as a professional pianist, together with mothering the children, and the domestic duties. Her attributes are best described as industrious, persevering and honest, and she has deep sympathies. Indeed, I can think of myself as the chief beneficiary of her gifts in this direction, and can remember how her mother once said '*Gailėjo, gailėjo ir įsimylėjo!*' (she fell for him because she felt sorry for him!), when describing the beginnings of our relationship. At times she could be firm with me, which was often very necessary, especially when I became more deeply involved in public life. This involved long hours in libraries and archives, and later work for the Lithuanian resistance, but it often meant that I gave less time to Gražina. As a result she often felt very alone and sometimes the tears would show in her eyes, yet despite this she supported me and enabled me to continue with what had been begun. Though she would sometimes scold me for neglecting our home life she would often then go on to type my manuscripts and comment on my books and speeches with an insight which has contributed greatly to my thinking. I will not discuss the periods of tension and danger which we shared, nor the problems and trials which we faced, but I knew that I always had the support of a wholly true and loyal friend. As time went by, we were more and more affected by what had developed between us and began to reflect deeply on the influence of Providence on our lives, and one day I was moved to propose that we should have our wedding properly blessed by a priest. She was overjoyed, and our minds were as one. We both knew it was entirely the right move, and wasted no time about it.

After 1939 the oppression of foreign powers had torn many Lithuanian families apart. Whereas my closest relatives had retreated to the West in 1945, most of Gražina's had regrettably ended up in the East, although an elder brother had escaped being sent to Siberia and had reached Canada. She never saw him again, as he died before Lithuania regained independence. When it became possible for our exiles in the West to return home at last, the question of whether to do so or not was often a cruel dilemma, but it was quite different for the Siberian deportees. Many of them succeeded in coming home, even when it was illegal for them to do so. Despite the hardships they had endured there was often a cruel and incomprehensible paradox in their homecoming, when many of them experienced discrimination, and even scorn, from those who had been touched by the Communist mentality. Gražina had been a first-term student at the Kaunas Conservatoire when she was deported to Siberia in the spring of 1949, and she shared the experience of many other Lithuanian deportees, being separated from her parents, sisters and brother, who were deported separately. They were allowed to form a family unit again only after a prolonged period of separation. Gražina first found herself with other Lithuanians on an island in Lake Baikal, where she was ordered to work in the fishing industry rowing a heavy boat and pulling mile-long nets. Despite this heavy work she still found time to play the accordion at dances in the so-called 'house of culture', and after a while she was noticed, and invited to teach music at a Russian school. Later she was granted a permit to continue her own education in the town of Irkutsk some distance from Baikal. Eventually she landed up at the conservatoire at Sverdlovsk, in the Ural Mountains, but was still forbidden to return to Lithuania.

A few years after Stalin's death and Khrushchev's denunciation of his criminal acts and injustices, the surviving deportees began at last to come home. Gražina took a gamble at this stage, and returned without official permission to complete her studies at the Vilnius Conservatoire. Although she was back in her homeland the 'deportee' stigma still seemed to mark her career, as she discovered when she was rejected on the two occasions on which she applied for a lecturing post at the Conservatoire. She was by then rewardingly engaged, however, as a pianist with the National Opera and Ballet, playing at rehearsals, and helping singers prepare their parts. For over thirty years she prepared concert programmes for soloists and choirs, often going on tour with them, first inside the Soviet Union, and then outside it, though still inside the Soviet bloc. At that time every application to travel outside Lithuania, even to the 'People's Socialist Democracies', had to be discussed by a committee of the Communist party's Central Committee, and Gražina's 'stigma' was often an obstacle for these people. Though they would let her travel to East Germany or Czechoslovakia, she was always rejected when she and the choir were invited, say, to France. Whenever this happened she would enquire what the problem was, asking why she was discriminated against and why she was again being refused permission to participate in a professional activity for which she was well qualified and to which she was completely dedicated.

Eventually a senior official told her bluntly: 'You should be grateful that we allow you to work at all!' Such remarks can be really humiliating: they degrade a person, and the hurt can last a long time.

Another injustice which touched us personally was the fate of her parents. When they returned from Siberia, they found themselves living near Panevėžys, not in their former home but in a small farm belonging to someone else which we often visited with the children during the summer holidays. Gražina's parents originally lived at Anykščiai, where before the war they owned a shop which was attached to their house. Later they bought a farm of about twenty hectares near Panevėžys. The house was lost to them after the occupation in 1940–1 when they fled to avoid the first deportations imposed by the Soviets. When the Soviet army returned in 1944, they fled again. After this they dared not claim the house or even show their faces in Anykščiai, so they went to Panevėžys, where they rented a flat and worked on the farm until the luckless night in 1949 when deportation finally caught up with them.

The farm at Panevėžys was eventually incorporated into a collective farm, and when the couple returned from Siberia they tried with our help to claim some compensation for its loss. Some of the deportees did obtain a little, and a few even managed to reclaim their houses if they had not been pulled down in the mean time, but Gražina's parents were not among these lucky ones. Their house near Panevėžys was still standing, but the chairman of the local farming collective simply refused to allow them to settle there. We discovered that there were excellent reasons for this, though they were not explained by him or by anyone else for that matter. In fact, he and his family were now living in Gražina's parents' former home. He was secure in his greed, and would not even consider allowing them to take shelter in the dilapidated sauna shed on the farm which they asked him to allow them to use as a temporary home. Shortly afterwards a general meeting of the workers was called to consider the case. The members decided to allow Pranas Ručys to settle on the collective farm because they remembered my father-in-law well, and thought of him as a good person. They were fully prepared to welcome him back, but their chairman was now the ruler of this domain, and he overruled their decision peremptorily. So Gražina's elderly parents were forced to find another place. Her father was given work as a caretaker in factories, but eventually he had to depend entirely on his children.

At the time he began his new work, the old man applied to the authorities asking them to recognize the long years he had worked on collective farms in Siberia as counting towards an old age pension, but the fact that he had been refused work on the collective farm in his home area now counted against him, because the chairman's refusal to allow him to return meant that he had been placed in a different labour category. This meant that he could only work in a factory, and the system did not allow service in the factory to be added, for pension purposes, to service in the collective farms. His pension was tiny as a result, and when he realized this it became a major aim of his life to demonstrate that he had been unjustly deported. If he could prove this, he could be rehabilitated. For one brief moment, when he happened to be ill in hospital, it seemed that his search for justice might be rewarded. He was visited by some Russian KGB officers who appeared friendly. They took down details of his original property, the number and type of animals on the farm, the condition of the buildings, how much land had been sown, and so on. But after another long delay, he received a further negative answer and was told that rehabilitation had been refused, and no compensation was due. We learned later that the chairman of the collective farm had gone to Vilnius to put his side of the case. He came back with a ruling that a collective which had benefited through requisitioning a deported farmer's wealth had no obligation to pay compensation or return anything. It meant that old Pranas Ručys had achieved nothing at all, and a relative of the chairman who was living snugly in his former home went around crowing about the decision, saying, 'The collectives, which must be protected, are being supported!' Soon afterwards Gražina's parents both died without recovering their home, and owning not a single room between them. By then they were forced to seek a corner in their children's homes, and, worse, they were usually separated from each other, her mother staying with one family and her father with the other because we were all desperately short of living space.

Over the years I have learned a lot about Gražina's father indirectly from other people. The story of his deportation is worth telling and reads like a novel. In the months after the war ended he spent his time working on his farm, tending the buildings, the animals, the orchard and the fields, while his wife and the children stayed in Panevėžys town. The period was dangerous and sometimes violent because country farms were often visited by local partisans and, at least as frequently, by the NKVD and *stribai* (as Lithuanian collaborators were known) who were pursuing them. Armed conflict was frequent, and rural homes were often set alight. Farmers were shot, burned alive or transported to Siberia on the smallest pretext. Eventually Pranas Ručys's name was placed on a list, and in the early summer of 1948 he was deported. A Russian officer and soldiers arrived on motorcycles one morning, to tell him to pack his belongings into a cart. Gražina's father was in a state of shock and too numbed to know what to do. The Russian lieutenant saw that he was getting nowhere and showed real human feeling, telling him to take some clothing, and some food, saying: 'It'll all come in handy in Siberia.' A human relationship began to develop, which was not usual in such circumstances, since soldiers were trained to conform to a Soviet stereotype. Father indicated that he would not be able to take much food, since he had no meat in the house. He said he had been making bread, but it was not yet baked. Hearing this, the officer told him to fire the oven and bake his bread! He then asked whether there were any pigs, and ordered the soldiers to slaughter a couple of them and to salt their meat so it that could be 'deported' as well. At this stage Gražina's father found a bottle of farm-distilled *degtinė* (vodka) and some home-brewed ale. It was all highly irregular. The occupying forces became wholly preoccupied for a little while with the task of assisting the older man to go on his long journey into a hopeless future. He himself felt neither anger nor the need for revenge as he feasted the men who were both his deporters and helpers at the same time. Eventually the cart was full, though many items remained to be loaded. At this point, the lieutenant ordered his soldiers to commandeer a horse and cart from the nearest neighbour, and to load everything remaining. It was sunset before the convoy was at last ready to move. Pranas was taken to Miežiškiai, near Panevėžys where, with others who were facing the same journey into exile, he would be expected to load his possessions into railway trucks. But as the party moved through the forest it was met by a group of soldiers which was armed and ready to shoot. They had been sent out to look for the lieutenant because his men were late returning. As the neighbour who had come to ensure the return of his commandeered cart helped with the unloading, he saw Gražina's father being taken to the army commander's headquarters where he was admonished by a higher officer for getting the lieutenant and his soldiers drunk!

While all this was going on, a large crowd of people who had also been forcibly torn away from homes and families were being loaded into lorries near Panevėžys railway station. Gražina's father was still waiting to know his fate, but towards midnight he was called again to see the commanding officer, who told him that he was being released, and was now free to go home. It is difficult to imagine his thoughts as, quite alone and in the depths of night, he reloaded his belongings and drove his cart back along the starlit road towards his empty and by now ransacked home. One might well ask what lay behind this miracle. The story was actually a simple one. His wife had been on her way to visit him when she was stopped by villagers who told her that he was being deported to Siberia. She had hurried back to Panevėžys to find a senior party member whom she had known from the time she lived in

Anykščiai. He knew Gražina's father well, and phoned the commanding officer to say that he must let him go!

Sadly his release was only a respite, because the entire family was to be ruthlessly deported in the second great wave of deportations which took place in 1949. This time the soldiers did not go to the farm, but went to the Panevėžys house where Gražina's mother was living, and it happened that he was there visiting his family. It was a different gang of soldiers this time, and when the officer checked his list he found that Pranas Ručys's name was not entered with those of the rest of the family. He knew well enough that an order is an order, and a list is a list, so he simply told him to get lost. Pranas then begged the officer to allow his smallest daughter to stay with him to save her from Siberia, but the officer insisted on keeping to his orders because the names he had been given were those of subversive persons whose continued freedom would be dangerous to the Soviet Union. The logic was clear: everybody named on the list must be deported, including the little girl. Pranas, who was now quite desperate, asked that he should be named as well so that he could go with his family. This honourable decision was to count against him later when it was argued that he had gone *voluntarily*, and should therefore not be treated as a deportee because his name had not been on the government's list. His own explanation cut no ice, nor did it help his case to explain that there had been no choice but to work on the collective farm at which he was dumped on arrival in Siberia, or that he had been directed to work in the factory on his return. He had left Siberia voluntarily too, and that was that, so the years on the collective there were never added to his pension. Despite the hardships and dehumanization, and the fact that it was eventually 'acknowledged' that the deportations had been unjust, the returned deportees never won official recognition of their sacrifice and their predicament. It meant that they were in effect, *not rehabilitated*.

It was only after Gražina's parents died that this issue of rehabilitation was finally faced. Until then the children who had been deported were stigmatized just as much as their parents. They had committed no crime, and had come before no judges, yet they were labelled as deportees, and the shadow remained to affect their professional future in a system which was quite unremitting in its attitudes. I have explained how it affected Gražina, but her brother was also dogged by the same problem. He was a graduate geologist of considerable ability, but despite the Soviet arrangements for sending specialists to work abroad, was refused opportunities to work in Algeria and Morocco. It was further evidence of how the deportees, a group which had committed absolutely no crime, continued to experience discrimination. In most cases property which was stripped away from them as they went into exile was not returned when they came home. Even after independence, when laws had been passed to ensure a just settlement, many of the former deportees experienced intimidation. When they attempted to reclaim their properties they met consistent and intolerable barriers of red tape, refusal to comply with the law, and even blatant abuse from people in the local government system who had been active contributors to the Soviet repression. Those who had benefited from the communist system, and had made 'something on the side' for themselves were deeply resentful of those who were naturally eager to reclaim the things they had lost in a time of grave injustice.

During the democratic interlude after 11 March 1990 we used our parliamentary powers carefully to redress many of the injustices which affected former deportees, and were largely successful in securing formal arrangements for the return of lands and property to the former owners. Unfortunately the parliamentary election in the autumn of 1992 which reestablished the Lithuanian Seimas also returned the former Communist party to office, and this new government immediately began to undo what we were trying to accomplish, first by limiting the award of compensation, and eventually ending it altogether. It was awful to know that people who had been forcibly removed from their farms, but who had now returned to claim what was rightfully theirs, were being pushed away and treated as if they had deserted their properties. Gražina had been one of those deportees. She grew up far from home, but the severe conditions did not break her, and she continued to believe in the future. She had persevered, educating herself and maintaining the hope that she would return home one day to work in her native Lithuania. Her nephew, who was born in Siberia, came to Lithuania after Stalin's death to grow up in this country. He began work as a driver, but now farms his grandfather's land with love and affection. It has been justly returned to him.

People who went through the experiences which I have described often have a very strong character and iron willpower, and are acutely sensitive to the big questions of justice and injustice. Sadly, these are traits which the communist system feared. I have been close to many of the returned exiles, and have learned much from them about what is an important part of the Lithuanian experience. I remain deeply impressed when they speak of the harsh and sorrowful years of exile in Siberia. Yet they also remember that time as having been a period of joyful togetherness and youthful solidarity. While they feel pain at the injustice done, they harbour neither spite nor the desire for revenge, and the act of returning to them their family properties was straightforward reparation, a restitution in justice which acknowledged their human loss. When one considers the enormity of their experiences the compensation is more moral than material, but it still means a great deal to them. The programme has already been achieved in part, but it must be carried further until each and every one of them has received its benefits.

As we remember the colourful episode which accompanied the first attempt to deport Gražina's father, it is worth recalling what his neighbours told his daughters about their father's last moments before leaving his farm. They saw the elderly Ručys going around a circle of birch trees which he had planted himself, hugging each one of them individually and saying goodbye sorrowfully. He was leaving everything that he held dear and everything that he had lived for, thinking he would never return to Lithuania. Many of those who shared his plight did not return, and in the vast wildernesses of Siberia between the icebound ocean and the Altai and Kazakhstan, there are innumerable unmarked Lithuanian burial grounds as well as cemeteries which can still be identified. People visit them to tend the graves, and sometimes to bring the remains of their relatives back to the land of their birth. Gražina's brother-in-law returned there to see the graves of his two brothers who died of famine, and set up a cross (since he could not find the grave) in memory of his father, a village policeman in independent Lithuania until he was deported in 1941. This was the fate of many people, not just Lithuanians. Having been torn away from their country countless numbers died of malnutrition and exhaustion. One wonders why the world has seemed incapable of perceiving the magnitude of Soviet crimes, and why it has not condemned them as it has condemned Nazi crimes, which they equal and in some respects more than equal. When, in August 1991, I signed on behalf of our Supreme Council an 'Appeal to the Parliamentarians of the World', calling for a Nuremberg-style International Tribunal to be held in Vilnius to condemn Soviet crimes and those who had been responsible for them, my call fell on ears which were entirely deaf. Time has passed since then and the idea, which was then ignored, is at least discussible in some places now. Similar thoughts have been voiced in other post-communist and neo-communist countries, but one wonders whether this is because they believe in truth and justice, or whether it has happened only because some people fear the resurgence of communism, of which there is still a danger. I greatly doubt whether there will ever be a concerted attempt to deliver the justice which was eventually meted out to the Nazi leaders. There are activists in Lithuania today who wish to revive the Communist or Bolshevik party, and they assert that it is wrong to compare Bolshevism with Nazism. While I can agree in part, it is also true that Bolshevism applied its own policies of extermination and that these continued for much longer. In fact the system succeeded in exterminating a greater number of human beings than did Nazism; it applied its brainwashing techniques to larger populations, and developed a technology of oppression which penetrated and corrupted the human spirit over a longer period of time. When all is considered and weighed in the balance, I conclude that the sufferings of the casualties of the system and the threat to the future of human liberty were proportionally greater. However, now that we have seen the pervasive power of that system brought to an end, we should be able, at least on the European continent, to learn from those events in the way we respond to the continuing parallels which are to be found elsewhere in the world. We have clear choices between ignoring injustice and playing it down, or else recognizing injustice where it occurs. We shall not learn this lesson unless we recognize the truth about the Soviet era, that these crimes happened, on a catastrophic scale and to a degree unheard of in the earlier history of human civilization, and that the human community is in danger when such facts are not understood and heeded.

During the First World War, when Russia and Germany were contesting the territory of Lithuania, my grandfather Jonas used to say: *'Abu labu tokiu'* ('both are the same'). How much more is this true of the two ideologies which have so dreadfully threatened the human spirit during my lifetime. From my childhood, a doggerel ditty which people used to sing around 1940 (though not very loudly) floats back into my mind:

> Dvi birbynės, vienas tonas.
> Tai Berlynas ir Maskva.
> Viens raudonas kaip šėtonas,
> Kitas rudas kaip šuva.
>
> [Two reed pipers, but they have a single tone.
> One's from Moscow, the other's from Berlin.
> One wears red, he's Satan in a frock,
> The other's dressed in brown, and he's like a shitty dog.][7]

There was also a verse which I remember from my excursion to the villages of Dzūkija in 1959 where I noted down some folk-songs of the resistance period. A girl addresses her tormentor, a *stribas* (a collaborator of the type found everywhere in occupied Lithuania) who, being ordered to 'exterminate the enemies of the people', had gleefully used the opportunity this order gave him to strip his victims of their possessions:

> Ar ašarota aš tau graži,
> Kad mano kraitį imi, veži?
>
> [I'm deep in my tears, but do I attract you? Say!
> As you grab at my dowry, and cart it away.]

In my lifetime Lithuania has survived all kinds of extreme experience. Her deportees went through the crushing machine of a totalitarian system, and when they returned from Siberia they found their country morally and spiritually fragmented, divided between two spirits. One of these had remained human, and had struggled. The other was a spirit of resignation and acceptance of the system, of tolerance for its degeneration. Those of our people who survived by retaining their deeper human values intact had endured their tribulations in hope, and in the end they realized their dream. However, there are still some who await the fulfilment of their hopes because they have not yet been able to return home. We acknowledge that the experience of those who still live abroad in exile also reflects the historic experience of the Lithuanian nation. We also cherish the thought that what this nation has gone through in this century can work for the good of the whole world, if we draw properly on what it has taught us as a nation and learn how to share its meaning with other human beings.

Those of us who are still alive to speak and act must do what is necessary to explain what our nation's terrible experience has taught us about the human condition and the struggle for justice. The many graves which lie in the vastness of Siberia will not give voice to Lithuania's message. No one will preserve these cemeteries for posterity's sake, and when a little more time has passed they will not be listed as monuments to history. The eternal flame will not burn there in the wilderness to preserve the memory of the gulags, which will never be turned into museums like Auschwitz and Dachau, because they are too far from selfish Europe. It is, however, to be hoped that the prayers written on scraps of brown packing paper by the deportees will leave a message that we can understand and that neither Lithuania, nor any other nation, will ever need to send its messages of personal survival, of despair or of hope, in this way again. The poignant song of the girl who saw the *stribas* cart her dowry away reminds us of our freedom fighters, of our partisans, and of the painful longing of the exiles and their sufferings. Now that we are free again their bravery is the true dowry of the nation. In the fullness of time such songs as this will be treasured monuments, because they will speak to the next generations of hope, of belief, of human longing and patient endurance.

CHAPTER 9

The origins of Sąjūdis

To ask how and where Sąjūdis began[8] is to ask how political movements are born. There is a sense in which our movement appeared like a river in full course, which tells little of its origins. When we trace a stream back to its source we may find a clear spring, though it might equally flow from a muddy lake. Whatever its origin, the strength of the river quietly increases as the tributaries add their volume to its flow, until it is large enough for people to notice it and to insist that it has a name. Sometimes it can be difficult to tell which of the tributaries of a stream is the most important, and which of them should carry the name of the river. Similar considerations apply to Sąjūdis. The movement was formally established by resolutions passed at a public meeting on 3 June 1988, but it had really began a good deal earlier. Even in the spring of 1988, there were models to emulate, like the People's Front in Estonia which began as an umbrella organization linking like-minded movements. Lithuanian activists from the 'Rebirth movement' had already held meetings with the Estonians, and had taken note of their organizational infrastructure and their projects for economic reform. Similar reforms were being considered in Lithuania, perhaps even on a scale more ambitious than elsewhere in the Soviet Union, and our Academy of Sciences had already ventured to draft a new law, which would incorporate both civic and sovereign rights into the constitution of what was still the Lithuanian Soviet Republic.

In reflecting on the origins of the name Sąjūdis, we must also remember the Lietuvos Laisvés Kovos Sąjūdis, the Lithuanian freedom fighters' movement, which had put up armed resistance in the immediate post-war years. The memory of its bitter struggle must have influenced the naming of our new movement. Then again a decade before Sąjūdis was established individuals and groups had begun to engage in public campaigns against the endless problems of our society. A good example of our people's persistence was the struggle to draw attention to the ecological effects of the large-scale exploitation and destruction of Lithuania's natural environment. My father was prominent in this struggle. It was his belief that nature has a higher intrinsic value than anything that human beings can create, and he argued that nature and architecture must live in harmony, claiming that we are under an obligation to adapt and live in harmony with nature. Because of these beliefs he supported other architects who had become active in this field where it was urgently necessary to protect the environment from misguided planning decisions, and from the self-interested *apparatchiki* who often benefited personally from the badly planned urban expansion which was going on all over the country. I can recall a whole series of awkward situations in which he challenged major projects. He felt impelled to do so because the communist planning authorities had an established tendency to locate major schemes in places where rational consideration might suggest that preserving the beauty of the natural environment would outweigh the benefit from the construction project.

These conflicts began very shortly after he came back from Australia, when he was working in Kaunas. He started writing to the papers protesting at the behaviour of the municipal councils, often challenging their chief architects, whom he accused of promoting schemes which should have been rejected. However, with only a single exception no newspaper in Kaunas or Vilnius would publish his arguments. But later, in 1973 when he celebrated his eightieth birthday with an exhibition of his architectural achievements and was invited to appear on television, he used the opportunity to express feelings which he had suppressed over the years, and denounced a whole series of bad decisions, and 'crimes against nature and the environment' and then announced blithely that the newspaper editors had been 'forbidden to publish his point of view' except for that one paper in Vilnius which had been 'daring enough' to publish his articles! While this tirade would be regarded as fair comment nowadays, such open criticism on the television screen was then quite unheard of, and the entire republic experienced an unaccustomed shock at hearing this sweeping attack on the planning officials. There were of course others who had tried to argue for action to protect the environment or buildings which embodied some aspect or other of our cultural history, but they had usually found themselves on the losing side. Despite their frequent failures, these earlier protests had a moral and educational effect, and many of my father's fellow architects now told him that they appreciated his outspokenness and responded to his initiative by forming an unofficial group whose members were ready to protest, and to prepare the case against unsuitable projects by taking photographs and writing articles.

These actions led to the first unofficial protests which Lithuania had seen being organized, beginning in the early 1960s with demonstrations against major Soviet construction projects planned in Jurbarkas and Klaipėda. At Jurbarkas, plans had been advanced to construct an oil refinery on the banks of the Nemunas which would pour effluent into the river. It was clear that this would pollute not just the river, but also the unique enclosed environment of the Kuronian Lagoon, the long sea-lake which lies behind the coastal sand spits where the river approaches the Baltic Sea. The plan also involved damming the river to allow a hydro-electric station to be built, and drowning the entire historic valley with all its ancient hill-forts and castles. In the end this protest was success-ful. The refinery was eventually located at Mažeikiai in the north of Lithuania, and the building of a dam was abandoned. A further battle also loomed when a petition was prepared against a scheme to construct a major oil depot at Klaipėda. There were solid arguments against a project which would have a ruinous effect on the entire environment of the port, the bay and the sea, with pollution flowing northwards to cont-aminate the tourist zone along the Baltic coast, and this protest was widely supported by our Lithuanian scientists and architects, and some-times unofficially by members of the government, though it was an uphill struggle against the Soviet bureaucracy. The opponents of the scheme suggested an alternative location at Šventoji, a site at which a second port for Lithuania had been proposed even before the Second World War, but this battle was lost, and the oil depot was constructed at Klaipėda.

There were many other campaigns along similar lines, but I particularly remember the occasion in 1978 when Klaipėda's municipal corporation blew up its historic eighteenth-century fire station, a small but stylish and extremely beautiful building, which had long stood at the centre of the town. The planners wanted to erect a large hotel in its place, to face a large square which would be dominated by a statue of Lenin. This complex project was intended to bring a new character to the place, and its support-ers naturally pushed the arguments of their political ideology to the forefront, but there were protests from the inhabitants of Klaipėda, who wanted their unique and beautifully constructed fire station to be preserved for posterity. They kept vigil at the building, and were supported by many protesters from Vilnius and elsewhere. Eventually, the council promised to relocate the planned construction elsewhere in the city. The people were pacified by this news and discontinued their vigil of the building, but as soon as they had relaxed their guard the council took advantage of the situ-ation and demolished the old fire station. There was then nothing left to keep a vigil for, so the hotel was built, together of course with the statue of Lenin.

A long series of such skirmishes inspired the preparation (under my father's guidance) of a memorandum of protest which listed the histor-ical monuments that had been destroyed. We engaged in discussions with the Ministry of Culture and produced evidence to show that the Council of Ministers had often issued demolition permits in contravention of both Soviet and local laws. This campaign resulted in a National Monuments Preservation Office being established with responsibility for making recommendations to the Council of Ministers. However, as one might expect in the closed system of Soviet bureaucracy, the new office continued to be very accommodating when issuing demolition permits to the municipalities, and the Klaipėda fire station was an example of this. The city bureaucracy had a registered monument which it was itching to demolish, in defiance of the law and local opinion, because it stood in the path of a grandiose scheme. We were told that the head of the Monuments Preservation Office had prepared a directive requiring the architects for the project for the hotel to explore all avenues for the preservation of the fire station. It sounded fine, but in the double-speak of the time what it actually meant was: 'After you have considered the matter, please reply to me saying that you have discovered no possible way of preserving the monument.' Once this little paper ritual had been completed the destruction of the monument could of course go ahead without regard for public recommendation or the opinion of the architectural profession.

People everywhere in Lithuania suffered from this obnoxious bureaucratic oppression, but it was the inhabitants of the Old Town of Vilnius who finally lost patience. This happened when a powerful group of *nomenklatura* formed a co-operative to build an underground car park near the heart of the Old City. It was well known that this was an area where the unexplored foundations of the medieval city lay, but the necessary permission was given without regard either for archaeological considerations or the quality of the buildings which were to be demolished. Work started without delay, but at this point my father began to object and asked for my help in making his protest effective. We approached architects, writers and artists, asking them to voice their opinions, and soon groups and societies joined us in expressing their disapproval. The fight against the garages was then discussed in the Communist party's committee in Vilnius where the functionaries condemned the protesting intelligentsia as 'obstructers of this useful project' in a way which made it plain that we were considered to be nothing more than a nuisance. Fortunately the issue had now caught the public imagination, and the strength of opinion behind us became forceful enough to get the construction stopped. At first the stay was temporary, but the dispute dragged on, and as time passed, the excavated hole filled with water, forming a pond which was eventually filled in some years later. But while the argument was going on, pupils from nearby schools, including my own teenage son, used to look into the hole as they passed by. They would argue about who was going to win. This time it was a victory for the resistance. It was an early sign that things were beginning to change.

Another project which came up at the meetings of the Society of Architects around this time was a plan to bulldoze several streets in the Old Town so that a six-lane highway could be driven through Cathedral Square. It was a development which would have ruined the entire appearance of Vilnius Old Town, which is the most extensive historic quarter in the entire Baltic region. When the matter was discussed at meetings of the Society of Architects it became clear that the traffic generated by the scheme would eventually cause major damage to the cathedral and its bell tower, and to the nearby Gediminas Hill. Again it was the intervention of the intelligentsia which stopped the project, but this time students and young people were increasingly drawn into the fight. I recall a meeting at which staff from the so-called Monuments Preservation Office presented their case for the project at the University of Vilnius. They were articulate officials who believed in their cause, but their arguments sounded increasingly pathetic and they patently failed to prove their case in a hall packed with students and their professors. The societies of Writers, Artists and Composers also entered the arena. This had always happened to a greater or lesser extent behind the scenes, but now the discussion was in the open, and their influence in this struggle for culture enlarged the opportunities for debate. Freedom of thought was extended little by little as a result of this process, and gradually more democracy was achieved in the learned societies themselves. My own part in this process was played in the Composers' Society, which held its general meeting to elect new officers and a chairman only once in every four or five years. Such gatherings sometimes saw signs of struggle as groups from the different generations took their stand in defence of a particular musical style or outlook, but the state to which we were accustomed was one which offered bribes to cultural workers to ensure their compliance with its ideology. Such procedures promote compliance, and the Composers' Society was as much a part of the system as any. It was possible to gain advancement, favours and material advantage through holding office, although there were specific expectations from those who had been elected. It is still extremely difficult for westerners to understand just how fully the state controlled every aspect of one's life through such channels as the allocation of housing, or permission to make a journey abroad, or even to buy a car or a refrigerator. It was a system under which one's opportunities for enjoying earthly possessions were almost wholly dependent on how well one co-operated with those in office. This meant that the election of officers, even in the Composers' Society, had to be played out according to the set Soviet scenario. Thus officials of the Communist party took care to nominate the committee members and chairman to be elected, selecting the officers in advance of a ballot in which members were obliged to ensure that everyone, or almost everyone, was elected according to the list. In order to be additionally sure that everything turned out as expected, the head of the cultural branch of the Central Committee of the Communist party or a similar high official always attended the general meeting, and this meant that most members were effectively excluded from nominating candidates. It was useless to step out of line or protest, as the party would 'have its way come what may', and artists knew the consequences of stepping out of line very well. Nonconformity of any kind had clear penalties; for example, a composer would lose out on new commissions if he did not comply, while performers would find that their income would decrease because remuneration was based on *two* scales. It meant that what one was paid, say, for playing in a quartet depended on the whims of a committee which was sensitive to 'reports', while that committee itself had of course to deal with its own superiors and managers who had their own means of controlling those who might step out of line. The system was so devised that a rigorous authoritarianism was in play from the top to the bottom.

Despite the entrenched character of this rigmarole, some of my generation of composers and musicologists were prepared to rebel against this demeaning, mechanical and artificial method of selecting officers. We began by being critical, and later started to propose alternative names for election, though it soon became clear that this tactic would achieve little unless we prepared a strategy. Even then we knew that embarrassment would be unavoidable because the procedures had been carefully constructed to prevent anyone moving to a more democratic style. If we nominated a candidate who was not on the prepared list, we would be asked, 'Which name do you want replaced by this candidate?' This was a powerful controlling device, because if you gave a name the person was usually present, and might even be sitting next to you. It took us some time to discover a formula which helped us side-step this manipulation, but eventually we learned to say: 'Though I like and appreciate our listed colleague, it would be of more benefit to the society if so-and-so were elected', and this tactic enabled us to move gradually to a position where elections could be held on the basis of a list of candidates longer than that prepared by the party. This was the first sign of democracy in the ballot, as one could then cross out, for example, the name of the Communist party secretary, who might then be voted out.

Despite our progress in this direction there were further constraints on real democracy in the election procedure as the supervising officer would normally announce the number of officers to be elected and his appointee would then immediately stand and read out a list of fifteen names, all of them 'approved' candidates. If we were swift enough to react, an additional candidate could then be proposed from the floor. However, the chairman would usually follow this with an immediate ruling that 'the number of candidates has to be agreed in advance', and our game was then up. We might stay silent if this happened because, although we were aware of being cheated, protest of any kind had to be handled obliquely in a diplomatic way. But it was difficult not to be angry on these occasions, and we often felt that we were being treated like simpletons. The real question we faced at this stage was whether to conform or not. We often found the courage and the determination not to, and this was naturally when the cost of nonconformity no longer included deportation or the peril of losing one's job. However, the threats of unpleasantness remained, and one's enemies could still eliminate one's name from a delegation and prevent one from travelling abroad, or refuse the coupon which would allow the purchase of a refrigerator!

On the eve of one general meeting the younger musicians, knowing that the officials would, as usual, propose a single candidate, decided that it would help the society to have a new chairman. The past chairman was a good composer, but was intolerant and authoritarian, so we agreed to nominate someone else, so that a vote could be taken. Our candidate was widely respected and was also well known as a composer. A former pupil of his was selected to put his name forward, and I was chosen to second the proposal, but at the crucial moment the intended proposer panicked – he simply lowered his head and kept quiet when the moment came. I felt acutely uncomfortable, but realized that our group would lose all credibility if our intention was not carried through, so I raised my hand and declared: 'I nominate another candidate.' At a stroke, the order of submissiveness which had endured so long that it had begun to seem entirely natural was challenged and destroyed. The chairman of the meeting saw his position threatened and attempted to ridicule me. Rolling his words for effect, he offered a vote on 'one candidate proposed by the Central Committee and the Ministry of Culture of the Lithuanian Republic and another, proposed by . . . Comrade Landsbergis'. However, his manœuvre did not work, as both candidates immediately declined their nominations. The real effect of our move became apparent a fortnight later when a third person became the new chairman of the society. The doors had opened just enough to allow us to glimpse the fact that a little more democracy was now possible.

Before Gorbachev announced *perestroika,* another event took place which confirmed that a new atmosphere was developing in the creative arts. We had realized that we were a group of like-minded close friends in the musicologists' section of the Society of Composers. We were able to elect our own committee and chair every four years, and in 1984 I had the honour to be elected chairman. In that year the section planned its work well, and we were able to make careful arrangements for an annual conference of Baltic musicologists, and to plan a series of festivals and concerts to promote the traditional music of our countries. Our activities developed within this framework, which was to embrace ancient and medieval as well as more modern music. This definition allowed church music into the programmes, which would not have been possible otherwise. It was a major breakthrough because centuries of history lay behind these works, and much of it was unknown to our young musicologists, who were soon learning a great deal about things which had found no place in the official curricula. Our aim was to encourage the widest possible interest in the continuity and development of our Baltic cultures from their earliest beginnings, and to involve the faculties of music in this interest. Needless to say we had an immediate fight on our hands. First we had to defend our decision to group Lithuania, Latvia and Estonia into a shared annual conference, but, as it happened, we were successful in handling this potentially awkward geopolitical question despite the tough opposition. Our difficulties were always political, and even in small matters such as writing musical review articles it was often necessary to choose between tampering with the truth, which was the only path to personal reward, or to speak one's mind. The cost of integrity was always painfully clear. To follow its requirements always meant paying a price. One would have to say goodbye to that hoped-for refrigerator or something like it for yet a while longer. In the end one became inured to the situation. One simply learned to say, 'The devil can take the refrigerator, his needs are greater than mine!'

In the fullness of time more and more of our Lithuanian composers, the younger generation especially, shrugged off the musical restrictions imposed on them, to become the musical avant-garde of the Soviet Union. However, a wedge was driven between members of the profession as this process developed. Many of those who had little creative individuality continued to please the state in the approved manner, receiving in return commissions from the Ministry of Culture for compositions, song festivals, public concerts and so on. Meanwhile a vigorous new generation of talented composers busied itself with altogether more significant and often larger compositions. Though their work should have been rated highly, the tariffs applied at the time spread the funds available to pay musicians more thinly as the output of fresh new music increased. Nevertheless the work of younger musicians was in demand, and they were being called on increasingly to represent the new trends in the Lithuanian music scene abroad. A situation developed which sent the old guard, which often disapproved of the new musical trends, into a rage, and this occasionally resulted in turbulent scenes. One incident was widely reported, when a senior party official went to listen to a recital of modern Lithuanian music, and left announcing his total confusion. We were very diplomatic, and had learned that it was best to arrange concerts which included cantatas dedicated to the party to cater for the needs of these people. We also did our best to avoid inviting them to music festivals, or to the recitals which our society arranged for composers to hear each other's new work. We even became unwilling to invite members of that unsympathetic clique to symphony concerts, because we knew in advance that they would understand little, dislike what they heard, and would then create a fuss. It was entirely natural for these mighty officials to react negatively to modern music. They seemed to believe that anything which did not conform to their set and rigid views involved an intentional snub to their authority as 'representatives of the people'. How dare the musicians and music reviewers perform or praise any music that 'workers could not understand'!

Some members of the musical fraternity kept in with officialdom by writing banal music, 'which ordinary people understand'. They were often supported by reviewers and journalists who knew where their political advantage lay, and tried to prove the worth of such music by explaining how to appreciate it and how to teach people to understand it. One arts magazine in particular maintained the official line in an editorial which said: 'All our Lithuanian composers should be praised for their productivity. Praise must not be reserved exclusively for the self-selected "chosen few" among the modernists.' It was of course an attack, and the writer then accused us of manipulating the critics and the reviewers 'by creating a clique of our own'. The communists also tried to undermine us by finding composers who would 'respond to the needs of the masses', and a new wave of restrictions followed in which our articles were simply rejected for publication, or edited to the point where we refused to have them printed. Derogatory attacks on composers of meaningful contemporary music were then mounted, and in 1985 the confrontation moved to new extremes. Some of the party's high-ranking officials were returning to attitudes reminiscent of Khrushchev's time. As chairman of the musicologists' group I made some effort to explain modern trends in music, with the support of the vice-principal of the

Conservatoire who was a party member, but the articles which we prepared were refused publication. Shortly after this, crudely insulting articles appeared in the press attacking 'incompetent musicologists whose praise for bad composition is misleading the public'. The implications were obvious, and we responded to this abuse by arranging a meeting to redress the situation. I proposed two ideas to this gathering: first, to establish an annual prize for the best modern musical composition of the year. As our Ministry of Culture was clearly not prepared to do anything like this, we suggested a small cash prize, or that a picture bought with donations from friends would serve to establish it. It would at least provide a moral reward for the composers, and help to establish the fact that that it was possible to take an independent view of truly artistic work. My second proposal was to collect for safe keeping musical articles which had been refused or censored each year and to send copies to the Lithuanian Communist party, its Central Committee, the Ministry of Culture, and the Society of Composers' office. We had been asking the authorities for more than twenty years to re-establish the leading Lithuanian musical journal, which had been closed by the Soviets in 1940, but Soviet functionaries had long refused us this right, saying that it was 'not needed because no worthwhile articles were being written!' Our collection would of course prove them to be quite wrong. The discussion had seemed useful, but shortly afterwards we found that there had been an informer in our midst, who had returned to brief his masters. On the morning after our meeting, Communist party headquarters issued a statement to the effect that our section of the Composers' Society was preparing *samizdat* (a word with overtones of subversion and dissidence), and threatened to disband it immediately. Shortly after this the minister for Higher Education called me to his office, where he shouted at me, saying that he was 'going to crush' me. The omens were not good; we realized that people's emotions were running high, and so in order to end this silly sequence, we agreed that the chairman of the musicologists' section of the Composers' Society should be sacrificed, and I yielded at once to allow my successor to be elected immediately.

The steady trickle of ignominious events of this kind was the source from which the Sąjūdis movement flowed. Neither I, nor anyone else, can tell you exactly when the movement was born, but as I have suggested, its spirit was already implicit in Lithuania's will to resist and was there in the dark days of 1940, as it must have been when our people faced earlier threats a hundred and even a thousand years ago. In my view Sąjūdis had no definite beginning, nor will it ever have a final end, because it embodies the spirit of Lithuania. However, in 1988 it emerged as a broad political movement supported by the people, and it moved, first to capture the local Soviet for the people of Lithuania, and then to challenge the entire totalitarian oppression of the Soviet empire. At times our movement was blessed with great good fortune, and never more than when we first contested elections to the Supreme Council of Lithuania, and when we confirmed Lithuania's independence. Sajūdis was not merely a reform movement, although we used that term as a cloak for our real aims. We acted within the law, but our intention was not the reform of the Soviet system. What we were working for was the establishment of Lithuanian law. This was the foundation of our movement and the basis of its future agenda. We were a puny David, but we resisted our Goliath with all the strength we could muster. We had been pushed into a corner as a nation, but we fought that corner and were not overcome. In a chess game, the time to counter-attack is at the moment when the opponent's offensive has expended itself and it worked that way for us. Lithuania did not allow herself to be checkmated at the beginning of her game because she wanted to live and not to be exterminated, but she held out without using force, allowing the enemy to make the wrong moves. The Soviet strategy was aggressive. It required more energy than did ours, and inflicted damage, but we were not extinguished, and in the end it was they who weakened first, albeit gradually. The old games were still going on when Sajūdis began, but we learned from playing them and discovered soon enough how to move from a defensive to a pre-emptive strategy by going out to meet the oppressor, and making his life unpleasant. Two years after this discovery, we were playing this game strategically move by move, growing steadily in experience and understanding, and beginning to change the direction of events.

It could be said that our initial strategy was simply to hold on. To have opened a full offensive would have seen our annihilation, so we chose to remain alert until the enemy's force had lost its momentum. Our opponents were among the mightiest forces in the world, and we endured their presence with forbearance through the long years. In the end, however, they seemed to have lost sight of their purpose. The Soviet bear had become increasingly confused and did not understand its plight. Its leaders scorned us because, in the imagination of their hearts, they believed that they were still in control and felt they could put up with the mere pinpricks which their humble opponents might inflict upon them. Our strategy was, by comparison, much more far-sighted. We had already recognized the underlying facts, and foresaw that this evil empire would sooner or later fragment into many states. We also knew it was necessary to broadcast and promote this understanding, but we had recognized that revolutions and coups entail bloodshed and are therefore abnormal and essentially inhuman events. In consequence we had reflected deeply on what we were doing. It was our hope that, when the time came, the dissolution of the Soviet Union would proceed as normally as circumstances would allow, and that the various interests would then proceed carefully, attempting to avoid mutual threats, and that the nations would talk and negotiate with each other wherever possible. It was our belief that human beings should always attempt to understand each other, and the basis of our moral stance even in relation to our powerful opponent was the idea that we were dealing with human errors and mistakes. Because of this, we tried to avoid suggesting that we were dealing with a deranged monster, even though our experience sometimes made this the most plausible interpretation. We knew above all else that we were not alone in our struggle, and that our progress must always take account of our natural allies, those forces throughout central and eastern Europe, and in the Soviet Union itself, which hungered for humane values and for the normalization of life. Knowing this, we supported the democratic movements in all our neighbouring countries, co-operating closely with the national movements in Latvia and Estonia, giving help to the Polish Solidarity movement, and maintaining contact with our counterparts in Belarus and Russia. This was the most important solidarity of all, and our strategy did not change even when we came under extreme pressure towards the end of the struggle. We gained fresh impetus when we defined our position as being that of an *occupied* country which was *de facto* and legally outside the borders of the Soviet Union though actively oppressed by it. This stance had practical implications for other people's perceptions of our actual status, and when they finally understood that we were more than a peripheral force *within* the Soviet Union new factors came into play which enabled us to exploit the changing relationships which emerged from the East–West *détente*. Indeed we discovered that this reassertion of our identity was our sharpest weapon.

All these things are now water under the bridge, but having held out against an attack which had continued for fifty years, we planned our counter-offensive with great care. We anticipated that the other side might well want to reconsider a situation which promised nothing but a stalemate, and to strike a new balance. We hoped they would agree that there was no point in leaving things as they were. We even hoped that they might realize that there were more important things in life than their sullen attempt to dominate their neighbours, that they would shake hands and declare a draw. Such things happen in chess, and the Soviet game could clearly not continue for much longer in the way to which we had all become accustomed. But I often wondered whether circumstances might force us towards a checkmate situation; it was still not unthinkable that our enemy might attempt to crush our resistance suddenly, and in the crudest and cruellest way. It was still capable of behaving unpredictably, and if events had gone that way we might well have taken some very foolish decisions. Any precipitate reaction would almost certainly have wiped out the progress we had made and then there would have been yet another checkmate imposed by our enemies. However, when we dared to hope for success, we knew that it was not a case of winning against an all-powerful and wise opponent. Powerful it remained, but the bear had become decrepit and dangerous, and our hope was now that it would lose its way through stupidity. That would have been the best outcome, but in the meantime we needed to be mightily patient, facing the constant frustration of our position with as much fortitude as could be found. It is interesting now to see how things worked out in the end. When we consider the whole panorama of events, it must be said that Gorbachev's *perestroika* provided an excellent framework in which our tactics could develop. It gave us an opening because it meant that the situation had changed sufficiently to allow us, and others, to perceive that we all stood 'for' and not 'against' *glasnost, perestroika* and even Gorbachev! Yet though we agreed with what was proposed, and even with those who wanted to implement it, we learned that our enemies had not really changed. Essentially the same old guard that had opposed reconstruction and openness everywhere in the past remained in position and continued to meet every fresh contribution to the debate with suspicion, resentment and refusal to budge. In these matters the Lithuanian *nomenklatura* was also, to say the least, very provincial, and it acted as a brake on developments. Not being with us, they were against us.

Not surprisingly the first signs of the openness stimulated by *perestroika* appeared in the official journal of the Society of Writers, but it gradually spread across the country. The new freedom of thought and speech gathered force, and then became a tidal wave as people found a new spirit in their meetings. It washed around them, and when I was invited to address a meeting of philosophers and artists which took place at that time I quoted Eduard Shevardnadze at length, describing how his vision of *perestroika* would work out in internal affairs. My speech was given at a time when it had become apparent that the Lithuanian government was committed to avoiding the issue, and a member of the audience asked me what I thought of its stance, in a way which implied that there was not much point in talking about *perestroika* in Lithuania. It was a provocative formulation, but I seized the opportunity with pleasure and insisted:

Perestroika provides an opportunity which we must not reject, but there must be no illusions ... This drive for openness from Moscow may well get crushed, and if it does, the same fate will overcome Lithuania. Anything is possible at present, but it would be cowardly and irresponsible to remain as mere bystanders at such a time. An opportunity has been offered and we must take it!

It was a timely comment, if only because the trickles were now turning into torrents, and discussion clubs were springing up everywhere. People were discussing everything. This opportunity to express oneself was obviously a major advance. Lithuania was coming alive with the excitement, and in Vilnius in particular such open discussion was in full spate. If one had been debating with the philosophers yesterday, one would be with the writers tomorrow, and with the architects at the weekend, but today one was with the young musicians, and if there was time, with the artists. Invitations to speak were just pouring in, and the notice boards everywhere were full of posters announcing meetings at various times and places. In this atmosphere, the Philosophers' Club was like a beehive. Some of its discussion covered the moral needs of the rising generation, and the necessity for a reformed and humanistic education in Lithuania. I also recollect a very impressive meeting at the Society of Artists, in which Arvydas Juozaitis, a young philosopher, struck hard at corruption in Lithuanian local government and the Communist party. His lecture was copied and read widely. Some ten years earlier this kind of openness would have landed him in a mental hospital, or in Siberia, but by 1988 these penalties no longer applied, and this young philosopher was already a symbol of change, a hero with his name in the public eye.

It did not take us long to realize how valuable it was for our cause to have ideas breaking through in this way, or that we had to continue to support each other if the advances we had made were to be secured. I responded to the excitement by posting a set of proposals on the notice boards of all the cultural associations with a note requesting that their members should convene a joint conference to discuss and adopt them. The proposals declared the necessity of establishing constitutional sovereignty for Lithuania, the need to ensure the protection of the rights of religious believers, and the adoption of Lithuanian as the official language of our country. They also asserted that Lithuanian law must in future have priority, in every case, over any decrees or legislation which came from Moscow, and especially over any promulgation from that quarter which might threaten Lithuania's existence. When these proposals were being drafted we were actively considering how to follow the

Estonian example by establishing a People's Front. A group of determined young people took the proposal to heart and set about organizing a public meeting to establish just such a body. As this initiative was beginning, they learned that the Academy of Sciences had announced a debate on the economic situation, and on social reconstruction in Lithuania, which was to be held in its conference hall at the very centre of Vilnius, and they decided to exploit this event for their own purpose. Thus, on 3 June 1988, over 500 people attended the meeting. Eduardas Vilkas, the academic who was in the chair, opened the meeting by declaring that the discussion was to be confined to the scientific examination of economic questions, but it was soon apparent, in that electric atmosphere, that the topic would be extended, especially when the concept of national reconstruction was supported by Antanas Buračas and Juozas Bulavas, both of whom were members of the Academy. Doubts were expressed as to whether the new organization would be permitted to work and if so, within what limits. Should we not, it was suggested, seek permission from the Central Committee first? My reply was that we should act, not ask. Then, if force were used to stop us, we should know what limitations would be imposed upon us. At the end of the meeting a committee of thirty-five people was formed which we later called the Sąjūdis Steering Group. This committee responded to the intense interest which had been generated by publishing its aims in a very short space of time. It defined its mission as one of working to speed up *perestroika,* and announced its role of co-ordinating the contributions of the groups which had already come into being in order to create a single national movement which would seek sovereignty and democracy for Lithuania.

The first meeting of this Steering Group was held in a dilapidated building near Vilnius Cathedral. Interestingly this place happens to be the only remaining part of the old Lower Castle of the grand dukes of Lithuania. A member of the Central Committee of the Lithuanian Communist party gatecrashed the first meeting and was politely asked to leave. Once it had established its independence in this way, the self-assurance and boldness of the Steering Group seemed to grow by the minute. Some of my friends and acquaintances became members, and the composer Julius Juzeliūnas was among the first. He is much older than I, but was always a very close colleague and had a history of difficult relations with the ruling party. His opera *Sukilėliai* (The Rebels) had been rehearsed in 1957, but was banned on the day before its première. It had told the story of Father Antanas Mackevičius, a Catholic priest who led a rising against the Tsar's yoke in 1863, and in particular had highlighted the contrast between the kindly priest and a brutal Russian gendarme. The affair put Julius in the government's bad books, where he remained; he had to wait another twenty years before his opera was staged, but he never gave in and often spoke out against the dogmas of our rulers. Also in the circle were the baritone singer Vaclovas Daunoras; artists Arvydas Šaltenis and Bronius Leonavičius; Algimantas Nasvytis, an architect who achieved renown for his efforts to preserve historic buildings; the poet Sigitas Geda, who had often been reproved for his modern verse; and the writer Vytautas Petkevičius, whom I had frequently met when we supported his ecological campaign against the construction of an oil platform in the Baltic Sea. We also had some philosophers, Arvydas Juozaitis, Professor Bronius Genzelis of Vilnius University, and Bronius Kuzmickas, who is a humanist of the widest horizons.

Half the members of the Steering Group were also members of the Communist party, but it must be remembered that the key positions in the professions were then open only to party cardholders whose attachment to it was therefore often superficial. When I first met Algimantas Čekuolis at one of these meetings, he immediately apologized that the paper which he edited had once refused to publish an article of mine on the danger presented by our atomic power station: 'I liked it very much, but I dared not publish it', he admitted. His paper, *Gimtasis Kraštas* (Native Land), circulated mainly among Lithuanian exiles in the West, and was soon to be one of the first papers to denounce the bureaucracy of our country and to call for its restructuring. Another member was Justinas Marcinkevičius, one of our leading poets. He had written consistently about our Lithuanian homeland, its culture and history, and all his writings referred to 'Lithuania', and never to the Soviet Union. He too was a member of the Communist party, but his participation in Sajūdis added an infectious patriotic excitement to our activities, an attitude which attracted further followers into our midst, upholders of our country, prestige and honour. Justinas's sincerity was obvious, and he had that special human quality of being prepared to admit the errors of the past. This disposition was even more valuable at a time when such personal qualities were urgently needed to inspire dedication to the common cause. Interestingly, none of the younger people in the steering group were members of the Communist party. Zigmas Vaišvila, a lively green activist, stood out among them; Gintaras Songaila, who had founded an organization for the protection of historical monuments, and Artūras Skučas were also prominent. Artūras was a resolute radical, and it was his insistence that we must unite our efforts in a single organization which actually led us to the founding of Sajūdis.

When it came to the actual foundation meeting of Sajūdis there were quite a few doubting Thomases present who questioned whether we would be allowed to function, or suggested that we must approach the government for permission before carrying on with our work! I recall saying that we must establish our movement properly before facing these questions. Only then would we learn exactly how much freedom we could expect to achieve and whether our actions were going to be tolerated or not. We had no intention of starting an anti-communist crusade, but we did want to establish an open reform front which would include those who sought independence; reasonable communists; non-aligned people; believers and atheists; ecologists; and everybody who was prepared to work for the nation's well-being. Sajūdis grew, and it was not long before embryonic political parties could be identified within our membership, as Greens, Democrats, Social Democrats, Christian Democrats and others declared their positions. However, Sajūdis itself had no intention of developing a narrow ideology: the entire purpose of our movement was to pave the way, to create a broad coalition and to seek reforms, and we knew that we had the backing of our community in general for these aims. It was this awareness which enabled us to develop our campaign against the bureaucracy within a short time. Once we had secured public support, we tested our position and discovered that the apparatus which oppressed us all was surprisingly weak. The bureaucrats had become paralysed by the inflexibility of the system which they operated, and had alienated themselves from the people by their privileges. Their shortcomings were obvious, and their methods of threat, terror and corruption, the main tools of their power, were primitive. We were taking on a colossus with feet of clay. The conclusions reached by the Lithuanian Communist party's Central Committee in 1989, and certainly the complaint they forwarded to Moscow, in which they declared that the 'Lithuanian working class is dissatisfied with the Party's diminishing role in society', today read like an Orwellian script written by leaders who had lost all contact with reality.

The width of the political spectrum which was reflected in Sajūdis helped us in many ways, and the participation of the learned societies, such as those of the writers and the artists, which included many high officials of the Communist party in their membership, gave us significant leverage inside the existing political institutions. This was a huge advantage when we began to open the question of how a parliamentary opposition could be developed. It is a paradox of the period of *perestroika* that Sajūdis was so indebted to Gorbachev's followers for providing the opportunity to form an opposition in the tradition of the western democracies. When we first began to discuss these things, however, we were not at all well equipped to take advantage of our opportunity. At first we had no elected leader, our meetings being presided over by members in rotation. Indeed we were actually against the idea of electing a leader at first, because we thought it was important to avoid too much structure since Sajūdis reflected many different undercurrents, and these were full of energy. We had many matters to draw our attention, and it was important to extend the movement, and to ensure mass support and a general sympathy with our aims. We had lost no time in organizing the many groups which now sprang up in the factories, offices and scientific institutions, and in the towns and villages. Eventually, these spontaneous groups were incorporated into regional structures, and these gave us coverage across the whole country. Many people attended our meetings, and while they still often felt intimidated by 'big brother', the fact that the visiting speakers could speak openly was a tangible proof that it was at last possible to live without perpetual fear. Yet while we set the best example that we could and publicized the evidence, we knew that openness such as we enjoyed was still not so easy for the country people. While city-dwellers could show bravery, villagers continued to live under the shadow of the Party, which still seemed almighty to them. In these circumstances every meeting had its impact and the membership of Sajūdis increased steadily. Many of those who joined us had suffered in the gulags, or endured exile, and they were now living for the internal revolution!

Growth in the membership, and the wide support for our movement, soon made it necessary to establish a regular publication, so *Sajūdžio žinios* (Sajūdis News) was born soon after the Steering Group was established. At first it was a typewritten publication photocopied by the efforts of Artūras Skučas and circulated by the movement's young people. The first issue contained only the minutes and resolutions of our meetings, but the second and third issues carried our replies to a government journalist who had attempted to rubbish our efforts. After this it became a platform for our ideas and plans, carrying controversial articles, reports of speeches and meetings, resolutions and notices of forthcoming meetings. While we wanted the movement to grow we were desperately short of funds for postage and simple things such as tape cassettes to help us record meetings. At one meeting we emptied our pockets, to find that we had only 163 roubles between us, but we were now rescued from this financial difficulty by our readership, which saw the periodical as a miracle and continued to support it even when competition began to appear from the mainstream press, which was progressively liberalized. However, despite this wide support and open distribution, our paper was technically an illegal *samizdat* publication as we had no government licence. This could have proved precarious for everyone involved because the first number had appeared only a few months after the time when even having a poem printed in such a place would have led to certain imprisonment. We were sending 1,000 copies a week to all parts of Lithuania even at the start, and there were piles of copies at all our meetings, each with a contribution box nearby to allow people to give according to their ability. Some would pay twenty kopecks, others ten roubles, others nothing. It was an arrangement which turned out to be very practical as it allowed us to claim that the paper was not being sold, and this saved us from being charged with illegal trading. This too was a breakthrough because we soon noticed a new trend in Lithuanian publications as dedicated volunteers emulated *Sąjūdžio žinios* in other parts of the country. Before long almost every town had its own Sąjūdis newspaper, and we naturally helped them as much as we could. Moscow itself was astonished at our success, because we soon had over 150 independent periodicals in circulation at a time when Latvia and Estonia had only five or six each. It was entirely in character: Lithuanians have always had an unquenchable thirst for free expression, and like to face reality on the basis of being properly informed!

It was early in the summer of 1988, probably on 17 June, during the fortnight after Sąjūdis had established itself, that the movement had its first brush with Communist party officials. A meeting was arranged with the agreement of both sides, at the premises of the Society of Writers, and Lionginas Šepetys, the party's secretary for Ideology, a more open and intelligent man than most of his colleagues, was given the task of bringing us back into the fold. He opened the meeting by declaring that the Central Committee of the Lithuanian Communist party 'fully approved of the founding of Sąjūdis'. He went on to say that we had embarked on a new phase, that there was much to do, and that the advice of Sąjūdis 'could be most useful to the party', which had decided that advisory committees would shortly be appointed to discuss plans for future reforms. These were important developments, and there was no need for Sąjūdis to spend its energy in working independently, as it would be more beneficial for its members to join in the work of the new committees. What we were attempting to achieve would in this way become an accredited activity; our standing would be improved and our advice listened to, because we would be official consultants to the government. Indeed, he elaborated, there was little point in our forming Sąjūdis groups throughout Lithuania, as we were intellectuals whose role was to plan reforms and to make decisions, not to become bogged down in the anonymous work of managing an organization whose members could not rise to our level of understanding! Of course, we listened to this carefully constructed attempt to reclaim us very calmly. It was a real education to learn that the Communist party was not merely interested in our work, but believed that 'Sąjūdis will not be successful unless it co-operates with the party and the government'. We were of course ourselves interested in the party, even deeply interested. We also hoped to help it out of its current dilemmas, but we wanted to do this in our own way, by destroying it! I remember replying to Comrade Šepetys: 'We see you as two Communist parties. The progressive Communists who want reconstruction are welcome to join us, but as for the others, the protectors of privilege and stagnation, we intend to fight them!'

At last, our movement had become a great river. From now on its flow was constantly strengthened by input from new tributaries. It was no longer possible for the communist bureaucracy to deflect its course. From now onward our meetings in Vilnius, our capital, and throughout Lithuania were attended by hundreds of thousands of people. It was a cause which would soon link millions of people in a hugely confident protest when people joined hands along both sides of the great highway which links the three Baltic states, known as the Baltic Way, in a great human chain which extended from Vilnius through to Riga, and then on to Tallinn, uniting three small but proud nations in a single declaration that their long oppression must soon end.

CHAPTER 10

Banknotes in umbrellas

Sajūdis now recognized that it was time for its activities to become public. We therefore announced its first mass rally for 24 June 1988, knowing that this would be a real test of our resolve and that of the nation. The nineteenth Congress of the Communist party had been called to take place in Moscow at the end of June. We felt this was as good an opportunity as any which might present itself for our coming out into the open, as we were aware that the Lithuanian Communist party had ignored Gorbachev's request that the election of delegates to this Congress should follow more democratic conventions than those which had been traditional in the party. He had in fact proposed that delegates should be selected by secret ballot, but our communists had complacently decided to retain the practice of introducing a prepared list of names to a selected audience for rubber-stamping. Such lists would of course include only the names of those who 'really mattered' and no one else stood any chance of selection because no other candidates were put forward. Our rulers had planned everything according to the old system with no recognition of the need for change, and we determined to seize the opportunity which it gave us to expose them.

So we acted, deliberately. Not long before the Congress was due to begin Sajūdis announced that we felt that the people needed to meet the Lithuanian delegates who had been selected to attend the Congress, and then invited them to come to a rally, to explain how they planned to represent the Lithuanian interest in Moscow. As they had been selected to represent the people of Lithuania at a Congress in which the whole future of the Soviet Union would be decided, our rally would provide a real opportunity to explain the line they were planning to take as decisions were made on the sovereignty of the republics. We then announced our invitation to the nation, adding that the rally would strengthen the position of the delegates in Moscow, as they would have discussed their positions with the public. However, at around the time we made our announcement we learned that strong forces were aligning themselves against the projected reforms and that disagreement and infighting had broken out in the highest Moscow circles. Within a short time reports began to appear in the Lithuanian press which echoed this tension, and some of these articles warned that too much public discussion of the misdeeds of the socialist past could only undermine public belief in communism. We then realized that most of the delegates who had been chosen to represent Lithuania at the Congress by our Communist party were die-hard reactionaries who would vote against any reforming resolutions. We were busy digesting the implications of this when we were advised that the City Council of Vilnius had refused us permission to use Cathedral Square at the centre of the city for our planned rally. We decided to press on with the rally regardless of the consequences. We therefore replied rather cheekily that we did not need permission to enter Cathedral Square as it was not the City Council's property, and added for good measure but in an attempt to soften the reaction which we anticipated, that while we were aware that the Soviet constitution did not allow demonstrations, this rally did not qualify as a demonstration as it was planned only as a means of sharing information. We also said that we could manage the event without help from the militia. The council need not worry about behaviour at the rally, since we would regulate ourselves using young volunteer stewards who would wear green armbands.

The Party responded to this message through unofficial channels, to advise us that the Congress delegates would not be coming to our rally. The implied suggestion was that we might as well forget about organizing a rally which had lost its purpose in the absence of the delegates. Of course, we reflected on this, but were determined to press ahead. We would express regret if the delegates failed to turn up at the rally, and then criticize them for deciding 'to stay behind closed doors without regard for democracy', a move which would expose them as being afraid of the public. After this we pressed on with our plans and sent individual invitations to each of the Congress delegates, though taking care to address them via the Central Committee's office to make quite sure that they were all recorded by party officials. We then scheduled the rally quite deliberately to take place on the day on which the Congress delegates would be gathered in Vilnius to prepare themselves for the Moscow meeting, so that we would be able to justify our claim that the Central Committee was a 'victim of inflexibility and inertia'. If that body did not change its mind about the delegates putting in an appearance we would announce that it was high time for its members to be sent packing! The irony involved in all this planning lay in the fact that we discussed all these matters in detail openly and loudly, knowing full well that the KGB had placed its microphones in every room in which we were likely to meet. Their equipment was always guaranteed to be in perfect working order, so we knew the Central Committee would be informed of our every decision less than five minutes after we had made it.

The Central Committee saw how our plans were working out, and changed its mind. We learned from official channels that it had reconsidered the situation and was going to send delegates to our rally after all! This changed the balance of the situation radically because we now knew that the militia would be most unlikely to use force. Nevertheless we faced a new dilemma about publicizing the rally because the newspapers and the radio were clearly not going to advertise our cause, and a Party directive had ordered that our posters were to be ripped down. We eventually hit on the idea of sending our young people, most of them students, on to the streets of Vilnius with sandwich boards. They agreed to help, and then walked around the public places of the city advertising the occasion for two days before the rally. We had some anxieties about this, but it was the only way of alerting everybody, and interestingly none of the bill boarders was beaten up or arrested, though many were stopped by the militia who clearly hoped to weaken their resolve. On the evening before the rally, I travelled home on a bus and sat next to a drunken Russian who wanted to talk. I chatted to him about the interesting rally which would be taking place the following day. I gave him no inkling that I was a member of the steering group, but I inquired if he was going to attend, and when he said that it was 'no good going to meetings as one can get beaten up by the militia for one's pains', I found myself saying, 'If you don't want people to be beaten up by the militia in the future, then you've *got to come* this time!' It was patently obvious that everyone knew what we would be up against. The threat of violence was real.

An hour before the rally began the Steering Group met Algirdas Kaušpėdas (who had been asked to marshal the event) for a last-minute discussion. He is an architect who is well known throughout Lithuania, especially among young people, as the founder of the rock group *The Antis*.[9] Algirdas had been asked to direct the rally because of his extensive experience in organizing rock and folk concerts. His group had been touring Lithuania with a repertoire of social and political protest songs and since 1988 had sported a Lithuanian flag at their concerts. Algirdas now told us that the poet Justinas Marcinkevičius, our chosen lead speaker at the rally, had backed out of the engagement at the last minute. We had to make a quick decision about who was going to speak first, and my colleagues immediately turned to ask me to do this. After brief consideration I said that I was happy to oblige, but wanted to know if they would let me introduce a new idea into my speech. We left for Cathedral Square to find crowds arriving there from all parts of the city, pouring from all directions like rivers flowing into a single lake. It is normal for Lithuanian people to sing on such occasions, but this time there was no singing. Everyone was very serious and solemn.

We pushed through this gathering crowd to reach the platform where we found four Congress delegates already waiting for us. They were Algirdas Brazauskas, from the Central Committee of the party; Alfonsas Macaitis, from the Komsomol; Kęstutis Zaleckas, first secretary of the Vilnius Communist party; and Juras Požėla, president of the Academy of Sciences. We exchanged greetings with them, but as we sat down with them the bystanders warned us that there were armed soldiers in the grounds of the Ministry for Internal Affairs, just behind us. They could just be glimpsed, and were dressed for action. I took this in, but decided to say nothing. Then I began to address the gathering, saying that we were all there to meet the delegates chosen to represent Lithuania at the nineteenth Congress of the Communist party of the Soviet Union. However, everyone present knew that these delegates had been selected by the Central Committee in the old way. Yet even if we felt that they could not claim to represent Lithuania properly because real elections had not taken place, we still wanted to meet them. I then suggested that they should have refused selection by such a discredited process, but explained that we knew they had accepted the procedures because they were the victims of that ingrained habit of submissiveness which the party had always encouraged. While we would like to be sure that this was the last time that selection would take place according to those methods, we did not now want to denounce them personally for having gone along with a now discredited procedure, because we would prefer to ask them about the attitudes they would adopt when they reached Moscow. It was essential that they were aware of the needs of Lithuania and the best interests of her people, and if they voted for good decisions there, we would be ready to acknowledge them as our nation's representatives, but they must be warned that they would be repudiated if they should vote in any way which was detrimental to Lithuania.

I could feel as I spoke that my speech was flowing well. People in the crowd shouted agreement and applauded, while others brought flowers to me. Encouraged by this response, I expanded on my theme and turned to discuss the ecological issues that were facing the country. I announced that we must fight together on these issues, whether we were Lithuanians, Poles or Russians, and then proposed (as the crowd roared in agreement) that the plan to build a third reactor at the atomic power station at Ignalina must now be discontinued. When I finished speaking other members of the Steering Group followed this lead, and all spoke with conviction and demanded change. They were followed by the Congress delegates, who spoke in turn. Each of them promised, in broad terms, to comply with what was being requested, and everything seemed to be going well until Juras Požėla spoke. He rebuked some of the people present for displaying the Lithuanian tricolour, and the crowd reacted in an instant, showing its feelings by booing magnificently! It became immediately obvious that we were surrounded by intensely patriotic feelings, and when, a little later, another Sajūdis speaker mentioned the poor financial position of our movement, the people again reacted spontaneously, this time by offering money. It had just begun to rain and a steward had opened his umbrella to shelter himself. Suddenly he sensed the mood around him and turned the umbrella upside down, passing it into the crowd! The idea caught on everywhere and soon the place was full of umbrellas, all inverted to receive an enormous collection of soggy notes which we gratefully stuffed into polythene bags with some enthusiasm at the end of the rally. The mood was marvellous and even when the rain began falling quite heavily, we simply did not feel it. It seemed as if all the clouds had dispersed, and the sun was shining everywhere in Lithuania again! I had brought an American record of the Lithuanian national anthem with me, and we caught this wonderful mood by playing it over the loudspeakers. It turned out to be a contribution which completed our elation. This was the first time that it had been heard openly at any public meeting for more than forty years, and because of this the younger people had some difficulty in finding the right words. Older people simply could not restrain their tears.

On 9 July we called a second great rally in Vilnius, this time in Vingis Park, to give delegates a chance to explain their actions on their return from Moscow. At this gathering I spoke about the future of our country, declaring that we must build a Lithuania which was more just than it had become, using the opportunity to denounce bad laws and double standards in environmental planning, though my real theme was the accountability of a free nation and its responsibility for protecting the part of our planet which history and Almighty God had given us. After I had spoken Algirdas Brazauskas replied, and the huge crowd of 150,000 people gave him long applause as he announced that the extension to the atomic power station, which I had denounced at the earlier rally, would now be stopped. In my opinion his performance that day was the reason why the Lithuanian Communist party appointed him as its leader some time later. Brazauskas has always stood out among the other party *apparatchiki* because of his gifts of communication and persuasion. They had observed his charismatic ability to communicate with people and needed to exploit this skill.

A few weeks later, early in August, Gorbachev sent his senior adviser Alexander Yakovlev to Lithuania on a fact-finding expedition. Sajūdis was not then strong enough to demand conversations with him, though I was able to attend a meeting at which he was present because the Communist party had invited intellectuals of all colours to join the discussions. I went as a member of the Society of Composers and most of my Sąjūdis colleagues took advantage of similar opportunities. We took the chance to explain some issues to him, and I remember telling him that Griškevičius and Songaila, the former and current leader of the Communist party in Lithuania, and all their entourage were still unreconstructed supporters of the values of the Brezhnev era who had simply not changed. To put the record straight we also told him that Sąjūdis was fully committed to *perestroika*. Yakovlev responded rather honestly, and made a short statement which brought the way Lithuania was then being governed sharply into question in a way which showed just how much things had changed. These observations gave everyone, including the most ardent Communist party conservatives, a great deal to think about, and the significance of what had been said was immediately taken up. At that time the second secretary of the Communist party of Lithuania, like those of all the Soviet republics, was appointed directly by Moscow. In most of the other republics this direct appointment by the Kremlin put the second secretary in a position to dictate policy to the first secretaries, who were locally appointed. From Moscow's point of view this was an ideal arrangement as it left each Soviet republic with a powerful political overseer whom no one could leapfrog in the scramble for personal gain, and was therefore a way of ensuring that the local clique always followed the party line. The second secretary in Lithuania was a Russian called Nikolai Mitkin, a short-sighted, crude man who tried to control everything. Vytautas Petkevičius, a man who was renowned everywhere for his bluntness, was present at the meeting. He took immediate advantage of Yakovlev's remark in a way which caught everyone's breath. Obviously referring to his superior, he asked boldly whether it might be possible to get rid of this Lithuanian anomaly. Yakovlev was no fool and knew exactly what was implied. He responded deftly: 'Please correct me if I'm wrong, but I believe that Lithuanians are people of great culture. I ask whether it is fair of you to criticize Mitkin just because he is a Russian? If I were appointed Second Secretary for Lithuania, would you also try to get rid of me?' It was a nice play on the tension in the situation, and the audience began to laugh heartily. They shouted their reply: 'No, we would be pleased to have *you*.' I could not hold myself back at this point, and joined in the fun. I found myself shouting: 'There's only one flaw in that argument. *You* wouldn't allow yourself to be dropped into our laps like a Christmas present. We would have to *elect* you ourselves if we wanted you!'

On 23 September 1988 we held yet another huge rally in Vingis Park, this time to commemorate the pact between Hitler and Stalin, by which the dictators carved up eastern Europe and the Baltic states, an act which

had led to the outbreak of the Second World War. It was hugely important for us to commemorate the millions who had perished on that
account, but not unexpectedly the organization of this important meeting
became a problem. We had originally planned to gather in Cathedral
Square, but a demonstration was already in progress there. It was a
hunger strike organized to support a demand for the release of political
prisoners, and was organized by Lietuvos Laisvės Lyga, the Lithuanian
Freedom League, an organization which was opposed to Sąjūdis on the
basis of a more radical nationalist programme. The movement had a
much smaller membership than ours, and was less effective, but its
supporters were often abusive to us because we were prepared to use the
parliamentary process, which in their opinion was a road which led
nowhere. The League wanted to organize general strikes, hunger strikes,
or whatever would attract the attention of the world, hoping that the
Soviet Union and its forces would be shamed into leaving Lithuania as a
result. We believed them to be naïve idealists who were somewhat in our
way. Their current activities had probably affected the decision of the
Central Committee of the Communist party to decree that it did not wish
Sąjūdis to organize its meeting in Cathedral Square on the grounds that it
would not hold the anticipated crowds. The City Council then redirected
our rally to Vingis Park. This did not really displease us, but we used
the change of direction as a bargaining counter pretending to be unwilling to move, but agreed to the proposal on condition that we were
allowed to speak on television to announce the changed location. We
were delighted when the bargain was accepted. Not only was there more
room, and a concert stage in the park, but this would be Sąjūdis's very
first television broadcast and therefore a historic moment. I used those
few precious minutes very effectively to emphasize Comrade Stalin's
crimes, and his brutish complicity with Herr Hitler!

Over 250,000 people turned up in the park for this rally, perhaps even
300,000, and I was asked to take the chair. We took pleasure in the fact
that Justinas Marcinkevičius was able to come on this occasion, and he
gave the meeting a beautiful introduction. Another poet, Sigitas Geda,
followed him with a denunciation of the communist system which he
described with the fervour of an Old Testament prophet as 'satanic'. Our
list of speakers included communists, the platform being carefully
balanced by the inclusion of senior Lithuanian churchmen. However,
when a young priest came forward and spoke harshly about 'atheists and
unbelievers', I felt it necessary to make it plain that Sąjūdis stood firm
against dogmatism of any kind. Some of the clergy and the members of
Lietuvos Laisvės Lyga later showed open disapproval of my views, but
the young speaker remained friendly towards me. This incident caused

something of a stir, but it was soon upstaged. A few of us had met in a small flat in the suburbs of Kaunas a few days beforehand and had prepared a tape-recording as a contribution to the rally. I sensed now that the moment was ripe for its use, and indicated that it should be played. Then I raised my voice to announce the next speaker: 'Mr Juozas Urbšys, the minister for foreign affairs of the government of *Independent Lithuania*, will now speak!', I said. The audience was then astonished to hear the recorded voice of this historic witness telling them plainly how our country had been forced to submit to the Soviet forces in 1939, while Stalin and Molotov gloated over their agreement with Hitler. His statement neatly summarized all the dissatisfactions and demands of our movement. Other speakers described the painful story of the deportations of the past, the imprisonment of innocent people by the KGB, and the Communist and Nazi conspiracies against Lithuania, going on to demand 'justice in the present and a new vision for the future'. The many faces in the crowd were concentrated and quietly angry, and in between the national flags I saw the wreaths of rusted barbed wire which they had brought with them to symbolize what our nation had endured. It was a historic moment: these facts were well known, but in over fifty years this was the first time that they had ever been repeated in public, let alone announced to such a rally of our countrymen. As soon as the proceedings were over, we prepared an abridged version of our demands and telegraphed it to Gorbachev.

After this, the enthusiasm of the audience was unbounded. A spontaneous collection was made to finance the movement, and I remember one elderly enthusiast declaring later: 'I had no money in my pockets, so I said goodbye to my camera!' An unforgettable atmosphere had developed. We had asked people to come with candles, to be lit in memory of all the martyrs of Stalin's pact with Hitler, and as the speech-making continued into the twilight, a quarter of a million candles were kindled to illuminate the scene with a beauty which could never have been anticipated, and which is emotionally indescribable. As if by the wand of a magician, the park lit up. The massed candles flickered in gentle unison with the stars in the night sky above, and as they burned down, a soft mist descended to envelop us all. When the crowd finally dispersed, people gathered the litter they had left behind, and it was noticed that there was not so much as an empty bottle, or even a piece of paper, to be found lying in Vingis Park the morning after.

When the rally was over I reached home at around midnight. The telephone was ringing, and the call was from Marijonas Misiukonis, deputy minister for internal affairs. He spoke urgently, asking me to go to Cathedral Square at once. There was tension there, he said, which might become an unpleasant incident in a moment. I phoned two Sąjūdis colleagues, Vytautas Petkevičius and Arūnas Žebriūnas (who is a film director), asking them to meet me immediately in the square. When I arrived in the area it was extremely dark and rain was falling heavily. I noticed that the militia and other soldiers had surrounded the square. Every other street from the Old Town to Lenin Prospect was empty, but the square was filled with people who had come from the Vingis Park rally with flowers and candles for the hunger strikers, who were huddled under the walls of the cathedral, and completely surrounded by militia-men. The crowd was rumbling its discontent, its members actively voicing their desire that the building, long sequestered for secular purposes, should be returned to the Catholic Church, and people were shouting: 'It's our country and it's our cathedral! Let us kiss its walls!', to the uncomprehending militia. As I watched, some women made an attempt to reach the hunger strikers, only to be pushed aside roughly, an action which inflamed the crowd's anger to the point where it was clear that a riot could erupt at any moment.

Petkevičius had arrived before me, and I heard him trying to appease the crowd. I too began to speak, attempting to calm the situation by saying that a fight would reverse the progress we had made that day and prevent us from achieving more. At first I was not recognized, and people began to shout at me, but when I asked them 'in the name of Sąjūdis' not to be impulsive they quietened down. Sąjūdis had become a magic word by now. As soon as they relaxed, I turned to the militia, and asked why they were not allowing people to pass through their lines. They replied that they were under orders, and I asked why such orders had been issued. 'Who needs to forbid the people to walk on the pavements?', I said. 'It's not our business,' they replied. 'Whose responsibility is it then?' 'It's the minister's', they replied. 'He decides, we obey.' I then asked them to look around, to see what was happening in front of their eyes: 'It's not enough to follow orders without using common sense! Why don't you let a few go through? They can't do any damage.' My remonstrations were in vain, and they still refused, saying that they had their orders. 'What if I get them changed?', I asked. 'Go on, try', said the officer, who had the sense to see that the crowd was again getting agitated. So I told everyone to be patient, and went to the other side of Cathedral Square, to the Ministry of Internal Affairs. I went straight in, only to discover that Petkevičius had arrived before me and was already in discussion with Stasys Lisauskas, the minister.

I entered the room to find Lisauskas very comfortably ensconced in a comfortable chair. He was drinking brandy, but he left us standing, both dripping from the rain outside. When eventually I was offered a chair, I took advantage of his discourtesy and refused, 'because I was so wet'. In the meantime the minister briskly set about explaining his philosophy to us: 'We are the government', he said, 'and we'll show a strong hand, to teach that crowd a lesson. If we give in to them we'll lose everyone's respect.' I was upset, and said drily: 'A ruler is in control when he uses wisdom rather than force', and begged him to exercise his discretion, advising that he should follow a course which would avoid unnecessary confrontation by showing some flexibility. He was clearly unmoved and just sat there, his face flushed. The next day I told the Central Committee that he had been drunk. He reacted with anger, but my accusation was actually investigated. I told the Central Committee quite plainly that Lisauskas should be sacked, that he was dangerous, and had been hell-bent on demonstrating his power at a difficult moment. A member asked how I knew that he had been drunk. I retorted that I could not *know*, but he had *looked* like a drunk, and had *spoken* like a drunk, which was quite as bad, and equally dangerous. However, this was all a question of bolting a stable door after the horse had fled, because the problem was already over. The orders to the soldiers had in fact been withdrawn shortly after I left the ministry building. Lisauskas, it seems, had actually responded to my suggestion that a few people might be allowed to visit the hunger strikers in turn. A garbled message had reached me, and I had rushed over to see the deputy minister, who checked my story, and then gave permission for just ten people to be allowed past the guard. The message was relayed back to the square, and there was a move forward by the crowd. Many more than ten of its members pushed forward. The militiamen counted those nearest them and then tried to shove the excess number back, but the crowd then turned nasty, so that a much larger group actually got through. When we asked for a second group to be allowed in, the militia insisted that the first group had to leave before this could happen, so I went in to negotiate, and encouraged those who had seen the strikers to go home from the square immediately to prevent the militia from becoming more irritable. By three o'clock in the morning several groups had visited the hunger strikers in this way, and tension was subsiding. People then began to disperse, and it was at last clear that conflict had been avoided. It was a huge relief. A dispute with the local militia was one thing, and could be resolved, but a contingent of Soviet internal forces was standing on the other side of the square throughout the disagreement. Their involvement would have been something quite different. Those Russian soldiers did not understand, and cared less, about our Lithuanian problems. If the crowd had rioted that night it would have been quite impossible to negotiate with the Soviet army.

For a while after this incident the tensions seemed to lessen, but a month later things took a downturn when the Lietuvos Laisvės Lyga announced a meeting to be held on 28 September to support the hunger strikers, whose protest still continued. As soon as they had made the announcement the movement was precipitately banned by the authorities. Like Sąjūdis, the movement had consistently avoided asking for official permission when it planned its meetings, its stance being that this was necessary only to inform the authorities. Now that they were faced with an order not to hold meetings, they simply went ahead with the banned meeting as if nothing had happened. This time, however, soldiers were sent in to disperse the crowd as soon as their leader, Antanas Terleckas, began his address, and started to lash out at bystanders, beating people and dragging them away. This brutality pushed the body of the crowd towards the Ministry of Internal Affairs building. It was an involuntary movement, but the soldiers who were inside reacted as if they had come under attack. The situation became exceedingly dangerous in a very short time as they were armed with automatic weapons. Meanwhile another part of the crowd was being driven in the direction of the nearby river along a road lined with piles of stones because it was under repair. When I saw video tapes of the scene I was shocked at the way things had been handled, and astonished that not a single soldier was killed, because these heaps of stones seemed to be dangerously easy to pick up and throw. It would have surprised no one if a riot of stone-throwing had broken out in these circumstances because the situation was so volatile. Later the soldiers complained that stones had flown through the air, not just verbal abuse, and claimed they had no alternative but to attack the crowd after a girl had knocked a soldier's helmet off. Of course the official reporting agreed that they had no option except retaliation in self-defence, and condemned what it called 'the hooligans', though everything we had heard and seen contradicted these claims. The film showed that the soldiers had attacked first, and that it was only at the very end of the affair that the people had responded to their violence. It was only after the soldiers had started pulling their victims across Cathedral Square that the situation had deteriorated. In the end the tables were turned and the situation then became so dangerous that the minister for internal affairs ordered the soldiers to retreat.

We pieced the day's events together later, and learned that the militia had begun their work that day at around five o'clock in the morning, first by attacking the hunger strikers, whom they transported away along with a few other people who were around at that time after beating them. Most of these were young people who had joined the strikers, and I received a telephone call that morning to say that they were being held in a militia building. Cries of pain had been heard coming from this place, and a crowd had gathered with the intention of liberating them. I responded to this information by going down to see the evidence for myself, but when I arrived there was no one around, and I heard no cries. As the building was open, I went inside, and found a room where one of the hunger strikers was sitting on a chair, his face bloody and badly damaged. It was Algimantas Andreika, who lifted his shirt to show me the bruises he had received when he was kicked by the soldiers. To my surprise I was allowed to talk to him, and he told me that one of the young women arrested with him had been dragged from the room by her hair only minutes before my arrival. She had been driven off to an unspecified place, which alerted me to the possibility that some of the victims of the day's events might disappear. I then tried to find out the names of everyone who had been arrested, and wrote them down so that we could keep track of things. While I was doing this, members of the militia were busy writing out charges, with the intention of taking these people to court.

I left the militia centre with a heavy heart, and after giving my news to Sajūdis over the telephone I went back to my workplace. A little later I was beginning my lecture when they rang back to tell me that our council was discussing the situation in our rooms on Cathedral Square, and had called for a protest meeting outside the Ministry of Internal Affairs. My presence was urgently required. They had also decided to send a delegation to the public prosecutor's department to demand that charges should not brought against those who had been arrested, and that those guilty of beating the hunger strikers should face the courts instead. I left for the square at once, and arrived to find a mere handful of our people there. There was a priest standing with them, accompanied by another man who was holding a megaphone. We had not met before, so I shook his hand and the next day *Tiesa*, the Lithuanian *Pravda,* the official newspaper of the Communist party in our country, printed an article headed: 'Sajūdis extends a hand to the extremist Terleckas.' This was so obviously untrue that I wrote to *Tiesa* (ironically the name means 'Truth') the next day to explain just what had happened, and that Terleckas was 'not a leper', but the paper did not print my letter. I had to content myself with pinning my letter up on the notice board which we had earmarked for Sajūdis notices at the Institute.

Our statements to the meeting on the square declared that the militia officer responsible for the arrest and beating of the hunger strikers, together with the officials at the Ministry of Internal Affairs who had sanctioned his action, should be dismissed. We then moved on, walking to the offices of Liudvikas Sabutis, the chief prosecutor. He was a very decent man, and Moscow later dismissed him from office, though he became a Sajūdis deputy two years later, and was to become the chief secretary of our Parliament, the Supreme Council of Lithuania, in March 1990. He received our delegates courteously, and listened very carefully to what we had to say. Eventually he agreed with us that an investigation must take place, adding that the courts 'must avoid taking decisions which might result in his office having to review their proceedings later'. In the event, the court which heard the cases found the strikers innocent of the charges brought against them, an exoneration which was received with rapture by the crowds, who treated them as heroes on their subsequent release. Dreadful though that day's events were, they achieved a further concession for us in the longer term after an official inquiry was called to look into what had happened. To our surprise Sajūdis representatives were invited to sit on it, and its probings brought many things to light when government ministers and other witnesses confirmed that both the first and second secretaries of the Communist party had actually seen and approved the action plan before these disgraceful events took place. We learned that the order for the operation had been issued by Marijonas Misiukonis, the deputy minister for internal affairs, and deduced the fact that the orders had actually originated in the offices of Songaila and Mitkin. This was enough for us to demand their removal from office. News of these revelations reached Moscow, which responded by sending a commission charged with carrying out further investigations. The hearings for this second inquiry then took place in the council chamber of the Communist party's headquarters, to which representatives of the Central Committee were called, together with Sajūdis representatives. We were quick to take advantage of this unusual situation and used it to repeat our earlier demand for the resignations of the first and second secretaries of the party, and to our total amazement this call was effective. At a significant moment in the proceedings Comrade Songaila was suddenly called from the room 'to receive a telephone message'. Shortly afterwards he returned with a very long face. For a moment the significance of this was lost on us, but we soon realized that comrades from Moscow were sitting next door listening to the proceedings as they were translated. They had called him out to deliver their own verdict to him directly! Both the party secretary posts became vacant shortly after this and, more surprisingly, our Sajūdis Steering Group (which was meeting almost daily by now) received an invitation from the Communist party to discuss the applicants for these positions, as they needed to know whom we would support, or rather whom we would not oppose! The outcome was that Brazauskas and Beriozovas replaced Songaila and Mitkin – and the party had almost asked Sajūdis's approval for making these appointments!

Until this time Sąjūdis had not been registered as an official organization, and this exposed our members in government offices and in the rural areas and the smaller towns to being accused of anti-Soviet or anti-communist activities. Of course, we encouraged them to resist this bullying and to disregard the threats, telling them not to be afraid because the time had come to bring the party's monopoly of government without opposition to an end. However, though neither Soviet legislation nor Lithuanian law forbade the establishment of political organizations, the government played a long 'cat-and-mouse' game with our application to be registered and was clearly reluctant to agree. We complained about the delay, but were told that a Soviet law would 'soon be passed', which would clarify our position. Our response was to point out that such a law had been 'in the planning stage' for at least ten years, and nothing had been achieved by Moscow in all this time. We urged that Lithuanian legislation should fill the gap, and suggested that this could easily be co-ordinated with Soviet law when the time was ripe. A lot of argument ensued, but the government eventually accepted our proposal and proceeded to pass the necessary legislation. Once this was done, Sąjūdis's constitution, its manifesto and its programme could claim established political legal status. The government clearly resented our achievement. Though its members did not say it openly, it was obvious that they were preparing to tolerate a legalized Sąjūdis only because they recognized that we would create difficulties if they did not, and that their prestige would suffer in consequence. We had pushed hard to achieve this basic security for our movement, and had used all our flair for publicity in doing so. We had also handled the issues creatively. During one of our demonstrations in favour of this legalization, we had opened a 'new Sąjūdis office' by placing a desk and a chair on the pavement and conducting our business right next to the front entrance of the Supreme Council!

At the beginning the Sąjūdis Steering Group had operated without a chairman, on the principle that we were all equal. However, on 22 October 1988, only fifteen days after the Lithuanian tricolour had been triumphantly raised to its proper and proud position above Gediminas Castle in Vilnius, delegates were called from all parts of Lithuania to a Founding Congress in the capital city which was to establish Sąjūdis as a formal movement. It was a gathering which attracted a multitude of guests and extensive media interest, and its opening sessions were presided over by the poet Justinas Marcinkevičius and Professor Meilė Lukšienė. I am very happy to record that my father made the opening speech on this historic occasion and boldly stated, 'We are here to restore Lithuania's independence.' The delegates approved our constitution and programme and elected the 220 members of the Sąjūdis Seimas (Parliament), which afterwards elected a Council of thirty-five members, which contained many members of our original Steering Group, including me. This gathering was intended to consolidate our movement and received huge public attention. The proceedings were broadcast at length with many people remaining glued to their seats all over the country as they watched the proceedings. It was an occasion which heralded normalization and the return of democracy to our country, and many wept tears of joy and kissed each other as the events unfolded. The emotions accompanying the day's events were so strong that a few heart failures accompanied the excitement. Two scenes from the Congress remain riveted in the memory. The first was when Rolandas Paulauskas, a delegate from Kaunas, told us that even Sąjūdis could betray Lithuania, and that the Soviet Union would not have allowed it to function were it otherwise. The other was the declaration that Vilnius Cathedral, which had long been used as a museum and art gallery, was to be returned to its former sacred function. Several speakers had already declared their resentment that the cathedral had been used in this way since the Communist take-over, their feelings being focused by the fact that a mass had been arranged for the second morning of the conference, to be sung in the open air, in the square *outside* the cathedral. The government, recognizing the strong feeling of support for these speeches, had attempted to forestall further criticism, and made a suggestion that the celebrating clergy might like to spend an hour, and perhaps hold a service, in the cathedral. The Church authorities had declined this invitation promptly, Vaclovas Aliulis declaring on behalf of the bishops that they would only hold a service in the cathedral when they had got it back. In an unexpectedly swift response, Algirdas Brazauskas called a handful of Sąjūdis Council members together during an interval in the debate, and proposed that the cathedral should be returned to the Catholic Church. Our response was to say that this was an absolute necessity, and that this news would be met with the utmost joy at the Congress. We broadcast this good news in three languages, and this time I spoke in Polish.

Algirdas Brazauskas was at this time newly appointed by Moscow as first secretary of the Communist party of Lithuania, and his invitation to the Congress of 22 October had seemed an important gesture. Of course the return of Vilnius Cathedral to its rightful owners was a gesture of huge importance and added much to our movement's credibility. However, Brazauskas's presence did not speed our registration as a political movement, which took a further five months to come through. It was when this recognition of its legitimacy was finally gained that the movement renamed itself as Lietuvos Persitvarkymo Sąjūdis (Movement for the Reconstruction of Lithuania – the word Sąjūdis means 'the Movement'). While these developments were very hopeful and influenced our momentum, it is important to note that we were facing the old impasse with the Communist party once again, even before the second half of November. This became very evident during a debate in the Supreme Council when we proposed that Lithuania should pass a declaration of sovereignty, emulating what had already been achieved in Estonia. During the debate, Algirdas Brazauskas, Justas Paleckis and Lionginas Šepetys manœuvred to prevent our document from being voted upon. It was a blocking tactic, but in the sequence of events it was this incident which made it quite clear to us that the hitherto informal organization of Sąjūdis could no longer sustain the pressures which the responsibilities of our parliamentary position entailed. It had become necessary for the movement to formalize itself still further, and to elect a chair of its Council who could be identified as able to speak on its behalf with full authority whenever the need arose, whether in parliamentary debate or elsewhere. The idea came about without previous discussion. At an ordinary meeting of the Council Algis Čekuolis, a journalist, proposed me for this post. Vytautas Petkevičius disagreed and responded immediately, by walking out in protest. At the meeting of our Parliamentary Council which followed, the matter came to a head in a much fuller discussion in which everyone present had something to say. At the end of this debate two nominations were put forward, and an election took place in which Romualdas Ozolas and I were both nominated. Everyone present spoke to support their preferred candidate. During this discussion Romualdas Ozolas, who had been proposed by Jokūbas Minkevičius, decided to support me himself. This changed the balance of the debate, and I then made a statement in which I observed that our general situation required that the chairman of the Council must be *seen* to have the support of every one of its members. I would therefore accept this position only if I received unanimous support, adding that if this was forthcoming, I should like to have Romualdas Ozolas as my deputy. Then I retired from the meeting, in order that the proposals could be debated without the embarrassment of my presence. When I was called back, I was greeted as the chairman of Sąjūdis and told that I had been elected unanimously.

As I remember these events, I also recall the worried faces of a group of young members of the Sąjūdis Steering Group and Seimas Council, who had gathered in a group at my flat late one evening some time before this. They had told me that they possessed fragmentary information about a plot to destroy Sąjūdis, and demanded that I should immediately take on the chairmanship of the movement. They offered me every support, but they were not representative of any faction or group with influence. As to what happened to their proposal afterwards,

I am still ignorant. When the actual nomination for the chairmanship came, I noticed that it emanated from a totally different source. Then, some eighteen months later, it dawned on me that the two most prominent of my would-be supporters of that evening were now among my main detractors.

CHAPTER 11

True and false deputies

When Ringaudas Songaila resigned as first secretary of the Lithuanian Communist party on 19 October 1988, he was quickly replaced by Algirdas Brazauskas. Brazauskas was a member of the Presidium of the Supreme Council, but our country's status as a Soviet Socialist Republic meant that this body was subordinate to decisions of the Communist party of the Soviet Union, so Brazauskas now became Moscow's chief representative in Lithuania with the duty of passing on its instructions. A number of the deputies of the Supreme Council had actually joined Sąjūdis, and a few were members of its Executive, and it was possible for other members of Sąjūdis's Seimas Council (elected after the Founding Congress of 22–3 October 1988) to attend sessions of the Supreme Council, where they were sometimes called on to give their opinions, though not to vote. Justinas Marcinkevičius the poet was one of the deputies who had become a Sąjūdis member and our Sąjūdis Seimas Council put him in charge of the arrangements when it was necessary for us to submit proposals to the Supreme Council.

It was 16 November 1988 when Estonia's Supreme Council confirmed its earlier declaration of sovereignty by changing the constitution in such a way that Estonian law should prevail whenever any contradiction appeared between its national laws and those of the Soviet Union. This Act made it plain that Estonia was fully on its way toward independence and Sąjūdis recognized this, and decided that Lithuania should follow the lead which had been given. With this in mind, members of the movement signified that we would be proposing similar changes to Lithuania's constitution at the next meeting of the Supreme Council. This had already been arranged for 18 November, when we put forward motions which proposed firstly that the raw materials, water, airspace and territory of our country should be declared as belonging to Lithuania rather than to the Soviet Union; secondly that Lithuanian citizenship should be a precondition of permanent residence in the country; and thirdly, that Soviet legislation should be declared invalid if it was not in accord with Lithuanian legislation. We knew that these proposals would give rise to difficulties from the other side and made a show of being reasonable and getting ready for negotiations, though we were agreed among ourselves that we would not give up until this last item was adopted.

Our resolve was steeled on this point by the knowledge that Gorbachev had called Brazauskas to a meeting in Moscow on 16 November. We told him that we wanted to discuss the business arrangements for the Supreme Council's discussion of these constitutional proposals as soon as possible after he had returned from his Moscow meeting. When we sat down, however, he told us straight out that Gorbachev would almost certainly overrule the Supreme Council if it supported our proposals, explaining that Gorbachev had many enemies in Moscow, and a programme such as ours would threaten him personally if it was allowed to go ahead. Brazauskas said that it would be very unwise of us to press the issue because he believed Gorbachev to be committed to achieving virtually everything we wanted. We should therefore avoid forcing him to move against us. We heard him out, but before the end of the discussion we had made it clear that we planned to do everything possible within the existing rules. Brazauskas was equally direct in return, and brought matters to a head. He told us, without beating about the bush, that if we insisted on a vote, he would himself certainly vote against the changes we had proposed. It was obvious that he did not want the issues to be debated, but we eventually persuaded him to agree, even though he understood that we were determined to put our proposals to the vote. However, we were well aware that his opposition could well mean defeat for us.

The discussion of constitutional issues began abrasively in what was otherwise a rather dull parliamentary session on 18 November. When we reached the appropriate point in the agenda two Sąjūdis representatives were given leave to speak, and I rose to tell the Council that it had three choices: first, to adopt a completely new constitution (and Sąjūdis was already working on that idea); second, to accept the proposals under discussion; or third, to adopt the last of the three proposals on its own. I pointed out that this last option meant that Lithuanian laws would have superior standing in future. This I said would *imply* a declaration of sovereignty and then invited the deputies to declare support for the action already taken by our colleagues in the Estonian Republic on the question of sovereignty, pleading that our Supreme Council should unite in a common cause with them. Brazauskas declared that he could not support this course of action. It was unfortunate, but he clearly needed to stick close to Gorbachev's directives on the matter. As he showed his disapproval Justas Paleckis, who was a well-known *apparatchik*, jumped to his feet to say that he too opposed constitutional change. Obviously he wanted to turn the debate against us by a manipulative appeal to the sentiment of the collected members. He turned his head towards a prominent deputy and said, in an appealing tone: 'The decision is a difficult one, but there is one person in this assembly whose judgement I respect particularly. I often defer to his opinions when I face a dilemma and would therefore like to turn to ask his opinion on the matter. I am speaking of Justinas Marcinkevičius, our greatly loved poet, whose judgement I value and will respect in this matter along with the opinions of First Secretary Brazauskas.'

Paleckis clearly hoped that his words would take Marcinkevičius by surprise, putting him in a position in which he would make an instinctively conservative response. Marcinkevičius was clearly taken aback and visibly sank into his chair as he took in the huge responsibility which had been thrust upon him so unexpectedly. His discomfort was plain, and a prolonged pause followed. The silence was electrifying, and it became obvious that the *nomenklatura* would be in a very difficult political situation if he raised his hand in favour of our proposals in the vote which followed. Paleckis's move had been clumsy, but it meant that Brazauskas had to fill the gap, which he did by declaring himself to be categorically *against* the motions and by giving it as his opinion that Moscow would overrule any change to the constitution, so that it was pointless to vote for any proposals of this kind. It was clear by now that the debate had reached its end, and Lionginas Šepetys, the chairman of the session, who was also the Communist party's secretary for ideology, now spoke. He asked members whether they felt that the time was ripe to vote, and suggested that it might be better to postpone the matter. It was a clever move, and many of the members voiced their agreement immediately, although others shouted against the proposal. Šepetys affected not to hear these dissenters and Brazauskas, who was sitting above him in the tiered seats of the platform from which members of the government faced the body of the assembly, nodded his agreement. That was that. The vote was not called. The opportunity for which we had waited so long had simply passed us by, and the chairman, after the briefest of pauses, called for the next item of business.

Normal procedure in the Supreme Council required that motions which had been agreed for debate were put to the vote before the next item on the agenda was called, so we were somewhat dazed by this sudden shift in the proceedings. The matter was now to be postponed until the Council's next session. In those days it was only once in six months that members came to raise their hands in the approved Soviet manner, so it was obvious that the collusion between Šepetys and Brazauskas was intended to kill our proposal off. We had no recourse except to leave the chamber in protest, so we got up in a body and left with dignity. Typically, no comment on our walk-out reached the media either then or later in the day, but as soon as we left the building we came face to face with the crowd which had assembled outside in eager anticipation of a historic announcement confirming a major step towards the re-establishment of the nation's sovereignty. Its members had been listening to every word of the proceedings in the debating chamber and were still holding their transistor sets in their hands. It was soon obvious that they had failed to pick up on our protest because it was a silent protest and had not been commented on. As we met them it became obvious that they believed we had gone along with the decision not to take the vote, which would have been the obvious implication of our having remained in the chamber. We stepped out of the building to noisy expressions of disapproval, even contempt, and it was obvious that these people felt badly let down. However, it took only a little time and explanation for them to understand how we had been outmanœuvred, and soon everyone knew exactly what had happened. When the comrade deputies appeared a little later they at first showed every sign of being satisfied with their day's work, but feelings had begun to build in the crowd, which now reacted angrily. The deputies were called traitors, even spat at. Of course, we were accused of incitement, but the truth was out. These people had waited all through the day and listened intently to the proceedings. They required very little explanation of what had happened, nor did the country.

I still place the responsibility for this squarely on Brazauskas's shoulders. He had already decided to oppose our ideas and to prevent the vote during his visit to Moscow. For some reason he did not believe in independence, and was always ready to argue against it. When we met he would regularly explain the disadvantages, list the impossible demands which would be placed on the country, and detail the strong measures the Kremlin's advisers had prepared in case we ever went for it seriously. The voteless debate which we had now experienced was, however, the first serious conflict I had with him in his capacity as head of the Supreme Council. In the event it was not as dreadful a mishap as we feared. Even though we had obviously lost one battle, we had gained the people's admiration, and our work now moved forward faster as a result. We were increasingly becoming a viable political opposition, and soon that was how we began to describe ourselves. The eventual outcome of that day's events was that our work and initiatives became increasingly reflected in public affairs. When we left the Supreme Council after the debate that day, we had tried to lead the crowd away with us to avoid an excessive reaction to what had happened. Many of them followed us to Cathedral Square where further discussion took place in the open air. We did not restrain our criticism of the Supreme Council in this public airing, and said that they now represented nobody. When the discussion appeared to come to an end, we went across the road to Sąjūdis headquarters where we continued to review our position and to consider our options. Sąjūdis then issued an official statement condemning the cowardice of the Supreme Council, and its leaders' submissive attitudes to the Soviet Union. This statement was widely read, and very well received, and we followed it up by collecting signatures from members of the Supreme Council on a petition for a reopening of the previous day's session and further debate on the proposals on which discussion had been so improperly interrupted. We also decided to call for votes of no confidence against the chairman (Vytautas Astrauskas) and secretary of the Supreme Council, and Lionginas Šepetys who had taken the chair at the meeting, anticipating that this would have a marked effect on their supporters if it was carried. A public demonstration was also planned for the next day, a Monday. At least we would stop all traffic in the streets of Vilnius for a few minutes at noon, and if possible, in all the other towns of Lithuania.

It is sad to recall that the events which I have described, and the action which followed the next day saw the beginnings of a split within Sąjūdis and the alienation of some of its members. These troubles began when Vytautas Petkevičius, a writer and a personal friend of Brazauskas, attempted to manœuvre Sąjūdis into becoming a complement of the Communist party. He was an abrasive operator who tried to exploit all the ambiguities of the situation, and bluntly dubbed those who did not share his views as 'stupid', even as 'destroyers of Sąjūdis'. This turn of phrase indeed was rich in irony. His activities caused a lot of tension, though those whom he criticized quickly learned to be careful, and went out of their way not to confront him head on, knowing that the party would eagerly exploit any obvious divisions in our movement. Attitudes became increasingly unpleasant, and after the debate in the Supreme Council, Sąjūdis was increasingly accused by the administrators of the Communist party of being a 'radical and extremist organization', while its members were described as 'unrealistic idealists'. We were represented to the local Russian and Polish populations as nationalists who would oppose and restrict their vital interests. We were accused of various illegalities and threatened with prosecution. Our Seimas Council discussed the increase in these problems and decided to restrict our contacts with the government to just a few members of the Central Committee of the Lithuanian Communist party. We had been faced with a problematic situation, but our discussion made it obvious that our movement must establish a resilient structure if it was going to survive. This was the background to my appointment as chairman of the Sąjūdis Seimas Council, to represent the movement, organize its work and decide on the priorities. When I embarked on this role the libellous Moscow press and television reacted immediately, coming to the assistance of the local party with an article in *Izvestia* which claimed that 'the best brains of Sąjūdis had now left it, or had been pushed aside by the "Landsbergis extremists" who were now in charge'. It is interesting to recall how, as Christmas approached, these 'extremists' suggested that those who favoured Lithuania's rebirth should light a candle after dark on Christmas Eve, and place it in a window. Petkevičius, still posing as a member of Sąjūdis, scorned the idea, announcing that it was 'a dangerous proposal', and saying that he feared that those who opposed the movement's ideas would smash such candle-lit windows in angry reaction. The irony of his protest lay in its twisted character, because he pretended to be speaking in Sąjūdis's interest as if he was our protector, though his 'advice' was given in a threatening way and sounded dangerously like an order. However, he was not listened to. Windows were illuminated with candles all over Lithuania that Christmas Eve, and nobody went out to smash them.

This was the atmosphere in Lithuania at the time that the country was preparing for the election of deputies to attend the Peoples' Congress of the Soviet Union. However, by the time the New Year had dawned we discovered that we were enjoying new international attention. Interest in our situation seemed suddenly to have spread, and we found that important guests were flocking to visit our movement in numbers which we had not experienced before. Significantly, a delegation came from the European Parliament. Members had formed a group there to keep the situation in the Baltic countries under review. Unfortunately its members took it upon themselves to explain how long our road to independence was likely to be. They said that everyone would be most helped if we agreed to come to an agreement which kept us within the Soviet Union and learned to live in harmony with Gorbachev. Initially this message seemed very depressing, especially as it came from the European Parliament, but we soon learned that the visit had been organized by a Lithuanian exile who was employed as an adviser to that Parliament. We had already received warning signals about this man, and they turned out to be true. We discovered much later that he was a KGB agent and had been sent to undermine Sąjūdis. Moscow had seen him as a valuable tool in its strategy of manipulating the European Parliament. His attentions were unwelcome, but they brought us little disadvantage in the long run because his schemes had put us officially in touch with the European Parliament for the first time. As a result we discovered that we had friends and supporters there.

On 15 February 1989 we convened a major meeting of the Sąjūdis Seimas at the Music Theatre in Kaunas. It was ironic that this building was the very place in which the leading communists of the time had declared our country to be a part of the Soviet Union in 1940, as our meeting was to mark a significant step forward in the process of unstitching the unholy bargain which they had struck at that time. We were careful to ensure that the event was well prepared and we held thoroughgoing discussions in the fortnight leading up to the opening. A declaration was carefully prepared for the Seimas to discuss, and we were rewarded by a rich and comprehensive debate on the text, which lasted all day and into the small hours of the morning. The intensity and fervour of this discussion were such that its formal proclamation took place after midnight and a day later than planned. However, we suddenly realized how auspicious this was, because that day, 16 February, had been celebrated in pre-war Lithuania as our National Independence Day! The resulting solemn assertion of our country's right to be independent was then made unambiguously and unequivocally with this anniversary at the forefront of everyone's mind. The purpose and goal of our movement was to be the achievement of full independence. Once the Seimas had given their wholehearted assent to this historic declaration, the delegates snatched a few hours of sleep. They then rose to attend a special mass celebrated by Cardinal Vincentas Sladkevičius, the archbishop of Kaunas and primate of Lithuania, in his cathedral. Immediately afterwards a huge procession wound through the streets to the open square which stands before the Kaunas War Museum, where our national Statue of Liberty had been restored and was waiting to be unveiled. It was a moment of rich portent because this powerful symbol of Lithuanian independence had been pulled down during Stalin's regime on the orders of Antanas Sniečkus, a prominent Lithuanian quisling, but the sculpture had been stored in Kaunas Art Gallery. Now, on Independence Day, 16 February 1989, the statue stood high on its pedestal holding the nation's flag in one hand and broken chains in the other. A crowd of more than 100,000 people had gathered, and my father had been chosen to unveil it as a veteran of Lithuania's War of Independence of 1918–20. The leaders of the Lithuanian Communist party, Algirdas Brazauskas and Vladimiras Beriozovas, came from Vilnius to watch the celebrations. They had received permission to participate from Moscow! We saw the event as the beginning of a moral revolution, something which was emphasized after the unveiling, when Cardinal Sladkevičius delivered an address which spoke of Lithuania's independence and its rebirth. His words were followed by a further cere-mony in which members of Sąjūdis Seimas swore an oath (of which I was the author), in which they promised to strive for Lithuanian independence and vowed, if called upon, to sacrifice themselves for it.

Later that day another huge crowd of people was to repeat these words in an evening ceremony in Cathedral Square in Vilnius. My father was again called on to perform an unveiling ceremony there, this time of the commemorative plaque which had recently been attached to the house where the Lithuanian Council had proudly met to proclaim the independent state of Lithuania in 1918. When this celebration of our national past was done, another huge procession moved on to the Rasos cemetery, to visit the grave of Jonas Basanavičius, the founding chairman of the Council, and those of soldiers who had lost their lives defending our nation's independence. Later, at sunset, I made a speech at the City Sports Hall to open the commemorative concert which was being televised that evening. It was an opportunity to publicize Sąjūdis's declaration of Lithuania's independence, and I took some pleasure in the knowledge that the communist ideologists were turning white with anger as I spoke. We had already recognized that our celebrations would bring into the open the tensions between *our* beliefs and *their* ideology, and had moved boldly knowing that Sąjūdis would find no better opportunity to launch its campaign to get its nominees elected as deputies in the forthcoming election to the Peoples' Congress of the Soviet Union. Our moves had, however, been carefully observed, and the Communist party's fundamentalists now began to press Brazauskas to find a way of crushing Sąjūdis. He reacted by aligning himself more and more with the conservatives, and the Central Committee passed resolutions against Sąjūdis. Our financial backers were warned about the 'dangerous path' being trodden by our movement, and soon our access to television programmes was withdrawn. The explanation was that the election campaign had begun, and we were informed that this meant that those concerned could present their views in the scheduled election broadcasts, so that 'Sąjūdis had no need for special treatment'. This of course implied blatant inequality because the communists could have access to the screens at any time and on any subject of their choice, and would claim that they were 'speaking outside the election campaign'! We protested, of course, and then responded by deciding to call the people to a rally at the Kalnų Park, Vilnius, on 8 March. There I told the crowd that the communists would soon be refusing us access to the press, the only medium now left to us, if things went any further. I then reminded my hearers that our people had still not forgotten how Tsarist repression had been outwitted by the illegal book-distributors, and said that we would revive that tradition if necessary, because the best weapon in our fight for democracy was openness! My comments might be construed as headstrong, but I was past caring and determined only to demonstrate that our resolve would not be broken by any campaign of suppression.

When the election actually began we faced the same old tiresome communist charade of lies and slander. We found ourselves being told that Sajūdis could not be named as an official body on the ballot papers as candidates were to be nominated from places of work, factories, collective farms and other organizations. The message was that the Communist party was going to retain its monopoly control of the whole process, and that the real selection of candidates would be conducted by the government. This was true to form, but the outcome had all the makings of farce. We were determined to make the best of our limited room for manœuvre, prepared lists of people in good standing in our movement, and then got local Sajūdis branches to nominate them as candidates. We did not restrict our activities to organizations in which we were strongest, but sought nominations in as many places as possible. These activities, not surprisingly, met with resistance, but when our candidates were refused registration in some of the districts, we took journalists with video cameras along with us to record just how the electoral commission was treating our attempts to register candidates. Many of the electoral officials simply lied to us, or looked for ways of avoiding responsibility, and there were a number of interesting incidents. In one case Kazimieras Motieka was attacked by a newspaper for speaking against the party and communism in general in an article which described him as 'against the constitution', and it asked for his name to be removed from the list of candidates. He was still a member of the party, and was summoned to appear before the Central Committee, but he avoided this by taking rapid pre-emptive action. He resigned by returning his card to the general secretary! One would have thought he would be cast into outer darkness after snubbing them in this way, but the party machine then produced a surprise. When their list of candidates was published, his name was still included as one of their members. It may have been inefficiency but was probably an attempt to pull him back into the fold by giving him a second chance, but he saw it as an attempt to wrong-foot him, and responded with vigorous condemnation of their audacity in putting his name forward after he had left the party. His protest was dignified and public, and made at exactly the right time, because he had severed his link with the Communist party just before its spin doctors declared its 'rejuvenation'. His move was widely acclaimed.

Arvydas Juozaitis found himself in an even more complicated situation. He had been nominated to stand in the first round against Brazauskas, and it even looked as if there might be a good chance that he would win, though neither he nor the rest of us were quite certain whether we really wanted that result because Brazauskas clearly had his part to play in our dealings with Moscow. The matter hung in suspense, but our decision was made for us when his signature (as a member of the Sąjūdis Seimas Council) on a contract for the publication of a calendar which we had not authorized was discovered to be a forgery. We already had wind of a campaign to compromise him, so we took advantage of this discovery by arranging the immediate withdrawal of his candidature, a move which interestingly enough was commended for its wisdom by the foreign diplomats who were now to be found in Lithuania from time to time, visiting us from Leningrad or Moscow. They clearly regarded the decision as a sign of prudence!

Under election law as it then stood, our candidates needed to be nominated by 'workers' collectives', meetings of hospital doctors and nurses, or school or factory staffs. It was planned that I should stand in Panevėžys, where over thirty such groups put my name forward. Despite this general support, however, some of the collectives there introduced a divisive element into the procedure by supporting other Sąjūdis members for the constituency. The names of the poet Justinas Marcinkevičius and the academician Raimundas Rajeckas were unexpectedly put forward. The intention seemed to be to confuse and complicate matters, a process which would benefit the administration in power. However, the ploy did not work as both men withdrew from the contest, despite their continuing membership of the Communist party, in order to avoid having the Sąjūdis vote split on election day. In the end I was left facing only a communist *nomenklatura* candidate. As the campaign developed, Sąjūdis candidates explained our intention to represent the movement and its principles in Moscow, in the Supreme Council of the Soviet Union. We said that other candidates might sell their country down the river, but our sole interest would be to defend Lithuania. We gave solemn promises, sometimes in writing, that we would concede nothing with regard to Lithuanian sovereignty, reminding the electorate that we were wholly committed to Lithuanian independence. This was of course in line with our movement's recent declaration, but we needed to state our case radically because Laisvės Lyga (the Lithuanian Freedom League) was still urging the unrealistic policy of boycotting the Soviet elections. In the week before the election we were exceptionally active throughout the whole country, and our posters were on show everywhere. This huge effort paid off handsomely when we came out as the victors. Of the forty-two constituencies contested by Sąjūdis we won thirty-six, and I was elected too!

After the elections we naturally expected to get back the hour of television broadcasting we had enjoyed on Wednesday evenings before the election campaign, but which had been withdrawn on the pretext that it 'might conflict with the campaign'. However, we were now briskly informed that this was not to be the case. We had been successful in the all-Soviet election, but elections to the Supreme Council of the Lithuanian Soviet Republic were now pending, and we were to be excluded from access to television broadcasting until this was over, on the same basis as before. The Communist party had realized that our recent success would be a prelude to a campaign to capture the Supreme Council for Sąjūdis, and this of course was the last thing that they wanted. The message was not unexpected, and our response was rapid. A general call was immediately sent out asking our supporters to assemble at eleven o'clock that same evening, on the steps of the Vilnius television studio complex. The protest was planned to coincide with the transmission of a programme called *Atgimimo banga* (The Wave of Rebirth). When the appointed time arrived there was a vast gathering. We had already learned how to make the most of our demonstrations, and this one was designed as a happy celebration which would declare that while our opponents might not want to let us into Parliament, ours was now a movement with a highly successful election campaign behind it. We had been triumphant and were going to use their obvious obstruction of our path to further electoral success by showing everyone our disapproval of the government's attempt to deny us the means of communication with the very people who had just given us their confidence. So we set out to tell everybody that Lithuania's television service was paid for by taxes collected *from* the people, and was therefore there to provide a service *for* the people. I opened the event with a series of questions:

> Whose television service is it anyway? Whose money built these studios? To whom do they belong, and whom should they serve?
>
> The Communist party claims that television belongs to the state, so whose state is it? Members of this government have persuaded themselves that they are the state, that it belongs to them, but we are returning Lithuania to *democracy*, which means that it must belong to you. Democracy claims that the state belongs to the people by their own efforts and thoughts, through the constitution and the law. Our television is maintained from the people's funds, so it should serve them ... If the government tries to prevent television from serving the people, then the people have the right to change the government.

This blunt message got through. The government woke up to the fact that our 'live spectacular' would damage them if the protest was sustained. The following week the doors of the television centre were opened to us, and our weekly hour was reinstated. Our friends inside the television centre were once more in a position to help our movement.

We had videotaped the rally which led to this success, and planned to show the film on television during the election period, but the authorities in the broadcasting service, who were under government supervision, were clearly determined to avoid this. They told us when the time came to schedule the programme that they had no time-slot available, but before we had really digested this information we learned that the government had commissioned a propaganda video of its own, which was to be broadcast as a matter of priority! We were suitably angry, but not outwitted, as our friends in the studios set about preparing a new broadcast for us, which included our video with shots of other Sąjūdis mass meetings at which the national flag was flown. On the day before the government's propaganda film was to be shown, they cheekily slipped this into the peak-hour transmission slot in place of another programme. As a result, it had a large audience, while the communist video broadcast on the following day reached an audience which had been prepared by seeing shots of our meetings. The result was useful because the government film pretended, however preposterous it may now seem, that the communists had supported the national demonstrations. Indeed, their footage claimed these as their own! As we had already shown the true picture, we had stolen their fire, and the dishonesty of their propaganda was made plain for all to see. Their film had little impact.

In general, the election period was a happy time for us. Sąjūdis was still a young and lively movement. When set-backs came we were able to respond to them with a song in our hearts, because our belief was strong. Those of us who were involved in the movement were deeply committed. Though we were all very different as individuals, we were like-minded on the really important issues. Some of our most active supporters were white-haired and elderly; the names of Professor Juozas Bulavas and Dr Meilė Lukšienė come to mind as I write. Both were widely admired in our movement, but there were always much younger enthusiasts, such as Zigmas Vaišvila, alongside such older people. Though Bulavas was enjoying his seventieth spring and Vaišvila was in sight of his thirtieth, the gap in their ages was forgotten because they shared the same youthful spirit, and the vision which Sąjūdis offered of a future green with hope. When the elections were finally over, we were in a new, very challenging and excitingly different situation for the result had demonstrated the strength of our movement and our people's support for it. There was uncertainty no longer, and we could also rest satisfied in the knowledge that we had at last ensured for ourselves a greater degree both of personal safety and of real political standing. It meant that our deputies were able to attend the Peoples' Congress of the

Soviet Union confident in having the nation's mandate behind them. We could also attend the Lithuanian Supreme Council and act with authority there, knowing that we had rights which must sooner or later be acknowledged, even in that bastion of the Soviet system. Having been elected by the people, we could assert that we were their true representatives. We could therefore be bold in dealing with our opponents, the unelected *apparatchiki* of a usurping ideology. They might continue to carry their false credentials for a while, but we knew democracy had once again become the real source of moral and political authority in our nation. We were therefore fighting from the high moral ground.

CHAPTER 12

Between the steps of the Kremlin and the Baltic Way

Elections to decide who should represent Lithuania at the Peoples' Congress of the Soviet Union took place in March 1989. The outcome was that Sąjūdis won against the Communist party of Lithuania by a ratio of six to one, and some of the most prominent of the *nomenklatura* lost their seats, including the chairmen of the Supreme Council and the Council of Ministers. This final indignity only served to rub salt into the government's wounds, especially when the new deputies defined the new political balance by choosing not to appoint Algirdas Brazauskas as leader of the Lithuanian delegation. My name was suggested for this position, but I was firmly against being nominated for that post and also refused to be one of the Lithuanian representatives on the Supreme Council of the Soviet Union.

In May the successful candidates attended a session of the Baltic Assembly in Tallinn, where we met the Latvian and Estonian deputies who had been elected at the same time. At this meeting the representatives of the three national movements (the People's Fronts of Latvia and Estonia and Sąjūdis) prepared a communiqué to be sent to the United Nations Organization and national governments around the world, calling for the restoration of the independent states of Lithuania, Latvia and Estonia. Copies of this declaration were also sent to the Supreme Council of the Soviet Union and to Mikhail Gorbachev. As the memory of the Tbilisi massacre was fresh in everyone's minds at the time, we prepared a statement urging the Soviet government 'not to wage war on its own peoples', and then I joined the chairmen of the other two national movements in signing a concordat committing our countries to a closer relationship, including the development of a common market between us in the future. We went on to discuss a common strategy for defending our interests at the Peoples' Congress of the Soviet Union, and though we failed to agree a statement committing us to a joint policy, I persuaded our Lithuanian deputies to overlook our disappointment and sign the draft document. This had attempted to define our common position and would now serve to define our own, since it affirmed that 'no one outside our countries could have any role in deciding our futures'. It was a position which both asserted our national sovereignty, and made it clear (in advance) that we held the Moscow Congress legally incapable of pronouncing on the sovereign rights of Lithuania. In this way we set out the case we would argue and the course we would follow, that is, that no decisions could be made affecting the Baltic states without the agreement of their elected representatives, and that our future was not to be determined by the majority vote of a Soviet Parliament. From our point of view it was vital that these principles were openly stated in this way well before business began in Moscow, because the first duty of the Congress would be to elect 270 deputies from its 2,250 members to serve on the Council of the Soviet Union, and a further 271 to serve on the so-called Council of the Nationalities. As the electoral rules allowed only four Lithuanians to become members of the first body, and a mere twelve to represent us in the second, we knew already that we had no chance of having a deciding influence in any debate on the constitution, or on matters concerning national sovereignty, unless we took scrupulous care to ensure that our negotiating positions were uncompromised.

There were other dimensions to our weak position in the Congress. We knew that we must be particularly circumspect with regard to any 'democratic proposals' which might emerge in the forthcoming debates in this stronghold of Sovietism. Any enthusiasm for them might well be seen as supporting decisions which could harm our own national interest. We were not prepared to compromise our position in these matters, as we were now in a strong position at home, where our own Supreme Council had adopted Sajūdis's Declaration of Sovereignty immediately after our electoral success had been confirmed. It had also recognized the principle that Lithuanian law must have precedence over Soviet law in every case. Interestingly enough, it was not any constitutional problem which eventually gave us most trouble, but rather the argument about who should control the raw materials produced in our territory. The Soviet Union was naturally concerned above all else with the protection of the economic interests at the core of its colonial rule. Gorbachev had already tried to tell the Estonians that the raw material wealth of their country was a property which 'belonged to all the Soviet peoples' under the provisions of the Soviet constitution. They had refused his claims gently, but we Lithuanians did not believe that soft words were the right way of dealing with this issue, and declared plainly that his argument was a legal absurdity which merely reflected the interest of an occupying power and nothing else. It was interesting that the Soviets did not bother to engage deeply in arguing about this disagreement with us once we took that firm stance, though it took almost a year before I noticed this. The psychology involved was complex, and was one of the paradoxical effects of the bureaucratic arrangements through which Russia arranged the exploitation of its colonies. This experience was a useful strategic lesson which helped me to emphasize our solidarity with Boris Yeltsin's stand when the time came.

The Soviet Congress opened on 25 May 1989, and our first clash came in the opening sessions during the elections of the two Councils. Once again, despite the moves towards reform, we were expected to follow the old procedures of voting on a *single list* of candidates which had been prepared in advance. There was a brazen assumption that the Executive's recommendations would be accepted unanimously and without question by every one of the 2,250 deputies. As the procedure was set in motion, we recognized what was afoot, and decided to seize the opportunity to ask for an alternative method of selecting candidates. Before the vote was called I therefore asked to speak on behalf of my delegation and pointed out that very few in that large assembly knew the members of the Lithuanian delegation. Like the other delegations we were expected to supply a number of candidates to fill seats on the higher Councils, and an election was about to take place to accomplish this. We had anticipated this and followed appropriate procedures to select our own candidates, but these nominees were now to be passed over by a procedure which selected candidates by an obscure process which would soon involve us in voting for names which meant little or nothing to us. We were troubled by this procedure and asked Congress to respect our national judgement and allow us the opportunity to choose our own members. We had not voted for candidates to represent Tajikistan, Kazakhstan or the other republics, and by the same token we had no wish for others to select our delegates. We believed that the election of the Lithuanian representatives to the two Councils in Moscow (the Council of the Soviet Union, and the Council of the Nationalities) should be the concern of those who had been selected by the people of Lithuania to do just that, and no one else. As I spoke, Gorbachev's anger became apparent to everyone present. Suddenly he roared, 'What is this? A blocking manœuvre or an ultimatum?' Then shouting broke out around the hall: 'Doesn't Lithuania trust us?' Some deputies yelled abuse, others tried to calm things down, but nobody seemed to want to examine our challenge to the system. It soon became apparent that the majority of deputies wanted to ignore the fact that we had raised a question of *principle* about how elections should be conducted. However, this was the very ground of our objections. We had decided to take a stand on principle, and were much less concerned with *who* was elected than with avoiding blind compliance. In particular, we did not want other people to elect representatives to speak on behalf of Lithuania without registering our disagreement.

It did not escape us that some of our own Lithuanian colleagues were unhappy with what I said. Some of them told me that I had 'spoken out of turn', and others attempted to apologize 'on behalf of the delegation'. Their reactions prompted me to request leave to speak again. I said that my words were not intended to reflect on decisions taken by deputies from other republics. We Lithuanians were concerned with issues of national sovereignty and constrained by our own circumstances, and the congress must not be surprised to find a majority of our deputies failing to vote according to the procedures which had been prescribed. In fact, when the vote actually took place, most of our delegation abstained. This was entirely consistent with our decision to maintain a stand on principle for the duration of the Congress, even with regard to formalities and matters of procedure, because we had determined to press for proper political and parliamentary procedures, come what may.

Congress sessions and meetings took place daily. We were accommodated in comfortable rooms in the Hotel Moskva in the centre of the city. It had a good restaurant (by Moscow standards), and the Kremlin buffets offered food which was wholly unobtainable in Soviet shops, such as caviar, mandarins, oranges and pineapples. All deputies received good expenses allowances, but despite these comforts the sessions dragged on. Many were happy to use the free tickets provided, and took time off to fly home to their families. Deputies enjoyed a very comfortable life-style, and many of them were seduced into compliance by the pleasant opportunities which life in Moscow offered and the privileges they had in the community. All that those who wanted to be reselected had to do in order to return was to vote as they were told. Yet times were changing, and we at least were determined not to be rubber-stamping deputies whose vote could be reckoned on in advance, or who left for home at every opportunity while allowing the system to rumble on regardless. We had determined to use every opportunity for change, and made arrangements to discuss our plans carefully. A Baltic Deputies' Club was founded and registered, and once this was done we met there every evening to reflect on developments or to work out what our strategies should be. We were not alone in making such an arrangement and even before the club had opened, the Russian democratic forces, with Academician Andrei Sakharov and Boris Yeltsin among its leading members, had established what it called an Inter-regional Group. They asked us to join it, but we replied that while we would support any of their proposals which reflected our own concern for democratic principles, there were big differences between their position and ours, because while they planned to reform the Soviet Union they saw its future as a single unitary state. Our policy was different. We wanted to see the break-up of the Union, and our participation in Soviet politics was intended to be strictly time-limited. We saw ourselves not so much as deputies of the Soviet Union but as a Lithuanian delegation which was temporarily camping out in Moscow to promote our country's national interests and to fight against centralism. Although they were disappointed by this answer it was clear that our position was well understood, and indeed the idea of collective representation was not yet always obvious to all members of our own delegation, who needed a lot of persuasion to hold to the general position upon which we had agreed. I can remember one of these weaker brethren exclaiming, 'Landsbergis wants to force his will upon us'. However, there was no alternative, although holding the group together was not always easy. But, despite the tensions which inevitably emerged among us, the small Lithuanian tricolour which I had taken with us to Moscow was a powerful unifying force, and helped a great deal. We always placed it in front of our delegation at Congress meetings, and though Gorbachev and Lukyanov seemed to look at it with some disdain, no attempt was made to remove it. I think that they got used to it eventually, but I often wondered if they saw our behaviour as childish and felt they were humouring us by letting us display the flag. It is possible that they imagined that we would be pleased to remain citizens of the Soviet Union while holding on to this one symbol. Our national flag meant more to us than that, however. We were made of rather sterner stuff and were more strategic in our thinking than they had perhaps allowed for. It happened that our delegation's allocated place in the Congress Hall of the Kremlin was in full view of the television cameras. We took full advantage of this position and placed our flag strategically to say something, both to Gorbachev's followers and to our own people. As a result, even the Muscovites on the streets used to recognize us and cheer enthusiastically.

The delegation was always careful to discuss Congress business in advance in order to decide priorities, and we were very diligent in doing this. We went to the Baltic Club each evening to consider the agenda, to work out our tactics and to decide who would issue statements or make speeches. Early in the Congress a procedural concession was made which allowed for individual statements at the end of each debate. Every request to avail oneself of this opportunity had to be made in writing with the support of a delegation. We used our opportunities to the full and had a supply of these applications prepared in advance. If ever Lukyanov put an end to the discussion from the chair when we still had things to say, we would hand a prepared request to him. This device provided a useful way of getting around the many fraudulent efforts of the Congress managers to limit our contributions, and in the end we were open about it to such a degree that one of our deputies told Lukyanov that it was 'not worth his while trying to gag us' because we had a collection of these requests ready for every occasion. When we had concluded our own meeting each evening we would normally meet the Latvian and Estonian Front deputies around 11 p.m., to try to establish a shared viewpoint. We noticed after a while that we were disciplined in our opinions by comparison with our neighbours, who often came with issues unresolved among themselves. Some of their delegates seemed very ready to compromise with Gorbachev, especially when the going was tough, but we were consistent in our belief that compromise 'for the sake of good relations' would do no good. We remained firm because we knew that Moscow had always failed to recognize our needs and would continue to do so, unless it was quite clear that we and others would be prepared to defend our position, to which we were totally committed. We expected few concessions from that quarter even when this was clear, and had come to terms with this very real constraint, so we argued against compromise from the start, especially if it was grounded in the wish to avoid giving offence. We knew that soft compliance would always give the wrong impression, and would virtually guarantee that we would gain nothing. Our stand, however, carried the possibility of our being left in splendid isolation, and this danger was accepted. We noticed, however, after a while, that some of the Latvians had accepted official posts, but he who sups with the devil may need a long spoon!

We wanted to notify the Soviet Congress of the changes to our constitution as adopted on 18 May, and applied for leave to present our Declaration of Sovereignty to the Congress. Neither Gorbachev nor Lukyanov replied. We waited a while, and then asked for copies to be distributed to the deputies. Again, there was no response. Their silence did not, however, deter me from taking the opportunity to read its key statement aloud in an address to the assembly, in which I declaimed the sentence: 'Legislation is valid in the territory of the Soviet Socialist Republic of Lithuania only when it has been enacted or confirmed by the Lithuanian Supreme Council.' In the same speech I warned the republics by describing Lithuania as having been 'invaded by a blood-stained monster which crashed in through the door carrying a grave-digger's spade in one hand, a bad constitution in the other, and with its army following behind'. For good measure I added: 'It has behaved in this way without let-up since 1944. Though it has finally begun to propose *perestroika iki galo* [*perestroika* to the end!], do you *really* think that this fine phrase means that they are asking for the enforced slavery of the Soviet Union to be replaced by a voluntary union of friendly neighbours!'

Again I was not mincing my words, and this stance obviously did not endear us to the majority of delegates. We were not liked for what we were doing, but as the first session of the Congress came to an end we began to sense some change in attitudes. This first became apparent when a plan to establish a Committee for Constitutional Control was proposed. It came with very little warning, and it was clear that the Congress was expected to accept it without discussion, as a full list of nominees for this body had already been prepared. It included people from Moscow at the top, with a sprinkling of names from the other republics, and even one Lithuanian representative, a lawyer from Vilnius, whose name had been included without his being consulted. He was quick to sacrifice this unexpected preferment, and asked for the nomination to be withdrawn. We understood from what was going on that a war had already begun behind the scenes over the constitutional arrangements, which was why the names of representatives from the Baltic republics had been included in the list of proposed members. It was to some degree a papering over the cracks, because the designers of that list knew as well as we did that both Lithuania and Estonia were already legislating for themselves, and had unilaterally declared Soviet laws invalid within their territories. The underlying message was that Gorbachev's followers were rushing to put their Constitutional Committee in place, anticipating that it would act in the near future to declare these actions of both our governments to be invalid. The Congress was being expected to rubber-stamp what the Executive had already decided, even though we were absolutely determined to oppose these proposals. We began to fight them piecemeal and wholesale, arguing from the start that such a body should only be formed on the basis of consent between sovereign states. What we were saying was, of course, that the rulings of such a committee could not be applied to Lithuania if our Parliament disagreed, and that it was virtually a foregone conclusion that we would reject its formulations. Our opponents countered by arguing that our objections were out of order, and telling us that a Constitutional Supervision Law *already* existed following changes to the Soviet constitution passed in the autumn of 1988. We countered this with the reply that we had collected 1,800,000 signatures against those very proposals at the time, and had subsequently presented the petition to the Kremlin. We said that this had made it crystal-clear that those changes had been explicitly rejected in Lithuania by the whole nation. We also pointed out that it was constitutionally improper to appoint a committee to supervise a law before the law had itself been passed! It was only too easy for us to envisage provisions being included in the next phase of constitutional legislation with which we would be quite unable to agree, and we foresaw that in all likelihood the planned committee would be armed with powers to pressurize us into conformity. We could not go along with the proposals on any account. We would therefore not co-operate with a vote to establish a body whose duties were not defined.

Gorbachev became very angry at this, and turned to ask Congress whether a vote should be taken. Interestingly, he put the question by asking 'whether a vote for the establishment of the committee should be taken or not' rather than for a 'vote for the formation of the committee'. The subtle choice of words did not escape us, and we were worried by this manœuvre, fearing that we were close to being outwitted. Congress could easily have viewed our positive response to this proposal as implying a vote for the subsequent formation of the committee. If we were to participate in the voting, even by voting *against* the establishment of a committee, our consent to the process being followed would have been implied, since we would have no option but to accept the majority decision. As we could not allow ourselves to be put in this position, there was only one way to deal with the resulting dilemma, so we simply stood up and walked out. We left just two or three communist Lithuanian deputies behind, but it could be said that we took the Estonians out with us, as most of them went too. Derogatory remarks followed us, but the eyes of the world were immediately turned on us as our withdrawal was televised and discussed in the newspapers in every corner of the globe. In fact we had managed to destroy the project, though we only knew that we had scored a victory when Gorbachev dropped the idea of an immediate vote. An ineffective working party was set up to undertake preparatory work on the constitution of the committee, but after a while the matter was quietly forgotten.

Another dramatic event around this time was the walk-out of one of our deputies, Egidijus Klumbys, in obvious protest at a speech made by General Rodionov, who was responsible for the atrocities committed at Tbilisi in Georgia on 9 April 1989, when soldiers under his command murdered twenty peaceful demonstrators and wounded a further 200. Rodionov was elected to the Congress by the Soviet army units under his command in Georgia and he attended as a member of the Georgian delegation. In a speech which made his satisfaction with his butchery evident to us all, he launched into a crude attack on Georgians. For us Lithuanians his arguments were tortuous and unbearable, and we shuddered with horror when his words gained first one ovation, then a second, when he praised Stalin's repressions of 1937. The applause seemed to come from a majority of the deputies, and Klumbys took this as his cue for stalking out. As he went, the Georgian delegation as a group moved away from Rodionov, leaving him sitting alone. After a while Rodionov left too, and the Georgians then began to take part in the proceedings once more. They had been embarrassed, and had been protected from being shamed at home by following the example of one principled Lithuanian. The incident had a further valuable outcome later, when a commission was set up to investigate Rodionov's butchery in Tbilisi.

We seized an early opportunity to demand the condemnation of the Molotov–Ribbentrop Pact. Our detractors in the Congress denied that such a pact had ever been concluded. They said there were no secret documents, that this was a historical fiction, that there was no proof. They asserted that the story was the product of the febrile imagination of the enemies of communism, and that it was a good example of bourgeois lies being spread. Even Gorbachev took the same line, speaking vaguely of dubious photographs which could be falsifications. He must have known of the existence of documents, but preferred to lie publicly by saying the accusation was unproven and that no original document had been found. Nevertheless, we pursued the matter openly. We were forthright, saying that the whole world knew of the pact and that if this Congress failed to condemn it, it would imply that the Soviet Union had still not entirely left behind the old ways of Stalin's time, and was therefore not to be trusted. We explained that we had raised the issue on the instructions of our Lithuanian Supreme Council, which had received the report of a commission set up to investigate the question. Its conclusions had demanded not just the condemnation of the pact, but a campaign to eradicate some of its consequences. From our viewpoint, these were developments of the greatest importance, as the Lithuanian commission had included representatives of the Communist party and the Academy of Sciences as well as of Sąjūdis. Its work had brought us to a political consensus, within which every group was ready to demand that our independence, so unjustly removed, should be re-established. We needed to bring the commission's findings to the attention of a wider world, and enlighten the Congress in Moscow, so Sąjūdis had 2,000 facsimile copies of the original Russian text of the secret protocols printed in Vilnius, which we then distributed by hand to the other delegates at the Congress in the foyer of the Hotel Moskva.

At this point Gorbachev began to see that the issue had to be faced, and he began to search for some accommodation with us. As a result, a Commission was appointed, with Alexander Yakovlev as its chairman. When we learned of this move, we insisted that representatives from all the Baltic countries should be included. Many deputies, especially the armed forces officers, were hostile to this suggestion, but Gorbachev surprised us by going along with our demands. Kazimieras Motieka, Zita Šličytė, both advocates, Justinas Marcinkevičius, the poet, and I were appointed. Estonia was represented by Edgar Savisaar and Professor

Endel Lipmaa, an eminently sensible person, a shrewd diplomat and a skilful politician who came to the meetings fully prepared with a case full of documents which he used to refute the Soviet arguments. Gorbachev had designated us the 'Commission for Evaluating the Non-Aggression Agreement between the Soviet Union and Germany', but when our terms of reference were being discussed he implied that there was no need to investigate the question of 'secret protocols', claiming again that nobody had ever seen the original documents. He told me that the copies printed from microfilm which we had circulated were of dubious origin and unconfirmed validity. My position was naturally different, so I stood up to argue that as there were no doubts about the existence of a pact, the existence and content of the secret protocols was precisely what the Commission must investigate. I then affirmed that the commission's title must refer to the 'secret protocols', as this was the heart of the matter. Gorbachev dealt with this by pretending that he had not heard this proposal. We had already noticed that this was a device which he often used in order to manipulate meetings. He and Lukyanov were good at pushing through whatever was in their interest, and avoiding what they deemed to be 'unsuitable to the Centre'. We felt that further discussion of the title was pointless at that stage, and did not protest, but this led to later difficulties, when some of the Commission's members took the title literally and continued to argue that we were not there to discuss the 'secret protocols', only the pact itself. This was not our only frustration: we had hoped when the Commission was set up that it would report before September, to be ready for the fiftieth anniversary of the pact, but officialdom seemed to want to delay the outcome. For a while Yakovlev, its chairman, disappeared on other business. We were quite unable to contact him and his absence meant that the Commission did not meet for a long time. When he was interviewed by the press late in August, he blithely set about describing the Commission's work, though he had scarcely attended its meetings. His statements were, not surprisingly, only partly true. He even stated that if secret protocols had existed, they would have meant very little; the future of the Baltic states was decided because their peoples had disliked their governments at the time. He then played other clever cards, but it was demeaning to hear an otherwise serious politician regurgitating these discredited arguments. After this, Yuri Afanasyev and Edgar Savisaar, the deputy chairmen of the Commission, called us to Moscow, and a report signed by twenty of the twenty-eight members was issued in Yakovlev's absence. Its publication went unnoticed, and no internal newspaper or television service bothered to mention our conclusions. However, we called a press conference on our own initiative for foreign journalists in Moscow at which we blithely announced that 'the government had interfered with the Commission's work', and then distributed our conclusions. It was a move which put Yakovlev in a difficult situation since the official line had previously claimed that he would speak for the Commission. However, for the time being, both he and the system he represented were able to shrug us off, and no report appeared in print.

At the second session of the Congress the process repeated itself. It was obvious that the Commission had bypassed attempts to control its conclusions, and it was now clear that our conclusions had flown in the face of all the propaganda previously issued by the Foreign Ministry. Despite this, Gorbachev's adviser, Valentin Falin, was determined that the report, if and when published (it had still not been submitted to Congress), would avoid any mention of the violations of international law which were the basis of our case. Indeed his evasion went further, as he also asserted that no such law had existed at the time of the pact, and that the discussion of the Commission should therefore have concerned itself only with the individual international agreements which had been concluded. The situation was unhelpful and complicated, and so in order to make the best of things, we did not press too heavily. We firmly made the point, however, that the Soviet Union had broken some of its previously agreed international commitments by agreeing to the secret protocols. We argued that during our final meetings Yakovlev had summarized our conclusions and then presented his alternative viewpoint. The subsequent voting had rejected his formulation, but he remained unimpressed. By now it had become abundantly clear that our opponents were not prepared to accept any evaluation of the pact other than that which had long been current in the Soviet Union. The situation seemed to be one of stalemate; indeed when the issue was next taken back to Congress, it was openly said that the Commission's conclusions must not be adopted and that we had manipulated the evidence in order to facilitate our leaving the Soviet Union. Against all the evidence, we were again being told that there 'were no protocols', that there was no evidence, that no proof was to be had, and that there was certainly no need to give in to 'those Balts', as they sneeringly called us! As the debate proceeded and the time for voting got closer, the situation became a clear 'heads – they win, tails – we lose' alternative, and it was quite obvious from the mood of the Congress that the Stalinists were expecting victory. However, at this point the Congress managers must have noticed that we Lithuanians and our friends were astonishingly happy. This must have surprised them, and it was clear that Gorbachev himself was puzzled by the oddness of our demeanour. Why were we so obviously happy when we should be preparing to lose the day? Eventually he must have realized, probably rather suddenly, that we were laughing at the stupidity of the

Congress. Its members were compromising the Soviet Union more and more effectively with every new contribution they made to the debate, showing that the whole system was as Stalinist as ever it had been. The penny seemed to drop suddenly, and Gorbachev must have realized at the last moment that he would be facing political ridicule if the Congress proceeded to reject the Commission's findings. He turned quite unexpectedly to Yakovlev and the Commission, and asked them to 'resume their unfinished work'. Yakovlev responded by saying that he had 'nothing further to contribute'. He was withdrawing! The tension was clear, but what followed next was more reminiscent of a novel or film than of a parliamentary meeting. There was an interruption of the proceedings, and an elderly man was suddenly ushered to the microphone. He announced himself as an archivist from the Interior Ministry, and then produced a sheaf of documents from the Molotov archive, which he began to introduce to the Congress. As he proceeded, he named all the secret protocols, one by one, even providing the dates of their requisitions and movements. The effect was stunning, especially when Yakovlev then agreed, 'moved by this new evidence', to continue to chair the Commission 'in order to investigate these documents'. So the commissioners met finally on the next day, to vote on our conclusions all over again. This time the report to Congress was agreed, with an added mention of the protocols which had now been 'proven to exist'. The discussion was naturally brief. The other side were tight-lipped, but we were less restrained. The victory was sweet.

We regarded this Commission and its conclusions as vitally important for our future. The debate had also demonstrated very clearly just how Yakovlev had received his directions from above. Though he was a reformist, he still followed the party line and had obviously tried to maintain its slanted interpretations of the Molotov–Ribbentrop agreements. The story which he had so recently peddled had, of course, begun its long currency as a Stalinist lie, its purpose being to tell us that the Soviet Union, in its unending search for peace, had tried to come to an agreement with Germany in order to eliminate the possibility of war and to defend other nations from fascist slavery. During one of the Commission's meetings, I had asked Yakovlev about the identity of the person who had drafted the document we were then discussing which repeated this fable. He had hesitated, and then said: 'You might consider it to be my work.' I continued with my observations on its content, using the expression 'according to Yakovlev's document' more than once. He seemed to find this description embarrassing, and after a while he protested, saying that the document was not actually his. I retorted: 'Is it anonymous then? Why should we pay attention to a presentation for which no one takes responsibility?' There were many similar incidents during the Commission's deliberations.

When the fiftieth anniversary of the Molotov–Ribbentrop Pact came along we made great efforts to give prominence to its fateful consequences in the commemoration which was arranged. It was on that day that the people of all the Baltic states joined hands right across the three countries, along the great highway which connects Vilnius with Riga and Tallinn, which has become known as the Baltic Way. The idea of this link-up first came from the Estonian People's Front, and was planned by the national movements of the three states, each in its own manner, but co-operating with each other. Our great human chain began from Gediminas Castle and the cathedral in Vilnius, and stretched through Riga and on to Tallinn, linking three whole nations in a common act. At 7 p.m. on 23 August 1989 some two million people, men, women and children, linked hands in one continuous chain, and stood for a moment, in silence and meditation. Over a million people participated in Lithuania, and for the first time Poles came to join an event which was arranged by Sąjūdis, bringing their own flags and emblems. For some time before the joining of hands began, every side road leading to the Baltic Way was jammed with people coming by coach and car to their predetermined places, and some people just could not reach their destinations on time because of the overcrowding. I myself remained busy right up to the last moment trying to calm down people who were stuck in traffic jams, using the radio to advise those who could not reach their appointed places to leave their vehicles and join hands. As I spoke to them I reminded them that all of us in this great gathering wherever we might happen to be, were joined in a special togetherness, that we all shared the same road to the future. Gradually a continuous and unbroken human cordon was formed along the main highway, and there were many smaller line-ups along the side roads. Later in the evening there were mass meetings in all the larger towns, and bonfires were lit on the borders of our three countries. At many places in the Lithuanian countryside people erected wayside crosses to commemorate the event, and many had prepared themselves by attending mass. Just before 7 p.m. I finally joined hands with a group of young Lithuanian Scouts on my left, and with my wife Gražina and a group of former Siberian exiles on my right (Gražina herself having been a deportee). At the chosen moment we all stood still, enjoying a profound silence, lost in deep thought.

The Baltic Way demonstration stretched out over 600 km, and as we savoured that moment we could sense the millions of linked hands and hearts and feel that their will was now unconquerable against the Soviet onslaught which had drained our hope for so long. It was an additional joy to see many Lithuanians who had returned from abroad to share in the event, among them my brother and his wife, and my sister and her husband, who had come that summer on a visit from Australia. However, there were obviously some who did *not* join us along the Baltic Way, and they included the bewildered local leaders of the Communist party, among them Algirdas Brazauskas, Vladimiras Beriozovas and Justas Paleckis. It is probable that Gorbachev had refused them permission to join hands in this momentous demonstration of the people's will in which three nations joined! They had been allowed to take part in the earlier unveiling ceremony of our Statue of Liberty, but our movement had taken the country to the point where they must have sensed that control was slipping from their grasp. They absented themselves therefore from this peaceful demonstration of human solidarity. However, none of us considered ourselves poorer for their absence. Indeed, on the contrary, had we thought of them we might have conveyed our condolences for their loss, because they were rapidly becoming less important to the nation.

When dusk fell the candles were lit, and their flames illuminated the entire length of the Baltic Way from the flower-strewn steps of the cathedral in Vilnius, through its cobbled streets, and on through the main highways along the long road to Riga, and onward to Tallinn in Estonia. It was further moving testimony to our common resolve, our confidence, and our hope. Perhaps it was no surprise to us to learn that the reaction to this news from Moscow was surly and resentful. They were angry at this huge achievement of the Baltic national movements. The Central Committee of the Communist party of the Soviet Union then stoked up its threats, and went so far as to plan drastic action. Its press and the other media were busy meanwhile with virulent denunciations of us Lithuanians as 'nationalists and extremists', and put it about that our action was leading to a 'nationalist hysteria' against Russians and the other nationalities, and against socialism, and the 'friendship of nations'. We were told that we were leading our nation 'towards an abyss', and that our country would not be able to exist without the Soviet Union. 'You will not survive!', we were told, again and again.

Against the background of our history, and in these circumstances, such words could not be interpreted as being anything other than a murderous threat, but we were already embarked on our journey and following a peaceful course along the Baltic Way to independence.

1. *Gabrielius Landsbergis-Žemkalnis, Landsbergis's grandfather.*

2. *Members of the Varpas movement, 1894. From left, the first and fifth
    are Landsbergis's grandfathers Jonas Jablonskis and Gabrielius
    Landsbergis. On the right is Dr Vincas Kudirka, the author of the
    Lithuanian national anthem.*

3. *In front of the family home in Kaunas, 1934.*

4. *Five generations of the family, February 1990.*

5.   *Vytautas Landsbergis with his wife Gražina, 1960.*

6.   *With his first-born son Vytautas, 1963.*

7. *A protest outside the Ministry of Internal Affairs, 29 September 1988.*

8. *Vytautas Landsbergis with his father, aged ninety-five, at the Founding Congress of Sąjūdis on 22 October 1988.*

9. *The Sąjūdis 'office' at the front door of the Supreme Soviet of the Lithuanian SSR in early 1989; this peaceful demonstration demanded formal recognition of the movement.*

10. *With the architect Algis Nasvytis just before the first Congress of Sąjūdis.*

11. *Hands held from Vilnius to Tallinn: a glimpse of the scene near Vilnius on the Baltic Way, 23 August 1989.*

12. *A closer view of the Baltic Way demonstration. With his wife Gražina and members of the recently re-established Lithuanian Scout Movement.*

13.   *A sword garlanded with roses! A gift presented by the Estonian Popular Front at the second Congress of Sąjūdis, 2 April 1990.*

14. *Addressing the rally at Vingis Park in Vilnius, autumn 1990.*

15. *On the way to the Moscow negotiations: comparing notes with Prime Minister Kazimiera Prunskienė, 2 October 1990.*

16. *The meeting with President Havel of Czechoslovakia in Prague, 30 May 1990.*

17. *Early hours of 13 January 1991: Soviet tanks move against unarmed people.*

18. Waiting for an unknown destiny: an anxious scene inside Parliament in the early hours of 13 January 1991.

19. Crowds surrounding the Lithuanian Supreme Council building on the morning of 13 January 1991.

20. *January 1991: the barricades around the Supreme Council building.*

21. *The Council of the Baltic States meeting, Jurmala, 14 April 1991.*

22. Moscow, 29 July 1991: after signing the treaty with Russia.

23. The funeral of the murdered Medininkai border guards.

24.   *President Bush gives a handshake across the negotiating table, Washington DC, 8 May 1991.*

25.   *Vilnius says goodbye to Lenin, August 1991.*

26. *The United Nations Assembly acknowledges Lithuania's acceptance into membership, 17 September 1991.*

27. *Expressing satisfaction that Lithuania's flag is flying among those of the sovereign nations outside the UN Building, 17 September 1991.*

28. *The Houses of Parliament, London: signing for Lithuania's member-ship of UNESCO on 7 October 1991 (Laima Andrikienė, member of the Lithuanian Seimas, and Eimutis Šova are on the right).*

29. *A meeting with His Holiness the Dalai Lama in the Lithuanian Parliament, 1 October 1991.*

30.   A meeting with His Holiness Pope John Paul II in the Vatican, November 1991.

31.   Reviewing the Lithuanian Volunteer Force: Kaunas, spring 1992.

CHAPTER 13

An independent nation once again!

The character of the Supreme Council of the Lithuanian Soviet Republic changed dramatically when it was joined by the thirty-six Sąjūdis members elected to the Soviet Congress in 1989. Although we had no voting rights, we were entitled to participate in the debates and speak on any matter of our choice. Whereas the handful of representatives who had previously represented our movement had to struggle to gain a hearing, we were now *Soviet* deputies and needed only to raise our hands to be called to speak! Yet it was obvious that the old guard resented our new freedom and were determined to prevent our progress, and it soon became evident that they were voting against Sąjūdis proposals in order to show that they were still the masters. However, the mood of the nation had changed and they knew this, so they softened their attitudes on a number of important questions, especially on the legislation concerning Lithuanian citizenship and the restoration of private farms. In particular they went along with us on the question of re-establishing Lithuanian as the official language of our country.

Despite the caution of those who opposed us, development was rapid, though many long-standing difficulties remained. Most importantly the amendments to the constitution, which had been denied proper discussion on 18 November 1988, were adopted along with the Declaration of Lithuanian Sovereignty by the Supreme Council with improvements in May 1989. The final text of the Declaration referred unequivocally to the secret protocols agreed between Molotov and Ribbentrop and the consequent occupation and annexation of Lithuania, and affirmed our nation's right to full independence. We established a Commission to investigate the pact of 1939 comprehensively, and our local Communist administration co-operated with our proposal but then undermined it by voting to refer the matter to the Supreme Council of the Soviet Union! Eventually it was obvious that they had realized that they had no alternative but to go along with us in the end.

This was a time when many new organizations were coming into being, and some of them reflected the communal aspirations of the Jews, the Poles and the Russians in Lithuania. As our policy was to work for the whole community, we hoped that Sąjūdis would attract them all.

However, there was a division of opinion among the Russians in Lithuania. Some of them had aligned themselves with Sajūdis and its democratic path, despite receiving abuse from conservative and chauvinistic elements in their own community. Others were so much against us and all that we stood for that they were prepared to organize and arm groups of *provocateurs*. Many of the Polish nationalists within our country became active against Sajūdis, and their leaders did not hesitate to allege that our movement was hostile towards them and was planning to expel the Polish community from Lithuania. Nothing could have been more untruthful, and this development was entirely deplorable. Even some intelligent people in their midst participated in a press campaign which systematically maligned our aims and misconstrued our policies. In the face of this campaign it was understandable that our campaign for political openness and reconstruction appeared to be undermined. Many people who should have been our instinctive allies were marginalized by this campaign, and it was late in the day before we realized that we must take a firm initiative if these tensions were to be overcome, so that our smaller communities were not left feeling that 'to be a good Pole was to be against the Lithuanians and their Sajūdis'. However, we needed little prodding to make us recognize fully that these communities also needed to express their own national identities. Their claim for education in their own languages had its proper place in the general national awakening.

The Jewish community seemed to have no problem with Sajūdis, perhaps because most of its members had already recognized that any help they might need was most likely to come from our movement. However, there were complications, because they were divided between those whose origin was Lithuanian, and those who had arrived more recently from Russia. This second group were Russian speakers who often had the same attitude to the Soviet Union as other Russian newcomers. By contrast, the Lithuanian Jews had a natural sympathy for Lithuania, although this was a time when many of them were leaving us to go to Israel. I saw some in tears as they left our country. Their community had seen great tragedies during their lifetimes, and most had lost close relatives, but they were now separating themselves from everything that they had lived through, and from all the failures and opportunities of their native land. Although their culture was their own, we had always seen them as a part of the community of Lithuania, while they too wanted to see Lithuania free and independent. A Sajūdis colleague once told us about a party of Lithuanian Jews which went to Israel to take part in the Maccabean games, and how they had appeared in the stadium carrying the Lithuanian tricolour at a time when it would have been politically prudent for Israel to have presented them as having 'come from the Soviet Union', but they were not prepared to be used in that way and had proudly announced themselves as 'Lithuania's team'.

By now, our goals were clear, and we were firmly on the road to independence. While we had some initial illusions about what was implied by the policy of *perestroika,* these quickly disappeared, though we did find that it provided opportunities which we were able to turn to our own advantage. Our experience was very similar to that of the Estonians, who also set about recreating their own economy, only to realize as we did that the Russians were prepared to allow only limited freedom at best, and would set firm limits on what we might achieve. Although the people of Russia were increasingly aware of the stultifying effects of their centralized command economy, it had encouraged general attitudes which reflected only too closely the economic arteriosclerosis which was its final result. This mentality was so widespread that it deeply affected the new plans for Russian and Soviet development, which had no real drive about them, although they now intended to allow greater independence to state-owned companies, and the authorities were busy nominating special economic zones which were to be outside the jurisdiction of the republics. Our common Estonian, Latvian and Lithuanian responses to this policy involved vigorous opposition, because the special zones would operate purely for Moscow's benefit, while our countries would at best be allowed a few regional variations of economic policy. We had no wish to remain dependent on intermediate structures which could be manipulated from Moscow, and were consistently in favour of re-establishing ourselves as fully independent countries which could control our own economies. Because of this we persisted in our arguments, and eventually the Soviet Union appeared to accept the idea of conceding a limited kind of independent economic base for the Baltic republics. However, at the last minute it clawed back even these few concessions, and the changes turned out to be cosmetic rather than real. We learned from this experience, and understood that Moscow would block our path to political independence because it wanted to ensure that our economic development remained subservient. Its self-interest was unchanged and unchanging. For as long as the political and legal power to concede or not to concede, to give or not to give, to defer or to delay, or to decide just how much to give to our countries lay in the hands of the men who controlled the Kremlin, our efforts would yield nothing. If we remained content with the very limited economic concessions now proposed by the Soviet leaders, the result would be economic and social stagnation. Independence was now the only solution which would permit us to achieve anything solid, and the alternative was some sort of pseudo-autonomy, a mask for continued dependency and exploitation.

As the economic arguments for independence became clearer, it also became increasingly obvious that political independence was the only practical guarantee of our legislative rights. Gradually this realization dawned even on the Lithuanian communist *nomenklatura* and was reflected in their political activity. So, in December 1989 the Lithuanian Communist party decided to separate from the Communist party of the Soviet Union, forcing the obviously reluctant Brazauskas to comply with their decision. When this was announced, Gorbachev is said to have reacted with scorn, though it was not quite clear whether his anger was real or not. Shortly afterwards, in January 1990, he visited Lithuania on the instruction of his Central Committee. We had long been familiar with the Kremlin's rituals, and this visit bore the signs of being an important occasion. As the 'great reformer' was known not to travel empty-handed we waited, wondering whether he would present us with an important decision or disappoint us with a meaningless gesture. During the visit he met ordinary people as well as party intellectuals, and was left in no doubt that the Lithuanians wanted to 'separate' from the Soviet Union, even though he had refused to meet the leaders of Sąjūdis. Naturally, we felt that this did not help him to use his visit to the best advantage, so we did all we could to be hospitable, and invited him to meet us in Cathedral Square. A great crowd gathered there to greet him as 'the leader of a neighbouring country', but he did not turn up. This was of course regrettable, but he seemed to make up for it when he unwrapped his present to Lithuania just before his departure. It was an announcement that a new law was soon to be drafted which would allow the republics to secede from the Soviet Union. It sounded as if a real concession was being made, but we were sceptical and waited to read the small print. When the draft of this 'new law' was published, our caution was justified because it was clear, even from the preamble, that this was yet another communist gimmick. It was passed into Soviet law, as he had promised, by the Congress of the Soviet Union in April 1990, but it had been designed with considerable care to make it impossible for any country, even Russia itself, to secede from the Soviet Union. It was true that there were provisions for secession, but an initial referendum with a majority of two-thirds of all eligible voters in the country was required, and this had to be followed by a second referendum after a transitional period of five years. Even then, it would be necessary for the Soviet Congress to agree before a republic's plea for separation could be finalized. We knew that Lithuania had only fifty votes out of 2,250 eligible to be cast at the Congress, so it was apparent from a first glimpse of the text that this was a law that might have been drafted on Orwell's *Animal Farm*!

This was not the only danger creeping up on us at the time. We knew that Gorbachev was busy preparing a revision of the Soviet constitution in order to create a presidency, and of course to ensure that he would be elected to that office! He was arming himself in other ways too, and soon after his visit to Lithuania his Soviet Peoples' Congress gave him power to declare a 'state of emergency or a curfew in any part of the Soviet Union'. On learning this we perceived it as a provision which had been drafted with the Baltic states in mind. We were clearly running out of time and must act with speed. We needed to ensure that the forthcoming elections would produce a Supreme Council whose membership was capable of taking the radical decisions necessary to uphold Lithuania's legal rights without regard for Soviet assumption of power if the Soviet president should decide to curb a Lithuanian government with which he disagreed.

An election campaign followed which produced no major surprises. There were 472 candidates standing for the 141 vacant places. When the election began, Algirdas Brazauskas was chairman of the Supreme Council of the Lithuanian SSR as well as leader of the local Communist party, to whose will the Supreme Council was effectively subordinated. He had achieved these exalted positions when his party's rough process of internal change had relieved his predecessor Vytautas Astrauskas of the chairman's position in the Supreme Council. When a television journalist asked my opinion on how a president should be elected, I replied: 'It should involve the whole nation', an observation which was very near the bone at the time, because we were acutely aware that the current (unelected) Supreme Council might well attempt to appoint a president and to change the construction before handing over the reins, in order to retain power in the hands of the Communist party. We also feared they might declare some kind of phoney independence before the elections of 24 February 1990, in a pre-emptive strike against Sajūdis which would destroy our negotiating position. This idea was actually discussed by press and television reporters in lobby interviews with members of the Supreme Council in January 1990, when it was suggested that the Soviets might allow Lithuania to call itself an independent state, and even permit us to open some consulates abroad as a sop to our yearnings for independence, while retaining us in some kind of continuing union. We saw this prospect as a real danger because it provided a formula which would have permitted the Soviets to appear to respond to national feeling, but in a way which did not affect the stability of the USSR or its economic relationships with the West. If 'independence' had come this way, it would have been steered by the Communist party, but fortunately things turned out otherwise; our insistence on open debate ensured that other alternatives were explored. Effectively the idea was stopped in its tracks, and we kept reminding the nation of the Molotov–Ribbentrop Pact, and of the illegality of Lithuania's incorporation into the Soviet Union. We knew that the pseudo-Parliament which we had in Lithuania at that time would certainly fudge the issue of statehood if given the chance. In our view it needed to be discussed by a properly elected Parliament which was backed by a real mandate from the people, and at a time when the majority of its members were confident of their ability to use the powers which belong to a legally sovereign state.

The Lithuanian election had an advantage over those in Latvia and Estonia, where Soviet military personnel still had the right to vote and to stand as parliamentary candidates. We had already succeeded in persuading even the old Supreme Council to pass legislation which defined our specifically Lithuanian citizenship and electoral laws. This meant that soldiers of the Soviet army were not regarded as permanent inhabitants of our republic if they came from elsewhere and were therefore not allowed to vote in our elections. Brazauskas and his party had opposed this change in the law and had forecast that it would provoke dangerous retaliation. However, members of the newly founded Democratic party agreed to take advantage of the provisions in law for a referendum by collecting signatures petitioning for one to take place on the question of removing these soldiers from our electoral rolls. The *nomenklatura*, foreseeing the likely result, conceded our demand without a referendum taking place, the matter being agreed by the Supreme Council, probably because Moscow recognized that a massive referendum majority would follow and wanted to avoid the humiliation which that implied. Of course the new legislation did not prevent some of the officers who were 'permanent' inhabitants of Lithuania from voting, as its principle was concerned only with defining Lithuanian citizenship, and the elections were supervised by a new electoral commission, although some unofficial foreign observers were present in the country as the guests of Sąjūdis when voting day came. These visitors were parliamentarians from Austria and Canada who travelled all over Lithuania to see what was taking place. They were not interfered with, but when Moscow realized that we had arranged international observation of our elections, they arranged to stop four American congressmen by having them delayed for three days in Berlin. As a result, this deputation gained entry only on the evening the votes were finally being counted, so the Canadians, who were a larger group, bore the brunt of the task. They have remained firm friends of ours, and it was on their recommendation that the Canadian Parliament adopted a resolution on 12 March which acknowledged the Act for the re-establishment of Lithuanian independence passed by our Supreme Council the previous day, and gave support to what we had done.

The results of this national election were published late at night on 24 February. They showed a landslide for Sajūdis. In the first round it led in 80 of the 141 seats, and out of 90 prospective Sajūdis candidates 72 were finally elected as deputies. We had hoped to start our parliamentary work as soon as possible, but needed to wait until the conclusion of the second round of voting, as 95 deputies were needed to make up the quorum. The second round in the election was for candidates with less than a 50 per cent share of the votes cast in the first round. We applied for these electoral run-offs to be moved to 4, 7 and 8 March, and the results gave us the necessary parliamentary quorum. As a result, 10 March saw the opening day of our new session. This was an achievement of crucial importance, as it meant that our proceedings began two days before the opening of the new session of the Congress of Peoples' Deputies which was about to resume its sittings in Moscow. For us the timing was critical as we were contemplating decisions of fateful importance. We needed some time to sort out procedural matters, so we were forced to leave the all-important business until 11 March. The first issue to be established was the question of whether we had the right to issue a declaration of independence. There was much to discuss on this matter. Some of our people were keen that we should follow the Estonian example. Estonia had two influential organizations with elected members in the Congress of the Soviet Union: the People's Front, which was similar to Sajūdis, but more inclined to compromise, and the Estonian Congress, which was more radical in its politics than we were. This second group had discussed the abnormal constitutional situation existing in the country, and had decided that their existing Supreme Council was not equipped to deal with the question of independence because of its Soviet constitution. As a result they had determined to establish a completely new parliamentary assembly, and to hold a new round of elections to bring this body into existence. It would then be endowed with authority to determine the necessary constitutional questions independently of any entanglement with the Soviet constitution. Some of our members held that we in Lithuania were in the same situation, and advised that we must follow a similar route. They asked whether we, the deputies who had been elected under the Soviet constitution, had the right to act as non-Soviet deputies, and whether it was really possible to transform the Lithuanian Soviet's Supreme Council into something else. They also asked whether the existing Supreme Council could really express our nation's sovereign will in the presence of the occupying regime.

We wrestled with these important questions with an acute awareness that we were working against the clock, as the Soviet Congress might well be asked, within a matter of hours of its business beginning, to pre-empt our decisions. It was necessary that we should establish our right to manœuvre before that body claimed the right to overrule our actions. I therefore proposed that we should accept a document which had been drafted by Sajūdis proposing that the Supreme Council should be formally reconstituted *before* it proceeded to debate the re-establishment of national independence. This document described the duties and competence of deputies, and declared that the independence movement was 'committed to returning sovereign rights to the Lithuanian nation by due process, using the *existing institutions*, despite the fact that they had been imposed by a foreign power'. It declared clearly that elected deputies were part of this process, and that they had received the people's mandate in free elections. This empowered them to express the sovereign right of the nation, and to re-establish the independence of our Lithuanian state by this authority. Once agreement was achieved we were free to proceed with our most pressing business, and at six o'clock in the evening of 11 March, Parliament formally abandoned the term 'Lithuanian Soviet Socialist Republic' and declared itself the 'Supreme Council of Lithuania'. Only a few minutes afterwards we passed the Act for the Name and the Emblems of the State, which declared our assembly to be the 'Supreme Council of the Republic of Lithuania'. Our Parliament was now ready and able to decide for independence by passing the Act for the Re-establishment of National Independence.

These were profound changes, but they implied that it was now essential for Lithuania to have a new constitution. The Soviet model was unsuitable for our purposes. We had, however, already drafted a document which emphasized Lithuanian sovereignty within the framework of the existing constitution. This had been discussed in the time between the first round of the election and this first session of the new Council. While there were some among us who wanted to work on a new constitution immediately, it was my view that this was not feasible, and that it was best to adapt the existing constitution to the present situation by purging all mention of the Soviet Union, and to leave fuller concentration on a new constitution to a more favourable time. Sajūdis had put a lot of work into exploring this solution through an earlier Commission of the Supreme Council, and there was a working document ready. It would have taken far too long to discuss even this constitutional solution paragraph by paragraph, and I therefore proposed that we should adopt it through a shortened procedure immediately after our Independence Act had been approved, leaving consideration of changes until fuller discussion was possible. This is what my colleagues then agreed, and though it was difficult to follow the plan through exactly as intended, we did eventually find time to make selective changes whenever this was absolutely necessary. The process of resolving constitutional issues is normally a protracted one, but on 11 March we postponed even the discussion of what might have been considered essential constitutional procedures because of the urgent need to act immediately. We moved forward with great care, but perforce we moved swiftly. With great deliberation, therefore, we removed the Soviet constitution and reinstalled the 1938 Lithuanian constitution in its place (to emphasize the fact that it had never legally been superseded until now). Once this was done, we immediately suspended that constitution, in order to adopt what we termed the Temporary Basic Law as a provisional constitution to deal with immediate issues. The proceeding was complex, but was put through as a matter of urgency, and if the result was not elegant, it served our immediate purposes.

Neither the Latvians nor the Estonians followed our example of attempting to reform the existing constitution. However, we were concerned to do the most we could to resolve an ambiguous situation during the foreseeable future in which some elements of the Soviet constitution continued to have at least partial validity in our country. We were all attempting to find routes to the same goal, but the Estonians explained that they could not proclaim their country to be independent while it was still occupied. They argued that they were going through a transitional phase towards independence. I used to ask them: 'If you are in a transitional state, then when and where are you going? If you are in a transitional state from being a Soviet republic, does that mean that you are still a Soviet republic or not?' Our stance was consistently different from theirs: we maintained that the Soviet Union had occupied Lithuania and annexed it by force, and that it had never legally been a Soviet republic. We were now re-establishing the suspended independent Lithuanian state, and this was why we had formally reinstated the Lithuanian constitution of 1938. Our subsequent substitution of a more contemporary (but deliberately temporary) constitution was a device to defend ourselves from the Soviet Union, while maintaining our momentum. It meant that we had our own constitution, which was that of an independent state, and that in virtue of this fact the Soviet Union had no constitutional jurisdiction in Lithuania. The process was far from perfect, but it provided us with a political weapon by establishing the legal ground on which an independent state could be built. In Estonia and Latvia the situations were more complicated, as there Soviet military representatives were present among their deputies, and their populations included a much larger number of Russian nationals than did ours. As a result, their legal and political moves were often compromises, half-measures of a kind which could be legally dangerous. Our circumstances were different, but our road was rougher. However, it was a more direct and obvious route. Two months after we Lithuanians had taken these decisive steps we joined with the two other countries to form a council of the three Baltic states, to co-ordinate our rules and regulations, though politically we continued to act as three independent states. Despite this preparedness to work with Lithuania, my colleagues from Estonia and Latvia were still willing to travel to Moscow whenever Gorbachev invited them. Unlike them, I always refused such invitations, because Lithuania had passed her Acts of Independence and was now a different country.

Before business began on 10 and 11 March, we discussed how we would elect the chair, vice-chairs and secretary to the Supreme Council, officers who would be responsible for the conduct and recording of the meetings, and for procedures to ensure that items for debate were properly presented and that motions were voted on. As Sąjūdis deputies we had to agree beforehand whom we would propose for the chair, and for whom we would vote, as there was a very good chance of our being obstructed by the Communist party, which was almost certain to try to capitalize on Algirdas Brazauskas's personality and experience. In the event they exerted pressure by collecting signatures on a document which suggested that he was the only man up to the job, and that the whole of Lithuania expected him to become the chairman of the Supreme Council. He was, they said, the 'nation's choice'. The situation threatened a split which we could ill afford, so we carefully discussed how we could respond to his candidature and the role he might play in future. We then formed a Sąjūdis Deputies' Club, on the lines of the arrangements we had made in Moscow, to ensure that we could work as an organized faction. It was a good project, but unfortunately it was only partly successful. Though we all carried the Sąjūdis ticket, we differed among ourselves as our ranks included Greens, Social Democrats, Christian Democrats, Democrats, even Communist party members, and others who were non-aligned. This extraordinary variety prevented us from achieving a consensus on the proposal that voting together in the Supreme Council should be a condition of the club's membership. A significant number of members insisted that they could vote only according to conscience, and the eventual outcome of this undisciplined individualism was that the Sąjūdis majority in the new Parliament was cut progressively, as this freedom led to the development of an internal opposition, which sometimes prevented us from having an overall majority. The issue of collective discipline was of course a difficult one in a fledgeling democracy.

The Sąjūdis deputies nominated me for the chair of the Supreme

Council. We had a majority there, and everyone was aware that Brazauskas would also be a candidate, but it was obvious that progress would be impaired if he was elected, as the authority of a chair can influence a meeting and he was known not to be keen on true independence. Even though the Communist party had incorporated national independence in its manifesto, he saw its coming as a gradual process which must be agreed by Moscow in advance so that existing relationships with Gorbachev would not be disturbed. This knowledge led to a call for the chair to be chosen from the ranks of Sąjūdis. Weak interpretation of national independence was the last thing we wanted, because there was real anxiety that some kind of dictatorial action might be taken against us sooner or later. This was not an unrealistic worry. We knew the crude working methods of a system which could always call in the military and the KGB to help it out. It had already interfered brutally in other republics where developments had taken place which were disliked by the Kremlin. Moscow had recently appointed a direct representative with absolute powers to rule Armenia, and an official with similar powers might well be introduced in Lithuania. This kind of take-over was implicit in the way the Soviet state was run, so we knew that this was a real threat. It was also an immediate one, and the legislation on independence and the constitution which we rushed through the Supreme Council was in anticipation of the fact that Gorbachev would acquire additional powers on 12 March. The 11th was therefore the optimal date for the proclamation of our Lithuanian independence.

All these questions were in our minds when the Sąjūdis deputies met in the Deputies' Club before the new session began, to prepare for the election of a chair for the Supreme Council. The wider political context provided important strategic considerations, and I pointed these out. I then proposed that it was essential that only one candidate should stand against Brazauskas – not necessarily myself – but when the assembled deputies had considered their options the principle was agreed, and I was duly nominated. Later, in the Supreme Council proceedings, the communists proposed Brazauskas as expected. Ozolas's name was also put forward, but he declined in my favour with a speech in which he said that the voting must be conclusive in the first round. Despite our previous agreement in the club, someone then nominated Motieka, but he also declined and invited those who might have voted for him to support me. Two candidates remained: Brazauskas and Landsbergis.

The real contest now followed and both of us had to present our programmes to the Supreme Council and then answer questions. As alphabetical order was observed, Brazauskas spoke first. He answered all the questions, but evaded some issues. While he was speaking, I prepared myself, and was afterwards told that my answers had made the better impression. As a result, a number of communists changed their minds, and the final tally was thirty-eight for Brazauskas and ninety-one for me. Some members of the former government showed obvious disappointment with this result. I had known for some time that my election was virtually a foregone conclusion, but they had not expected the communists in Sąjūdis to vote against their party leader in the secret ballot. Of course I was glad they voted for me, and once the declaration of the result was over, I took the chair from Professor Juozas Bulavas, who had conducted the election as chairman of the Electoral Commission, and thanked the assembled deputies. Business now began in earnest as my chairmanship of the Supreme Council entitled me to appoint its three deputy chairmen. I immediately offered the position of first deputy to Brazauskas in order to diminish the pressure of the opposition. He declined the position courteously and proposed Bronius Genzelis in his place, but I would not accept this and pointed out that the chairman alone had the prerogative of nominating his deputies. Though Genzelis was a member of Sąjūdis, he was also a member of the Central Committee of the Communist party, and I knew that he was not always the easiest person to get along with. This made him unsuitable for the collective task which we faced, and would have impeded the activities of the Presidium. Brazauskas's tactic in proposing him was clever: however I reacted, it would do me harm, and my refusal to choose Genzelis gained me an immediate enemy. In the event I chose three men on whom I could rely and whose skills were complementary. Bronius Kuzmickas, an erudite philosopher, steady in character, quiet, honest and conscientious, was still a Communist party member, but I was certain that he would not cheat or lie – I learned later that he was already contemplating the best way of leaving the party, which he soon did. Kazimieras Motieka was chosen for his legal mind and determined stance, and I thought I would be able to rely on his support. Česlovas Stankevičius, an engineer by profession, was to be my third deputy. He was a wise person and a good statesman, who already had experience of drafting government papers, and was meticulous in his every action. Such a man would never let a politically incorrect or weak point pass by when legislation was being drafted.

Once I had made up my mind, the Supreme Council confirmed these three men as my deputies. I then proposed Liudvikas Sabutis, our former public procurator, for the post of secretary of the Presidium. He had been dismissed from his earlier post on Moscow's instigation for having defended the demonstrators who were beaten up after the hunger strike in Cathedral Square, and for allowing Sąjūdis to form a group among his office staff. Romualdas Ozolas wanted a high position in the Supreme Council, but his threat to change sides if he did not get it ended his chances. Algirdas Brazauskas's similar attempt to angle for the prime minister's position was also objectionable to my mind, but I had to acknowledge these men in some way, so we made them vice-premiers. Once these appointments had been made we proceeded to the first legislative session, in which we defined the responsibilities of deputies, and then renamed the Supreme Council by removing the words 'Soviet Socialist' from the name of the state, thereby restoring the name of the Republic of Lithuania to what it had been before the Second World War. We also reinstated the *Vytis* as our state emblem (a white knight on his charger with a raised sword in his hand, which is set against a deep red field). As we proceeded with the discussion of these profoundly signifi-cant changes, I was not alone in being increasingly aware that a large Soviet emblem with its hammer and sickle, red star, oak leaves, wheat sheaves and its intrusive motto 'Proletarians of the word, unite', contin-ued to hang above our heads, dominating the Supreme Council chamber while these things were going on. It was obviously impossible to disman-tle this now superfluous anomaly without disturbing the proceedings, but I devised a neat solution which was implemented during the debate. A wide screen, painted in the yellow, green and red colours of our national flag was prepared by workmen who then raised it slowly until the provocative emblem finally disappeared – to the sound of a spontaneous outburst of applause!

Once these preliminary tasks had been completed, we fully legitimized our work by adopting the Act of the Supreme Council of the Republic of Lithuania for the Re-establishment of the Independent State of Lithuania. Its text began with the following very important words:

> The Supreme Council of the Republic of Lithuania, expressing the will of the nation, decrees and solemnly proclaims that the authority of the sovereign power of the Lithuanian State, heretofore constrained by alien forces in 1940, is restored, and henceforth Lithuania is once again an independent state.

A little later on that proud evening of 11 March, as the chairman of the Supreme Council, I had the enormous pleasure of announcing the result of the vote. Of the 130 deputies present on this historic occasion, 124 had voted for the Act and 6 had abstained. There were none against. The Act was passed! I congratulated the Supreme Council, and exclaimed: 'Lithuania, I salute you!' We stood to sing the national anthem, hardly restraining our tears of joy. Rapturous applause followed, and I addressed the Chamber: 'Honourable deputies, Lithuania is *free*: she is free in spirit and in law. We can also shout out aloud, that Latvia will also be free!' The deputies immediately echoed my words, repeating them again and again in a loud chant. 'We can say that Estonia will be free' (again my words were loudly repeated) 'and that all countries which are still not free shall become free!' Again loud cheers followed. When they had died away I announced: 'And now we shall continue with our work!' We had fully savoured the significance of our historic step and now lived in the hope that, because we were not alone, we would be more secure.

The six deputies who had abstained were all Polish, and all faithful members of the continuing Soviet Communist party. Later, they explained their voting behaviour: the declaration had come as a total surprise to them, they had had no chance to consult their electors, and had not known which way to vote. I responded that they were not to be condemned, but rather congratulated: after all they could easily have voted *against* the Act. However, when the full story was told we learned that three Polish deputies had actually voted with us. They had discussed their decision with their colleagues beforehand and had persuaded at least six of the others not to vote against it! These details were, however, lost in the euphoria of that crucial evening. We went on to adopt the provisional constitution to give our new 'Lithuanian dawn' a secure legal basis, and then worked on through the night. When I was finally able to return home, morning was breaking. As we stepped outside Parliament people greeted us with flowers and wished us good luck. The crowds were small, but we held back from inviting masses of people to share our joy because we needed to avoid advertising our achievement to the whole world lest Moscow should get wind of what we were doing too soon, and take retaliatory action before we were fully established. There was a crowd outside Parliament, but the population of Vilnius had not yet come out into the streets. It was noticeable that there was still uncertainty in the air. Gorbachev's behaviour seemed to be threatening, and other people were unhappy when they learned that Brazauskas had not been elected chairman of the Supreme Council. However, as I reflected on the situation, I felt that things were much as they should be. We had been given the people's support when it was needed, and we had done the best we could, the best possible at the time. We did not need to parade through town and country when what we had done was simply consonant with what our whole people was also striving for, especially when our immediate future was still uncertain. So in our moment of triumph we were reticent. We noticed, however, that Brazauskas held aloof from the rest of us and interpreted events differently. He talked to a *New York Times* correspondent on 12 March, just before his regular trip to make his dutiful report to Moscow, and said at length that Lithuania was not overjoyed by its Supreme Council's 'irrational decision'! He then admitted to voting for it, but explained that he had done so against his better judgement, and because of moral pressure!

We were unaware at that stage that a KGB special agent was also on his way to Moscow on the 12th, to report on a plan for the armed forces to remove Lithuania's 'independence seekers'. It had been prepared by General Zhitnikov, the commanding officer of the Soviet division garrisoned in Vilnius, in co-operation with Vytautas Sakalauskas, a former prime minister of the Lithuanian Soviet Republic, and two other persons, and included clauses allowing the release of 6,000 criminal prisoners, who would no doubt have been expected to pay for their freedom by joining in the mayhem which was being contemplated. It only needed permission from Moscow to put this plan into operation. With hindsight, we realize that Moscow refused its sanction only because it knew that Washington would not have remained silent. We had no idea what was afoot and passed the day profitably by abolishing conscription to the Soviet armed forces within Lithuanian territory. This Act followed naturally from our assertion of sovereignty, and was as important to parents everywhere in our country as it was irritating to the Soviet regime. We also sent a letter to His Excellency Mr Gorbachev to tell him that we had proclaimed the renewed independence of our country, and to express our hope of developing friendly international relations with the Soviet Union on the basis of bilateral talks. The letter also asked him to show concern for those young Lithuanians who were already enlisted in the Soviet forces, and to ensure that no reprisals would be taken against them.

These circumstances made it necessary to waste no time in forming a government. As it was my prerogative to name the prime minister, I had forewarned Sąjūdis deputies that my choice would be Kazimiera Prunskienė, an economist with great energy and the will to lead. She had already been a deputy prime minister of the Lithuanian Soviet Socialist Republic, and had support from influential Sąjūdis members and our Deputies' Club. She seemed therefore to be the most suitable of the possible candidates. While we did not really want a member of the Communist party in the post, there was no one else with so much experience of government, and anyway she resigned from the party after I had talked with her. Romualdas Ozolas was still a communist and a member of their Central Committee at this juncture. In any case to have a woman in such a post seemed to underline Lithuania's European credentials and to distance us from the Soviet embrace. While I could see little difference in practice between those who had resigned from the party earlier and those who were doing so now, I felt it was essential to reassure the

West that we were conducting a peaceful transition to democracy, not rehabilitating a communist regime. However, I was faced with a real situation in which it was very difficult to find people with suitable experience who had not been in some way tarred with the communist brush. When it proved virtually impossible to find someone competent to fill the crucial position of minister of finance, I decided there was no option but to call in the previous minister, and he did his job well.

It was not easy to form an administration in the circumstances which we faced, lacking as we did any reserves of experience in government, and I had many problems in finding a minister for social security, and other positions. Few Sąjūdis members were suitable or willing to enter the government, and the press was unfavourable to us. It grumbled disapproval at most of my new appointments, especially those of younger people. It was a real shortcoming in our movement that we had not prepared lists of suitable candidates beforehand, but in reality we had little time to prepare ourselves for office, and while some conversations had taken place, few of them had gone much beyond the debate about who should be prime minister. Forming the Cabinet therefore caused me difficulties, especially as our national situation made speedy decisions necessary. With the wisdom of hindsight, I now understand why established democratic states often make the formation of a new government an extended process, but our situation was fragile, indeed dangerous, and I felt acutely apprehensive when days and weeks passed by and we were still without a full government team. Part of the problem lay in my belief that the international recognition of Lithuania would be advanced by multiple contacts with other states, and that it was therefore essential for us to resolve all these issues as soon as could conveniently be arranged. Kazimiera Prunskienė was helpful to me in this work and, as prime minister, was equally active in looking for suitable ministers. We often discussed the candidates together, sharing problems. One of these was the appointment of a minister of internal affairs. The previous incumbent had hated Sąjūdis actively, and was hostile to everything we stood for. After deliberation we appointed Marijonas Misiukonis, who had been his vice-minister. He had not only been a member of the Communist party but had worked for the KGB. We, however, saw him as an undogmatic figure by comparison with other militia officers, and he impressed us as an honest manager. I also recalled how he had phoned me after our rally in Vingis Park on the night of 23 August 1988 with the invitation to go to Cathedral Square urgently to help resolve the difficult situation there, and how he had later withdrawn the militia units of the Ministry of Interior on 28 September in order to avoid a bloody confrontation. We saw gestures such as these as indications of a willingness to co-operate, and he now said he was with us on the issue of independence, and believed that there was no way back into the party for him. Others were not convinced about Misiukonis's candidature, but I agreed with Prunskienė's urgings and felt it was a wise decision. He quickly identified with us and prevented a dangerous split between a faction of the militia loyal to Lithuania, and another which wanted to remain subordinate to Moscow. We were in a genuinely difficult situation and there were relatively few people of experience whom one could honestly rely upon so I had to take some risks. However, what I did not realize was that the prime minister herself had also been a KGB agent.

The question why I did not make a clean sweep of the government by giving office only to people whom we could trust implicitly has often been raised. My answer to this has always been that there were very few such people. Sajūdis was a mass movement, not a party. Its membership was completely open and we had no enrolment selection or scrutiny of applicants, and no one checked anyone's past. We were working together, and shared the same experiences, and our trust in one another developed from this. There were some who trusted no one, and there were certainly a few who purposefully set about spreading mistrust about me. There were also those who theorized about democracy in abstract terms, without regard to our real situation. At times one wondered whether the more outspoken people really lived on the same planet as the rest of us; whether deliberately or otherwise, they certainly created difficulties. We were repeatedly told that the presence of Prunskienė and Ozolas, both elected deputies, in the Council of Ministers 'violated democracy', because of the confluence of legislative and executive responsibilities. We were also reproved because we had kept on a large number of people who had held office under the previous government. Essentially, we had to compromise. We called the resulting situation 'a coalition' while I tried to persuade a number of sensible and honest friends and acquaintances to co-operate and to accept ministerial posts. Most of them declined. I even offered a diplomatic position to Arvydas Juozaitis, regardless of the fact that he had written an article attacking me, but he refused and remained in opposition. As a result, the government included ministers from past administrations as well as new names. Even though the resulting mix was criticized, I am ready to defend it. Indeed I would say that even if the Council of Ministers had been made up of Sajūdis members, things would probably not have worked out very differently, because many of the civil servants remained in post. However, the elevation of Algirdas Brazauskas to the position of vice-prime minister, which I had arranged for the sake of peace and consolidation, turned out to be rather riskier than I had expected.

One problem which we faced with Communist party members in key governmental positions was that they continued to be organized, influenced and directed by their leaders. There was a danger of their becoming a law unto themselves because the whole party machinery was still in position from top to bottom. The party included elected deputies and parliamentary and local government officials to whom the structures and workings of both the Supreme Council and the Council of Ministers were an open book. They were of course its managing directors, and precisely the same situation prevailed in Poland, Czechoslovakia, Bulgaria and all the countries of the old communist empire. Wherever the civil servants remained in their posts, they carried on with their work, giving no obvious indications of whether they were working for or against our policies. If suspicions arose, they would declare their commitment to work for the state, since they wished to keep their jobs. While some shared in the spirit of national rebirth and sincerely believed in the future of Lithuania, others wished to avoid the new responsibilities involved. We often found them forgetting what was now expected of them, or muddling things up. Sometimes this must have been deliberate, sometimes it clearly was not, but if challenged they would laugh the matter off. Some of them clearly hoped that the interruption of routine which had come about as a result of our success in the elections would only be temporary. If they were patient, perhaps everything would fall back into its former place! This entrenched spirit of opposition was to continue to bedevil our efforts, undermining our efforts at reconstruction and weakening the people's trust in us.

I knew all this was going on, but it would scarcely have been appropriate for me to turn up at one ministry after another to clear out unsuitable civil servants. However, the new minister for culture and education, who was a young man, began to sack some of his department's employees and reshuffle others. Hostile articles appeared in the newspapers expressing incomprehension and a sense of injustice, or saying in effect: 'Look how unrelenting independent Lithuania is becoming. Just what have we been fighting for?' We then found ourselves being described as dictators and even Bolsheviks! Yesterday's men made good use of the weapons of demagoguery which were available to them, but the whole incident showed that we could not set about sacking all the civil servants working for the Supreme Council. If we had done that, we would of course have had to take them all back again because there was little alternative talent and experience available. It would have demanded immense radical conviction to make such people redundant. Many of them were old and near retirement, and could claim to have faithfully performed their duties throughout their working lives. It is not that simple to sack people, and despite our frustrations, we knew it. We were not courageous managers in that sense, though there were plenty of radicals who accused us, and still do, of having been too tolerant.

Another problem loomed in the municipal councils. Only a month after the elections to the Supreme Council, the Sajūdis elections section warned us that we were going to lose the forthcoming local government elections, and proposed that we should postpone them to avoid defeat. This did not seem feasible to me. There was evidence that the municipal system was in a bad state, and that many officials had embezzled public property. However, we were fully occupied with other issues, and the proposed solution did not appeal to me. It seemed evident that in making this suggestion my colleagues had not yet broken out of the Soviet mentality which seemed to have a somewhat low regard for local government. Though they clearly did not appreciate the implications of delaying the elections, I did not agree to the proposal, and the election went forward. As expected, we lost every regional municipality but one, and in consequence there was opposing political control of the two tiers of government. This soon made its effect felt when we found our efforts at commercial privatization and land reform frustrated.

To round off the achievements of 11 March, we had prepared and sent an address to the Supreme Council of the Soviet Union, and to the nations of the world. This needed no reply, but several came, notably from the Canadian Parliament, which had immediately adopted a resolution in support of our Act of Independence. Similar positive responses also arrived from Poland and the Scandinavian parliaments. Many government departments, organizations and political parties also responded from around the world. Shortly afterwards we decided to write to the various states directly. The Australian foreign minister, Gareth Evans, replied in words which seemed to give full recognition to our stand. We publicized this fact, but then learned that his administration had called a press conference and issued a statement to the effect that we had misinterpreted this matter. His statement of goodwill had been more personal than official. While we were entering a new era with the broad goodwill of people in many countries, we had no actual promises of governmental support from abroad. In the United States of America, the good offices of Stasys Lozoraitis, the ambassador of pre-war Lithuania (who was still officially recognized there), had kept awareness of our cause in the public eye. Yet, despite the fact that Lithuania's independence continued to be recognized there, and despite his position as a link with the American government, we had much less support than we expected. While our address announcing national independence was received favourably by the White House, President Bush remained more cautious than we could have hoped. At a time when he might have influenced events considerably by a few words on his hot line to the Kremlin, he seemed to say little. The line must certainly have been used, and of course we do not know what was said. But we did notice that, after his discussions with the Kremlin, he spoke evasively whenever the question of Lithuania came up.

We Lithuanians always have had, and always will have, a cautious attitude towards the policies of the West. Our history has often taught us bitter lessons, and we have learned not to expect concessions from fate, because we have frequently known the experience of being left alone, or forgotten, or sold down the river. That was what Roosevelt did to the Baltic nations at Yalta. We knew from the minutes of his conversations with Stalin that Roosevelt had told the dictator that he had internal difficulties with the many immigrant voters who would take part in the elections he was facing. They were lobbying at the time, demanding that he should defend the nations which were then being threatened by the Soviet Union. Stalin had said: 'Explain to your voters that these nations will get the right to self-determination and will be able to elect their own governments, whatever their choice. Tell them to calm down.' It had ended there, and the bargain was simple and elegant: Roosevelt had something to tell his voters in the short run, and the oppressed nations remained under Stalin's rule for the foreseeable future.

The awful truth is that the fate of the suppressed nations was of no interest to Roosevelt. Yet in later years, armed resistance in Lithuania was kept going for ten years on American promises. Such false hopes were fostered, if not directly from the White House, then certainly by the American secret services and radio broadcasts. Our freedom fighters were encouraged to fight on, and they did not capitulate because of the hope they were given. They struggled bravely, even through the years when all hope had disappeared, to the bitter end. *Vienui vieni* (Absolutely alone) was the title of the moving tribute to these Lithuanian resistance fighters which was later published by émigrés in the West to record their heroism. The title is poignantly appropriate to what they endured, so bravely and for so long. It often comes to my mind.

When we were at last able to redress the balance of our history, the attitudes struck towards us by many countries remained ambivalent. Denmark, Norway and France made friendly noises but gave no written response to our appeals when we turned to the western world for help.

Statements were made, by their foreign ministers to their parliaments and by officials in other places, acknowledging that they had recognized Lithuania in 1920 or 1923, and had not withdrawn that recognition by recognizing the Soviet annexation. Against that background, such response was very strange. Though the Republic of Lithuania was recognized, the responsibility seemed to end there, almost as if there were no need to do any more. As time went on, it became apparent that the problem was not one of recognizing a state, but of recognizing our government by renewing formal diplomatic relations. It was particularly unfortunate that Sweden had recognized Soviet annexation *de facto* many years before, as had distant New Zealand. Sweden had at least tried to explain to us, even before 11 March, that they could only co-operate, or give us practical help, through the Soviet Union. The Swedes believed that practical assistance was more important than political recognition. While many of the democratic western countries were favourable to our claim of independence, our requests for proper recognition of our government met with ambivalence and prevarication, or the declaration that our problem was complex and was a matter to be resolved with the Soviet Union. As a result, our occupiers continued to dictate the rules. As there was so little foreign response, it was clear that any change which might come about could be achieved only as a result of our own initiatives. Eventually, however, the western proposal (issued by Mitterrand and Kohl) that there must be negotiations between us and the Soviets actually helped us. The Soviets had, at first, no intention whatever of entering such negotiations. Indeed at one point an irate Mikhail Gorbachev announced that there would be 'no negotiations with Lithuania'. This slip of the tongue eventually proved embarrassing to him, and of some benefit to us, because it revealed a fundamental intransigence, which worked to our advantage in the long run.

Moscow was naturally furious beyond measure at our Declaration of Independence. Brazauskas had been told this in the autumn of 1989 by Gorbachev, who had already decided to teach us a lesson in 'the political realities'. We were to be faced, 'should Lithuania wish to separate', with a series of financial and territorial demands which were so extensive that there would have been virtually nothing left of our country if they had been met. His clear objective was to ensure that the act of leaving the Soviet Union would become impossible because it was dependent on unrealizable procedures. Had Brazauskas been in control of our government, Gorbachev would probably have brought him into line easily enough, as the position he took was ambivalent, but Gorbachev's approach was such that it never for a moment led me to think of changing my view. I can still hear him raising his voice to me and shouting:

'Nobody will recognize you, *everybody* is laughing at you!' The only effect his arrogance had was to bring home to me the fact that we needed to phrase things differently. We quickly found a new formula and announced that the real issue was 'not so much our leaving the Soviet Union as persuading the Soviet Union to *leave us*'. The idea had actually come from an old farmer, who had visited me at the Supreme Council in the spring of 1990. Before he left my office he had paused and said: 'Why do they make all this fuss about *us*, it is *they* who must leave *our* country!'

Having dispatched our address, and all the appropriate documents to Gorbachev on 12 March 1990, to put him fully in the picture, we also sent a letter to Nikolai Ryzhkov, the prime minister of the Soviet Union. At this stage, Gorbachev was still chairman of the Supreme Council of the Soviet Union, not the president, as he became a little later. The third session of the Soviet Congress was still meeting in Moscow, and a few Lithuanian deputies were attending it. They were there, however, not as deputies of the Soviet Union, but as a delegation from the Republic of Lithuania. They read our dispatches to Gorbachev publicly at the Congress, and uproar began when it was noticed that our address began with the words 'To His Excellency'. This is the diplomatic convention used in communication with the head of a foreign state, but my adoption of this tiny formality created a small shock-wave in the proceedings. The Congress later went on to elect Gorbachev president of the Soviet Union, and we responded to the news by sending him a note of congratulation. Our courtesy was not reciprocated, and on 15 March we received a very different communication from the Congress, amounting to a curt demand that we should rescind our Act of Independence, which it described as 'invalid from now'. The message also included a fresh declaration of Soviet sovereignty over Lithuania. Our reply was laconic. It read: 'The resolutions of the third Deputies' Congress of the Soviet Union have no legal validity in Lithuania.'

On 14 March the chief of the Soviet forces in Lithuania met us for the first time. At subsequent meetings he was joined by three other senior officers, one of whom was the chief commander of the paratroop forces located in Lithuania. Their faces showed anger from the moment of their arrival, and they backed up meetings with military manœuvres, which included movements of tanks and other armoured vehicles, and a visit to Lithuania by General Varenikov, with whom I had a telephone conversation. It was our policy not to invite Soviet officers to my office, but they came there unbidden. Their line of conversation was always the same. They adopted an authoritarian and threatening tone, and punctuated the discussion with dogmatic phrases. The message was clear: according to the Soviet constitution they were charged with protecting the indivisibility of the Soviet territory, and were responsible for conscription to the armed forces. They would carry out the orders of their president to the letter. I played my part by explaining carefully, over and over again, that their president's orders had no more legal force here in Lithuania than for instance in Finland or Poland, and the same applied on the matter of conscription, where they had no right whatsoever to conscript the young men of another nation into their own forces. Clearly I recognized that they had the power to crush us at any time, but that would be to continue Stalin's aggression, and we were convinced that the present government of the Soviet Union would neither wish nor dare to adopt Stalin's methods. In the end this was a political problem which must be resolved politically, as Gorbachev himself had already said. For our part, we would do everything to reduce the tension between Lithuania and the Soviet garrisons which these officers represented, but we would ask them to exercise caution, and avoid all provocation to conflict, because such an outcome would not be beneficial to the Soviet Union and its policies, or to us. All these sessions with the military began with cold, strained formality, but ended in a normal businesslike atmosphere. However, the discussions with Moscow never came to a real conclusion, since so far as Moscow was concerned, this was a confrontation which was destined to continue and which would have tragic consequences. I came to refer to it as a 'creeping occupation'.

When the Soviet Union occupied Lithuania in 1940, they began to change the street names in our towns. I can recall how our family friends had gathered at my parents' house, and how conversation turned to the Laisvės Alėja (Liberty Avenue) in Kaunas. Its name was being changed to include Stalin's name. When I heard this I had interrupted the adults with the question: 'Will they call it "Nelaisvės Alėja" now?' (This was a play on the word *nelaisvės* which means 'slavery' or 'imprisonment'.) The adults, it seemed to me as an eight-year-old, were much impressed by my precocity! Our road to freedom was long blocked, but now Lithuania has its *Laisvės Alėja* again, which is not just a local Freedom Avenue but one which became a road of liberation for the whole country in 1990. Though the path which we trod over the years was full of treacherous pitfalls, though it took much effort, many tears and much blood and sacrifice to follow it to the end, in the end it was our 'road to freedom'. We insisted on taking that road.

CHAPTER 14

The storms of March and the struggle for control

A war of nerves began immediately after 11 March. It was first mani-
fested in unusual movements of the Soviet army. A propaganda
campaign then began, spearheaded by a newspaper which, despite drastic
paper shortages, never seemed to run short of newsprint, and supported
by the Russian-language radio station. Both sources were unrelenting in
their campaign to spread the view that only Soviet law was valid in
Lithuania. At the same time Gorbachev's ultimatum hung over us,
although we made it plain that we had no intention of complying with his
blackmail when we issued a statement on 23 March blaming the Soviet
authorities for increased tension in the Lithuanian Republic. They had
sent additional troops into the country and were using their military
resources to threaten us. Armoured cars were regularly paraded through
our streets, their machine-guns and cannon ready for action. Soldiers
were breaking the law – there were many reports of abductions and
looting. Sports clubs and places with similar shooting or hunting connections were raided all over the country and their guns and other
equipment were seized. A particularly brutal episode took place on 27
March when hospitals were attacked. All this went on without the military commanders even attempting to communicate with the local
authorities. All we could do was to instruct our prosecutor-general's
office to treat all such episodes as 'criminal activity', and we also
announced that what was happening could only be construed as Soviet
aggression against Lithuania, a policy which had been continuous since
1944, or indeed since 1940.

Naturally we feared that all this activity might end in some kind of
coup d'état, and our fears were intensified when we learned, on the
evening of 23 March, that army units had been issued with live ammunition and tanks were being moved from Kaunas to Vilnius. Shortly
afterwards we received a further report that around a hundred armoured
troop carriers filled with soldiers were on the move. We knew it would
take them around two hours to arrive at the outskirts of Vilnius, where
their aim would become apparent depending on whether they turned
towards the barracks or took a route which led directly to the heart of

the city. The movement of the column was watched intently as that choice of direction would tell us if we were to expect an attack on the Supreme Council. As we waited for this news, the Council continued its debate, everyone there being conscious that our period of government might soon be brought to an untimely and perhaps tragic end. In this surreal atmosphere members busily discussed my proposal that Stasys Lozoraitis, who had originally been appointed independent Lithuania's ambassador to the United States and to the Holy See, should be officially reappointed as our representative in Washington. It was imperative that this man of strong character, long experience and endless dedication should be given renewed authority to speak on behalf of our country in the event of renewed repression.

The prospect of attack naturally made us concerned for the safety of our deputies, but we judged it more logical to remain in session than to disperse. We had been elected to the Supreme Council to defend the rights of our nation as stated in our Act of Independence. There was little doubt in our minds that we would have to carry out our duty in the place to which we had been elected, so we stayed to face whatever fate might be ordered by the commander of the Soviet forces. We knew that they were drawing nearer by the minute and that it was probable that they would try to occupy the place in order to prevent us from continuing our work. We expected to be dispersed, perhaps arrested, perhaps even shot. Whichever way we looked at the situation we knew that we would soon be put to the ultimate test, and we determined quietly that if our enemies did decide on coercion, we would respond to them publicly on our own terms. We knew that whatever was in store for us as individuals, the events we were about to face would be a turning-point in our nation's history.

Our own militia were armed and guarding the doors of Parliament. I am still not clear if they would have used their firearms against the superior power of the army. Most of them would have considered it to have been their bounden duty, though much would have depended on how their officers interpreted the situation. The rest of us told each other that we would resist the advancing paratroopers by forming a human shield. We knew that such defiance would be crushed in almost no time at all, perhaps bloodily, but the stand would at least be recognizable as resistance. I stayed outside the debating chamber through most of this sitting, as I was busy using the telephone to appeal to governments and presidents, and writing letters in the same vein, but I left my office from time to time to keep in touch with developments. We knew the Soviet habit of taking immediate family members hostage, and we all tele-phoned our families. Gražina was at home looking after our little granddaughter and I asked her to leave, but she did not want to frighten the child and stayed put. A little later, at around 2 a.m., I spoke with a reporter from Moscow. After she left she wrote an interesting report on the prevailing mood, with a generous description of my bad character!

We learned that an armoured column had paused briefly at a cross-roads on the edge of Vilnius and had then begun moving towards the centre of the city. Soon we heard the tanks rumbling down the hill towards our Parliament building. Next we saw the lights, the machine-guns, even the faces. We expected the worst but they did not enter Parliament Square. Instead, they went around us, entered the road tunnel which lies just beyond, and disappeared! As the roar subsided and we breathed a sigh of relief, we felt exhilarated. It had only been a display to intimidate us, though the threat remained. We had won a moral victory. Faced by this crude show of force we had remained at our posts, true to our duty, to our oath, and to Lithuania.

On the next day Moscow ordered all the inhabitants of Lithuania to surrender all sporting guns and hand guns. The decree was carefully considered, and our Ministry of the Interior was told not to comply with such an order from a foreign nation. We then learned that the 'duty of implementation had now been passed to the Soviet army', which was worrying. In the prevailing atmosphere an incident might easily be provoked which would allow the army to use force. When we realized this I decided to use television, and appealed to 'people to behave peace-fully at all times and not to resist the army whatever the provocation'. We knew that the Soviets held the address of every member of the Hunting Association, and therefore the whereabouts of every registered gun in the country, so I asked everyone to report every detail of any suspicious burglaries or other infringements of their rights. Interestingly, no further action was taken after this by the other side. The system seemed to lack the will to further action. It seemed that we had passed another test.

When Sajūdis was in opposition the Soviet newspapers had regularly claimed that we persecuted Russians and aimed to reintroduce capitalism and bourgeois order. The vilification continued. Just after the Baltic Way demonstration had shown the unmistakable feelings of the three nations to the wider world, photographs appeared in *Pravda* and *Izvestia* which showed me standing in Cathedral Square with a uniformed group of Boy Scouts. The scene was innocent, but the story reported the concern of people in the Soviet Union 'at the reappearance of *Fascist youth*'. Then a Moscow television programme was broadcast denouncing the World Scout Movement as a 'Fascist organization'. This was an unpleasant incident, but it gave one of the youngsters a chance to appear on Lithuanian television, and everyone was reminded that only two

European countries have ever forbidden the Scout Movement – Hitler's Germany and the Soviet Union! A little later a leaflet attacking the Soviet Union, the Communist party and the national minorities was distributed. It is likely that it was produced by the KGB and its *provocateurs*, but it was given widespread publicity as 'evidence of the dangerous trends promoted by Sąjūdis'.

The Moscow media caused constant difficulties. They regularly followed the official Communist party line, asserting that Lithuania's behaviour was illegal, and that we were obliged to obey the Soviet constitution and laws. The newspapers also informed us that there was no chance of our leaving the Soviet Union unless we conformed to the law laying down the procedures for doing so. Our reply to this propaganda was always direct and simple: we were not part of the Soviet Union. Since 11 March, its decrees did not apply in our country, and we repeated again and again that Lithuania had been illegally annexed. This meant that our country had *never been* a part of the Soviet Union. We also declared, with equal consistency, that the Act of the Soviet Congress which had recently specified procedures for leaving the Soviet Union had been passed *after* 11 March and was therefore *subsequent* to Lithuania's Declaration of Independence. We invited Soviet representatives on numerous occasions to share in a television link-up between Moscow and Vilnius so that our position could be fully explained and made clear to everybody, but the proposal was refused on each occasion. We knew that the real interest of our opponents was to manage public opinion. They were not interested in transmitting our arguments because they wanted to be able to say that 'nationalists and fascists threatened Russians in Lithuania', and that we were 'working illegally against the Soviet Union in order to destroy socialist society'. These same circumstances would be used to justify their actions later, when words became deeds. They would then be able to say that their president had acted 'to put the house in order'.

One of the first laws passed in our newly constituted Supreme Council after the Constitutional Acts was that of 13 March, which ended enforced conscription to the Soviet forces. We announced that Lithuanian youngsters were no longer obliged to serve in those forces, and draftees began to remove themselves at once, many of them returning to Lithuania in secret. The Soviet command responded with an announcement that those who did not return to their units would be arrested and tried for desertion by military tribunals. We knew they would be judged according to Soviet law and treated harshly if their cases reached court. It would be difficult for our new state to provide protection for young men caught in these circumstances, so we advised those in this situation not to stay at home or in any other place where they might easily be found and identified. It was best for them to go to other towns or stay with relatives. When a number of them approached our government for protection, the best we could offer was accommodation at a hospital on the outskirts of Vilnius where a Red Cross flag was flown to indicate sanctuary. Our militia stood guard there, but on the night of 26 March the premises were suddenly attacked by a Soviet unit which beat up the militia and the escaped recruits. The young men were dragged away leaving blood-stained clothes and bedding behind. The event, the premises, the blood-stains and everything else were filmed as they happened by visiting foreign journalists, and though Soviet soldiers brutally confiscated most of the film on the spot, some of the footage saved was shown on the international networks. Of course we were then accused of making political capital out of the incident, and of failing to protect our young men! However, the Soviets showed more than average clumsiness because a second psychiatric hospital at Kaunas was also attacked that night. No conscripts were hiding there, but the premises were devastated and patients and staff were frightened beyond all reason.

Our law officers were instructed to take out criminal charges against the Soviet officers who issued orders to beat and abduct people in such circumstances, though in reality we could do little to defend our people against these outrages. In desperation, we appealed to the international organizations, including the Red Cross, for help. This appeal to the wider world seemed to bring no response from outside, but it had one positive effect: the Soviet military commanders told us that they would not, after all, prosecute the young men whom they had taken into custody. This seemed like a concession, although less of one than we originally thought, for the young men were to be stationed far away from Lithuania without leave until the end of their military service. When parents wanted to visit their sons they found they had to travel to the far north of Russia. Though such journeys were expensive, they were subsidized by the Lithuanian government because it was the least we could do to ease their anguish.

The propaganda machine of the Soviet Union claimed that its actions reflected normal military procedures for apprehending and sentencing deserters. That was to be expected from such sources, but their interpretation was accepted uncritically by western politicians even when we told them exactly what happened. We cited the 1949 Geneva Convention (which had been signed by the Soviet Union), which laid down that 'an occupying force has no right to enlist conscripts of the occupied country', and argued that these young people could not be accused of desertion. I recall one of our deputies telling us that his mother had seen the attacks on the hospitals on television. She had been an inmate of a ghetto during the German occupation, and had experience of the struggle against the Nazis. Now, having seen the documentary evidence, she criticized us for not having given the young men new identities and supporting papers. Her comment on what she had seen that evening was that 'the Soviets were acting just as the Nazis did'. It has stuck firmly in my mind. The Soviet Union was anxious to portray its actions in as favourable a way as possible, and on 3 April the Soviet foreign minister arrived in Washington for a three-and-a-half-hour meeting with Secretary of State Baker, during which he described the situation in Lithuania as a catastrophe comparable to an earthquake.

The whole question of compulsory military recruitment developed its own rules. It became clear that a potential conscript who did not present himself for registration was not likely to be bothered further, but deserters were ruthlessly hunted down. Their homes and those of the immediate family were often broken into and searched without warning. There were some episodes in which enraged neighbours took matters into their own hands in the attempt to save young men from arrest, or to free them from the hands of the soldiery. In one incident a group of soldiers surrounded one of our militia stations where a youngster was hiding. The soldiers started arguing, and while the argument was going on, the young man they wanted managed to escape. When the soldiers discovered he had fled, they left in low spirits. In a very different incident, a young man was accused of theft and should have been taken before a civil court. However, the militia realized that he had deserted from the Soviet forces and handed him over to the Soviet soldiers instead. He then tried to run away, but the soldiers shot him dead in broad daylight while he was running. Later, our procurator's office not unreasonably charged both the militia and the soldiers with manslaughter. Yet while these things were happening all over the country, there were officials in our Ministry of the Interior who were chiefly concerned with pleasing the occupying power, and were prepared to co-operate in tracing conscripts in hiding. We learned of such betrayals after the event, but the ministry was reluctant to punish the culprits. We also learned of other members of that establishment who behaved in an unprecedentedly flexible manner. The situation often gave rise to suspicions about where their real allegiance lay.

Our internal opposition was not slow to exploit this complex situation. They accused us of 'taking on too much' by refusing to countenance conscription to the Soviet forces when we had no real means of defending our own citizens. Aware of this accusation, the Supreme Council published a declaration it had prepared reminding everyone that Lithuanian citizens had no obligation to serve in a foreign army. It said plainly that the Supreme Council opposed such service and suggested that our citizens should not enlist, but also advised the community that we did not forbid enrolment by those who wanted it. We knew that many young Russians, especially those who were the sons of officers, saw it as their duty and a matter of honour to serve, and while we did not know quite what the majority of the Polish community felt, we supposed that many were favourable to the Soviet viewpoint and would allow their sons to enter the Soviet forces. However, some Lithuanian parents were afraid of non-compliance, and we knew of parents with a problem teenager, perhaps with a criminal record, who might feel that it was best to 'allow the army to sort them out' even though there was some danger that the youngster might return in a tin coffin. This was a growing problem, and such military burials often presented a double political problem, because people were no longer confining their feelings to the expression of grief at such funerals, but using them as an opportunity to express protest. Soviet officials presented parents with certificates stating that the soldier had died in action, and this was happening much more frequently than in the past. Though strict instructions were invariably given to the contrary, parents would want to have the coffin opened to have a final glimpse of their sons whom they had perhaps not seen for a long time. Many had found a severely beaten and mutilated body inside, and realized that their son had not seen the field of battle but had been brutally murdered. I still have a letter from some soldiers which reported their experiences: 'We are not allowed to leave our camp in our free time, and we are contemptuously called Germans or capitalists. We are being mistreated because we are Lithuanians. Do we escape and run back home, or just endure this horror?' Sąjūdis received shoals of such letters describing atrocious conditions and treatment, all providing proof of the way recruits were treated in the Soviet forces. But what these lads suffered in retaliation for our declaration of national independence went far beyond the standard indignities imposed by the Soviet army. On 12 March I wrote to Gorbachev, asking him to intervene and help such conscripts to return home, but he ignored my plea. Instead he decided to terrorize us further.

When the boycott of conscription intensified, Moscow ordered all foreign correspondents to leave Lithuania. Most complied and left, one by one, over the next few weeks, because they were afraid to lose their Soviet visas and permits to work in Moscow. Edward Lucas of the London *Independent* was an honourable exception. Having received the first visa issued by the Foreign Ministry of the restored Republic of Lithuania, he took the opposite path. When he arrived in Vilnius, the Soviet border guards had not woken up to what was happening and accepted his documentation. He was later particularly proud of being the very first person to have obtained a Lithuanian visa, but his arrival was soon spotted, and he was swiftly expelled, and at that stage it was beyond our means to control the situation. Shortly after this, Senator Alfonse D'Amato also attempted to reach Vilnius from the United States, using one of our visas. In his case the border guards, who had received new instructions from Moscow, refused to let him in, and when a delegation of French doctors flew in from Warsaw a few days later, they were put on another plane and taken on to Moscow. Each of these actions was a further expression of contempt for our stand, and a form of psychological warfare. However, the process served the Soviet Union very well politically, as the most significant factor in gaining international recognition after establishing control of the country is a government's ability to control its borders. This requirement was constantly asked about by the governments whom we most wanted to recognize us, but the Soviets had expressly ordered their border guards to prevent us from exercising any kind of control of our own. This became a particular concern of theirs, and they were instructed not to tolerate even a single militiaman wearing Lithuanian insignia, or allow even a shed to be erected if it could be construed as a border post. However, on 20 March, the Supreme Council charged the Council of Ministers with the task of marking out the borders of Lithuania. It was perhaps symbolic, but two additional checkpoints for goods in transit were established after a little effort. This minimal arrangement was sufficient to confirm within a few days that there was a considerable traffic in illegal exports across our borders. It was an alarming revelation, and we acted swiftly to proclaim the need for tighter control over the flow of goods before the whole wealth of Lithuania was removed. We had discovered by then that many of the factories in Lithuania which were under Moscow's direct management had received orders to dismantle their new western production lines and equipment and to shift them out of the country. I have to say that the fight for our national borders, which extended over a year and a half, was very difficult. It did not have a promising beginning because as soon as we attempted to erect our border control posts, the wooden sheds or portable units were immediately set upon by Soviet Interior Ministry soldiers and knocked down or burned. In many cases our guards were severely beaten, and the summer of 1991 saw the first murders of Lithuanian border guards. This was the way in which the Soviet Union demonstrated its refusal to give us control of our national borders, and its use of force on this issue was, as always, accompanied by a show of vindictiveness and sheer hatred.

Despite these severe difficulties, our attempts to establish border controls were increasingly supported by our people, who recognized that we were standing up for the principle of sovereignty. On 23 August, 1990, we commemorated the fifty-first anniversary of the Molotov–Ribbentrop Pact, and Sąjūdis organized a demonstration on both sides of the Lithuanian–Polish border at Lazdijai. Since Soviet guards were still in position there, we presented them with a petition which asked them to leave, so that control of the border could be taken over by Lithuania's Defence Department. This was a form of political pressure, but it was also a nation's personal challenge to soldiers who were under orders to remain at their posts. There was a swift response. Reinforcements were moved in, and then lorries turned up to pour reels of barbed wire around behind which the guards could defend themselves. However, I was very careful to ensure that this confrontation did not develop into open conflict. All the members of our Sąjūdis Council came to this particular demonstration, and in order to hold the interest of the large crowds which had gathered, we addressed them in turn. I was kept very busy as I was asked to speak on legality and the justice of our country's demands, but was also expected to remain in control of the situation when our Sąjūdis representatives negotiated with the border-post commander to allow people to cross the border briefly to meet those on the other side. We achieved our aims that day without conflict, and the gathering attracted particular international attention because this was the Polish–Lithuanian border, not a border shared with the Soviet Union. We considered this to be another constructive political event which usefully added a little more weight to the pressure already exerted by Sąjūdis on the Soviet system.

The war of nerves in which we were engaged now took a surprise turn, involving buildings owned by the Communist party. The Lithuanian Communist party had separated itself from the Communist party of the Soviet Union by now, but had split again. The smaller group, those remaining faithful to Moscow, were commonly known as the 'Platformers' (because of their 'fundamentalist platform'). The larger of these two Communist parties continued to occupy all the properties belonging to the former united party, and saw no reason to ask the state to provide security for these buildings. However, Soviet soldiers suddenly began to occupy them, explaining that they were there to 'provide security'. This was obviously a pretext to hand these places over to Moscow's Platformers, who had indeed 'asked the army to protect "their" buildings'. We interpreted this as meaning that both the Platformers and the army had received orders from Moscow. We then asked the Soviet army authorities if they would perform the same kindness if the Social Democratic party made a similar request, and noted with amusement that they were, for once, at a loss for a reply. However, the propaganda machine was busy exploiting the situation, telling the West that Communist party property in Lithuania now needed to be defended from the threat of seizure. The story implied that the Soviet Union was now defending the private ownership of property, a principle which would of course be well understood in the West!

The larger Lithuanian Communist party was naturally not well pleased by this unexpected pantomime, and its representatives argued that these buildings had been built with Lithuanian funds and therefore could not be claimed by the Moscow loyalists. They acknowledged that financial help had been received by these places from the Soviets in the past, but claimed that any support received had long since been repaid, but the disagreement rolled on and widened. I advised the Lithuanian Communist party leaders Brazauskas and Beriozovas more than once that they should start court action against the illegal seizure of buildings, but they were obviously reluctant, and I interpreted their response as reflecting deeply ingrained habits. They could not see how their attempt to sort out this dispute about property in their own country by appeal to the Communist party of a foreign country echoed the broader problems of their own nation, nor explain why their conduct of the affair disregarded their own government and their own national legal system. As a result, the issue dragged on until Brazauskas eventually settled for a mutual agreement with Burokevičius, the Platformers' leader. They then decided to divide the properties between them. Significantly the deal was clinched in Moscow, but the real end of the saga came in August 1991, when we declared with some satisfaction in the aftermath of the *putsch* that all Communist party properties now belonged to the Lithuanian state!

Among the other premises which the Soviets occupied by force that spring, was the publishing house in Vilnius in which were located the editorial offices of many of our newspapers, journals and book publishers, together with the largest print workshops in the country. A squad of soldiers turned up to occupy these premises one day without warning or obvious authority, except that they were accompanied by a group of Platformers, who claimed to be the rightful owners and forced their way in. The seizure was a severe blow to the Lithuanian newspapers, and crowds of people reacted to the news by surrounding the buildings and holding a vigil of protest. The situation could have become very difficult if the soldiers had not decided after a while to abandon the premises.

The next point of attack in what had become a rolling programme of seizures was the prosecutor-general's office. Moscow now decided to install its own 'prosecutor-general for the Lithuanian Soviet Socialist Republic'. It was an act designed to cause confusion, as we had appointed our own nominee to this important position under the provisions of the temporary constitution, and he had settled into his duties after being sworn into office before the Supreme Council. However, the Soviet constitution required this appointment to be made by the highest authorities of the Soviet Union. Moscow therefore deemed him a usurper without authority, and installed its own puppet. Next they attempted to bring our district prosecutors into line with him, though few co-operated. The courts, however, took their own view of the justice of the situation, and would hear only cases brought by Lithuanian civil servants. Communications from Moscow's appointee were ignored, and fortunately the legal officials continued to answer to the country's rightful prosecutor-general. This acknowledgement of our authority was of the greatest value, because it meant that Moscow's attempt to install an alternative legal system had failed. Despite its futility, there were very sinister implications to this whole charade, which could well have been a first manifestation of Gorbachev's threat to create a whole parallel governing structure. This might have been achieved by setting up a puppet administration dominated by the Platformers, or some kind of 'Salvation Committee', and the threat remained, with significant sections of national life like the Lithuanian railways still under the control of the Soviet militia. Gorbachev did not give up his attempts at disruption, and attempted to use the Naujoji Vilnia Bank in eastern Lithuania to create a secondary fiscal system which would dislocate our own. These attempts continued throughout the summer of 1991 and there also was some effort to separate our eastern region from Lithuania. The worst threat of all, however, was the fact that the KGB still functioned from its huge building at the very centre of our capital city. As yet we had no levers to remove this sinister Soviet institution, and we did not wish to sacrifice lives in attempting to do so.

Vilnius Airport was also seized by Soviet military units. This was scarcely a strategic necessity because everything there was already in the hands of a staff who belonged, almost to a man, to the Moscow-orientated and KGB-dominated Yedinstvo (Russian for 'unity') organization, which was the channel of much of the opposition to us. We had our own small government plane for journeys to and from Moscow, so we used the airport regularly, even though we were warned that the mechanics there might well attempt to eliminate us by sabotage. We were even told by well-informed friends that the whole Cabinet should never travel together on the same flight. It was sobering advice but we ignored it and flew as we needed, because we had come to the conclusion that if the KGB really wanted to liquidate us, no precautions of ours would stand in the way of their plans. Meanwhile their current priority was to establish a viable opposition to us, and they used every opportunity to frighten people by portraying our government as fascist and vengeful. It was predicted that we would end up hanging communists and persecuting Russians and Poles, and sensible people were warned that they must unite to defend themselves against us! It should have been generally realized by this time that we were not set against any national group, and wanted every citizen to share in the process of renewing and democratizing our country, but this steady drip-feed of provocation did find a response among a minority. Few of these were Lithuanians, and most belonged to a rough fringe which was happy to be controlled by the KGB. Many of them fitted nicely into the noisy, often violent Yedinstvo faction, which followed Moscow's hard line in blind obedience out of love for the great 'Soviet motherland' which embraced 'everything from the Polish border to the Kurile Islands'.

Yedinstvo, in its frantic desire to oppose our reconstruction of the state, seized every opportunity to provoke unpleasant incidents. Its members' faces would swell with anger as they vowed to 'defend the Soviet government' or 'to overthrow Sajūdis's bloody Supreme Council'. We could see that a few thousand such people could well, given coherent instructions and military advisers in civilian clothes, be incited to try to sweep us aside. From the communist viewpoint such a scenario could be presented as an outburst of 'popular discontent'. On several occasions members of the movement tried to frighten deputies, and even to take over the Supreme Council on one occasion. Sometimes army helicopters unexpectedly flew over Vilnius, scattering leaflets which called on people to come to the Parliament 'to overthrow the fascists', and 'to get rid of the Landsbergis government'. This involvement of Yedinstvo was clearly no accident, but Mrs Prunskienė was prime minister at the time, and the disturbance came to nothing, perhaps because the KGB would have had no advantage from the overthrow of her government. On another occasion Yedinstvo called on the Poles to 'defend their rights which had been infringed'; and we could identify assault troops in civilian clothes at this meeting by the army-issue boots which they were wearing. We learned that the main body of demonstrators planned to break into the Supreme Council, and prepared a defence plan involving our militia and defence volunteers, and then called on the people to protect Parliament by keeping vigil outside. They responded very generously, and huge crowds hurried there and kept the vigil going day and night for several days – indeed their songs could be heard for almost a week afterwards. When they came, Yedinstvo members began to assemble in a dense phalanx, and we feared a clash between the two crowds. We had emphasized ever since 1988 that violence and rioting would not serve our cause in any way, but we knew that Moscow needed fights, clashes and riots, so that they could claim that the situation had deteriorated and was dangerous to life. We were facing a situation in which an aggravated response to their provocation was a distinct possibility, and would be used to justify intervention.

I recall Mikhail Gorbachev assuring Senator Edward Kennedy that 'force will never be used in Lithuania'. However, his rhetoric did not prevent Lithuanian youths from being abducted and beaten by Soviet troops the very next day. Gorbachev had added a caveat: 'unless there is a danger to human life'. The last thing which we wanted to give him was any excuse for using this option, so we were extremely anxious when members of Yedinstvo paraded that afternoon. However, their performance was so clumsy that it bordered on the comical. Early the same day soldiers in armoured vehicles had formed guards around the statues of Lenin which stood in every city. Just a few weeks earlier Kaunas City Council had decided that the Soviet decree making Lenin's statue a compulsory part of their civic provision was now obsolete, and with some pleasure had moved swiftly to demolish their local statue. His statue in Klaipėda also needed protection, and a small cannon mounted on a concrete pedestal to commemorate the Red Army's taking of the town in 1945 was also being provided with special military protection. This monument was a monstrosity, a Stalinist hangover. Even before our challenge to the system began, its removal had been planned by the City Council, a decision taken on aesthetic grounds. Klaipėda Council was actually doing no more than implement a decision which had already been taken, but the local Yedinstvo stepped in to demand its protection by the military. That could be seen as amusing, but uglier news arrived from the same city. Someone had poured paint over a monument in the nearby Soviet military cemetery, and another armed unit had been placed there by the commander of the nearby army barracks. We sent a team to investigate, but they were not allowed near until a Moscow television unit had finished its documentary report which explained that the memory of our Soviet liberators was being defiled in Lithuania! The way this situation was handled seemed to suggest a great deal about who were the real authors of the damage. It seemed not at all unlikely that it was the work of a KGB *provocateur*, and the suspicion grew when we learned that leaflets bearing the name of Sajūdis had been distributed in Klaipėda. These called for a blockade of the army barracks there, and the military responded by announcing that any such provocation would meet with an immediate and larger retaliation. We contacted the Klaipėda branch of Sajūdis, and learned that nothing of the kind had ever been considered, though members had planned to light bonfires for a barbecue and to have a singsong on a beach not far from the barracks which dominate that corner of the city. It was another example of the provocations and distortions which abounded, and could be heard or read about every day. Our people had, however, never resorted to beating anyone, used no physical violence, and were not provoked into fighting. Our only retaliation to provocation, even to force, was to sing in the time-honoured Lithuanian manner.

On Holy Saturday, the eve of Easter, Gorbachev gave us an unannounced ultimatum. We were to return immediately to the constitutional situation of 10 March, that is to the legal situation before the re-establishment of our nation's independence, and would face severe consequences if we had not agreed to this by Easter Monday. On hearing this news, foreign journalists flocked to hear my response, and I told them that my countrymen were celebrating a religious feast which was neither acknowledged nor observed in the Kremlin. Since we wished to observe this religious holiday, our reply would come *after* the festivities. However, in the event, Gorbachev was not prepared even to wait that long. He had raised his whip high and now brought it down hard; on Easter Monday, 18 April, at exactly half-past nine in the evening, the entire oil supply and 80 per cent of the gas supply to Lithuania was cut off abruptly and without warning. We learned later that the energy crisis which this intervention precipitated had been calculated to inflict maximum damage within about a fortnight. However, there was an element of miscalculation because Easter was late that year and the spring and early summer were warm enough for us to get by with reduced use of electricity. We were in fact blessed by good fortune, though there was a natural anxiety that our industrial production might grind to a halt, or that our autumn harvest might fail if the problem was not resolved quickly. Some people, however, emphasized growing fears about the situation, and chief among these ministers of gloom was Algirdas Brazauskas, now chairman of the committee set up to combat the blockade.

We learned later that Moscow's experts had calculated that Lithuania would be forced to capitulate within a week, or at the most two, and that the West could not respond to any cries for help in that short time. The oil and gas blockade which they had imposed was underpinned by their preventing the supply of over fifty other types of raw material and essential produce. When we asked what was happening and offered to pay cash for these goods in the normal way, we received no reply, so in an effort to circumvent the state distribution machinery we sent agents out to buy materials which were urgently needed directly from individual companies in the Soviet Union. We also began negotiating with the districts and the republics, offering cash or bartered agricultural produce and had considerable success in our efforts. It took Moscow some time to realize what we were doing, but when it did, the Soviet Railways were ordered not to transport goods to Lithuania. Clearly the situation had become a real political and economic blockade. It was a critical time, and we attempted to minimize immediate problems by switching from a command to a market economy as quickly as we could, and the idea caught on fast. Tanker lorries were soon crossing into Lithuania from Belarus in droves to sell off their loads by the roadside. The prices were much higher, of course, but soon petrol markets developed to supply the much needed fuel at a more reasonable cost. After a while, the soldiers cottoned on to what was happening and started helping us as well; they could not resist selling army fuel to earn something extra. The adaptation to this free market was so widespread that even the KGB found it impossible to stop business, and may even have joined in. We also considered using more dramatic means to make an impact on international opinion. There was a plan to send an oil tanker to Klaipėda. I mentioned this in a letter to Mitterrand, and the possibility that the Soviets might sink it caused grave concern to George Bush.

As a result of the petrol shortage private transport almost came to a halt throughout the country, and public transport had to be cut to the bone. At this time the idea was floated that we could be rescued by the bicycle. Taking up the idea, I used my tape recorder to prepare a message for the people of Sweden, because we had learned that a demonstration was held in Stockholm every Monday in support of our struggle. I decided to ask the people of Sweden to give Lithuania practical help and supply us with 100,000 used bicycles. I suggested that this project would surprise the world, and win them a reputation as generous friends. It came to nothing, and the Swedes probably thought I was joking. (Two years later, however, I reminded the Queen of Sweden of the project. Shortly afterwards our Supreme Council received a present of – bicycles!) In fact I was not joking, because the hardships of the blockade were growing rapidly, and were reflected in falling standards of living, unemployment, insecurity regarding the future, and the rise of internal opposition.

This last was of course rooted in the Communist party, and was now being guided and fomented by the capable hands of the KGB. One of its eager agents took the opportunity to found the organization Ateities Forumas (Future Forum). Their tactics also showed themselves more openly in the Supreme Council. In essence they were very simple: they were against anything and everything which might strengthen the independence of our country. Their criticism was focused particularly on our legislative achievements, on what they called the 'paper laws' which had been passed by the Council, but which could not be implemented because of the confusion into which we had been thrown. My arguments also were simple. I pointed out that the laws which we had passed were designed to replace the previous Soviet laws. It was true that we had not yet been able to implement many of them, but we were fighting for *our constitution*. Whenever we were told that the Soviet constitution or Soviet law applied to a situation, we could now reply that this was not true, because a Lithuanian law had been substituted in every case. I also argued that if we had not replaced Soviet by Lithuanian laws, we would have been in a significantly worse position. We had set out to make the law our *own*, to make everything new, and the concept of the law of Lithuania, the *law of our own people*, was therefore a political tool. Though we may have enacted some unsuitable legislation at that stage, we could not ignore the pressures which the blockade was putting on us. The fact was that we were still under the influence of Soviet agencies which had dominated most of our lives. Soviet law had to be expunged and replaced, and it would have worked out very badly for us if we had not begun to remove it from the statute book. It was essential to the exercise of our nationhood that our government took responsibility for the whole apparatus of the Lithuanian state into its own hands, accepting responsibility for its own actions and even for its own mistakes and the tensions arising from them. This was all a part of growing into the political maturity of independence.

People do not change overnight, but despite our difficulties, the movement which took place in people's attitudes and feelings was very gratifying. On Sunday 29 April, at the height of the blockade, a concert took place in Cathedral Square in Vilnius. A symphony orchestra played, free of charge, and its members were wearing formal dress for the occasion. The conductor was Juozas Domarkas, an artist of some renown, and Beethoven's Ninth Symphony was being performed. This work is a universal cry of hope and freedom, but this particular performance distilled a message which had been conveyed to many parts of the world that spring, the message of Lithuania's long struggle to become free. A little earlier I had been asked to contribute over a satellite link to a chat show in the United States. The host had asked what music I would like to have played at the summit meeting between Bush and Gorbachev which was about to take place. I had replied: 'Beethoven, the Ninth Symphony.' Interestingly, these words were heard as a challenge from Vilnius to the presidents of the superpowers and were widely reported. It was a breakthrough, but my reply meant more than that to me. Our nation was busy defying the Soviet blockade, and while the superpowers sat down to decide our fate *we were not even represented at the table!*

Yet as I stood in Cathedral Square in our capital city that Sunday afternoon, with thousands of my country's people standing around me, in rapt attention yet in festive mood, I shared their appreciation of the great power of Beethoven's magnificent work in the depth of my being. As I listened I suddenly felt wholly in touch with what I had said to that American audience. Above all I knew that everyone present sensed the deepest meaning of that majestic music without needing to have it explained. When people enter into the spirit of such music, when it is understood and *felt*, it transmits its spiritual strength to them. Was it too much to hope that even Bush and Gorbachev, sitting at their negotiating table in Iceland, might also have to respond to the music of our souls?

CHAPTER 15

Gorbachev and the difficult path to negotiation

The decrees of the Lithuanian Supreme Council made on 11 March meant that our deputies could no longer serve as parliamentarians of the Soviet Union. Nevertheless the Council instructed the existing deputies to attend the Third Congress of the Soviet Union in Moscow as representatives of independent Lithuania. They were to inform the government of the Soviet Union and deputies of the Congress of the re-establishment of the Lithuanian state, and to present them with copies of its foundation documents. Yet though the decisions taken by our Supreme Council were quite clearly communicated, Gorbachev continued to insist that Lithuania was still a Soviet republic. It meant that our representatives retained their official status in Moscow and were able to enter the Kremlin as members of the Congress. They were alert to the opportunities this status offered, and were assiduous in representing our national cause in the Soviet capital and in rejecting Gorbachev's position.

Our representatives collected information, and made statements on Lithuania's behalf whenever and wherever they could. As they were a group with considerable negotiating skills, and had acquaintances in the Soviet capital, they had no difficulty in contacting important people, and set about trying to develop a new working agreement between Lithuania and the Soviet Union. However, the Kremlin remained totally inflexible and its key decision-makers, particularly Gorbachev and Lukyanov, the vice-chairman of the Supreme Council of the Soviet Union, rejected every proposal our representatives made. Gorbachev in fact publicly rejected any negotiations with Lithuania. In the end, their blocking strategy was so obvious that we felt forced to change our tactic and decided to send a delegation led by Romualdas Ozolas, our deputy prime minister, to Moscow. He was given a free hand to begin a dialogue, and we were quite prepared to make major concessions in order to open the door to formal recognition of the Lithuanian state. Indeed, we had reached the point where we had agreed among ourselves that we would change our attitude to providing supplies to the Soviet forces while they continued to stay on our national territory if it meant that serious discussion could begin. However, Moscow steadily dismissed everything we offered.

Though we were stoical, this was a very dispiriting and frustrating period, but, despite constant set-backs, we continued to believe that our case was based on natural justice. We also trusted that the wider world would sooner or later recognize that our independence was valid. In the mean time the doors we knocked on all remained shut.

The general situation was clearly not very promising. At about the time the economic blockade of our country was due to start, Alexander Yakovlev, the secretary of the Central Committee of the Communist party of the Soviet Union, invited our delegation headed by Romualdas Ozolas, deputy prime minister, to a meeting. It was nominally unofficial, but the fact that it was taking place was made public, and a flock of journalists appeared. It was clear that some of the participants had tipped them off, perhaps because they were obviously optimistic when they arrived, and were clearly expecting a scoop of some kind. Their arrival scarcely seemed important, but when Yakovlev was faced by reporters he announced that he was making no promises and added darkly that our meeting had been intended to be private. When I asked him what he meant, he observed that this had been a lost opportunity, 'because your people were unfortunately unable to keep their mouths shut'. That may or may not have been the case, but I now believe that, even if every delegate on our side had been totally discreet, the hard-liners were working to ensure that we left empty-handed. The allegation of indiscretion on our part suited the Soviet leadership well at that stage because even the suggestion of real negotiations would have produced powerfully hostile reactions from Soviet fundamentalists. Whatever the value of these speculations, it was clear at the time that Gorbachev now had a pretext for putting the blame on us. It was a feeble excuse, but for a man in his position it was quite sufficient to dismiss the need for dialogue.

The 'university of life' was now teaching us fast, and as we struggled to clear the ground for negotiations, we learned a great deal about the place of semantic ambiguity and allusion in the diplomatic game. In an unguarded moment at an earlier stage Gorbachev had said that 'negotiations were quite out of the question', but we discovered the existence of a terminology which distinguished 'negotiations' from 'conversations', and then found that there were even finer nuances which included 'consultations' and even 'contacts'. This range of 'alternative routes' seemed to be useful and we entered more deeply into the game, though we sometimes felt that the Soviets were entangling us in a web in which we were 'talking' in every kind of place without ever 'negotiating'. Having realized this, we started to describe all our contacts with the Soviets as 'negotiations' whenever we spoke with western diplomats and reporters. It was a description which reflected the language of normality and suggested that our position was recognized, and after a time Soviet spokesmen also used the expression. When the West urged them to settle their disagreement with us, they would say that 'negotiations were being held'. It meant, of course: 'our side is doing everything correctly', but '*they* were being intransigent'. We would then say that they were not declaring the real state of affairs and were evading the real issues! This went on and on, but in the mean time evidence of what was really happening was steadily accumulating in our files, and eventually we decided to tell the world of the web of duplicity in which we had become ensnared, by publishing papers which revealed the nature of our negotiations. At this point we collected most of the letters, applications, statements and proposals which had been exchanged while we attempted to arrange talks with the Soviet leaders. We then published this comprehensive collection under the title *The Road to Negotiations with the Soviet Union*. It was very noticeable that most of the documents reproduced carried the laconic rubber-stamped endorsement, 'No reply received'. The book was distributed among Western heads of state and diplomats and we found that it was a useful weapon.

One document of ours which failed to get a reply (unless the reply was the economic blockade) was a letter which went to Moscow by air on the day the blockade started. It was drafted in the hope of forestalling the worst outcome. Its every phrase was cautiously formulated, and it was scrutinized carefully by the Supreme Council to ensure that it was as conciliatory as possible. It asked the Soviet leader to authorize consultations concerning negotiations with a delegation from the Republic of Lithuania. It also stated that the Supreme Council agreed 'not to enact any new political legislation during the period of preliminary parliamentary consultations between Lithuania and the USSR', and invited the Soviet Union 'to refuse to use any type of coercion, including economic, against the Republic of Lithuania and its citizens'. Its formulation could scarcely have been more emollient, though we were careful to indicate that we were not in the business of appeasing the Russian bear by deliberately inserting the expression 'economic coercion' into the text. We had used this expression on other occasions, and we included it now because, knowing that the West had warned the Soviets against using force against Lithuania, we hoped that the term would convey an impression of Lithuania's plight which would be taken up in the broader discussion. We were clearly implying that any economic pressure used to threaten us would also be a form of violence. Unfortunately no one picked up on this implication and we failed to lodge the term in the international agenda.

An extremely important letter, which asked us to 'be patient', was sent to me on 26 April by the president of France and the German chancellor acting jointly. The two leaders observed that the Lithuanian nation had unequivocally announced its decision to implement independent rule and asked that it 'should now have the patience to use the traditional modes of diplomatic dialogue'. It was interesting to notice that the letter included phrases such as 'conversation between the leaders of Lithuania and the USSR', and 'the *beginning* of negotiations', nuances which reflected our position accurately; but from our standpoint the message carried worrying implications because it also asked us to 'suspend temporarily the implementation of the decisions of the Lithuanian Parliament' in order to enable a dialogue and negotiations to begin. At first reading it seemed that we were being asked to rescind the Independence Acts which we had passed on 11 March, and because of this its suggestions were examined very carefully before we replied. Many of our number saw it as reflecting Gorbachev's demands, but I read it differently, as it was precise in its commendation of Lithuania's decision to choose independence and contained statements which explicitly recognized the expressed will of the Lithuanian people and our independent rights. Because of these features it seemed that it could serve as a guarantee that we would not ultimately lose out if we should agree to a *temporary* suspension of the implementation of the legislation which had *followed* our declaration of independence. Our parliamentary secretariat prepared a reply which reflected this reading, but I found this draft unattractive and sat down to write my own reply without further delay. This letter told François Mitterrand and Helmut Kohl that Lithuania was quite ready for talks with Moscow, and that we were prepared to 'negotiate on all the issues, *except* the independence of the state of Lithuania, which had been fully and finally re-established on 11 March 1990'. As I wrote I was careful to treat the two leaders, the signatories of the letter to which I was replying, as eventual intermediaries in our dialogue with the Soviet Union and as guarantors of our Lithuanian democracy. My efforts in this direction seemed to go unrewarded. Neither leader wished to take up this role actively, at least at this stage, and this call received no direct response. However, it did not pass unnoticed. I responded openly but hostile journalists suggested that 'Landsbergis had not understood the letter nor replied to it in an appropriate manner'. Helpfully, the French Foreign Ministry immediately issued the statement that 'Vilnius had understood everything correctly'. This squashed the insinuation.

A little before these developments, Vaclav Havel had made the noteworthy proposal that we could use the good offices of Czechoslovakia as a neutral participant in any Soviet–Lithuanian dialogue. I had accepted his suggestion with considerable gratitude, but the Soviets made absolutely no response. In the context of the letter from François Mitterrand and Helmut Kohl, and with the knowledge that George Bush was standing behind them, his offer assumed an even greater value. Yet these tokens of international concern were not enough to prevent the blockade starting, and we were confronted with the stark reality of our political situation. Within a week people from many countries gave tangible evidence of their support for our actions, showing their sympathies by demonstrating and lobbying their governments. They collected money and goods which reached us as aid, but no direct help was received from their politicians, who were prepared only to give us good advice from all sides, with the journalists joining in the chorus. We had already been told often enough that we had no grasp of *realpolitik*, and now the West began to give additional advice about how to behave in response to the blockade – as if *they* knew Gorbachev and the Soviet system better than we did! To exacerbate the farce, we could now hear the tired clichés which the Soviet propagandists had applied to us (which described our actions as 'rash', 'unthinking' and 'undermining the process of *perestroika*') being recycled and achieving new life in the messages of caution which were reaching us from our western friends, who were busy telling us *ad nauseam* that 'Gorbachev's aim is peace and democracy', or 'Gorbachev is in difficulty because of pressures within the Soviet Union'. Some people also told us that 'our resentment might hinder his reforms', and that it would be 'better for everyone if we cooled down'! The concern of the West was quite clear: Gorbachev was not to be criticized because nothing must stand in the way of *glasnost* and *perestroika*. Meanwhile other voices joined the chorus against us, notably the Lithuanian Communist party which was now clamouring for 'a political solution'. Of course this implied that we should seek a quick compromise. It hardly needs saying that no one from that quarter could explain what the nature of the compromise would be. Their 'solution' was, however, crystal-clear to us: they wanted Lithuania to return to the Soviet fold, where its future would be decided by *internal* negotiations, and if we did not comply, the swift removal of Vytautas Landsbergis was to be the next priority.

A continuous campaign of propaganda was now being waged against me. I was described as unbending and unwilling to consider compromise. As a result, I found myself being asked to explain my position by politicians from the West such as Senator Lugar, who phoned one day at George Bush's instigation to ask about our position. I explained in very simple terms that we would accept almost any kind of compromise but could not climb down on the question of our national independence.

Compromise, yes, but not capitulation. It is worth recalling that Gorbachev similarly never minced words when referring to us. When visiting America he had told journalists: 'Your president would have resolved this question of independence in less than twenty-four hours if Lithuania was one of the United States!' He had regularly referred to what he called the 'Federation of the Soviet Union' during that visit, and mentioned more than once that President Lincoln had 'gone to war to maintain the integrity of the nation'. The implication was obvious: a wise and infinitely patient Soviet president was being wonderfully tolerant of Lithuania and its perverse behaviour. What was worse was that this charade was still being sustained as the blockade developed. However, it was already obvious that Gorbachev had acted on poor information when he clamped down on us in this way. He obviously believed that our economy would collapse almost immediately under the pressure, and therefore that armed intervention was unnecessary. Much later a record of a conversation from this time between Vytautas Sakalauskas, the ex-premier of 'Soviet' Lithuania, and Algirdas Brazauskas was found in the office of Gorbachev's secretary, which showed clearly how Gorbachev had reached this conclusion. Brazauskas had reported to him that 'Lithuania's resources will run out before the middle of May, and the subsequent crisis will only be resolved by presidential rule from Moscow'. Gorbachev, who was eager to show himself as 'the man who saved the situation without using force', was preparing for this outcome, and took his whole entourage along with him. His Soviet system had great skill in manipulating public opinion, and was now busy describing our Lithuanian government as 'amateurs, playing politics for their own pleasure'. They successfully manipulated the American press into describing us as 'a mixture of politicians, musicians and actors', while their own Soviet press often insisted on calling me 'a dangerous man who wants to be a martyr'. They were even sometimes kind enough to suggest that I might soon achieve this goal, and many vicious anonymous letters arrived which, like the newspaper reports, carried the unmistakable imprint of KGB propaganda. We were accused of Nazism, nationalism and 'the persecution of minorities', and articles putting this view appeared whenever a foreign leader expressed sympathy for our cause.

The Soviets stuck firmly to their line on contacts and negotiations, insisting that they would talk to us *only* as a republic of the Soviet Union. The fact that we had already exercised the right to self-determination and had left that coercive state was wholly ignored. The Federation Council of the Soviet Union, which consisted of the chairmen of the Supreme Councils of the Soviet republics under the chairmanship

of the president of the USSR, therefore continued to invite me to participate in its meetings. Though I had *no* intention of going, they even went
so far as to telephone me to ask me to explain my absence! Of course I
told them firmly that they had no power to require the head of a foreign
state to attend their meetings, and just as they did not invite the leaders
of Poland or Finland to their deliberations, they need not invite me
either. However, I did attend one more meeting of theirs, though for my
own reasons. After the Council of the Baltic States had been inaugurated
on 12 May 1990, I arranged with Arnold Ruutel, chairman of the
Estonian Supreme Council, and Anatolijs Gorbunovs, chairman of the
Latvian Supreme Council, to go to meet Gorbachev. The idea was to talk
with him on a 'three-plus-one' basis, as it would allow him to negotiate
on the broader issues which affected us and strengthen our own position
at the same time. I knew that the legal status of the decrees of independence promulgated in Estonia and Latvia was rather weaker than ours.
However, we were also aware that western European countries saw our
peoples as having shared a similar fate, and that they had floated the idea
that our problems might be resolved through a *regional* approach. At
first Gorbachev had not troubled to reply when we made the same
suggestion, but Ruutel eventually received an indication that he would
see all three of us together if we attended the Federation Council's
meeting on 12 June. Gorbachev was of course keen for it to appear that
we were returning to the fold and wanted to discuss the principles of his
'new Union'. Thinking of these issues may have led him to overlook the
fact that he had actually started to negotiate with us simply by making
this arrangement. The opportunity implied by his invitation was,
however, not lost on us, and we accepted it. For the first time real possibilities of negotiation seemed to be on offer.

We met in Moscow on 12 June to decide on a common strategy before
going to the Kremlin, and resolved from the start that we would not
accommodate all Gorbachev's wishes. It was impossible for us to avoid
entering the Assembly Hall, so we agreed that we would define
ourselves as observers by not making any contribution to the discussion.
This seemed a good way of showing that we were independent, but on
the way to the Kremlin we found ourselves surrounded by journalists.
Their questions quickly showed that our arrival there was interpreted as
a surrender, and they seemed to be anticipating a ceremonial confession
and absolution of our sins in the Council, with Gorbachev presiding over
the ceremony! Everyone knew that such a spectacle required the utmost
publicity, so we were being welcomed as prodigal sons returning. We
entered the Assembly Hall to be greeted by Gorbachev's advisers, and
many of the national chairmen seemed genuinely happy to see us there

again. Yakovlev's face in particular showed undisguised joy, probably because he now felt certain that the question of the Baltic states would be resolved without further delay. Gorbachev's offer of 'independence in various degrees' had already been announced to the other states of the union, and they probably believed that the opportunity of more autonomy within the Soviet Union which this implied had been enough to persuade us to join the common agenda of *perestroika*. In other words they seemed to believe that we were prepared to compromise and settle happily for '40 degrees' of independence.

The debate which followed was concerned with the present condition and the future of the Soviet Union. The idea of a 'renewed Union' was on the agenda. We listened to Nazarbayev, the chairman of the Supreme Council of Kazakhstan, describe the exceptionally bad economic condition of his country, which had long supplied the Soviet Union with huge amounts of raw materials, including oil, gold and other rare metals. Now, after years of damaging exploitation, his people were suffering an extremely low standard of living, and the country's industry lay in ruins. There was extreme poverty, unemployment was rising, and dozens of new industrial towns had no cultural activities whatever. He criticized the present Soviet order, saying that such bad management was no better than plunder, but concluded his speech with gentle eastern courtesy and the observation that he had no doubt about the benefits to his country of remaining in the Soviet Union. The other chairmen then followed his example. Each began with criticism of the current situation, but all of them ended their speeches with a refrain of loyalty to Gorbachev in which his plans for reform and *perestroika* and his insistence on keeping the Soviet Union intact were praised. Gorbachev sat contentedly as they spoke, listening to the repeated message. Only the chairman of Moldova said anything even slightly different; in his view the Soviet Union must be reconstructed completely, because if things continued as they were, before long no one would want to belong either to the Federation or to the Confederation!

Gorbachev replied to the debate at this point, and discussed the meaning of the Union of States, and of sovereignty. As usual, it was hard to pin down the implications of what he was saying, but we heard him state that 'there was no such thing as sovereignty, and it would be useless to ask for it'. He also spoke disparagingly of the 'fashion' of 'parading sovereignty', and illustrated his disapproval by referring to the debate on sovereignty which had taken place in the Russian Federation's Supreme Council only the day before. 'Let's analyse what happened there,' he said. 'The Russian deputies are cautious about voting for it because they understand their responsibilities, and know that such a decision cannot be taken lightly.' However, it was not long before he was upstaged; even as he was speaking, there was a noticeable stir in the Hall as Boris Yeltsin, who had arrived late, asked leave to interrupt the proceedings. He looked at his watch, then made the dramatic announcement that his Russian Supreme Council had voted only forty minutes before on the very issue which we were debating at that moment. They had, he said, 'passed a declaration of Russian sovereignty'!

Ruutel now felt forced to speak, though in doing so he was defying our earlier agreement to eschew participation in these proceedings, because Gorbachev had turned and addressed a series of direct questions to him in rather an insulting way. Ruutel responded by standing up to reaffirm Estonia's declaration of independence; he also said that his country wanted to develop its current friendly relations with the Soviet Union. When he sat down Gorbachev turned on me: 'Well, Mr Landsbergis', he sneered, taking me aback, 'and how does *Lithuania* see the future of the Federation? . . . What changes would you propose for the Treaty of Union?' I had been given no warning that this challenge would come quite so suddenly, and knew that I had to respond on the spur of the moment. I was bound by the earlier agreement that we should stay out of the debate, but answered: 'Mr President, I cannot comment on the internal affairs of the Soviet Union: that would be an interference.' As I said this both Gorbachev and I remained seated. It was more usual for people to stand when addressing him, but as far as I knew there was no written convention requiring this to be done. Many of those around showed that they thought I was insulting the president, but I knew that if I were to stand at this juncture it would imply my acceptance of a subordinate position, because a sovereign remains seated when he talks to his inferiors and they stand to reply! Being the head of an independent nation I addressed the Soviet president as an equal. To stand up would have been to humiliate my country, which would be unforgivable, and so I replied from my seat and said: 'Lithuania takes a close interest in the changes in the Soviet Union, but she cannot contribute to the decisions needed to bring them about.' I wanted to leave my comments there, but Gorbachev was not prepared to give up so easily, and he shot the question back to me in another form, asking my personal opinion. At this I retorted:

> There is no question of our agreeing to participate in the Soviet Union either now or in the future. I am sure that you understand that we are unable, and indeed refuse, to participate in any such agreement. You must not think that the future of the Soviet Union is unimportant. If you invited us to contribute to your proceedings as observers, we would at least try to give you our advice.

Then, hoping that a soft answer would deflect the tangible anger building up around us, I injected some Socratic logic into the situation by pointing out that the more definite the demand for reform within the Soviet Union became, the happier we Lithuanians could be, *as neighbours.* Finally, I said that if the Soviet Union was really changing, the best proof of its transformation would come when it stopped interfering with the change which was taking place elsewhere, and in particular terminated its blockade of my country.

As soon as I had delivered these words a heated discussion erupted around me, and I still regret having failed to place my cassette recorder on the table in front of me at the beginning of this debate. I had known that it would not work properly in my pocket, but I had avoided putting it on the table because our host might have required me to put it away. I certainly did *not* want to enlarge his ego at the expense of my own in that hostile arena. As the debate rolled on Gorbachev continued to dominate every exchange with his usual methods, interrupting almost every speaker. To be fair, he was rarely aggressive, but he knew very well how to make everybody aware of the authority the chair held, and to show that he was solely in command. He also had a repertoire of techniques for confusing speakers and for throwing individuals on the defensive. On this occasion he flew off the handle in no uncertain way, almost at the moment I reproached him for blockading Lithuania. I was taken aback by this retort, and said: 'What are you saying? Do you believe the blockade is civilized behaviour?' 'Blockade?' he yelled again. 'What blockade? You should choose your words more carefully!' The word was clearly unacceptable in Moscow circles, where oblique reference and allusion to what was going on was preferred to direct discussion and analysis. Expressions such as 'market controls', 'economic means' and 'partial restrictions' might have been acceptable, but I had clearly put my foot in it as far as they were concerned, and it was obvious that Gorbachev had been hugely enraged by my comment. He demanded forcefully that the word 'blockade' was not to be used. However, he did not get his way, because the representatives of the republics of Kazakhstan, Moldova, Belarus and Georgia all joined in together, declaring that they too were 'against the blockade'. It was clear that these national leaders had deliberately chosen to ignore his rulings. Their intervention meant that the debate which Gorbachev had opened by condemning Lithuania had ended up with a hefty rebuke being thrown at the Kremlin. The outcome was a general agreement that the blockade of Lithuania must be lifted. Gorbachev fell silent.

The session had lasted over three hours and Ruutel, Gorbunovs and I stayed on in the hall when it finished, waiting for Gorbachev to meet us as he had previously arranged. We had paid our entrance fee and wanted the second part of the programme, but Gorbachev seemed in no hurry and just went on chatting with his own group long after the hall had emptied. It is likely that he felt he had already gained enough from our presence to satisfy his own needs, because Moscow's television news was going out that evening with an item which showed that we had been present. Of course it showed us in the role of mere docile participants in the Council meeting! So we were kept waiting, his demeanour giving us no clue as to how he was going to respond or when he would be ready. It was not at all clear what was going on. Perhaps the long wait was a way of showing that he was still the ringmaster, or perhaps he hoped we would simply go away. We were not, however, prepared to do that. If we had backed out we would have been seen as cowards, so in the end Ruutel approached him and when he received this reminder he reacted as if with surprise. A further wait ensued before we were led by the prime minister, Nikolai Ryzhkov, to a small office nearby.

There were differences between the situation in each of our states. Lithuania had already made an explicit declaration of independence and we were paying the price for doing so by suffering the blockade. In distinction, Estonia and Latvia had declared themselves to be in a transitional state, 'on the way to independence', a position which could notionally allow more room for manœuvre. Gorbunovs had already declared that Latvia would suspend its declaration in exchange for a guarantee that the country's Supreme Council would not be disbanded. His offer seemed to reflect the difficulties of their politics and the threats and blackmail which he faced. As we began, Gorbachev clearly wanted to control the discussion, and talked first with the representative of Estonia, which he regarded as more flexible. When the conversation finally came around to Lithuania, I told him plainly that our decision was final. We simply had no legal means of annulling our Act of 11 March, and this meant that nothing would be achieved by the blockade or by any further ultimatum. I invited him to accept that the time for military and economic threats had long since passed, suggesting that he should begin a dialogue in search of a mutual understanding instead. I explained that this was all I could offer. Our people had given my government a mandate to proclaim our country's independence, not to retract it. It was therefore totally impractical to demand anything else. As I spoke, Gorbachev kept interrupting to insist that he knew, from his close relationships with the leaders of the United States, Britain and other countries, that nobody, but nobody, would recognize our independence. He even invoked the name of the British prime minister as a supporter of his viewpoint, adding curiously, 'I call her Margaret' – as if such a tone of familiarity would impress us into acquiescence!

At this point Ryzhkov joined in, asking whether I had any idea of the future costs of our raw materials and other imports. 'How will you pay for the gas and oil which you need? Have you got foreign hard currency?' he demanded. In what was rapidly becoming a cross-examination he treated me like a schoolboy facing an oral examination. I did not want to get involved in pointless economic dispute and, indeed, I could not reply to him with precise details. I soon got the message that he was looking for a way of putting me off my stroke. At that stage, political principle was more important to me than winning a futile argument about prices in which he was obviously trying to imply that the Soviet Union was subsidizing Lithuania, so I told him that we would find it necessary to earn the revenue to pay for our imports, just like every other small country. Ryzhkov saw this reply as a sign of my reluctance to give direct answers to his question on prices, and interpreted it as weakness on my part. This became evident very shortly afterwards when he gave an interview in which he expressed surprise at the 'considerable shortcomings' of 'many of the leaders of the Republics'. Indeed, on that occasion he used me as an example, and said: 'Landsbergis was incapable of answering even a simple question on international market prices!' It was his way of claiming that Lithuania had an incompetent leadership. Gorbachev and Ryzhkov, who were persistent questioners and unyielding responders by turns throughout the discussions, repeatedly insisted that their hands were tied by the resolutions of the Third Congress, and that it was absolutely necessary for us to give in. Nothing could be done for us, they said. The blockade (which they preferred to describe as 'the partial restrictions') would come to an end only when Lithuania found a way of denying and retracting the declaration of 11 March. This was their position, from which they would not move.

There was nothing new in these demands. But as the two men repeated the old phrases, I noticed that their mood had changed curiously. We still seemed likely to arrive at a stalemate, but the discussion was now conducted in a reasonably constructive atmosphere, which seemed surprising after what had gone before. The pressures were still strong, but much pointless argument was avoided because the heat seemed to have gone out of the situation. More importantly the threats seemed to die away, and we ended up agreeing that we needed to find a formula which would enable us to continue discussion. Even though I was unable to announce that the blockade had ended when I returned home, I was not despondent because the fact that Gorbachev had at last met with us had reduced the impact of the opposition's constant goading. It helped our position at home. People had been told repeatedly that Landsbergis was inexperienced, clumsy, impolite, a wholly incompetent politician who had insulted Gorbachev even from the first letter he had written to him by using the term 'Your Excellency'. Our detractors had insisted that Gorbachev would not forgive me, or even agree to negotiate at the same table. What they were really saying was: 'Landsbergis is taking unnecessary risks with Lithuanian independence', or: 'Landsbergis must be dropped quickly, for the good of Lithuania', so the meeting with Gorbachev was helpful because it showed that I was, after all, someone that he could do business with. Once I had sat down with him, the atmosphere in Vilnius became calmer. One may wonder why his attitude had changed. I cannot help feeling that it had something to do with the fact that the Communist party of the Soviet Union was preparing to hold its Congress. Gorbachev wanted to confirm that everything was in order and entirely under his control. Whatever the truth was, the practical implications were clear.

Certainly Gorbachev was becoming more active in his dealings with us. On 26 June I received another invitation to travel to Moscow for talks 'to find a way out of the present predicament'. I accepted, and went with Česlovas Stankevičius, my deputy, and Egidijus Bičkauskas, our permanent representative in Moscow. Though Mikhail Gorbachev came to this meeting I noticed that he often turned to his colleague Lukyanov during the discussion, almost as if to check whether he was marching in step with some prepared plan, and I had a curious impression of a man being supervised. During this session I told him plainly that the current Supreme Council of Lithuania was the first to have been elected democratically since the war, and that our people would interpret its actions as a simple betrayal if it went back on the decisions taken on 11 March and agreed that Lithuania was part of the Soviet Union. I added that our deputies had no electoral mandate to take such a course, and that it would therefore be illegal to take it, and he gave the stock answer once again, that we 'must act according to the Soviet constitution, because Soviet law prevailed in Lithuania as in any other Soviet republic'. He then told me that he was categorically opposed to our separatism, but 'understood our need to save face', and advised me that we needed, as politicians, to find an excuse which would convince our electors of the need to change direction. Hearing this, I told him that I had perhaps not expressed my points clearly enough, and repeated my position again, emphasizing that this was not a matter of saving face or of losing it, but of responsibility and accountability to our electorate. However, I soon realized that such explanations were a waste of time.

As this discussion developed, I believed at first that the honourable gentleman was *pretending* not to understand my arguments because such misunderstanding was expedient. In the end I saw that the reality was quite different: he simply *did not understand me* when I spoke about the accountability of democratically elected deputies. He spoke only of the future of the Soviet Union and painted a utopian picture of its principles of association, saying there would be an option for any republic which so desired to 'leave the Union according to its law' at some later time. More than once, he returned to this point as if lecturing us in the role of a more knowledgeable friend. 'Your Lithuanian deputies have problems', he said, 'because they do not know how to present their conclusions to the electorate without losing face.' He then explained that all we needed to do was to take the necessary decisions. He would then himself be very happy to help us out with any explanations and justifications which the resulting situation required, using his own experience to diagnose our problems and tell us what to do. It was as simple as that! As we listened to him repeating these directions it became apparent how he had become renowned as a master of obliquity and diplomatic excuse. At first it crossed my mind that he must have a panel of experts compiling his stratagems, but suddenly it became clear to me that Gorbachev and Lukyanov were not pretending anything. The truth was that they had no inkling whatever of the democratic principle which requires elected representatives to be fully and honestly accountable to their electors, and to carry out the promises which have been made to them. Such concepts were quite alien to both men, and I believe it was because of this incomprehension that the essential character of the Kremlin's rule never changed. Its central principle was that a government makes decisions without reference to its obligations or promises. They believed that to find a suitable formula, and the right words and sentences to deal with the immediate situation, permitted them to fool people for ever. When Gorbachev eventually brought our meeting to an end he was still exhorting us, right up to the last moment, to find a way of returning to the state of affairs which had existed before 11 March. Indeed as we left, he told us that there were to be no negotiations 'until you have achieved that result'. When I turned to go out of the room he kindly advised me to sleep on what he had said, and to find a way to circumvent the problem! I had no intention of leaving him with the last word after what had gone on inside, so I walked back to him from the doorway and asked him to consider the negative consequences which would follow if we were coerced into capitulation.

The obduracy we had met was rather depressing, and we returned home down-hearted. We had gone to Moscow after hearing the report of a meeting which had taken place on 12 June between Kazimiera Prunskienė, the prime minister, her deputy, Algirdas Brazauskas, and Ryzhkov and Lukyanov. They had given me to believe that the meeting I have just described would bring negotiations closer, but Gorbachev's attitude seemed to imply that the situation had taken a step backwards. We had the feeling that we had again reached an impasse. I had only been back in Vilnius for a day when Prunskienė phoned me to say that Gorbachev had rung to ask for another meeting that very evening to discuss the preparation for negotiations. She and I were to be present. The new manœuvre seemed transparent to me, and I divined that Moscow had learned through the KGB or senior Communist party members that there were large and increasing differences between myself and Prunskienė. Of course the least friction at the higher levels of our administration might well encourage our opponents to exploit this in their own interest. As there were to be only three of us at the meeting now offered, Prunskienė only needed to side with Gorbachev to leave me isolated. I could then be shown to be intransigent and set on preventing the solution which would be of greatest benefit to all. The prospect seemed awful, and I feared Gorbachev had been advised that this would be a chance to see the 'Lithuanian split' acted out in his presence. He was, however, robbed of this pleasure – both then and later – because Kazimiera Prunskienė had agreed that we should present a common front to defend the nation's independence on each journey to Moscow because individual visits by her would confuse Moscow as to the real issues.

Although notice was short, we met to decide that we would be accompanied by two deputies on this journey, which took place on 27 June. Mrs Prunskienė proposed, as prime minister, that Česlovas Okinčycas (a lawyer who had the reputation of being one of the centrists in the Supreme Council) should travel with her. The choice was acceptable because Okinčycas was a Pole, who might be presented as unbiased in the conflict between Soviet and Lithuanian interests. I felt that his presence might also help neutralize the Soviet claim that the Lithuanian Poles were against independence. Then Prunskienė proposed, I thought rather abruptly, that no other senior officials should be taken to this meeting. I believe that this was because she wanted to exclude my deputy, Česlovas Stankevičius, who had accompanied me on the previous mission. He was determined and honest, but I knew that he had no enthusiasm for Prunskienė, so I acceded to her request for the sake of peace and quiet. Having settled this, I decided to invite Saulius Šaltenis, a writer (to whom politics was a totally new subject), to come as a witness to the proceedings, selecting him because I knew him to be an honest man and acute observer, an intellectual who was totally committed to Lithuanian independence. As far as I could tell, there was nothing about him to irritate either Prunskienė or Moscow. These arrangements seemed to satisfy us both, even though they had been cobbled together in haste, but unfortunately no one had been able to reach Okinčycas before we were ready to leave for the airport. When we realized this I proposed taking

Vladimir Jermolenko instead. He comes from Kaunas and is of Russian descent. He was duly invited, but as we were boarding the plane Okinčycas suddenly turned up, which left us with a delegation of five flying to Moscow.

When we arrived at the Soviet capital we were immediately driven to Gorbachev's dacha. It was an elegant classical building with a columned portico, standing in the forest, and must have been a country house on a great estate in the Tsar's time and one of Stalin's residences later. It was redolent of wealth and power, adorned with landscape paintings and rich carpets. As we arrived, Gorbachev himself came out to meet us. He was informally dressed, wearing a pullover without a tie or a jacket, and he smiled pleasantly. I remember feeling that his manner conveyed a working atmosphere, and even had a fleeting thought that matters might be concluded this time. Ryzhkov, Lukyanov and Yakovlev followed close behind him and when they had greeted us they asked us to wait a little, as they were preparing for a Congress of the Communist party of the Soviet Union, which was to take place in two days' time. They said they had not quite completed their business, but it was not long before we were called into the conference room, where they were already seated on the other side of the table. The thought crossed my mind that they looked like a flight of crows sitting on a telegraph wire, the most conservative at one end and the most liberal at the other! Between them they reflected the main streams of communist political thinking. First, there was Lukyanov, a communist, rigid and unbending as an anti-tank defence; next came Ryzhkov, the *nomenklatura* technocrat; then Gorbachev, the arch-manipulator of the whole system. Last in the row was Yakovlev, the most liberal of them and a committed advocate of *perestroika*. We looked each other up and down, and I introduced my delegation. As we settled to business, we suddenly understood why we had been called to this place, though no one had uttered a word. They were meeting us in order to prepare their statement to the party. It was their most important current concern, and their meeting with us meant that the Lithuanian question must have assumed a new significance.

The realization that the blockade had begun to backfire against Gorbachev was what underlay their concern; it had come home to him that his friends in the West were obviously unhappy about developments. An American journalist had recently asked me, in a live programme transmitted directly by satellite, about the implications for the blockade of the forthcoming summit meeting between Bush and Gorbachev. I had replied tersely: 'It could be a second Munich.' I also used the argument that the blockade was perverse as a concept, though it was paradoxically a recognition of the Lithuanian state 'because no state would blockade itself'. I had rubbed this message in by repeating a joke about a madman who fell over while he was running across rough country. He had hurt his leg, but became uncontrollably angry that it had let him down so badly, and so started hitting it mercilessly! The tale was intended to characterize the ridiculous political predicament in which Gorbachev had landed everybody by maintaining his assertion that Lithuania was legally part of the Soviet Union. Humour sticks. These things floated into my mind as we talked, and I realized that it had now become important for Gorbachev to present himself as 'successful in Lithuania' at his party meeting. This was why he was putting so much pressure on us, even though it would have been cheaper to relent. As I mulled over these thoughts Gorbachev asked me to give my account of the meeting we had concluded on the previous day, for the sake of those who had not been present, and then gave an abridged version of his own arguments. I reminded him that *our* aim had been 'to begin a real negotiation', using the opportunity to emphasize the need for both sides to be clear about their objectives and the topics to be discussed if this was to happen. I said that we must establish exactly what was to be negotiated beforehand, and pointed out that the process of elucidation, the preliminary stage, had in some sense already begun. Lithuania's objective in such negotiation would be the entire recovery of the prerogatives of a sovereign and independent state, with no external interference. Our discussions could be conducted in one of two forms: either by Lithuania and the Soviet Union negotiating directly, or by the three Baltic states negotiating together with the Soviet Union. I then summarized and concluded by stating directly: 'The question is whether we are to be "one plus one" or "three plus one".' Gorbachev responded by urging us to *compromise*. Significantly enough, he told us that if we were prepared to impose a *moratorium on the implications* of our Independence Act, he would no longer demand that we must annul the Act itself. He then compared our current political situation to that of two people in a boat which was rocking dangerously, and proposed a 'moratorium' in order to stabilize the boat. If this was done, he would promise help to rebuild Lithuanian industry and offer an invitation to reconsider the new agreements on the future of the Soviet Union. If these proposals suited us they could be implemented and then all would be well. If they did not work out afterwards, we could make up our minds on the basis of our experience and apply to leave the Union if we were then still so inclined.

This withdrawal of the demand that we must annul our Independence Act and return to the legal situation which existed before 11 March was useful. The demand had first been made by the deputies of the Third

Congress in angry reaction to the constitutional decisions which we had taken then, but now Gorbachev was prepared to reconsider the situation. As he made these points he talked clearly about our 'establishing a partnership'. The situation looked as if it was changing, and it seemed that we had become participants in a real negotiation for the first time, but we were unable to relax, and when Gorbachev proposed that we should discuss the Union agreement as the first item on the agenda, we were wary. To accept this proposal could undermine all the decisions we had taken on achieving independence. We saw his idea that 'separation from the Union' should be discussed only under prescribed conditions, and at a later date, as an old-style Soviet ploy. I tried to bring the conversation back to the things that concerned me and talked about the possibility of *negotiations* which would be acceptable to both countries. Prunskienė usefully expressed her views on this, and tried with Šaltenis's help to persuade Gorbachev to discontinue the blockade before formal negotiations began, as a goodwill gesture. However, Gorbachev turned this idea down emphatically, exclaiming abruptly: 'No: the moratorium *first*', his impatience showing his irritation that he had been unable to control the direction of the discussion. While his comments to me were short and unpleasant, he was more friendly toward Prunskienė whose arguments and presentation were different from mine. It was interesting to see how her presence changed Gorbachev's mood, but as I observed their exchange I became even more certain that it would be a grave error to give in to him. Effectively Gorbachev was failing to impose his style on the situation and he was becoming irritated. The discussion became very lively indeed, and while Ryzhkov joined in, Yakovlev and Lukyanov spoke very little. In fact Lukyanov just sat there, keeping quiet almost to the end, and once again it seemed to me as if he was keeping a watching brief over Gorbachev.

I had no qualifications for analysing the personalities of the Soviet *nomenklatura* in depth, nor much interest in trying to do so, but it struck me that these colleagues of Gorbachev's were men who lacked intellectual stature, and that Gorbachev himself was only too well aware of it. He often seemed to regard himself as being taller by a head than they were, and as having a strong personality. He came across as the successful leader of a gang, confident in his cunning, and he would obviously have been only too pleased to have dominated us in the same way. Demanding complete obedience, he was highly manipulative when things did not work out his way and would make a careful study of his opponents' weaknesses so as to discover ways of changing situations to his advantage. I sometimes imagined that gifts such as these would have made him an even more successful public figure in the West. However, as I reflected on these things I recognized that the political scene in which we were involved was not a drama we were observing from the sidelines. There were matters of deadly earnest in play, and I dared not take my own contribution for granted. These were sombre thoughts, and when I had the benefit of another man's observations on my participation in this meeting at a later point, it gave me much satisfaction. This happened when Saulius Šaltenis gave an interview to a French writer, in which he said:

> I was surprised by Landsbergis's style of conversation with Gorbachev . . . he spoke with ease and without inhibition, courageously, and as an equal amongst his peers. We must regard Landsbergis as a special case: he could be described as relentless; like a mosquito, he was always on the move, always in sight, always buzzing. He had a chronic cold, which seemed to put him at a disadvantage, but he voiced his feelings by putting terse questions like 'What are we saying? What are we talking about here?' and Gorbachev seemed to have no idea how to defend himself against this irritable mosquito, and he didn't like it. When Gorbachev said, 'Let's sit down as friends representing both sides', Landsbergis homed in, saying, 'Shall we establish which side we are to represent, the Republic of Lithuania or the Lithuanian Soviet Socialist Republic?' Gorbachev knew very well that it was against his interests to get involved in such unprecedented and exact definitions, but the relentless mosquito Landsbergis was quite undeterred by his manœuvres and would keep coming back saying, 'But Your Excellency has stated . . . ' or 'Your Excellency, could it be that you have not seen . . .', pressing requests for precise definition and explanation which simply unnerved Gorbachev.

I must put the record straight on Šaltenis's suggestion here that I referred to Gorbachev as 'Excellency' in this discussion. While I did of course use the term, as it was less familiar to the Soviets, it was deployed sparingly and only in my correspondence. Some people in Moscow and in Vilnius, especially those close to Gorbachev, took offence when I addressed the chairman of the Communist party of the Soviet Union and the head of the pseudo-socialist state in this way. Party members were accustomed to be called 'Comrade', and the expression 'Your Excellency' was repellent and even seemed abusive to them. However, my first reference to Gorbachev in these terms, made on 12 March, was purely and deliberately formal, and intended to define our relationship as reciprocal, as equal to equal, and to represent myself as seeking to be co-operative. To the writer Šaltenis my stance was both amusing and esoteric. In my personal contacts with Gorbachev, I addressed him as Mikhail Sergeyevich, adopting that style of Russian address used by the respectful friend, to show that our relationship was normal, that I had no intention of building psychological barriers and that our relationship was even better than in 1989. The course that my country was pursuing was entirely normal, and I had no reason to fall out with Gorbachev at a personal level, despite the political need to react harshly from time to time. Gorbachev liked familiarity on his own ground, and even when he had delivered a thunderbolt threat or administered an admonition, he would usually revert to a friendly and familiar manner, even addressing me by my first name, Vytautas, as if I were an old friend. His polished style and tactics were tangible, and this enabled the West to 'do business with him', because they appreciated his manner. There are all kinds of level of relationship in public life and the possibility for friends to be on first-name terms, but I never ventured to call him Misha, the shortened and more intimate form of Mikhail.

The meeting held in the dacha on the outskirts of Moscow was conducted in a constructive atmosphere and ended on friendly terms. I liked Yakovlev, who had the livelier personality, rather better than the fossilized Lukyanov. The most important development, however, was that Mikhail Sergeyevich had changed his tone even from the previous day, and now at last had dropped his demand that we revert to the situation as it was before 11 March. He now spoke only of our finding a formula to delay the Act, or rather to postpone its full implementation until some unspecified time. This was really a very different proposal from his earlier requirement, and had been dictated at short notice, literally overnight, by his political needs. Even though Gorbachev had begun intransigently, saying, 'We won't budge from our present position until you invoke the moratorium we require . . . Explain the position to your people in whatever way you can, and we'll explain to ours', the reality of this meeting was that it had been called to cut a deal, and we were aware of this from the start. The Soviets interpreted this 'moratorium' as a freeze on all the legal and social developments which were rooted in the decisions taken on 11 March, but they did not make this implication clear. In Gorbachev's own words, a formula now had to be found which allowed him to start 'the process' of lifting the blockade which he had personally imposed on our country. Its outcome had become an embarrassment to him, and it was necessary for him to take this action without losing face, and once he realized this he was prepared to act quickly. For our part, the most important development was the recognition that the Soviet Union was at last prepared to negotiate with us once we had introduced the required moratorium. As Moscow had previously insisted that there could be *no* negotiations between Lithuania and the Soviet Union, we felt we had at last accomplished something tangible. We returned to Vilnius with some satisfaction at this achievement but an objective view of our future made it seem far from bright. On consideration, one might even feel that our prospects were frightening. As the delegation flew back from Moscow, Prunskienė showed that she was upset and angry because I had made no decision, and had promised Gorbachev nothing. I too was worried, but my concern was with the possibility that our report would divide our parliamentary colleagues. I had been under considerable strain through the meetings, and was now suffering from a hellish headache.

Gorbachev had demanded his moratorium. We knew that most Lithuanians would see this concession as an act of submission to him, and I was left to agonize over the question of how we could please Moscow without sacrificing the main interests of our own country. As we puzzled over finding a formula which might allow the moratorium to be turned to our benefit, Gorbachev was showering promises and deciding to terminate the blockade. The issues were serious for him too. The knowledge that this policy had failed brought him face to face with the spectre of even worse political losses, and we were soon told that he could not afford any further 'loss of face'. The president of the Soviet Union must now have something to show; so things had been so arranged that the next move was expected to come from us. We knew we must be very careful to do nothing which would imperil the opportunity which had at last opened up for real negotiations to begin.

CHAPTER 16

Moratorium: a waiting strategy

The word moratorium came into our political vocabulary for the first time on 27 June 1990. It was not Gorbachev who introduced it but rather our own prime minister, Kazimiera Prunskienė, when she issued the statement which announced a 'moratorium of our Declaration of Independence which will take effect on 29 May'. What exactly this announcement signified was vague, but its constitutional implications were furiously discussed everywhere. It was immediately obvious that the statement had a rather doubtful history because it had emerged on the prime minister's initiative, but had not been finally agreed by the Council of Ministers or by the Supreme Council, before being made public. As the question was explored more deeply we were unable even to discover whether ministers had voted on the statement or even whether they had all been given the chance to read the text before it was published. Indeed, the question about what had really gone on is still unresolved because the minutes of the Cabinet discussion which were taken by Algirdas Saudargas, the minister for foreign affairs, have since disappeared. When the public heard the announcement the outcry was so great that I felt obliged to intervene to calm the situation. When I did this, I announced, simply: 'Others may propose. We shall decide', and referred the matter to the Supreme Council for immediate review. The resulting debate reflected the public furore, and made it quite clear that Prunskienė's initiative was ill-prepared, while many suspected that it may have been the product of a Soviet directive. The crux of the problem lay in her statement that the moratorium which she had declared was to continue through 'a period of negotiations', a formulation which clearly failed to specify the period of time involved, and it took no imagination to foresee that it could drag on in the circumstances which we faced. To give the Soviets such an obvious opportunity for delay would be to provide them with unlimited freedom to undermine what we had achieved. We should have been virtually certain of waiting many years for the constitutional uncertainties to be resolved; indeed it would have been in the interest of the other side to postpone the answer for ever. These points weighed heavily and were discussed intensively. The government was fiercely criticized, because a clear suspicion that Prunskienė was implementing Moscow's policies had now penetrated the public mind.

At this point it is important to recall that the idea of agreeing to inter-pose 'a freeze in the consequences of the declaration of independence without losing sight of its merits' had already been proposed by François Mitterrand and Helmut Kohl in their correspondence with me. Various diplomatic advisers to the United States and Britain had also taken the same line, and Senator Lugar had also telephoned on George Bush's behalf to register his agreement. On 23 May the Supreme Council responded to these moves with a resolution reaffirming our wish to negotiate with the Soviet Union, and stating: 'Any consequences of the Acts of 11 March 1990 which may affect those interests which have been defined by both parties as the objects of negotiation shall be temporarily suspended from the time when talks begin.' This formula had been care-fully designed to reduce the opportunities of the Soviet negotiators to strike unilateral attitudes which might interfere with our freedom to achieve a reasonable outcome. Even at that point in the discussion I remember Prime Minister Prunskienė maintaining loudly that this provi-sion was not sufficient to satisfy Gorbachev's expectations. Now, before even a week had passed, she was busy introducing her 'moratorium' on her own terms. She believed that she had a suitable formula for resolv-ing the difficult issues and could certainly boast that she had special contacts in both East and West, but she still did her best to avoid being challenged, and it was not difficult to see that her proposal was muddled and dangerous in the extreme.

In late June Gorbachev made a dogmatic statement reiterating his demand for the moratorium and asserting that it was now 'urgently necessary to resolve the situation in Lithuania'. This statement, however, was accompanied by the declaration that his pre-condition for lifting the economic blockade was that we should 'turn back from inde-pendence'. The blockade was of course a tool deliberately chosen at that time in order to frighten our people into submission, and our influential Lithuanian 'opposition', influenced by deputy prime minis-ter Brazauskas, found it useful for this very reason, as did their friends in Moscow. These domestic scaremongers were now busy telling us that fuel supplies would rapidly become exhausted and that our trac-tors, combine harvesters and transport vehicles would soon be at a standstill, that a serious shortage of fodder would follow and livestock would then have to be slaughtered. Agriculture would then, they said, be in ruins, and we would have famine on our hands. We were clearly facing a spiral of ruin, or else a spiral of mischief, because these blunt messages sowed division. While many wanted to stand firm on principle and said we must not yield an inch, others demanded submis-sion, compromise, even capitulation. As a result tension increased everywhere. It became obvious that we needed to find a formula which would both include the concept of the moratorium and conserve the nation's independence, a formula that allowed negotiation to begin but which could not be interpreted as implying our return to the Soviet Union, nor give the Soviets any additional pretext for pushing their claim that their jurisdiction encompassed Lithuania, its territory and people. We had no wish to have our hard-won achievements legally reversed and destroyed.

It was necessary to find the right form of words, and we prepared many drafts for the promulgation of the required moratorium. I myself worked hard and prepared no fewer than four drafts. Each was different, and all were carefully discussed and amended. However, I gained no praise from our detractors for these laborious attempts to ensure the right outcome. They made propaganda of the delays and started claiming that I had no firm opinion of my own: 'he would not suggest so many alternatives otherwise!' When I learned of this criticism, I replied that we must explore every aspect of the problem and every possible response to it, if only to know which were the best ideas and that these and only these would appear in the *final* draft. In the end, I was satisfied, and took the document to the Supreme Council, where I explained that its wording would satisfy Gorbachev because we had conceded the word moratorium which was so important to him. However, we could also be certain that it safeguarded our achievements. The Council accepted my view but went on to protect its position further by declaring that my document was 'a statement', rather than a 'resolution of the Council'. We also decided that its preamble should be followed by the formulation that the Council, in seeking bilateral inter-state negotiations between the Republic of Lithuania and the Soviet Union, herewith declared a moratorium from the *beginning of such negotiations*, and for the next one hundred days. It was another safeguard which imposed a clear time limit on our concession, while the fact that it could not take effect before negotiations had actually begun implied that Soviet involvement in these negotiations was a recognition of our Lithuanian state. In addition, the fact that our moratorium, which was to be announced on 29 June, was to be *delayed* in its effect until negotiations had *actually started*, emphasized the fact that the Acts of 11 March and our subsequent legislation were not being immediately repealed. Of course the legislation which stemmed from the Acts of Independence was *suspended*, but it was also clear that this suspension applied only to subsequent legislation and was for a limited time only. Thus, we were manifestly not reneging on our fundamental legal rights, nor on independence. The statement implied a slowing down of the effects of certain actions of the Lithuanian state, but could not be interpreted in any way as an act of annulment of that state. Nor did it imply any discontinuity in its legal basis or jurisdiction, as it did not say that we would make no use of our legal rights, or that we were suspending the legislation which derived either from the constitution or the Independence Acts, only that we would not pass new legislation during the set period of a hundred days. None of these things would diminish or infringe our sovereignty. On the contrary, the formulation was designed to confirm that the Soviets acknowledged the legal force of our Act of Independence: they would not have demanded that we shelve it had it been otherwise!

Our statement was concerned with matters other than what was to happen when negotiations actually began, and it noted that there were preconditions to the aims and objectives of the discussions which must be acknowledged and agreed by the representatives of both countries beforehand. These were additional safeguards entered by the Supreme Council to ensure that everyone involved knew precisely when the real negotiation had begun and exactly what it was all about. They were also intended to make it plain that we Lithuanians would agree to begin the negotiations only when an acceptable protocol had been signed. The aim of our document was to establish the parity of the national delegations as lawful and equal representatives and to confirm that this bilateral negotiation implied an official recognition of our state. We had also included a clause authorizing us to extend or terminate the moratorium once it had been declared, a provision which gave us an additional flexibility to end the negotiations automatically if discussions reached breaking-point. In these ways we had considered every eventuality, including the possibility of a Soviet attack on Lithuania or of our Supreme Council being incapacitated by the imposition of a puppet government. Under such circumstances the moratorium would simply cease to exist! This outcome would be the completion of a set of ten cleverly devised safety precautions which would come into operation as a chain reaction if circumstances turned against us. Our motivation in all this came from the heart, because we had been on intimate terms with treachery and injustice over a long period, and had an intense awareness of the wrong that had been imposed by force on our nation in the past. Despite these precautions, however, the concept of the moratorium brought old fears to the fore, and I saw tears in many eyes as we struggled to find a form of words to protect our freedom of action in the potentially dreadful situation which we were facing. It was not just among our working friends in the Sąjūdis group of deputies that we saw this fear: it was present in the wider community. The very idea of this constitutional moratorium embodied something awful for Lithuanians as it touched on their deepest political and psychological sensibilities, so much so that there were people threatening to set themselves on fire when it was declared because they were afraid that it implied abdication of our independence.

My own heart spoke against any kind of moratorium, and I said as much when I called on the Supreme Council to vote on the statement. However, I raised my hand against myself because of the realities which we were facing. When the statement was adopted, our colleagues on the left congratulated me, and foreign journalists rushed to comment on 'my victory', and to ask if this outcome made me happy. When I told them that it did *not*, they seemed uncomprehending. Even when Gorbachev called the blockade off on the following day I remained unhappy because I was less than sure that he had analysed and fully understood our statement and the safeguards which it contained. However, I was reassured to the extent that I knew that he needed our assent to the word 'moratorium' more than anything else because he would now be able to present himself at the Congress of the Communist party of the Soviet Union with the message that 'Lithuania had relented'. Of course he would imply that he had broken Lithuania's will without bloody intervention, but this was very important to his line. I remain doubtful whether he fully understood at the time that the Lithuanian people's determination to retain their independence had not really ended. Nor did the foreign press understand. Its representatives thought we had made a concession which verged on capitulation, and Soviet propaganda made the best of this story-line. Such consequences were painful for us to observe and it was difficult to correct their perception because we were unable to say too loudly that we thought we had taken Gorbachev and the Moscow hard-liners for a ride. In our view, our statement embodied a certain sleight of hand because it outlined the moratorium as becoming effective *only* when the Soviet Union had signed the protocol with Lithuania *as a separate state* before beginning negotiations. It was a formulation which implied that they would have conceded our major aspiration before proceeding further.

For ourselves, we had no intention of signing any agreement which was not bilateral, or which would undermine our competence to act in our national interest. We certainly did not want to become committed to participation in a bright new communist dream of a future under Moscow's domination, though it was the wrong moment to trumpet these feelings abroad. While our statement had a steely core, its surface seemed to commit us to a rather bleak situation, and this realization overshadowed the relief we now felt at the lifting of the blockade. In other circumstances, this would have seemed a victory, but our hearts were somewhat heavy, and remained so until the end of December when both sides finally woke up to the fact that the fundamental issues between us had yet to be resolved. That, however, was a step ahead in the train of events, as the oil began to flow and our industries began to function once again. It had cost us hundreds of millions of roubles, and even though Lithuania had continued to supply the Soviet Union with meat and other foods throughout that difficult period, we received no compensation. Its ending meant that our people were able to relax and feel less frightened, but there was much resentment because many of them were naïve enough to believe the version of events which the Soviet news agency Tass put about. Its propaganda blithely purveyed the idea that we had retracted the Independence Act and made the country some kind of Soviet republic again. Many people therefore felt that our conduct had been outrageous, and we suffered their displeasure. Whether this criticism came from inside or outside the country, it was painful, not least when Yelena Bonner, the widow of Andrei Sakharov whom we admired and respected, announced her 'disappointment at our submission' in a public statement during a visit to the United States. The Estonian Parliament, which had often itself vacillated, also expressed 'astonishment at what had been done', and our recovery of esteem was a slow business, though we eventually achieved it by quietly explaining the subtleties involved. The passage of time also helped to show that our tactics had been rational. The pity was that people in the West saw only that Gorbachev had lifted the blockade on Lithuania, while almost no one seemed to take on board what we believed to be the much more important point – that the Soviet Union had at last actually agreed to start the negotiation as a result of our move. We had to run the gauntlet of endless criticism, but in the end it was a diplomatic triumph of the first magnitude for us.

On the same day, 29 June, the Supreme Council passed a resolution, which, despite its importance, attracted very little resistance, to suspend 'for the period of official inter-state negotiations', the implementation of any determinations which might result from the Acts it had passed on 11 March, which could be deemed to reflect interests which were to be the subject of negotiation by either of the parties involved. Having thus adjusted our image, we left for Tallinn for a meeting of the Council of the Baltic States on 30 June, in a calmer frame of mind because the announcement of the moratorium was accompanied by this new declaration. The meeting was notable for its active correspondence with the European institutions, whom we were asking to concede formal links at governmental level, a move which would of course imply recognition of our collective position. One of our letters asked the European Parliament to accept an accredited inter-parliamentary delegation to represent the needs of the Baltic states at Strasbourg officially. A positive response from Anders Bjorck, president of the Council of Europe's Parliamentary Assembly, to the request that our governments should be granted special guest status at its meetings allowed us to speak officially at its gathering at Helsinki in the following year, when we applied for full membership of the Council. Amid this flurry of activity we also issued an important general declaration which emphasized the independent statehood, *de jure*, of each of our countries, and protested the invalidity of the continued constitutional claims of the Soviet Union over our populations and territories. This last declaration was addressed to all the European governments and asked them to express their goodwill, but was directed especially to the Nordic Council with the request that it act as an intermediary between us and the Soviet Union 'in the organization of negotiations for the re-establishment of full statehood and the liquidation of the anomalies in north-eastern Europe which are the consequences of the Second World War'.

Our starting-point in making this request was clear. We were entering the crucial next phase of discussion with the Soviets without the assistance of any intermediaries. Lithuania had chosen to be an independent state, and we did not anticipate anyone attempting to change our minds on that matter, whatever discussions lay ahead of us. Nothing in any forthcoming negotiations with the Soviet Union could impede our legal claim to independence or our freedom to establish normal relationships with other states. While these assumptions seemed simple to us, I had to keep explaining them to the western media and to the officials of western governments, who seemed incapable of shrugging off the idea that the only real issue was our relationship with Gorbachev. As a result, I had to repeat the continuous message that we had only one mandate, which was to restore our independence unequivocally, and point out that the Soviet claim to rule Lithuania was based at best on the flimsy foundation of a bogus election in 1940 which had sent representatives to a puppet Parliament installed by an occupying army which had just dislodged our own government and brutalized the population. The resulting institutions had no real legal standing then, nor could the passage of time add respectability to those arrangements. Lithuania had never been a Soviet republic, but was rather an occupied country. The present impasse put us in a difficult situation because our consent, even on a temporary basis, to any proposal that we should remain in the Soviet Union or join its Confederation would convey the idea that our country had joined the Soviet Union legally and voluntarily. We were a properly elected government with no public mandate for such a move. If by some quirk the deputies of our Supreme Council should take leave of their senses, or submit to outside pressures and pass a vote to reject our independence, their decision would be illegal because they had been elected to achieve a contrary purpose.

In accordance with the provisions of our statement on the moratorium, both negotiating delegations would be required to sign a special protocol before being empowered to move further. On 5 July, a week after our meeting with Gorbachev, the Supreme Council passed a resolution committing itself to the forthcoming negotiation by establishing a preparatory commission. At this stage we avoided the selection of members for that delegation because of the earlier decision that both parties must be agreed on the aims and conditions of the exercise before the actual negotiations began. There was much careful reasoning underlying that determination, and we saw no purpose in proceeding further until there was agreement on these preliminaries. Our representatives would be fully accredited only when this hurdle had been crossed. The mechanism for deciding these matters was the special political and diplomatic commission set up for the purpose. Unfortunately this requirement produced a phase of difficult and even unpleasant discussions when we found that we had to explain the purpose of the negotiations time and time again and refer our parliamentary opposition to our statement, which indicated clearly that the negotiations were to be conducted by the Supreme Council itself. This had been declared previously, but now voices of dissent were heard and we were accused of 'not trusting the government', and arguing that 'such negotiations are usually carried out by governments'. We replied that we did not wish to prolong the processes of selection or negotiation. Political disagreements might arise between the government and the Supreme Council and they could be exploited. The situation we faced was unstable and could degenerate, and the world had not shown itself keen to support us. The Soviet Union might well put a governmental delegation in a position where it felt obliged to accept a deal which was unsuitable to the country. The Supreme Council had the duty of ratification and might well refuse to do so in such circumstances. We could prevent the Soviets announcing to the world that 'Lithuania was divided, the delegations have reached agreement but their stupid Supreme Council will not ratify it'. If tensions such as these could be expected, one could foresee how difficult it might be for the Supreme Council to reject anything compromising the government's position. It seemed quite clear to us that such eventualities should be avoided, and it was therefore better that the negotiators should report directly to the Supreme Council rather than go through the government, which would itself then have to refer issues on to the Supreme Council. There should be a single back-stop to the whole process so that problems in the negotiations would be dealt with immediately rather than indirectly. If there was disagreement it could be put to the vote, and the matter would be resolved in the public eye after a proper debate. Fortunately our members in the Council understood and agreed, and they confirmed the authority of the Supreme Council to take charge of the negotiations. The outcome was clear, but nevertheless the same arguments were furiously repeated on 21 August, when the Supreme Council selected its chairman to head the delegation of negotiators.

Before this phase was reached Prime Minister Prunskienė had asserted privately – to a wide group of hearers – that she knew things which she could not possibly reveal, and felt assured that she could get a suitable agreement for the whole country. Her demeanour in all this was somewhat mysterious, but she made it plain she must be allowed to negotiate without restriction if she was to procure this golden fleece. It was, however, her particular misfortune that general trust was not forthcoming, perhaps because her part in the recent involvement of the government in the potentially compromising affair of the voluntary moratorium was too well remembered. We now have the advantage of access to KGB documents which have since emerged, and they have yielded some insight into what was really going on in her mind. It appears that she had already given her approval to the Kremlin proposals to take Lithuania back into the Soviet fold, though in the form of the new 'Confederation'. Fortunately her ploy was side-stepped when on 5 July the Supreme Council decided that its Presidium should form a Preparatory Commission jointly with the government in advance of the negotiations. The question of the principles underlying the future relationship between Lithuania and the Soviet Union was to be put on its agenda, with the request that the discussions should be reported to the Supreme Council. It was also decided to establish groups of experts to undertake the preparatory work of discussing the operational structures for the negotiation in liaison with corresponding groups in the Soviet government. We announced that our negotiating team would be nominated only when Lithuania and the Soviet Union had come to full agreement on these necessary protocols.

Despite this clear announcement, there was now a crude campaign to pressurize us into naming our negotiators immediately. The pressures were huge, and a claim that our Supreme Council was ineffective was spread about, first in the Soviet Union, then in Lithuania, and finally on the world stage. We learned that the Soviet Union had chosen its representatives when a Soviet presidential decree in August announced a delegation led by Nikolai Ryzhkov. Rumours were then circulated that the Lithuanians 'could not agree among themselves' on their delegation. There seemed to be a conspiracy to rush us into forming a delegation, but we found these attempts to impose foreign expectations on us unacceptable and continued in our own way. We had decided on our priorities and we would stick to them. First the reports of the expert consultant groups must be received, and the work of the Preparatory Commission completed. We were determined that the delegation would not be named before we had achieved full agreement on the subjects to be negotiated and knew where our room for manœuvre lay. Until then we were not prepared to play silly games.

While this was going on I was asked more than once by interviewers from the press to compare politics and chess. They had probably learned that I had taken second and fourth place in our national chess championships back in 1953. In this case I explained our situation by analogy with chess as 'a tournament in which we did not accept our opponent's strategy'. We very definitely played this game according to our own Lithuanian strategy, which is always the best one for us, as was proved in our history as far back as the Battle of Grünwald in 1410. Two great armies had then faced each other, the Knights of the Teutonic Order and the allied warriors of the Lithuanian and Polish states. Neither side would start the battle, because both believed that the first to attack would put itself at a disadvantage by having to leave its well-prepared defences. At last the crusaders sent a knight forward carrying two swords. One was for the Lithuanian Grand Duke Vytautas, the other for his cousin Jogaila, king of Poland, and each was accompanied by the insulting message: 'Here is a present to arm the weaponless.' It was a provocation to which Vytautas, an experienced strategist and the acknowledged commander in the battle which was to take place, did not reply. The Teutonic Knights could not contain themselves; they advanced and were totally crushed. In every game and in every battle someone dictates the play or determines the style. Whether in football or boxing, in chess or in politics, in business or in war, it is important to impose one's style, and we refused to adapt to the Soviet style!

We were being pressurized to form our delegation from the day we established the Preparatory Commission on 11 July. Had we succumbed at that stage we would have had to face the next provocation only too quickly. We preferred to await the report of the Commission's work. Of course we had to give some sort of reasonable reply while we waited, so we said that the selection of the delegation had been passed to Landsbergis and Prunskienė, and that its accreditation would need to be confirmed. We did not elaborate further, although there were many prods and pressures from the Opposition and from those who clearly wanted to see a split between the government and the Supreme Council. At one point a group of prominent people presented a petition claiming that the Supreme Council was not only ineffective but was obstructing the government's work, and that it was time to think about new elections. The petition had been prepared by two of Prunskienė's allies. When this became evident, some of the signatories awakened to the fact that they had been duped into signing, and then asked for their signatures to be removed. It was an incident which reflected our disunity at the time, but despite these problems, some quiet movement was taking place below the surface. We were working towards agreement with Russia. In May I went to Prague by invitation of Vaclav Havel, and stopped over in Moscow for secret comprehensive talks with Boris Yeltsin which had been arranged informally through private contacts. We agreed to start negotiations with Russia at this meeting (which was followed up on 19 July when a delegation led by my deputy, Česlovas Stankevičius, was established). Having made this arrangement we then went on to meet the heads of all three Baltic states and Russia at Jūrmala, near Riga in Latvia on 27 July, and we agreed to begin work on mutual bilateral agreements without any preconditions. It was a move which exerted further pressure on Gorbachev.

August was one of our busiest times for visits and meetings, though it was a holiday month for the Supreme Council. We were on the alert for sudden moves by the Soviets and took the precaution of asking the Council to delegate additional authority to its Presidium during this period. What was requested was the power to legislate on an emergency basis, subject to appropriate endorsement when the Council reassembled in September. The opposition blew the matter up out of all proportion, claiming that the Presidium wanted to introduce a dictatorship. When they were in office, communists had recognized no limits to their powers, but now they were in opposition they had become zealous democrats. Led by Algirdas Brazauskas and Vladimiras Beriozovas, neither of whom ever seemed to say very much because their views were normally voiced by others, the opposition was vociferous, even brazen in its attack on us. They were a band of brothers who seemed to enjoy obstructing parliamentary proceedings by filibuster or by contriving questions which had little value but had to be answered because of parliamentary protocol. Their manner could be inordinately patronizing, as if they felt that nobody knew how the Supreme Council worked as well as they did. They often grated on everyone else's nerves by drawing out discussion to an intolerable degree. When the proposal to allow the Presidium to exercise temporary legislative powers was rejected at their instigation by only two votes, I responded with the proposition that the Supreme Council should indeed retain its responsibilities but that its members should forgo their holiday rather than leave the state without its legislative body at so difficult a time. The opposition had been overjoyed when it succeeded in defeating the Presidium's proposal, and was now hoist with its own petard. They were quite unable to change their minds, so they had to accept my offer and buckle down to work through what should have been their vacation!

On its own initiative, the Central Committee of the Lithuanian Communist party dispatched accusations about us to Moscow, and the Secretariat there passed resolutions repeating 'allegations made by comrades in Lithuania' about the 'dreadful situation there': decentralization, decollectivization, the dismantling of Soviet rule and the restoration of totalitarian, bourgeois dictatorship! Meanwhile, on 7 August we finalized our views on the protocol which we deemed would be necessary to safeguard the aims and conditions of our side in the forthcoming negotiations. We had to ensure that our delegation would be quite clear about its mandate and which issues could not be decided without authority from the legislature. Shortly after this, Ryzhkov agreed that our commission, led by Bronius Kuzmickas, should go to Moscow to prepare for the actual negotiations. They were met there by his representatives, Yevgeny Maslukov and Genady Ryevenko, who turned out to be most unhelpful. Their manner was abrupt, and they scorned our representatives, who they said were not sufficiently high-ranking to deal with the necessary business. On this basis they defined the meeting as an unofficial one, and were even more dismissive of our view that there must be agreement about protocol before the substantive negotiation opened. Even worse, at the first meeting to be convened on what they agreed was an official basis they insisted on describing the procedure as a 'consultation' rather than a negotiation. At this point I became involved because we believed it was necessary that the fundamental protocol should also reflect the understanding that Lithuania and the Soviet Union were two separate states preparing to engage in a bilateral negotiation to end an anomalous situation which had endured since 1940. My first act was to hand a copy of our delegation's draft proposal to Ryzhkov in person, this being done to ensure that he had been seen to receive it. When he responded to my gesture with a proposal for 'a new Union agreement', I immediately reminded him that our response to this suggestion had been given long since, and that *no* Union agreement would be signed by the representatives of Lithuania!

On 21 August we finally determined the membership of our negotiating team. It was to consist of eight people, three of whom would be selected by Mrs Prunskienė and three by myself. She showed considerable anger when she realized that she had not been appointed leader of the delegation, and even tried to decline nomination, though this must have been mere bluff because, when the Supreme Council approved all eight names, she calmed down. The first meeting was held on 2 October in Moscow, and its outcome was a communiqué on the forthcoming bilateral negotiations. Its text stated only that that 'negotiations would be held', and that the Soviet Union and Lithuania would participate, but the foreign press interpreted it as a statement that negotiations had actually started. Clearly they had not, though we felt well pleased with ourselves when the statement was signed, and felt it was a diplomatic achievement in its own right. Indeed I was sufficiently excited to offer Ryzhkov an autographed copy of the communiqué as a souvenir of the event, and to ask for his signature in return, while Aleksandras Abišala, another member of our delegation, claims to have cried out with joy when he saw Ryzhkov reciprocate. Indeed, that first day's work was useful, because we set up a joint Commission charged with preparing everything that was needed. One of the most important priorities on our side was to achieve an agreement about our trade relations for the next year, while the Soviets believed it was an urgent necessity to resolve the question of paying pensions to their retired army officers living in Lithuania. We managed to agree. They then tried to tell us to add members to our delegation, informing us that the views of those who opposed our aims, such as representatives of the managers of the factories in Lithuania which were still under the control of the Soviet ministries, members of Yedinstvo, the Russian–Soviet movement, and Polish Lithuanians who were against independence, were absolutely necessary to the discussions. We refused point-blank. It was, we said, the prerogative of the Lithuanian state to select its delegation, and I asked Ryzhkov bluntly whether such people would sit on his side of the table or ours. He responded evasively, saying it did not matter where they sat, but my point was made, and he gave in. It was no surprise, however, for us to find that the representatives of these Bolshevik fundamentalists, and other shadowy activists from Lithuania, were to be seen around Moscow and nearby in the offices of the Kremlin. These people had probably been promised their place at the table. Now they were lurking around the edges, and they were clearly being heard, because during our second meeting with Ryzhkov we were accused of being 'unwilling to listen to those of our own people whose opinions differed from ours', and attacked for refusing to incorporate them into our delegation. I countered these proposals by suggesting that he might set us an example by inviting representatives of the coal-miners from the Donbas who were then on strike, or some representative of the democratic forces who were in obvious disagreement with everything the Soviet Union stood for, perhaps Mrs Novodvorskaya, the dissident democrat who was openly and relentlessly opposing Gorbachev. 'Let them join your delegation, Mr

Ryzhkov,' I suggested. He immediately dropped the question and it was not raised again.

Our demand for a basic protocol was placed on the agenda of the second meeting, but the other side insisted that the starting date of the negotiations should be agreed and announced to the world first. Of course we were unable to assent. We had committed ourselves to a moratorium which would begin when formal negotiations opened, and the present proposal would have turned this situation to their benefit. For this reason we had a different priority and demanded that agreement on the protocol should come first. Such an agreement could well fix the starting date, but it would also state the purpose and the conditions of negotiation. The situation remained poised, and the Soviet delegation pretended to do some work on the protocol but failed to produce anything. In the mean time we prepared a number of drafts and indicated possible concessions. We then suggested that if we could not agree on a shared position, we could at least draft a document which showed both positions so that everyone knew exactly what we were dealing with. This was agreed, and the positions were set out side by side. Once the whole document had been put together their position looked rather ridiculous, because their thesis that Lithuania was a republic of the Soviet Union was placed alongside documents which referred to the peace treaty between Lithuania and the Soviet Union in 1920 in which the Soviet Union had given up all future claim to Lithuania, the account of the Molotov–Ribbentrop Pact and the annexation of Lithuania that followed, and their own eventual denunciation of what had happened then. It was clear that publication of documents telling both sides of the story, which laid our hard facts alongside their claim, would have damaged their credibility. They abandoned this idea, but were strangely stuck in their old position and continued to insist that Lithuania had volunteered to enter the Soviet Union. (Ten years later they are still doing so.) We saw that no movement was taking place, and again asked them to set down for us their own preconditions for proceeding. They agreed, but then had second thoughts, and nothing happened.

Ten days went by in this way, and the Soviets had still not found anything constructive to contribute to the formulation of a protocol. It is likely that they were stalling, believing that the world would admire them for setting no preconditions, while condemning Lithuania for losing so much goodwill by its insistence on essentially fruitless conditions so as to limit the Soviet Union's room for manœuvre. They saw us as being in a predicament, and were happy to let us stew in it without giving any assistance. While this was going on, we were pressurized by the fact that foreigners often seemed to be taking the Soviet view. Whenever this happened in my presence, I made a point of saying that the Soviet side *had* set its preconditions fifty years before. Soviet armed forces had been stationed on our soil since then, not the other way round, because there had been no Lithuanian occupation of Moscow. Then, when I was asked why we talked about 'equalizing the conditions of negotiation', I would explain that we were acutely aware that the Soviets had been blockading our borders, had interfered with our imports and exports, and were threatening yet more economic sanctions. These matters were the basis of our concern about the preconditions of discussion. We must some-times have seemed very unfriendly, but we had to be forceful to deal with these difficult points. We would get nowhere without being firm. Such questions had to be tackled repeatedly. Even when we seemed to get nowhere at the time, our frankness did win us respect in the end.

Increasingly we sensed that the reason the Soviets wanted to begin negotiations was because of western pressure. However, it was clear that they could not grasp the concept of two fully separate negotiating parties representing two separate states. As a result the distinction between 'them' and 'us' remained beyond them so far as Lithuania was concerned. They perceived the Soviet Union as a single nation and showed it in their detailed comments, as when they said that the negotia-tions should be minuted as taking place between two delegations, not two states! One could almost see them thinking that even if our delegation thought of itself as representing its country, it was our eccentricity because 'Lithuania is nothing but a region'. Their problem was a well-known one, but it seemed improbable that people with these attitudes would concede much to us on the question of sovereign rights. There were obvious compromises which could emerge from the negotiations, however, and even a general agreement would have enabled us to move towards fulfilling the requirements of our statement. However, the team we were facing seemed in no hurry to move the situation on and appeared happy to torment us with sarcastic warnings and lectures on political expertise, while failing to agree to anything positive. Soon it became plain that their procrastination was another means of exerting maximum pressure in the hope of compromising our position by attrib-uting the delay to our 'reluctance to accept compromise'. They wanted international approval, and at the same time to keep everything in their own hands. The discussion about whether the negotiations would or would not confirm Lithuanian independence was seen in terms of whether our country could be 'released' from the Soviet Union, the implication being that Lithuania was Soviet territory. We had to be forced to say that we were a part of that Union as a condition of being allowed to ask for permission to leave it. The casuistry was subtle. From a Soviet viewpoint we would be acknowledging what they had always believed about Lithuania, and we would be seen as having recognized the annexation of our country. From our point of view it would imply the retrospective legitimation of everything which they had done on our territory. Our case for independence would have been given away at a stroke and Soviet claims to Lithuania's territory would have been acknowledged in a simple act. Had we accepted this blandishment our independence would have been lost.

This black comedy went on and on, and nothing emerged. When the Supreme Council began its new session in Vilnius, our prime minister began to suggest that we had already missed the optimum moment for negotiation. She gave the impression that such negotiations would have already been far advanced if she had been chosen to lead the delegation, or if the required authority had been transferred to the Council of Ministers. As Kuwait had just been occupied by Iraq, the world's attention was fixed on the Gulf and interest had moved away from Lithuania. This shift in the interest of the world's press away from the Baltic countries improved Gorbachev's hand considerably. Prunskienė implied that Gorbachev had virtually 'agreed to allow us to leave', and increasingly insinuated that we had 'missed the boat because we had failed to exploit the opportunity he had given us'. These views were widely broadcast outside Lithuania, but the reality of what was going on reflected Prunskienė's understanding with Gorbachev more than anything else. Her memoirs, which express much self-pity and project much blame, say a lot about how Gorbachev promised to 'go on to lead Lithuania into Europe'. It is, however, a claim which simply does not bear scrutiny: Bronius Kuzmickas, who was at a meeting with Gorbachev, has described Gorbachev's conditions as being summed up in a single clause, i.e. 'subject to Lithuania's remaining in the Soviet Union'. To put things quite simply Prunskienė has conveniently suppressed this fact.

At this stage it would seem that Lithuania was regarded by the western powers as a stubborn nuisance. They were uncomfortable with what we claimed for ourselves, and thought that everyone would be better off if they ignored us, especially when we had dared to antagonize Gorbachev, whose personal charisma, some insisted, would even have made him acceptable as the president of the United States! Western politicians and journalists told us repeatedly that Gorbachev 'would like to help you, but is not in a position to do so at present', and described the Soviet situation as 'delicate and unstable'. They made much of the idea that the Soviet army and the communist fundamentalists represented a force which 'might well take over the government if given the opportunity'. Such an outcome would be catastrophic for the West and of course for

Lithuania. Of course, we were told, the West felt badly about our position, but we should understand the need, first to find a political solution, and secondly not to endanger Gorbachev's position. They would explain that we all shared a truly common interest, and I would patiently respond as before that the people of Lithuania had not given us any mandate 'to join the Soviet Union'. I would try to show that we were not intransigent, that we could see and appreciate the problems associated with Gorbachev's career and world policies. Occasionally there were people who took a less self-interestedly 'objective' view of our situation. I recall one American expert on eastern Europe proposing that our predicament could usefully be referred to the International Court of Justice at the Hague, where judges could decide the merits of our case. He considered this to be the best solution offered yet, and it is indeed a pity that no western country cared to consider taking the matter to that court. We would have welcomed the chance to do so for ourselves, but, of course, we faced the procedural difficulty that we were not yet recognized as a state, and therefore could not initiate proceedings. Such procedural requirements of course beg many questions. We had already been denied membership of the International Red Cross for similar reasons, and we soon learned that the International Football Federation was afraid to offend the Soviet Union, so our teams were unable to take part in its competitions, while Lithuania's chances of participating in the Barcelona Olympics also seemed slim. Our handicap was highlighted when our chess players were not admitted to the competitions at the Chess Olympics in Yugoslavia in the summer of 1991, despite having the support of every one of the participating grand masters from the Soviet Union. We can now deduce from all this evidence that the Soviet government, though not its decent citizens, had caught the world by its tail and was twisting hard!

Although the great powers seemed deaf to our problems, our case and cause were often well understood by the smaller countries. Vaclav Havel, the president of Czechoslovakia, sent me a letter just eighteen days after our declaration of 11 March, offering his country as a neutral haven for negotiations between the Soviet Union and Lithuania. A similar proposal, with an additional offer to act as intermediary, followed from the government of Iceland, and I visited that remarkable land in the autumn of 1990 at the invitation of Prime Minister Hermannsson. My attendance in an official capacity at the opening session of the Althing was the first such occurrence in Iceland's history (as my new Icelandic friends informed me), and it involved recognition both of Lithuania and of my position as head of an independent state. While I was there I spoke on national television and said that we needed one country to stand up before the world, to commend Lithuania's struggle, and to help us to break the Soviet diplomatic blockade from which we were still suffering. Even as I spoke, I well knew which country would be most deeply concerned to help our cause.

In October that year, a little after I had returned home, the Supreme Council of the Lithuanian Republic published a book in English entitled *The Road to Negotiations with the Soviet Union*. It contained some seventy-seven documents, each of which had significant reference to the re-establishment of our country's independence and the negotiations with the Soviet Union. All of them had been issued between 11 March and 2 October 1990. The introduction quoted John F. Kennedy's acute observation that 'if men and women are in chains anywhere in the world, then freedom is endangered everywhere', and the book itself was a chronicle of events which listed the thirty-three letters sent by Lithuania's Supreme Council and government to the president and governmental institutions of the Soviet Union in relation to the intended negotiations. Almost all of them bore our rubber-stamped endorsement 'No response received'. This publication went a long way towards convincing opinion-makers throughout the world that the failure to open negotiations was not Lithuania's fault, as had been so powerfully suggested by our opponents. I had been assiduous in explaining our case in this matter, and early in December I was asked first by Swedish and then by Polish television to appear in programmes which went out just before Christmas. In these broadcasts I took the opportunity to return to this theme, and said:

Today Lithuania is facing what is probably her greatest spiritual and moral trial. Her people have already sacrificed much on the altar of the nation's freedom, and I must tell you that while the world has heard a lot about my country recently, there is much more to learn. Lithuania has once again raised her battle cry in the past few years, and especially this year, but this call is not for her own sake only. What Lithuania is trying to achieve is the right to defend her freedom, and fully to re-establish her independent statehood, which was suddenly and forcibly taken away and abolished some fifty years ago by a foreign power. It is necessary to fight this good fight, but we do not do so for Lithuania alone. It is important to recognize that justice, which must be accessible to every single human being as a legal right, must also be freely shared by every human society and the whole of our human race. Where truth and justice stand chained and broken, so does society itself. If justice is denied to my people, there are implications for the whole continent of Europe and for all the nations of the world. When we began to liberate our small nation we knew full well that our actions had

231

implications for others around us, in the north, in the south, and also in the east, especially in the east. Many of the Soviet republics have already responded to our efforts, and their people have seen us as a shining example of the search for independence and democracy, and of the justice to which they also aspire. We have been told by many that we have started something important, and while only the future will answer our question whether the return to democracy which has begun in the Baltic states will expand into eastern Europe and across the Soviet empire, we can already ask what future awaits these reborn (and in some cases new-born) infant democracies. Will this fresh life survive until adulthood, or is it going to be crushed, to be left to await rebirth at some later time? There are many dangers which threaten Lithuanian democracy today, and the future is very uncertain for our land. There are many dangers which we face because the world has become more complicated, and because the enemies of democracy and liberty have the upper hand and have the power to use unrestrained coercion of one kind or another to keep our country oppressed and captive within their empire. Dangers lurk elsewhere too, not least in the indifference of the western world, but you must realize that our Lithuanian struggle is also a struggle for the liberty of your people, of western people. If you feel that you have no need of our example and no inclination to assist us, I will say this to you. If this small and delicate flower of democracy and liberty is allowed to be trampled underfoot before it has had a chance to bloom, will you not have second thoughts later? It will then be too late to be sorry that you did not protect it. Might it not be better to act now to that end?

Two days after this broadcast, Soviet forces entered the streets of our Lithuanian towns, and we protested – but to no avail. Though I paid visits to several Western capital cities at this time, travelling to Oslo, Reykjavik, Paris, London, Ottawa and Washington, I experienced the autumn of 1990 as bleak and depressing, even though I could claim on the basis of my travels that the recognition of our new state was already a fact in some ways. The Soviet threat was, however, looming over us again, though there were also hopeful signs. I had asked François Mitterrand about pre-war Lithuanian gold, locked in a French bank for safe keeping since before the war, and he had answered with no hesitation: 'It is your gold, use it as you wish.' He could not have been more emphatic, and his statement was as good as the president of France saying that our reborn Lithuanian Republic was the same state as the nation's pre-war Republic. I spoke in the same vein to Margaret Thatcher a little later, and she asked me to write a letter about the Lithuanian gold deposited in Britain in the same period. I wrote it in London that very night, and returned to Vilnius to find a friendly and positive reply waiting for me. When some Lithuanian journalists noticed that I received red-carpet treatment at Downing Street, they teased me, as if it was important to me. It was not, but it was important to Lithuania, though unfortunately only a few understood that. However, the Soviets *did* understand what was going on and it maddened them – to the extent that their line hardened.

Our opponents' next onslaught was calculated and precipitate. Our Baltic foreign ministers had been invited to participate as guests of the Conference for Security and Co-operation in Europe (CSCE) in Paris. They had already taken their seats when they learned that Gorbachev had brought pressure to bear to exclude them and they were forced to leave the hall when business began. One might say that communist totalitarianism had managed to control them even there. If this could be done in democratic France, it is small wonder that the Soviets did not need to mask their arrogance on the shores of the Baltic – or in Moscow. We had been forewarned. Maslukov, who was close to Gorbachev, had already said: 'We will act as an occupying invader', but we had continued to hold our position and stated firmly that formal fiscal connection with the Soviet Union would be cut from New Year. It implied the transformation of economic and trade links, even the transfer of tax obligations. Being outside Soviet state planning also meant moving outside their banking system. The announcement was not inconsistent with designs which we had already begun to hatch. As we had already passed a fiscal law the previous summer to reflect our commitment to a free economy, this was actually our first independent budget. We had also been moved to establish a commission, of which I was chairman, which was busy drafting a new constitution for Lithuania.

The Kremlin was now pouring its anger and threats down on all three Baltic states. It was urgent that the three governments worked together to consolidate our positions, so on 1 December the parliaments of all three countries assembled for a joint session in Vilnius. This historic meeting was wonderfully constructive and resulted in a series of joint declarations addressed to parliaments around the world, informing them of what was going on and asking them to use their influence to persuade the Soviet Union to stop threatening the Baltic states, and in particular to discontinue the political, economic and military pressure which had been applied to our three countries. We asked for dates to be set for the removal of Soviet military personnel and equipment from our territory, and we applied for the Baltic question to be placed on the agenda of the CSCE. We also used the occasion to confirm that we would sign no union treaty which would incorporate any of us into a legal Soviet structure, and at the same time we guaranteed the rights of foreigners in our territories. This was a considered response to the ugly Soviet slander, which continued to elaborate a myth of its own creation, that we intended to use our new independence to wreak an awful revenge on Soviet citizens who had made their homes in our countries.

This meeting of three parliaments was a unique event which had been brought about by the unprecedented pressure of our big neighbour's ultimatum. We now knew that we had to prepare ourselves for the possibility of a sudden attack, that we could all be dealt a mortal blow, individually or collectively. As Lithuanians we felt it necessary to settle our moral accounts immediately, and before events developed any further, by ending our promised constitutional moratorium, which had been extended by now to the point where it was bothering our national conscience badly. We had seen the situation worsen and now observed that the Soviets had terminated even the pathetically feeble negotiations they had begun with us, with no real notice. For some time they had been speaking openly and frequently about applying armed force against us, so we knew exactly where we stood with them. Faced with these many threats we passed another decree on 28 December on the question of bilateral negotiations between our countries. It made bold and visible concessions to the Soviets, dropping our earlier demand for a special preliminary protocol on the aims and conditions of negotiation. However, we now used this retreat from the concept of the protocol as an opportunity to revise the Statement which we had formulated on 29 June. After this historic paper had been redrafted only its preamble remained valid. The alterations meant that the promised moratorium was annulled. Its provisions had never been invoked and we now simply called them off.

There was no Soviet reaction to this, our latest decree. Whether they did not fully comprehend its content, or were deliberately ignoring us, it was still plain that they remained capable of deciding to resolve their 'Lithuanian problem' by force at a time of their choosing. The first of these possibilities was unlikely, because the implications of the new decree were too obvious to be missed by our own or the foreign press. The journalists noticed that we had abandoned the idea of a special protocol, but they failed to observe that the moratorium was now simply unnecessary. They responded as we hoped, noticing that we had removed the safety device while overlooking the fact that it had become redundant because we had also moved the explosives. We said no more. Our duty was done and we now awaited our fate with a clear conscience because the ambiguous history of the moratorium was over.

CHAPTER 17

The terror and the victory

The year 1991 began with the government at loggerheads with the Supreme Council, the disagreement having been precipitated by the sudden announcement by Mrs Prunskienė's administration of major increases in the price of food and goods manufactured by state-owned firms. As if this was not enough, Soviet influences were obviously at work encouraging the opponents of our independence to rebel and collaborate with the Soviet army, which was being prepared for an offensive. The tension was extreme, and the resignation of the prime minister completed the scenario. It was a crisis which left us struggling to decide who should be appointed to ministerial office, what kind of administration we would now get, and wondering whether we would after all be able to keep the affairs of state under parliamentary control.

The Cabinet drama

The pressures on the government at the beginning of January were obvious. Everything that was happening in Lithuania was influenced by dramatic tensions in the political environment. The wide differences of opinion in the Supreme Council played a key role, and the strain was most apparent in Vilnius, especially in the government offices. As the opposing forces in the Supreme Council realigned themselves, it was often very difficult indeed to work out what was happening, but every change had to be studied carefully. When Mrs Prunskienė resigned, nothing could be taken for granted. I was, however, taken by surprise when the centrist faction in the Supreme Council, which was dominated by a small but vociferous group of Social Democrats, refused to accept my nomination of one of its members, the economist Albertas Šimėnas, as prime minister. While I had already calculated that the communists, who might have tolerated him as a minister, would not want him as prime minister, the reason why the Social Democrats turned him down quite escaped me until Eduardas Vilkas of the Liberal party said disparagingly that he 'could not imagine Šimėnas chatting with Mitterrand'. It was obvious he felt that Šimėnas lacked experience, but I defended him, replying that it was only ten years since Lech Walesa had visited France as the voice of Polish Solidarity, and Giscard d'Estaing had greeted the unknown electrician from Gdansk as 'the future president of Poland'. Communist Poland had then seen his compliment as provocative flattery, but it was now seen as political foresight. This episode, however, was symptomatic of the dangerous fluidity of our parliamentary situation.

While my discussions did not end with Vilkas – and I still do not know whether my words influenced him – I was eventually successful in gaining the support of the Sąjūdis factions so that Šimėnas was finally confirmed as prime minister despite the combined opposition of his own faction and the communists. I have, however, to record the sad fact that our new prime minister did not remain at his post for long, as he disappeared on the night of 12–13 January. This extraordinary news reached me from the government offices at the same time as the reports of the bloodbath at the state television offices, and it was a dreadful moment both for me and for the country. We were actively anticipating an attack on Parliament. I had been repeatedly urged to leave the country for my safety. I was even told that a small aeroplane was standing by to fly me and my wife from Kaunas to Poland, but had refused the offer because I knew that it was essential for me to remain at my post, and I wanted our parliamentarians to stay at theirs. The situation was disturbing, and confused in the extreme, and I had scarcely taken it in. As I looked around me I noticed that a large group of deputies were anxiously gathered in the debating chamber of our Parliament building, and I remember they were all wearing long winter coats. We spent the rest of that night fearfully awaiting what might happen next. I had earlier made a somewhat clumsy attempt to persuade the women to leave the building, but they had refused. Now, on top of all this, we learned that the prime minister was not to be found, and we had to ask whether it was possible that he had run away. The news reaching us was extremely fragmented, but this was the story we were able to put together: the other ministers had felt the need for his presence at the government buildings and a car was sent to bring him from his newly acquired residence in Turniškės, which is on the outskirts of the city. Shortly afterwards the driver had returned, reporting that his passenger had unexpectedly asked him to stop on the way into town. He had then suddenly transferred his wife and their three small children to a private car which stood waiting in a side street and driven away without saying what was happening or where they were going. It was hard to digest, and equally hard to know what to make of this information, and we were left speculating about his state of mind and fate. Had he left of his own free will? Had he been duped, or kidnapped by our enemies? Was he in the hands of the KGB, which sometimes targeted people, blackmailing them by using their wives and children as hostages – and that was not their only way of breaking people. If Šimėnas gave in to pressure while still prime minister, others could make use of his name for their own ends. All these issues had to be considered there in the small hours of the morning, and we had to make immediate decisions. Though it had become obvious that Parliament was not going to be attacked immediately, because the action was elsewhere, it seemed very likely that we would soon be facing a new ultimatum, and be surrounded, isolated from the rest of Lithuania, and cut off from the world. We were now afraid that our enemies would soon be telling the country that it had no prime minister and that there was therefore no real government, or that the prime minister was prepared to abuse his position, or had been forced to collaborate. Such prospects were acutely disturbing because we knew that the authority he had might well be used to justify repression, violence, even the installation of a puppet government. We were not reassured when we remembered the precedents set by the Soviets in Lithuania in 1940 and in Hungary, Czechoslovakia and Afghanistan subsequently.

I went down to the debating chamber from my office to find a really militant atmosphere there. The defenders of Parliament were busy preparing for the anticipated attack by pouring petrol into bottles, and the entire building reeked of the smell. The deputies were also there, miserably cold and shivering in their winter coats because the windows had been thrown open to let the icy winter winds clear the petrol fumes. I bleakly informed members of the prime minister's disappearance and announced that I was calling a meeting of the Supreme Council to resolve the situation immediately. Darius Kuolys, the minister for culture and education, then confirmed that the prime minister had not reached the government offices as had been arranged. The former deputy prime minister, Romualdas Ozolas, announced that Albertas Šimėnas 'was now acting according to another plan'. The general dismay was tangible and members were profoundly aggrieved. No one in Parliament could have anticipated this situation, which was completely without precedent and until now beyond the bounds of imagination. The crisis had practical implications quite apart from our concern that Šimėnas had been abducted. He might now be manipulated for the enemy's benefit, and we knew that we could not function without a head of government. If Šimėnas had been captured, the outlook was grim both for him and for us. Eventually someone said that if he ceased to be the prime minister he would be of little use to our enemies. We then realized that it would be far safer for everyone if he were to revert to being an ordinary deputy, and that we had to impose that change of status without further delay for his own sake as well as our own.

Having heard this discussion I formally proposed that Albertas Šimėnas should be relieved of his duties as prime minister of Lithuania, 'because his whereabouts are unknown and he is absent from his duties'. The motion was softened by a clause which stated that he would be reinstated if he should return and be able to continue his duties, and that the new prime minister would resign immediately in that situation. Šimėnas was then dismissed by an almost unanimous vote. As we began to consider another candidate without further ceremony I was aware that I had a particular responsibility to take the person's experience, character and competence into account, but as I looked around the chamber trying to identify another centrist figure who would gain general support I realized that the centrists would be unable to supply a suitable candidate. While they had some prominent deputies in the Supreme Council, there was no one among them who would get the support of Sąjūdis, which had a near-majority in Parliament. It meant that my decision would be difficult, but eventually I spoke with Gediminas Vagnorius, an energetic economist who had already shown his capabilities in preparing legislation. I asked for his agreement that he would resign if Šimėnas should reappear and still be able to carry on as prime minister, and then nominated him. It was a good decision as he was a man of ideas, ambition, energy and determination. These were essential attributes in the situation which we faced, and he had often disagreed with Prunskienė and was reckoned to be her most obvious challenger. I was pleased to observe that even his most vigorous opponents seemed to recognize this, because they voted for him. However, I later discovered that their support was merely tactical, as many of our opponents believed that his government could not be expected to last for more than a fortnight before it faced internal disintegration and loss of public support. They had therefore helped to elect him in the belief that the imminent collapse of what they perceived as a right-wing government would discredit us, allowing left and centrist groups to take over, probably with the support of foreign forces.

This kind of reasoning was not new. Our opponents had voted against Šimėnas at an earlier election, with a similar logic. If they could avoid having a centrist prime minister, blame for the country's difficulties could be projected in a way which would create an opportunity for the left. Šimėnas had stood in their way. Now he had disappeared, opportunities opened up once again, and Gediminas Vagnorius was elected unconditionally to office, although when his position was confirmed he honourably responded to my earlier request, issuing a statement declaring that Albertas

Šimėnas would be reappointed to the premiership in the event of his reappearance, which in fact occurred on the afternoon of 13 January when he suddenly came into my office, unannounced and looking awful. His spirits were very low, and he seemed a broken man with a worried look. He spoke strangely and was barely coherent, and seemed to be asking what I thought of him, whether I condemned him, and whether we saw him as a traitor. Much later he gave a fuller interpretation of events, explaining that he had sensed a conspiracy against him. The idea had come to him just before he disappeared, and when he received news that the rest of the government was waiting for him and that a car had been sent to collect him, his suspicions were aroused by the absence of his usual driver. Some kind of persecution complex must then have got the better of him. He had hurriedly arranged his desertion by telephoning a close friend, urgently asking him to come to meet him, so that he could escape to frustrate what he believed to be a plot to install a puppet government by running the business of government from some secret location. He had transferred his family and the luggage to the other car and travelled to Ratnyčia, near to the Polish border, where they had stayed with the parish priest. The next morning he had listened to the news, which informed him of the Soviet atrocities and the appointment of a new prime minister. He had then realized his mistake and immediately ordered a car to bring him to Vilnius, where he came into my office to tell me apologetically why he wanted to stand aside. I could see the state he was in, and calmed him down, acting as a friend. The conversation came to an end when I told him that I understood his predicament and did not condemn his actions. I persuaded him to take a rest, offering him the small room behind my office where I kept a bed for my own use. He accepted my offer and slept for a good few hours while the Council and the government continued its intense discussion in the very worrying atmosphere which was threatening to engulf us all.

Within hours of these events Gorbachev's delegation arrived from Moscow at short notice for talks. The situation was extremely volatile. The Soviet army had declared a curfew, and the soldiers seemed likely to be provoked into opening fire on the people, who were defying it by remaining on the streets of Vilnius in large numbers. Since the attack on the television tower we were desperate to end a confrontation which threatened the future of our government and the lives of the many patriots who were gathered in towns throughout Lithuania, and especially around Parliament, which they were ready to defend with their lives. We urgently wanted the help of the Soviet delegation in reducing the level of aggression of the Soviet army. The announcement that it was on its way had extended some hope to us, though we had barely an hour to catch up on sleep before it arrived. Its members were all Supreme Soviet deputies, and the group included Nikolai Dementey, Boris Oleynik, Levon Ter-Petrosian and Vladimir Foteyev, one of Gorbachev's personal advisers. We had already been told that meetings had been arranged for them with the Soviet army commanders, and also with a delegation from the self-appointed 'National Salvation Committee'. Of course, these arrangements spelt danger for us, and had been made without reference to us, so we moved to reduce the threat by asking Gediminas Vagnorius to accompany them to the discussions. The Soviet officials had asked for two ministers to go with them and we were careful to appoint members of the government whose position would not be 'completely unacceptable' to Moscow. We also took care to ensure that these ministers went down to the airport to meet the visitors, to ensure that the 'National Salvation Committee', which clearly had a *putsch* at the top of its agenda, did not reach them first, and their closeness to the delegation proved valuable in an unforeseen way that same evening when one of them overheard Foteyev ringing Gorbachev to report his analysis of what they had seen and heard. He reported that 'the people and the government are on one side here, and the Soviet army is on the other'. I have to say that this information brought a huge sense of relief because it showed that the truth was beginning to dawn. Quite as importantly, it also confirmed that the myth that various groups in our population were actively confronting each other, with the army being obliged to keep the peace between us, was at last beginning to dissolve. Unfortunately for us, however, the Soviet machine was addicted to its propaganda and continued to spread its lies despite the evidence.

In parallel with these happenings there were equally dramatic developments elsewhere. While the ministers were awaiting Prime Minister Šimėnas at the government offices they learned that Algirdas Brazauskas, the former deputy prime minister, had telephoned Kazimiera Prunskienė, who happened to be staying in the country that night, requesting her urgent return to Vilnius. She had subsequently arrived at the government offices early in the morning, where, according to the ministers' account, she had taken it upon herself to declare that the Supreme Council was 'now inoperative and that the government had to take responsibility into its own hands'. She had then tried to browbeat the ministers into deciding to elect a new head of government, and had presumed to sit in the prime minister's chair. These actions had caused the ministers present to protest vigorously, and they had rejected her proposals outright. Pranas Kūris, the minister for justice, had bluntly asked her: 'What the devil do you think you are doing here?' He was of course on very strong ground, as Prunskienė was now only an ordinary deputy, and while she had a place in the Supreme Council, she was no longer in the government.

When the ministers refused to act unconstitutionally, her attempt to persuade them to change the prime minister fell flat on its face. Fortunately the danger passed, but it is easy to imagine how the situation might have deteriorated if our opponents had managed to drive this wedge between government and Parliament at the very time that Parliament was in a state of siege, and in serious danger of being dispersed. Had these moves been successful the outcome would have been as damaging as any *coup d'état*. A government of Brazauskas's and Prunskienė's choosing would have become the only source of authority in Lithuania, and it would have acted exactly as Gorbachev's supporters in Moscow and Lithuania desired. It is likely that it would have been forced to condemn the actions of the Soviet forces in order to gain political credit, but such a populist move would have secured its position, and the pro-Soviet Communist party chiefs would then have been able to negotiate for seats in the Cabinet. The resulting scenario would have fulfilled the aspirations of our opponents, while confusing ordinary people, as everything would have been more than half-legal, the government's continuity having been scarcely uninterrupted except for the convenient replacement of its new prime minister by Prunskienė. She was of course ready and waiting in the wings to resume the position. Had she done so, our period of rule would have been dismissed as a disorderly episode, and 'Soviet normality' would of course have been restored to Lithuania.

For the sake of the independence of Lithuania it was a very good thing that ministers rejected the unconstitutional step which Kazimiera Prunskienė had suggested to them. The actual decision may, however, have been a very close one, because it was quite apparent that the ministers had failed fully to comprehend just why the Supreme Council had been so determined to ensure that the government should not work without the explicit support of Parliament. This was a time of transition: their entire experience had been with a Soviet-style executive, and a tame, rubber-stamping Supreme Council. As a more democratic structure was developed there were some very strange undercurrents, and relationships were often strained. I can recall several curious incidents from around this time. One of them occurred at the time we declared the premiership vacant. I had scarcely begun to propose Gediminas Vagnorius as candidate for the position of prime minister when Česlovas Juršėnas, an influential Communist member, tried to stop the proceedings by declaring that we should not proceed 'until Mrs Kazimiera Prunskienė arrived in the Council to join the debate'. I wondered at the time why he considered her participation to be so important, but now when I think back, it seems likely that the incident implied that Juršėnas was aware of a conspiracy to make her prime minister once again. There was other evidence of such manœuvring. Just after Vagnorius was confirmed as prime minister, business was being rushed because we had little time to waste. It was his prerogative as prime minister to choose his own deputy premier, and he proposed Mečislovas Treinys as a good man who would also be able to preside over the urgent agricultural reforms which we proposed. However, Treinys declined the offer and Zigmas Vaišvila, an energetic young member of Sąjūdis, was then proposed and confirmed. This appointment closed the lists, and we prepared ourselves to let everyone know that Lithuania had a full government again. As the ministers were being called in to witness their newly appointed colleagues taking their oaths, the former prime minister swept into the chamber. Romualdas Ozolas, her former deputy, accompanied her, and I observed that both appeared to be confused by what was going on. Ozolas then left her to come to me, and asked in a breathless whisper: 'What is going on here . . . don't you *know*?' 'What should I know?', I asked. He seemed to be speaking about Šimėnas, but presented himself hesitatingly – as if implying that he was aware of something which I might not know. The moment passed without any further declaration, but the atmosphere was very strange, and continued to be so between us. Throughout this time of crisis, a momentarily interrupted or unfinished sentence, a movement of the eye, or an inflection of the voice might seem to convey profound understanding or else create tension, so I have no idea even now whether Romualdas Ozolas was privy to some conspiracy, or whether he was just trying to squeeze some information from me by hinting that he knew something at that moment! Both interpretations might have fitted his behaviour. However, I made allowances for him because his demeanour conveyed shock, though my response to that may have been complicated by the knowledge that he had lost a son only a fortnight before.

On the day following his visit to me it was obvious that Šimėnas had still not recovered, and his disorientation was plain. He continued to call on me for some time afterwards, and seemed unable to come to terms with the fact that he had been dismissed. At some level he must have felt deeply confused because he wrote a letter asking me to relieve him of his duties even though he had already been told that this had happened, and we had discussed the matter. It was hard to know whether he blamed himself or felt he was being blamed for deserting his post at a time when his country faced danger. However, he wanted it to be believed that he had resigned the premiership of his own volition, so I accepted his letter and then locked it in my safe. He was clearly not ready to assume any responsibilities, and needed help. After a while he went into hospital for a few weeks and then spent some time in a convalescent home. Later, when he returned to public life it was clear that he was not really ready to undertake any duties, though Vagnorius helped him by appointing him an economic adviser, which gave him some status. It took a while, but he did recover in the end and eventually Vagnorius nominated him minister for economic affairs.

The sudden change of prime minister on 13 January was an event which had repercussions that long continued to affect us. The question of what exactly had happened became the subject of ugly speculation, and this was tirelessly exploited by people who did not have the country's best interests at heart. Some claimed that Vagnorius should have resigned immediately upon Šimėnas's return, and that his failure to do so meant that the present Cabinet was illegal. Their arguments were intended to subvert the government's position and were compounded by a rumour that while the Supreme Council had had a quorum when Šimėnas's dismissal was discussed, this may not have been the case when Vagnorius's appointment as prime minister was confirmed. This rumour was actually contradicted by the fact that a count had been taken of the vote, but nevertheless Prunskienė and a Liberal deputy who was also a newspaper editor repeated it in print to suggest that Vagnorius and his government were 'illegally elected'. This irresponsible canard was repeated in January by people who wanted to wreak the maximum damage from the prevailing instability and tension. The campaign eventually subsided as there was no difficulty, ultimately, in proving the integrity of the government. The quorum and the vote had been confirmed by eyewitnesses, as well as having been recorded by the parliamentary secretariat. Someone also made a video of the proceedings.

Naturally we ordered a commission to confirm the facts behind Šimėnas' disappearance. It was held in closed session. Witnesses were called and extensive discussion took place on the draft report to decide whether it should be published. In the end it was agreed that we would not oppose the former prime minister's version of events and he was given the benefit of whatever doubt remained. Though it continued to be widely felt that some questions were still unanswered, it was this view which was published. There was no defect in the report or the way in which it had been drafted, but the issue was again actively manipulated by those who were against Sąjūdis and the Vagnorius government. A rather distorted story was circulated about this time in a publication of the Lithuanian Democratic Labour party (as the Lithuanian Communist party was now renamed – Lietuvos Demokratinė Darbo Partija, LDDP), which alleged that the ruthless Landsbergis had actually tried to kill Šimėnas. I could easily have used Šimėnas's resignation note, written on

15 January, to squash this libellous accusation, but forbore from doing so, not just because I felt that the note itself would then have been used to suggest that his dismissal had been improperly conducted, but also because I wanted to avoid causing him further pain. It was sufficient that events had resulted in his dismissal. He had been 'absent from his duties, and his whereabouts were not known', and Gediminas Vagnorius had been duly appointed as the new prime minister, subject only to his own commitment to step down in Šimėnas's favour 'if he should return and be able to carry out his duties'. These facts were in the public domain and it was quite obvious that Šimėnas had not been in any condition to carry out *any* duties when he reappeared, not even the ordinary duties of a parliamentarian. In these circumstances there could have been no question of his resuming the premiership. Those who lobbied to reinstate him were fully aware of his physical and mental condition and had ulterior motives. In short, they wanted to provoke opposition to the government – or to demolish it.

This was the atmosphere in which Gediminas Vagnorius began to lead the government. Despite these troubles, his administration survived as a viable government for a year and a half, an incredibly long time under such conditions. During that time there were many pressures on the government, and very many tense moments in domestic and foreign policy. However, his team provided a stable government and I could rely on his judgement and on our relationship, though I often longed for a closer working relationship with him and the members of his Cabinet, especially in the fields of internal politics and the development of the nation's economy. But we were all recognizably overloaded with work, and fully aware of the complexity of our responsibility.

The Volunteers

During those difficult days and nights in January the Lithuanian Parliament took charge of the defence of the entire nation. At the same time it had to learn to defend itself as best it could. Resistance was expressed chiefly in political terms, but preparation for armed resistance also began out of sheer necessity. A defence headquarters was established and a defence staff were appointed, though the Supreme Council avoided giving them wide powers. Meanwhile the lobbies and corridors of our Parliament building were systematically fortified with sandbags. Simple sleeping facilities for volunteers were also provided: many young men, and some not so young, had volunteered for duties in the building, hoping to defend our country and its independence by all means possible. They knew that in doing this they must be prepared even to face death, and they committed themselves by attending confession and mass, and then by taking a solemn oath. A group of them also established a field hospital inside the building and men were already being treated there when I visited it for the first time. Most of them had been wounded in clashes outside the state publishing house. In addition, barricades were erected all around the Parliament, and Lithuanian wayside crosses were soon to be found near them, together with a statue of the Blessed Virgin Mary, and an altar to which Father Robertas Grigas and other clergy often came to celebrate holy mass.

A special atmosphere of vigil developed around our parliamentary proceedings as people began to gather to sing hymns, patriotic songs and folk-songs. Soon our volunteers gained foreign support. A group of Ukrainians joined them, and I vividly recall an older man from this group dressed in full military uniform. After this parliamentarians came from other nations, from Poland, Hungary and other places, to spend some nights among us. They too came as volunteers, to share in our uncertainty, well aware of the danger to their own lives, and many of them commented on the sense of elation which filled the Supreme Council and the people who had gathered around its buildings. They all sensed this aura, which sometimes seemed to radiate throughout Lithuania. People were deeply affected, and arrived at all hours of day and night with food and medicine, or to relieve those who were on duty in and around the building. This manifest support continued throughout, with bonfires kept burning outside to ward off the cold, while resistance songs echoed through the building. Morale was extremely high, and those who spent those long nights there will always regard themselves as privileged to have shared in an unforgettable experience. Such an atmosphere is infectious. When I visited the volunteers informally I often found the words of their oath running through my mind. One day the chief of the Defence Department invited me to pay an official visit as new volunteers took their oath, and I took the opportunity to stand in line to commit myself publicly along with them.

The volunteers had taught us something important, but I still had to listen to the grumbles of leftist deputies. Our volunteers knew very well how much these men had fulminated against the idea of developing defence structures to support Lithuanian independence when the matter was debated by the Supreme Council. The volunteers knew of their contempt for the idea of a National Defence organization and a Volunteer Corps, but the boot was on the other foot now that these structures were in place, and it was not entirely surprising to hear that some deputies were treated to verbal abuse by some of our supporters. Some of them came to me with complaints, although Česlovas Juršėnas was not among them, because a volunteer who was standing guard outside Parliament had directed a robust, but extremely offensive epithet at him – an expression used occasionally by the ruder folk in Lithuania – as he tried to slip away from the volunteer guards. There are still some who fail to understand what the situation was really like as people gathered in the streets outside Parliament to defend it. One of them is the philosopher Arvydas Juozaitis, who resigned from Sąjūdis in 1990 after the elections. I asked him to 'stop opposing, and join the work of protecting the state', but he campaigned against our establishment of a National Defence Corps, describing our proposals as 'uncontrolled'. He still believes that our moves to create defence structures were detrimental to Lithuania and has even boasted: 'I joined the opposition to fight this type of Sąjūdis.' Gorbachev and the Moscow machine, together with some elements in the Lithuanian press and the state-controlled Vilnius television service, were delighted to publicize these views in the aftermath of 13 January 1991 as they tried to turn the blame on us for the outcome of the Soviet aggression. By then, however, we were beyond being deterred, and simply got on with our own agenda. As a result we passed several laws between 10 and 17 January to institute the Lithuanian Volunteer Defence Corps, a Defence Council and a National Defence Fund, as well as a resolution which condemned the 'open military aggression' of the Soviets in Lithuania. These formal enactments were a clear reminder to everyone that the Lithuanian Republic believed firmly in its right to defend itself against aggression, and was prepared to ensure the protection of key installations, and the structures of our state, whenever the need arose.

Our defenders had very few weapons and made the best of the poor resources they had. Our detractors denounced what they called 'madness' when Molotov cocktails were prepared inside the Parliament buildings and petrol fumes drifted through the halls. We were warned, perhaps with good reason, that the whole place would suffer instant conflagration in the event of an attack, and that all the deputies and civil servants inside would die in the resulting inferno. Whether or not that was true, at the time the question of death whether by one means or another seemed much less important than our common and overriding preoccupation. It had become utterly important to us all that we should neither flinch nor withdraw. We were deliberate in our preparations to ensure that our fortified barricades would withstand attack. Knowing that the Soviet army might quite easily deploy helicopters to land on the Parliament's flat roof, we placed defensive constructions there to prevent them landing above our heads. Everything was done quickly, and people had to be trained to shoot at helicopters in a way which would send the machines out of control. We had the help of a specialist military adviser, who worked out of the limelight but with great determination. He was a Lithuanian called Andrius Eiva, whom I met only once, a former American officer who may well have fought in the Vietnam War and had certainly taken part in the Afghan campaign on the partisans' side. He was also busy teaching defence tactics which could be used by partisans in the city of Vilnius. If we had ever been pushed to that extreme I am unsure whether our men could really have inflicted the damage he promised they could against a fully armed and well-trained enemy, but he helped to make sure that there would have been serious armed conflict if the Soviet Union had thrown its war machine against Lithuania. Our defence plans were designed to emphasize the fact that our independence was being threatened by a foreign military power, rather than by some internal *putsch*, though both contingencies stared us in the face at that stage. While the latter seemed to be the greater danger, both possibilities seemed very close, though by God's grace they were avoided.

We were soon to have the experience of being tested to the limit as we were now entering the period of tragedy which ended with a whole nation mourning its unarmed heroes. The defence of Parliament turned our defenders into a professional force, and they developed a system of military intelligence which was able in the hour of our greatest crisis to monitor the radio communications of the Soviet forces attacking the tele-vision tower. Their recordings of the events proved invaluable later on when they were eventually deciphered, as they could be used to indict those involved. They provided unquestionable evidence of the weapons used, and of the fact that the Soviet commanding officers had given defi-nite orders to shoot live ammunition. Our defence force also had special responsibility for my personal safety, and took this job seriously. Early in January they issued me with a bullet-proof vest which I was told to wear every time I left my office or ventured outside the building. I was also instructed not to stand near the windows of the Parliament building (even though they were now curtained), to avoid becoming a sniper's target. How real this threat was I cannot tell, but it was true that a single shot into my office from a Soviet gun might have resolved the Lithuanian question instantly at that time. My protectors were therefore firm in their instructions. When the martyrs of 13 January lay in state, our defenders were adamant that I should stay away from the funeral because I would have had to mingle in the crowd. As professionals they knew very well that they could not guarantee my safety in those circum-stances, and my closest colleagues also urged me not to join the cortège. They were so pressing that I agreed to delegate the job to Česlovas

Stankevičius, whom I asked to deliver a speech on my behalf. Despite all this I felt I had to pay my respects and went in the early hours of the morning to the lying in state at the Sports Hall, believing that hardly anyone would be about. It was the first time I had left the Parliament building since the events which had caused their deaths, and I went by car, seemingly unnoticed through streets which were patrolled by Soviet soldiers and units of the 'black berets', the infamous OMON troops. The hall was full of people, among them relatives in deep mourning, and it was difficult to hold back tears in these circumstances, though I managed a short speech which said simply that these were true Lithuanian volunteers, who had given up their lives for their country, unarmed. I spoke of how one of the martyrs, a young woman named Loreta Asanavičiūtė, had lifted her fragile hands against the cold steel. She had confronted an advancing tank armed only with her own bravery, and had sacrificed herself. Her action had saved many others, and her example had illuminated Lithuania's situation for the whole world to see. I then went on to honour each one of the martyrs, standing briefly before each coffin with the guard of honour before returning to my desk and the routine of the Supreme Council. I scarcely ventured outside again for a long time, but whenever I remember that day I am overcome by guilt and deep regret that I listened to my colleagues. I should have been present at the martyrs' funeral.

The propaganda war

We need to look in greater detail at the attack by heavily armed forces on the unarmed civilians who had gathered to prevent the Soviet take-over of the television buildings in Vilnius. The Kremlin had followed its usual strategy of orchestrating events, providing an 'interpretation' of what was happening even before it happened on the streets, though it soon became evident that developments were refusing to follow the Soviet master plan. They had designed a scenario by which constant provocation would make people respond in anger, which would then give an excuse for a full-scale attack by the armed forces, who would thus have a pretext for imposing the absolute control which they desired. Unfortunately for this strategy the people of Lithuania remained determinedly calm, and it was this which most upset the military plan when the army began to move into its predetermined positions though the planned scenario had failed to ripen. When Moscow began to broadcast its description of 'riots and anarchy in Lithuania', it claimed that workers had presented a petition to the Supreme Council only to be 'beaten up and dragged into the cellars of the building to be tortured there'. These allegations were of course completely untrue, but the propaganda machine had been switched on. It was producing ugly lies and distortions according to a blueprint which bore little or no resemblance to what was happening in the real world.

The difference between these broadcast accounts and the events on the ground in Vilnius was so great that it would have been farcical had it not been so serious. A group of drunken men had indeed attempted to enter the prime minister's office building to deliver a document which they described as a petition, but the broadcasts talked of a 'workers' delegation' going to the television tower to present a petition 'against the anti-Soviet programmes which were being transmitted', demanding that they should be banned so that the petitioners could continue to watch television in peace. We could not take this story seriously because it was clear from the way it was presented that it had been cooked up in Moscow. No one with the smallest knowledge of Lithuanian life would have dreamed of taking any kind of petition up to the Vilnius television tower, because they would have known that the studios and administration of Lithuanian television were miles away. The very idea of a petition of the kind described being taken there at midnight with the expectation that there would be anyone to receive it would have struck any Vilnius resident as ludicrous. Local people would have gone during office hours to the studios to see the staff. The whole nonsense was another example of how Moscow's lies failed to match the local scene, and was essentially laughable, though it had tragic implications because the system was manufacturing advance justification for an atrocity which was to come. We were at the centre of a process of disinformation and defamation which was designed to turn public opinion in the Soviet Union and in the West against us. This misinformation was relentless, no expense being spared. The machine had been switched on. Its design was clumsy, its mechanism imperfect and its sense of direction disordered, but the results were savage.

The Soviet intelligence system worked more subtly in the West, as a book published subsequently by one of their agents bears witness. According to the agent, he and his colleagues were instructed to influence public opinion in Norway in favour of Moscow. The January massacre in Vilnius came as a surprise to the Soviet embassy in Oslo, which had been concentrating on using their confidential channels of information to spread slanderous stories about the Lithuanian leadership, especially Landsbergis and the 'Kaunas mafia', who were accused of amassing large assets during the economic blockade of Lithuania, of using unconstitutional means to provoke conflict with Moscow and of pursuing discriminatory policies against national minority groups.

Directives from Moscow on 12 January ordered the Soviet embassy staff to intensify its propaganda and to blame the Lithuanian government for any ensuing confrontation in Vilnius, since they had by their actions provoked units of the Soviet army. One may wonder why these instructions reached Oslo only on the morning of 12 January. I do, however, remember hearing that Moscow could not decide which of the Baltic countries to attack first. Arnold Ruutel later told me that on the night of 12–13 January the sea-gates to the port of Tallinn were left open so that a special Soviet marine commando unit could have easy access to the town. This may have been true, but the action began in Vilnius and stopped there.

Documentary films were needed to supplement the propaganda effort, but much of the available material would have revealed the brutality of the Soviet soldiers and the policies behind their deployment. Moscow therefore sent a leading television journalist, Alexander Nevzorov, to portray the situation in a better light. The resulting film was peculiar, to say the least, though it may just have helped to mislead opinion in the Soviet Union. It portrayed the Soviet army and the 'black berets' of the OMON (the unit had originally been under the control of the Lithuanian SSR Ministry of Internal Affairs) as 'honourable defenders of the Soviet Union'. They had occupied the Vilnius Police Academy by force, ejecting staff and cadets before turning the place into a Soviet fortress bristling with armaments. From this base they had then begun a campaign of terror across the country, and in the capital in particular, which went on for more than six months. The defences which our people had organized for the Supreme Council had been mercilessly attacked in the Soviet media, but our entire organization was a joke when its equipment was compared with that at the disposal of this vicious group. However, Nevzorov's film portrayed a large and dangerously vindictive Lithuanian force trying to kill the 'brave OMON defenders of the Soviet constitution'. It presented this ugly gang as deeply loyal to Gorbachev and prepared to shed its last drop of blood in the defence of communism, while Landsbergis, who had signed their death warrant, attempted to have them picked off one by one by his snipers! These bullies were portrayed as the 'true heroes' of the Soviet Union.

When Nevzorov's work was done, video cassettes of his production were dispatched to Soviet embassies around the world to 'inform visitors and especially journalists about the events in Vilnius'. It was perhaps unlucky for the promoters of this propaganda that the actual events in our country were being transmitted live from Vilnius by a multitude of foreign correspondents who had gathered to witness events at first hand as they occurred. The evidence which they now sent home clearly contradicted Soviet propaganda, and the world at large was shocked at what it read, heard and saw. Soon we learned that Soviet embassies had begun to find the propaganda film embarrassing and had soon found it necessary to avoid showing it. A propaganda war was being fought for public opinion, and it was becoming clear that the political outcome was likely to depend upon its progress. A widespread debate about who was responsible for the events of January was being conducted internationally, and people had learned how our essentially unarmed nation was standing up to a brutal oppressor. While it is not too much to say that the world's conscience was deeply moved, it is a curious truth that our own movement was too deeply involved in the immediacies of what was going on to realize what was happening in the world. We continued to feel isolated, believing that the West was still unmoved, and I recall a cartoon in one of our newspapers which portrayed a heavy brute bashing the daylights out of his victim as western politicians stood by not lifting a finger. It was an expression of sentiment which was real enough, but it was no longer the right interpretation of what was going on. I am still disappointed that the West did not react more effectively, but I can confirm they had at last begun to register definite disapproval.

Moscow was busy presenting all opposition to its control as reflecting conflicts between ethnic groups and rival political forces, even suggesting there was a danger of civil war breaking out between factions in Lithuania. This was a line which could soon allow the Soviet army to be represented as 'defending the peoples from themselves', bravely interposing itself between the rival groups. The techniques of manipulation were well known; they had been used successfully in the Caucasus and Moldova, and quite recently at Baku (in Azerbaijan) and elsewhere. Now the strategy was being applied in our country, though it soon came up against unexpected problems because it was splendidly unsuccessful in fomenting tension between our various communities. Sadly, the architects of the policy were undeterred, and responded by investing more energy in their efforts to introduce an ethnic factor into our politics. On the night of 12 January, as tanks drove into the crowds and soldiers beat people up, we learned that many busloads of the roughneck followers of the Yedinstvo leader Valerka Ivanov were arriving from the Moscow-controlled factories to join in the fray. Few of these troublemakers were of Lithuanian origin, but they were all passionate supporters of Moscow. They were uniformly hostile to 'Lithuanian nationalism', which they described as Nazism, and their outlook reflected the primitive character of Soviet state propaganda, which often worked on simple minds to fill them with hostility to all who were different from themselves. General Varenikov, who took charge of the Soviet forces in Vilnius on 10

January, expressed exactly the same sentiments publicly, and we learned later that he had actually arrived in Vilnius with orders to use whatever force was necessary to finish us off.

Once the Soviet army had occupied the Vilnius television tower, it encouraged pro-Moscow Communists and members of the Yedinstvo movement to prepare television programmes attacking the Lithuanian state. A recording of one of these transmissions still exists, showing General Varenikov condemning our Supreme Council angrily over its declaration of independence. 'They *voted on it*!' he exclaimed. 'Even Hitler did not work the way they did, *it is fascism*!' The performance was an outburst which would discredit a half-wit, but here was a Soviet commander of the highest rank, the man entrusted by his masters with the future of our country. As events unfolded, more of his character was revealed.

The busing of *provocateurs* seems to have been a definite part of the strategy. Wherever they went scuffles and stone-throwing followed, though nothing too serious ensued. However, an incident on 13 January in a field near the main events at the television installation is worth mentioning as an indication of the role Yedinstvo played. It was not filmed because it was away from the focal point where the unarmed crowd resisted the advancing tanks and rifle butts of the KGB paratroopers, which is a pity because the record might help answer a few questions even now. It seems that Valerka Ivanov turned up with his hooligans to make trouble in a way which would provide the Soviet army with a clear excuse to begin military action. However, he actually arrived *after* the army had begun its dirty work. If they had turned up an hour earlier they could have caused serious damage, but the buses arrived too late for their roughneck passengers to be useful to Varenikov. It may of course have been the result of poor calculation of the journey time, but it is interesting that a legend grew up that the hour's difference between Vilnius and Moscow time was overlooked when the orders were prepared, and that the orders failed to specify that they should move in at local time. Speculation about the failure of co-ordination between the groups has continued to make people wonder, but one thing is certain: there was a Soviet plan to provoke civil riots. Had it been successful, their occurrence would certainly have become ammunition for the propaganda war.

After the event the Soviets naturally claimed that we had attacked them, still insisting that the army was involved in attempting to keep two warring crowds apart, one of which had been demonstrating against the Supreme Council before going on to continue its protest near the television tower! The style was again characteristic of the prepared briefings which came down from Moscow and said that 'Lithuanian extremists' had begun to shoot at soldiers, which had provoked the military reaction. It was, however, a description which did not fit the facts, as the Soviet troops sustained only one casualty, an officer with a bullet wound in his *back*. Later examination proved that the bullet could only have been fired by one of the soldiers as it came from an automatic weapon powerful enough to puncture his bullet-proof waistcoat. As no shots were fired by us it was clear that Lieutenant Shackich was a victim of his own side, though other rumours were put about in the months which followed. Some of these suggested that Lithuanian snipers had been shooting at both the Russians and our own people from distant roofs. This also was propaganda which we were able to disprove by studying the layout of the roofs around the area where the people had been standing and where Soviet tanks and paratroopers were deployed. Our review showed that it would have been quite impossible to target either the crowd or the military concerned from those buildings, and again we found that the dead had been shot with Soviet automatic weapons of the kind issued to their paratroopers. The bullets were army issue in every case, and had been prepared to tear tissue on entry into the body, to create large, potentially fatal, wounds. The use of such dum-dum bullets is forbidden by international law in war, let alone against unarmed civilians. It is a further instance of Soviet atrocities that their commanders were prepared to go to these lengths. The evidence was compelling, and we regarded these issues as being so serious that I asked 'Shchit', a democratic military organization in Moscow, to prepare an independent report on what had happened, but none of this could slow Moscow's propaganda, which continued to blame everyone except its own political establishment. Meanwhile the deeply guilty chiefs of our own pro-Moscow Communist party continued to urge the use of military means to take Lithuania back into the Soviet Union, calling for the intensification of any measure that might help them eventually to take over the government. Their leaders often went to Moscow for instructions, and the so-called 'National Salvation Committee' which had invited the Soviet forces to 'save Lithuania' was their creation. Mykolas Burokevičius, their leader, who had previously appeared on television claiming that it was he who was trying to prevent conflict, while we, the Lithuanian government, were hell-bent on confrontation, now began to blame us stridently for the lives lost. This story was circulated from Oslo but had been prepared in Moscow. The evidence to prove this came to hand some time later when a set of taped lectures was found a few days after the attempted *coup* in Moscow had failed. The tapes had been left behind by a senior political instructor who visited Vilnius just after the bloody events in January.

The lectures shamelessly rewrote the history of the situation and neatly absolved the National Salvation Committee from any blame, forgetting to mention that it had invited the Soviet military forces to intervene in Lithuania at the same time that the party for whom they were a front organization announced its intention of taking the government into its own hands. The only truthful accusation such people could bring against the Lithuanian government was the charge that we had steadfastly refused to comply, and had refused to capitulate! Unfortunately, similar allegations were also made by some of our own people and were echoed by the Lithuanian media, which blamed the Lithuanian leadership for the casualties which were sustained. Their agreement with the Soviet line gained them no credit either in Lithuania or in the West.

That there was a carefully laid Soviet plot behind these events became apparent in the light of what happened in Latvia and Estonia. Approximately a week before the atrocities occurred in Vilnius, Viktors Alksnis, a pro-Soviet Latvian with the rank of colonel, had informed a French woman journalist that armed *coups* were planned to take place in Lithuania, Latvia and Estonia. It had been anticipated that the price increases imposed a little earlier in the month would provoke extreme discontent, and that this would provide the occasion for subversive action aimed at overthrowing the governments. Parallel developments with some local variation were planned in all three Baltic states. When the Estonian government raised prices, large numbers of Russian nationals were bused to rallies outside the government building to demand the government's overthrow. At almost the same time the Soviet commander in the Baltic region, General Fiodor Kuzmin, accused the new Latvian militia, which was acting as a police force, of organizing repeated confrontation with his forces. After this he forcibly disarmed the militia, and an OMON unit, which was already notorious for terrorizing the inhabitants of Riga, was ordered to occupy the premises of the Ministry of the Interior. The attack took place on 15 January, and it left casualties lying in the street. Latvia was now experiencing what had happened in Lithuania, and it seemed likely that the same methods would have been applied in Estonia and even in Russia itself, where plans to crush the local democracies later came to light in places like Moscow and Leningrad where the local leaders were reformists.

It is one of the miracles of history that this far-reaching and complicated Soviet plan was finally unmasked in Lithuania. That bloody Sunday in January left little room for doubt that the Soviet armed forces were in the business of crushing unarmed civilian populations. It was a realization which caused a wave of indignation across the world, and mercifully it was this reaction which prevented the iron fist of empire from striking again. When this change in mood came, it was swift and decisive. Gorbachev acted by sending a Soviet parliamentary delegation of four to Lithuania. It included his deputy and it met the Soviet military leaders, local representatives and me in a tightly packed schedule. Its members came to my office, where we had a tense exchange in which I expressed my view of events and condemned the failure of the Soviet state to respond to my note of protest, delivered three days before the crisis. I did not mince my words. Having described the way in which Gorbachev had refused to speak to me on the telephone during the crisis, I then said bluntly that the Soviet state was inhuman and possibly out of control. Alternatively if, as its president claimed, he was still in control, then he certainly had blood on his hands. Later, I had the chance to express these views to Gorbachev personally, using the same emphatic language and demanding that the men who were guilty of these atrocities should be brought to account. My directness embarrassed him, and it was easy to see that he was avoiding a direct reply. However, he succumbed to the pressure a few days later and issued a belated denunciation of the violence in Vilnius and of the attempt to overthrow a lawful government. Until then he, like the others in Moscow, had avoided any acceptance of responsibility. He had tried to present himself as impartial, as the person who stood above all others. Now his climb-down was all but silent, though it involved a statement of the utmost importance to us, because it both acknowledged the legal authority of the Lithuanian government and condemned the Soviet Communist party and the other *putschists* in the country. Interestingly enough, Colonel Alksnis gave an interview some months later in which he said that he and his allies had done everything they were asked to do. He then added: 'But we were betrayed by Gorbachev.' The story illustrates the lateness of his conversion.

The possibility that the local Lithuanian communists had misled Gorbachev needs to be considered. Their propaganda had promoted the idea that the people of Lithuania were disappointed with their independence, with the Sąjūdis government, with Landsbergis as its leader, and indeed with everything associated with them. They were clearly taken in by their own propaganda, but Gorbachev himself seems also to have succumbed to the idea that a relatively small intervention would be sufficient to turn the clock back. Both he and his Lithuanian cronies must also have felt that our people would approve of 'order being re-established'. This, however, was essentially an unrealistic view of developments in Lithuania, and Gorbachev's delegation recognized this obvious conclusion after only one day in Vilnius. Once they had interviewed the two opposing forces for themselves it was plain even to them that it all came down to a fundamental disagreement between the legal government and the Soviet army. They were then forced to recognize that continued explanations and justifications on the old Soviet lines would bring no further benefit. Somewhat ironically I expressed these very sentiments to the delegation when it first arrived in my office at two o'clock on the afternoon of 13 January. I told them that the real opposition to us came from the self-appointed National Salvation Committee, acting on the orders of the pro-Moscow Communist party, and from virtually nowhere else. Other than this, there was no local support for the use of military force against us, and those who had invited it were not local people. Levon Ter-Petrosian, who was one of the more influential members of the delegation, had replied that he and his colleagues were 'trying to establish the character of the country's aspirations and would recognize the mood of citizens who had organized to defend their legal government'. My response was to say that our people were ready to sacrifice themselves for their legal government, not necessarily because they particularly liked its members, but because they knew that it embodied their country's sovereignty and freedom.

I had an abrupt and difficult telephone conversation with Gorbachev on 14 January. Its subject was the conflict between our two states, and he began by saying that Lithuania's troubles had begun 'because you have changed your government'. I replied that it was a matter for Lithuanians, and Lithuanians alone, to decide. I then told him that while our affairs were and would remain our own, we recognized that we shared common economic problems with the rest of eastern Europe, and he might usefully reflect on this as his own policies towards Lithuania had magnified those problems, which were really no different in kind from those, for example, of Russia. He must, however, recognize that we now had our own government and did not want it replaced by any arrangement determined from outside. He retorted that Lithuania's leaders were to blame for the difficult situation, and I responded by saying that we knew exactly who was to blame for our difficulties, but now wanted to move into constructive discussions. He then put me down by saying that he was 'unable to begin negotiations'. At this I slammed back at him: 'Haven't you already begun them, by talking with tanks and automatic rifles?' I threw in a few blunt observations on the way the recent atrocities had been ordered by his own military command and added that if he now wanted a different kind of dialogue with Lithuania he could begin it straight away, and on his own authority. I taunted him by suggesting that if his room for manœuvre in arranging such discussions seemed constricted it probably meant there was a second government in Moscow to which he was answerable and shot the question: 'Who rules the Soviet Union? The military or Mikhail Sergeyevitch?' I added that what lay at the root of the problem between us was the Soviet Union's view of the relationship between our two countries. He must recognize once and for all that the continued presence of Soviet forces in Lithuania was illegal and wholly unwelcome: 'The Soviet military has no right to shoot our nationals, and I am taking this opportunity to issue an official protest.' It was a conversation conducted under great pressure, and Gorbachev later dismissed my contribution in his high and mighty fashion in a report to the members of his Supreme Council in which he said that it had confirmed his opinion that it would be 'very difficult to establish a dialogue with any of the people currently controlling the Supreme Council of Lithuania'. Those who heard him must have discerned his enormous impatience with the key people in our government, whom he would obviously have liked to see removed from our positions. In his view only Prunskienė was amenable, and he said as much when reporting on the events in Vilnius to the Soviet Supreme Council in an aside which must be understood as an appreciation of her helpfulness. At the time we did not yet know that Prunskienė had suggested in Washington, as early as the spring of 1990, a 'postponement of the Lithuanian declaration of independence by two years'.

Despite their definition of the Lithuanian situation as a 'local conflict', its handling by Gorbachev and his advisers reflected a struggle which affected the whole Soviet Union. On the one side there was a growing band of democrats, on the other intransigent conservatives and Stalinists. Gorbachev wanted to play the role of middleman in this scenario, presenting himself as the centrist power-broker who would mould the situation by forcing the two sides to become reconciled. From this perspective, Lithuania and its problems were merely a pawn on a larger board. At a much later date a plan came to light which had been prepared by the KGB political forecasters during, or perhaps even before, the summer of 1990 to enable these objectives to be achieved. It explained how this power-broker role was to be constructed and promoted by marketing his attractive personality. Whether the KGB really viewed him as attractive or not is immaterial now, but it seems that it was quite clear to them that he was the only person strong enough to unite the profoundly conflicting forces within the Soviet Union. It was an added advantage from that viewpoint that he seemed to have the support of the West, where he was also perceived as the only politician able to stabilize that enormous state. Needless to say, his standing in these matters was not always to our advantage.

I recall two strange people visiting my room at the Supreme Council late in the afternoon of 14 January 1991, at a time when the building was full of defenders and visitors intent on showing solidarity with us. A group of patriotic Ukrainians had come saying that we were engaged in a struggle for the common good, and that they would happily fight with us and die if necessary. There were also parliamentarians from Poland, Hungary and other countries, who came believing that their presence made it less likely that the Soviets would launch an attack. I now found these two travellers from Russia in front of me, also claiming to be activists for freedom, although their ideas seemed out of harmony with what was going on around us. I had previously met one of them, Voronov, in Leningrad at an international conference on human rights held in the autumn. He had claimed so many titles on that occasion that one could be pardoned for wondering if some of them were fictitious, but he had implied a link with Andrei Sakharov and his human rights organization. He now told me that we must all join together to support Gorbachev as the man to resolve all conflicts and deliver us from the threat of total annihilation, in a Soviet Union-wide association. As I listened, I suspected that these men had not thought of this idea themselves, and concluded they were on a KGB mission. The second man was Vladimir Zhirinovsky, who was then known to few of us, and he scarcely opened his mouth throughout the interview, though I now understand that he boasted to an audience a few years later that he had come to see me in Vilnius.

Even this tiny episode shows how the KGB plan presented Gorbachev as a centrist. This idea soon disintegrated in Lithuania and in the old Soviet Union, but the man's image as a benevolent, positive reformer, rather than as a politician unable to control the militarist and Stalinist factions, could still dominate western opinion. Westerners were very reluctant to make things worse for him because they wanted to give him a chance to deal with his internal problems. This feeling was a very powerful one. Late in 1990 I was in Canada when someone asked me whether Gorbachev was 'a dictator or an opportunist, a humane man or a mere *apparatchik* who would do his best for the system even if it was malignant'. I have always felt that the man was very much the product of the system to which he belonged, and that it was impossible to consider him separately from a system would always revert to dictatorship and aggression in the end. It was this issue which was put to the test in Lithuania. We were the first country to experience the man's true character when the chips were down. The question I was asked was an important one, and some answers may now be obtained from his memoirs in which he describes what he calls the 'Lithuanian *putsch*', and claims that he was an innocent bystander in what occurred in our country.

The plebiscite

Many foreign governments reacted very rapidly to the news from Vilnius on the morning of 13 January. Norway, Iceland and Denmark responded at once, and the government of Canada suspended its programme of financial assistance to the Soviet Union the next day. We would have liked many more nations to have responded in similar terms, but a very clear political response came from the European Parliament. A resolution was adopted there in February which bluntly described the actions of the Soviet army as 'aggression and intervention'. Such terminology had not previously been used there, and was avoided when the casualties which resulted from the excesses of the OMON were discussed at a later date, but this recognition was enough at the time because the very use of the expressions 'aggression' and 'intervention against a state' implied a recognition of that state's existence.

Assistance now came to Lithuania from many places. Boris Yeltsin, the Russian president, bravely told Gorbachev 'to stop that disgusting business', and when Jon Baldvin Hannibalsson, Iceland's minister of foreign affairs, visited Vilnius soon after that bloody Sunday I asked him to take a further step by re-establishing formal diplomatic contacts between our countries. He willingly responded by sending Moscow a note saying that his visit implied recognition of the Lithuanian state. Our relationship with Russia was also of interest to him as formal documents of recognition between each of the Baltic states and the new Russian republic had been signed at Tallinn on 13 January. That important gathering had concluded with an appeal being sent to Javier Perez de Cuellar, secretary-general of the United Nations, which asked him to call a special conference on the Baltic states, and drew attention to the sovereignty of the Baltic states and the current dangers to peace. It stated that the four countries, having recognized one another's sovereignty, protested against the use of armed force against their citizens and announced that each had forbidden its citizens to take part in armed action against any of the other countries. Each of the four countries, being now committed to bilateral relationships which would be developed according to the principles of international law, appealed to the countries of the world to condemn any act of armed intervention directed against the sovereignty of the Baltic states. These documents were signed late in the evening of 13 January, and it is worth mentioning again that Boris Yeltsin had travelled to Tallinn after ignoring advice from his colleagues that he should stay away. As the serious events in Lithuania had not unnaturally prevented me from travelling to Tallinn, the final texts were sent to me by facsimile, and I returned them in the same way once they were signed. We were facing an extremely dangerous situation, and their publication brought us major political benefits, but the Soviet authorities were in an ugly mood when they received them, and a military attack on Latvia took place only a week later.

Immediately after the massacre in Vilnius, Russian democrats in Moscow organized a large demonstration in support of Lithuania. Like Yelstin's venturing to Tallinn, this was an indication of solidarity which warmed our hearts, raised our spirits and opened new perspectives for us as it gave practical and moral support which transcended the political immediacies of the day. Both events encouraged us to press on with negotiations to establish proper interstate relationships with Russia, a process which was concluded with a very important bilateral agreement signed in Moscow in the summer of that year. Other relationships were advanced by this development because Iceland was able to take further steps toward recognition of Lithuania once Russia had agreed to sign a bilateral agreement recognizing the sovereignty of the Lithuanian state. While progress on this front was slower than I had hoped, in retrospect I accept that I was over-optimistic about the pace at which full international recognition would come about. At first we anticipated that Russia would sign an agreement after the Icelanders, who were 'ahead in the race' as their Parliament was the very first to charge its government with the reinstatement of diplomatic ties. Reykjavik then prepared a joint declaration to be signed by the foreign ministers of both countries, which amounted to an announcement that diplomatic relations had been established, but this document reached us after the Soviets had learned of the Icelandic Parliament's resolution. On 24 January we sent an instruction to Algirdas Saudargas, Lithuania's foreign minister who was then in Warsaw, asking him to sign the restoration of our diplomatic relations with Iceland, expressing the hope that this would happen very soon. The Kremlin had reacted by recalling its ambassador from Reykjavik immediately, and that was enough to delay the next response. Our business did not then move forward again until the outcome of our negotiations with Russia had been clarified, but there were other reasons for the delay because the Estonians were also trying hard to persuade Iceland to include all three Baltic state in its initiative. So the issue dragged on until August. Of course we were unhappy about this delay, but in the end it did not put us at any real disadvantage because the whole world knew (and I did not hesitate to point it out!) that Iceland had already moved ahead despite Soviet objections. While the process which led to recognition seemed long drawn out to us, the delay was widely discussed and well understood. In the end Iceland proved the most independent of all the western countries, following a foreign policy which did not kowtow to Soviet pressure. Their concern for our predicament was a great asset to us in the end as one more factor which ensured that Soviet aggression against Lithuania was thoroughly debated in international forums. However, after 13 January and the casualties we suffered, there was a real change in attitudes. Wherever our diplomats turned up, and wherever I travelled, people of different communities and nations, their journalists and their politicians, all recalled the awful events in Vilnius vividly. The Soviets had precipitated their own crisis, and it had been shown to the world at large. Now they were unable to reverse the loss of political prestige which followed their actions. The memory of their brutalities had stained the general imagination, and would stay to haunt them.

One of the more important debates on the international scene was that which took place in the United States Congress when its Commission for Human Rights reported in May 1991. Its report had stimulated consider- able interest, and many congressmen participated. A group had been set up in Congress to seek ways of assisting the Baltic states, and its members now arranged for our leaders to attend the debate. As a result, I was privileged to address the gathering. My speech drew attention to the seizure of buildings in our capital and described the occupying army's atrocities, which involved looting and plunder as well as violence against unarmed civilians. I hoped that my comments would influence these politicians, as I was able to give very clear examples of how the Soviet army ignored both human rights and the laws of property. Their record in these matters would eventually cost them dear, but in the mean time they attempted to restore their dwindling prestige by accusing *our* government of infringing or ignoring human rights. Fortunately we could respond by showing that Lithuania was then the only country in eastern Europe which had already instituted a liberal and far-reaching law to guarantee the rights of its national minorities. Our sound reply on this issue did not, however, deter them from advancing on another propaganda front, and attempting to throw doubt on Lithuania's treat- ment of people who had moved into the country from other parts of the Soviet Union. Our response was to draw attention to the way the Soviet army regularly ignored the fundamental principles of human rights, including the right to life, and to point out that there is also a right to *have* a native country. This indeed had been my theme in the autumn of 1990 at the Human Rights Conference in Leningrad. My speech there asserted that our native country had been taken from us by the Soviets. It had since been denied to us. At every opportunity I repeated this obser- vation, telling people that the theft of a country is also a breach of rights, and that it is also a human right to demand that wrongs be righted. I said that we had a right to ask to have our own country returned to its own people.

I travelled extensively in the West in the spring and summer of 1991, and lectured widely on the tricks of Soviet propaganda. I also tried to interest prospective investors, explaining that Lithuania had a number of advantages to offer, not least because we already had our own independent legislature and law. My visit to Washington in May saw me addressing congressmen, businessmen and academics. Also, together with the prime ministers of Estonia and Latvia, I had a meeting with President Bush in the White House. I went on to Chicago where I had many interviews with journalists for whom Lithuania and Gorbachev were very high on the agenda at the time. We experienced real warmth, and much attention was paid to us. Later I visited the Richard Nixon Centre in Los Angeles where I particularly remember seeing the Lithuanian tricolour on display over the library. I also paid a visit to former President Ronald Reagan, whom I thanked for his firm stand against Soviet expansionism, and his defence of human rights in the Soviet Union which had given birth to *perestroika*. These events were followed by meetings with prominent Lithuanian exiles and the famous American-Japanese painter, Hiro Yamagata. We went on to Chicago where Loyola University presented me with an honorary doctorate and American Rotarians awarded me the Paul Harris Fellowship. The city has the largest concentration of Lithuanians anywhere abroad, and I met members of their many societies and talked with Lithuanian activists, whom I thanked for their unwavering dedication to our country's interests, and especially the efforts made over many years to ensure that the USA maintained its refusal to recognize the annexation of our country. The assistance given to maintain our embassy and consulates was also acknowledged, and I paid tribute to their continued devotion in bringing up their children in Lithuanian traditions and ensuring that they continued to speak our Lithuanian language. Many of them were eager to put their knowledge and expertise at the service of Lithuania, but I also met a cool and ironic element in these emigrant communities. Some intellectuals questioned whether the Lithuanian government should publish its own newspaper and told me that they considered this practice to be undemocratic – even when I reminded them of the legacy of the Soviet newspaper monopoly in our country. This did not seem to soften them, but their grudging attitude was more than compensated for by a group of young businessmen of Lithuanian descent who staged a traditionally American giant reception in my honour and Gražina's. Some eight hundred guests attended this feast, which took place in the Chicago Museum of Nature among the relics of dinosaurs and elephants! These dear exiles had earned the right to rejoice at having their own president with them. It was a kind of moral compensation for their long wait and hard struggle, to hear the news of my visit broadcast across the United States.

In June the chairmen of the Supreme Councils of the three Baltic states were invited to Brussels by the Benelux Council. A special council session was held in our honour and we were given a first insight into the work of NATO. Later in the month I went with a delegation of Supreme Council deputies and government officials on an official tour around France. It began and ended in Paris, where I met the president and prime minister on both occasions. The tour had been organized by our friends in the French National Assembly, and gave us a full and varied picture of the country and of its rich endowments in the sciences and technology. The French were truly open-hearted in their wish to establish links, and it later dawned on me that Lithuania had not yet fully prepared itself to welcome the extended hand of friendship. It was embarrassing to notice how we sometimes failed to recognize the gifts which were being offered to us from areas as far apart as the Vendée, Marseilles, Alsace and Lorraine. The Vendée has its own proud and tragic history, and the regional president, Philippe de Villiers, was extremely benevolent towards independent Lithuania. During a visit to a traditional Fire Festival he introduced us to Madame de Lattre, widow of the late marshal, a French national hero of the Second World War. The old lady recalled meeting Lithuanian students in Germany. As she did this her surname suddenly surfaced from the depths of my memory and I recalled my sister telling me how she and her husband had been with the rest of the Čiurlionis ensemble in the French zone of occupation just after the war. They had been given hospitality by de Lattre at his headquarters and had been well looked after by his staff. It really is a small world! At Nancy, the capital of Lorraine, an official choir met us singing our Lithuanian national anthem and the civic dignitaries drew our attention to a pediment displaying the *Vytis*, the Lithuanian national emblem. Above it was the statue of Stanislov Leszczynski, a king of Poland and grand duke of Lithuania who had lost his throne and ended his days as duke of Lorraine. On the last day of our tour we met the French minister for culture to discuss the forthcoming Baltic Festival and an exhibition of Čiurlionis's work, and while we were with him the news came that the OMON had occupied the main telephone exchange in Vilnius. Our country's connecting link with the entire outside world had been broken, and it seemed to me that this assault was even worse than events in January. The unexpected news caught me off guard, and my temper came to the boil. Before I had the chance to think things through I had spoken my mind to the minister, and said something like: 'We are here in France and you are being very kind to us. However, you do not want to displease the Soviet Union, so you and the other countries are afraid to establish formal diplomatic relations with us. Now, see what your friends the Soviets are up to while you hesitate!' Somewhat to my surprise he gave me a patient hearing and then suddenly picked up his phone and rang Roland Dumas, the minister for foreign affairs. He then asked me to repeat my observations. Once more my feelings spilled over, but to my surprise I now received a real answer for the first time, and an immediate promise that the question of establishing a permanent Lithuanian delegation in Paris would be addressed. Until then our only hope for early representation in Paris had been an information centre, funded by friendly French parliamentarians. Now at last we were to have renewed diplomatic contact and real recognition. It was a moment to be savoured, as we had already held a big press conference to discuss the Lithuanian embassy in Paris. The building had long been in the hands of the Soviet Union, but Michel Pelchat, a French parliamentarian, had attempted to reclaim it for us (even now the stolen building has not been returned to Lithuania). I used this occasion to slip in a statement that the West could usefully supply us with half a dozen anti-tank rockets to take home with us. It was my way of publicizing another bit of information which had reached us from Vilnius, namely that the Soviets had supplied the OMON unit occupying the Police Academy there with six new armoured vehicles.

It was in May 1991 that I addressed the American Congress in Washington, but the visit to the Helsinki forum in June was equally significant, and if anything a bigger step forward. We were invited on the initiative of Anders Bjorck, president of the Council of Europe's Parliamentary Assembly after two of his Council's experts, David Atkinson and Daniel Tarschys (who later became secretary-general of the Council of Europe) had been to the Baltic states to assess our human rights situation. They were well disposed towards us, and as the forum was to be concerned with all aspects of human rights, our presence there was appropriate. Of course the Soviets also received an invitation, but their initial response was to decline because they had learned that we would be present, though they later relented. This change of heart allowed the relationships between the Baltic states and the Soviet Union to be discussed in an international forum for the first time, and it soon became clear that things were not going the Soviet Union's way. It was a most important opportunity for us because it meant that our effort to internationalize our problem had at last been rewarded and showed us that ours was now seen as a European problem, with some hope of being resolved at that level. The Soviet Union had done its best to avoid this and would clearly have preferred to make a few concessions to the western powers while the real issues were left to negotiations which left us in a subordinate position, pleading like vassals for small concessions from their sovereign. To their chagrin it was now apparent that we were past that stage of the game. We were at last meeting them on equal terms when we arrived in Helsinki, and it was a wholly new and revitalizing experience. The Soviets were no longer able to pass us off as rioting provinces or infringers of minority rights, because our Baltic countries were now meeting with them on the basis of equality, as state with state. At last the shoe was on the other foot!

This new experience made it clear to us all that the tragic events of January had transformed perspectives both outside and inside our country. The communist plan now faced political defeat even in eastern Lithuania, where a significant population of other nationalities lived. Looking for opportunities to divide us, the Soviets had encouraged Polish nationalism in this area by suggesting that it might become an autonomous region with its own institutions, and finally even proposing that a separate state could be established there. In May 1990 Mykolas Burokevičius, the leader of the pro-Moscow Communist party, had told Alexei Lizichev, the chief political adviser to the Soviet army who was visiting the Baltic area, that his movement had 'declared the region of Šalčininkai independent of Lithuania', but complained there was 'no help from the centre' in furthering the plan. This policy was then further manipulated by the Communist party with the help of its advisers in Moscow, and some leaders of the Polish minority community had been encouraged to travel between Moscow, Warsaw and even Moldova to explore the potential 'separation'. Our opponents obviously hoped to make capital for themselves and to serve the Soviet Union by detaching this province of Lithuania. These threats of separation gave something of a boost to Moscow's propaganda against us. They seemed to believe that Lithuania might relinquish its own demand for independence as a result of this threat of internal secession. Moral deviousness and unpleasant intrigue often confuse the real issues when one is dealing with obstinate and devious people, but the miasma of suspicion which had come to cloud the nationalities issue in Lithuania was suddenly cleared by the January massacre. It was perhaps a paradoxical effect, but the sheer awfulness of what had happened opened the eyes of those representatives of the Polish community who had been most prominent in announcing, in Poland and elsewhere, that Poles were being discriminated against in Lithuania. They now showed solidarity with us realizing who was the true enemy, and that it was hostile not just to the needs of the nation but to the very concept of humanity. It was an awakening which affected Poles and Russians alike, and many of their leaders now joined in the general revulsion at the Kremlin's aggression and wished to dissociate themselves completely from this crime.

This was the first time that Lithuania's Polish leaders had shown this level of goodwill. Although they did not maintain this attitude for long, and later resumed their agitation, the fact that they showed solidarity at the darkest hour by denouncing Soviet actions on that occasion will not be forgotten. Lithuania's Soviet-orientated Poles were a complicated lot. Their disposition was in marked contrast with that of Poland itself, which held us in high regard and rendered solid help and support. Its government had given Algirdas Saudargas, our minister for foreign affairs, complete diplomatic protection when we sent him to Warsaw charged with authority to set up a government in exile if necessary. He was given facilities for a long stay there if the need should arise, and credentials which would have permitted him to fulfil our expectations of him in the event of the Soviet army invading us and suppressing our government. They were real friends in need, and it is likely that their concern helped to ensure that Moscow's plan to partition Lithuania's territory was halted. This backing was very important to us, and the developing situation brought other advantages when it became clear to everyone just how completely compromised the Soviet Union's institutions of law, order and justice were. We had learned that the Soviet Union's prosecutor-general had been charged with the task of investigating the army's crimes in Vilnius, but it soon became clear that this was less an attempt to control the process of investigation than a device for determining its outcome. Their so-called 'local prosecutor' was to be involved in collecting the evidence before sending it on to Moscow. While we would have been wholly willing to co-operate in an inquiry with a precondition of total parity and equal access to witness statements and other evidence, we naturally rejected this manœuvre out of hand. A shared investigation, with the Soviet prosecutor having equal status with his Lithuanian counterpart, would have been acceptable, but our suggestion for this procedure was not accepted, so we refused either to co-operate or to pass evidence to their experts, even for a trial period. We had been forewarned by the experience of others. The Latvians had faced a similar situation in which they not been cautious enough. Their legal officers had co-operated with Soviet prosecutors in a subordinate role and had handed over all the evidence to them, only to discover that it had all 'been lost', which was of course highly convenient for the Soviets. In our case we were happy to allow partial co-operation between the prosecutors, to allow their investigations to go forward, but little happened. The other side made virtually no attempt to investigate even the most obvious cases. There was a prolonged period in which inquiries were supposed to be taking place, but their staff never seemed to venture out of their offices. Yet despite this inactivity their officers came to conclusions which they eventually published. Curiously these results amounted to virtually the same statements as those issued by the Soviet authorities on the day following the massacre, and it was of course the old prepared scenario being repeated yet once again. The Lithuanians had attacked workers and had beaten them up; the workers had not been allowed to present an ordinary petition at the television tower; there were snipers shooting from the rooftops and the windows; we had shot our own people; the Lithuanians had pushed each other under the tanks, and so on *ad nauseam*. The report, though published by the prosecutor-general of the Soviet Union, was no better than street propaganda, written as if for the illiterate. It was a perfect demonstration of how their judicial system operated. The fruit was as rotten as the vine, and the product only served to prove that their highest institutions were still the wholly owned subsidiaries of the Communist party, which maintained its imperialist attitudes intact, and with complete commitment, whatever the propaganda about *perestroika*. Our Polish neighbours had their own long and bitter experience of this circular logic. Their government knew enough of our common history to avoid making sore places even sorer where wiser counsels might prevail.

After the Vilnius attack we wanted to emphasize the collective responsibility of the Soviet system for the crimes against people and property in our country, and after careful thought we took the unusual step of issuing a writ against Pugo, the Soviet Union's minister of internal affairs. Our critics considered this step to be pure political propaganda, but he was directly responsible for sending the army to our television buildings, while the OMON force which had seized the Police Academy building earlier also considered itself answerable to him. We therefore charged him with responsibility for terrorizing our people and initiating activities which were obviously criminal, and set the appropriate criminal proceedings in motion. Our action did not pass unnoticed in the world's press, and while the Soviets tried to shrug it off, it had a marked political effect. The fact that we had begun proceedings against a Soviet minister was likely to be reflected in any international forum where Lithuania's situation was discussed. After this matter was settled, we decided to hold a plebiscite on Lithuanian independence, and this took place on 9 February. This was really the most important political outcome of the disturbing events of 13 January, and we decided on it because the Soviets had announced that they would be incorporating into their constitutional law the principle that no nation could leave the Union without holding a referendum on the matter. They drafted their clause in such a way that two votes were necessary, and the second poll would certainly have taken place under unfavourable conditions. My reply to this effrontery was that Lithuania would indeed hold a referendum, but once only and under fair conditions. We were, of course, not 'preparing to leave the Soviet Union', since we were not in it, but nevertheless we would go to our people with a referendum on the matter on the same terms as if we had received an invitation to join! I was of course confident that the outcome would bring a resounding confirmation of Lithuanian statehood and independence.

There was a special background to my decision. On 10 December 1990 President Bush had asked me why, if the majority of our people favoured independence, we did not hold a referendum, and I had pondered his question carefully. We had refused earlier to comply with Gorbachev's demand that we should hold a referendum simply because we did not want to be seen to give in to his bullying demands. However, I realized that my argument had not impressed the rather straightforward thinking of the president of the United States. After this I spent a lot of time thinking about the form a referendum might take, realizing from the first that while it had to be different from the one Gorbachev was demanding, it must also reassure the world's politicians. In the end I settled on the idea of offering a plebiscite on the new Lithuanian constitution by asking the nation whether it accepted the first paragraph of our new constitution. To do this would be to ask the people of Lithuania if they wished their country to be independent. As we needed to avoid any question which might be construed as a concession to Gorbachev, we could not ask whether the country 'wanted to remain within the Soviet Union', which was where he supposed it still was! So my advice was that the people should be asked to confirm our draft constitution's declaration that 'Lithuania is an independent democratic republic'. This would at one and the same time satisfy the West and provide a highly effective rebuff to Gorbachev's plans for us – thus resolving two problems at once. When the plebiscite took place, it was in fact on these terms, and 90 per cent of the voters backed Lithuanian independence. It was a neat answer, and a peaceful and precise response, which gave a clear message to the aggressor. A thinking people had given a considered reply to those who believed that power grew from the barrels of their guns, by this simple democratic act. They had both snubbed the oppressor and won a new victory in the long battle for the nation's independence.

While the plebiscite emphatically demonstrated the strength of our position to the whole world it also had the advantage of protecting us from Gorbachev's plan to hold an all-Soviet referendum. He had announced that he would ask people to accept a new Union which would be 'improved by reforms', although the exact terms of these reforms was not specified at the time. From our viewpoint it was clearly justifiable to feel that the whole scheme was a pig in a poke, another example of the Kremlin acting in its own devious interest. It was an absurdity to ask people to express commitment to a state of affairs which did not exist and which no one had yet taken the trouble to formulate properly. The whole scheme was typical of a society which had only a one-sided social contract. It might have been appropriate to ask the people: 'Do you want to create a better Soviet Union, and if we are successful in achieving it, would you want to keep it?' Gorbachev's formula was nothing like that. The whole exercise was some sort of *trompe l'œil* designed to restrict the newly achieved freedoms of the Baltic states and much else, and with little delay. Naturally, we announced that no such referendum would take place in Lithuania. Gorbachev, however, ignored us, and the Soviet forces in Lithuania were instructed to make preparations. They received some co-operation from local authorities in the eastern part of the country, while unfavourable publicity was given to the fact that they got no help elsewhere. It was well understood in Lithuania that this was a desperate attempt to try to suggest that Lithuania's inhabitants wanted to remain Soviet citizens and were being prevented from expressing themselves. There were real dangers for us in this, but we had no option but to declare the referendum illegal, as a sovereign government alone has the authority to declare a referendum on its own soil. No national government could have faulted our action, but our decision also followed the outcome of our own referendum. It had served the nation very well and given an entirely satisfactory result. In reality it was the final plebiscite on our independence.

Everybody who took part in our constitutional referendum was fully alive to their feelings about their native country. The day saw the whole nation in festive mood, especially the older generation who remembered the past, and had experienced in very personal terms what it meant to lose their nation's freedom. The entire community came to the ballot box in its Sunday best or in national dress, and many infirm people who waited for the ballot boxes to be brought to them at home welcomed the officials with flowers, food and drink, to show their gratitude for being thus enabled to vote for the country's independence. In Vilnius we heard about two very old women who arrived at the polling station on the evening before voting day. While there was provision for advance voting for people whose business required them to be away from their district of residence on the day, the staff could not understand their problem. They lived nearby, and they would only have to wait overnight. The polling officer asked them, 'Why can't you come tomorrow?' The old ladies replied, very frankly, 'Look here, son, if we died tonight, two votes for Lithuania's independence would be lost!' This was the spirit which Gorbachev had decided to challenge. He did his best to tell the world that our plebiscite was invalid, meaningless, nothing but a mere opinion poll, but his words were wasted because he had not noticed that the world was changing around him. He was now becoming a bore. Lithuania's actions on the other hand had a new sparkle in the world's understanding.

The oppression intensifies

Although the central institutions of the Lithuanian state were not attacked on 13 January, the occupation of the television buildings was a determined attempt to undermine the government. Though the outcome resulted in a set-back for the Soviets, the occupying forces were undeterred and continued to interfere with daily life in Vilnius, and the news was regularly dominated by accounts of nasty incidents. One night a young driver did not obey a command to halt when he was challenged by a patrol and was shot in the back and killed. Doubtless he had been angered at the arrogance of the occupiers and had continued on his way. His disregard for their authority cost him his life, but there were lesser occurrences every day when citizens faced random interrogations, searches, insults and beatings. We regarded these as war crimes and began criminal proceedings whenever we could, though we felt stronger remedies should have been available. No one was immune from these unwelcome attentions and I recall Vidmantas Povilionis, a deputy of the Supreme Council, being stopped on the highway between Vilnius and Kaunas and ordered out of his car. He was searched roughly and then made to stand with his hands above his head in the freezing wind for two hours. After this he was carted back to Vilnius, but luckily he was released when he got there. There was no rhyme nor reason to these incidents, which were simply meant to keep everyone in a state of tension, and there were many casualties. Members of the corps committed to defending the Supreme Council were particularly prone to attack, especially those who had been put in charge of the sophisticated radio equipment which Canadian Lithuanians had sent to enable us to monitor the movements of military vehicles. They used to relay their observations back to a control centre, and the information was used to warn people if danger threatened. When the Soviets realized that this was going on they retaliated viciously. In one case they stopped one of our cars as it overtook one of their convoys and opened fire. One of the occupants escaped, but the other was badly wounded; he was beaten further while he was being interrogated. This was not an isolated case.

There were a number of foreign journalists in Vilnius who were keen to report these incidents. Some of them were also ill-treated, but they took the risk of being beaten for their pains and thrown into the cells, and Anatoly Lieven reported just such an experience in his book *The Baltic Revolution: Estonia, Latvia, Lithuania. The Path to Independence.* This form of terrorism amounted to an internal blockade on news. It was different from the economic blockade, but a deliberate extension of the Soviet aggression just the same. Indeed these tactics were a continuation of the military attack in January by other means, and reflected the same close co-operation between the Army, the KGB, and OMON. This last group had now been reinforced by deserters from our own police force. We had started to reorganize the service so that it would fit in with the needs of the new Lithuanian state, but some of its members had different loyalties, and when they saw what was happening, severed their links with their colleagues. Soon a number of these renegades acquired notoriety when a well-armed OMON unit commandeered the Police Academy on the outskirts of Vilnius in a move which made it clear to everybody that the highest authorities had instructed it to maintain a state of terror, since its officers were directly answerable to the Soviet Ministry of the Interior in Moscow. Indeed when its units moved into the Police Academy they were probably acting in accordance with a decree which came from Gorbachev himself who had recently ordered the 'disarmament of all illegally armed establishments in the territory of the Soviet Union'. While the declaration had mentioned the 'Soviet Union', the prevailing circumstances implied that Lithuania and the other Baltic countries were the target. His decree meant that every member of our Defence Department, those who had volunteered to protect the Supreme Council, our security services, even the Lithuanian police stood accused of being 'illegally armed establishments', and were therefore subject to attack without warning. Even policemen on night duty could be treated in this way, as they were regarded as being 'members of an illegal establishment' by extension. The policemen who had deserted to OMON were therefore guilty of double treachery when they broke into our main police arsenal to seize the weapons. They had been recruited by our oppressors to act as terrorists, and our prosecutor-general subsequently began proceedings against them for treason as well as theft. They should have known that they could not do these things with impunity, but their misdemeanours were part of a relentless process which gave encouragement to the criminal underworld to contribute to the general destabilization of our country. While these attacks on our ability to police the country were going on, Moscow's news agencies claimed that there had been a huge rise in criminal activity in Lithuania, publishing figures which were, ironically enough, inflated by our recording of *their* behaviour. They then used this misinformation as a further justification for their intervention! It was clear to us that this part of their propaganda drive had been packaged in advance, because such tales were circulating before the beginning of 1991. Eventually, however, we turned the question back on them and asked, in front of the civilized world, how policies which were deliberately designed to disarm our police force were expected to contribute to the reduction of criminal activity.

Although Moscow's Interior Ministry asserted that OMON was a local force, it was deployed alongside the regular army. The fact that its members were recruited specifically to oppose the Lithuanian government was another sign that Moscow's bureaucrats were closely watching what was happening in Lithuania, and carefully plotting to undermine us. At an early stage of Sajūdis's development they began to insinuate that we planned to maltreat national minorities. The accusation was designed to compromise a movement which did not fit into the marionette show of Soviet public life. While the accusation had no basis in fact, we were told that it was 'in the nature of a nationalist movement to hate other groups'. The script was quite subtle because, of course, our accusers claimed to know us better than we knew ourselves, and they intimated that while we were hiding our true colours at the moment, we would show them soon enough. The black-bereted OMON troops were then presented as being there to defend the interest of the minorities: they were the protectors of justice and truth whenever and wherever freedom needed to be protected. Unfortunately the real truth about these men was that they were ever ready to precipitate internal conflict to promote Moscow's interest, as were their equivalents in the Caucasus and in Moldova. The strategy was a recognizable one. In our case Moscow saw an opportunity to make use of the Poles in our eastern region, where they form the majority of the population in some places. When the time was ripe, the communists tried to proclaim that area an autonomous territory or an independent state with its own defence force in the form of the OMON. The same tactic had been used in other parts of the Soviet empire, where it was applied brutally and without any kind of human consideration. We had seen the pattern and had a dreadful apprehension that it would be used in Lithuania, and it turned out as we had anticipated. These special troops were to be the terrorist militia of the bandit Soviet state, and so the OMON drove around the country flying the Soviet red flag, busily persecuting our law enforcement officers in the name of the 'constitution' and using the crudest methods. Civilians came under fire on many occasions, as did our own police, and bombs were planted without regard for the danger to civilian lives. The strategy of provocation was so indiscriminate that one of these devices exploded on their own premises, while another went off at the heavily guarded headquarters of the pro-Moscow Communist party. Whenever the Soviet government made a reference to this movement it was described as 'an independent local force'. This was an empty assertion which I countered with a simple observation: 'Whoever provides troops with their weapons and their food is their master.' These men were in fact the mercenaries of the Soviet state.

The place most used by the opponents of Lithuanian independence to proclaim their defiance was the Vilnius county hall, the seat of the Vilnius region's local government. Many of the leaders of this regional council were Poles, who constitute a significant minority in the Vilnius area, and they announced their intention of establishing a local pro-Soviet Polish statelet with its own laws, constitution and citizenship within the borders of the Lithuanian Republic. However, even though the Polish flag was flown, the whole show was really another Soviet manipulation designed to give an impression that there were two, or even three governments running our country. These people were attempting to create an impression of extreme internal confusion in the hope that it would delay the international recognition of Lithuania and restrict our progress by deterring foreign investment, which of course abhors instability. It was clear that they hoped to undermine the government so that the flame of independence could be snuffed out, and the Kremlin itself gave positive support to their belief that their activities would dissuade the Polish government from helping us further. As we had no real option except to remain on course, we stayed cool in the face of this provocation and continued to insist that Soviet forces must leave the premises they had occupied, and pay for everything which had been looted or stolen, whether the booty was expensive portable television equipment or paper for printing. We announced publicly that significant supplies of newsprint had been taken from various editorial offices by Burokevičius and his shady followers, with some assistance from the Soviet military, for we felt it was important to take every opportunity of emphasizing that these forces were plundering the country and that their presence in Lithuania was illegal. We insisted that the agitation and terrorism which we were experiencing was nothing more than a continuation of the attack in January, and we missed no opportunity of pointing out that these pressures had a history which went back to the invasion of 1940, and were rooted in illegality from start to finish. When the *coup* against Gorbachev was staged in August, the rest of the world appeared to believe that it was an entirely new development, but we knew only too well that it was simply another manifestation of the forces which had long been at work within Lithuania, and a continuation of the tragic events which had engulfed Vilnius in January. The military attack which we suffered then had simply been transferred to Moscow.

A symptom of this process was an intensification of the vicious activities of the OMON in what now became a war for Lithuania's frontiers. We had decided that it was high time to separate Lithuania from the Soviet Union in practical terms by asking our police and defence forces to establish a system of border security. This simple move maddened the Kremlin because there had been no previous controls on traffic movements between Lithuania and Belarus and Latvia. They responded by ordering OMON to destroy our new border posts and eliminate our personnel, a move which forced us to direct close attention to the border with Poland, and to our sea ports, though we did not change the policy. There was a lot more than symbolism at stake, as a vast amount of contraband had begun to pass across our boundaries. These places were already controlled by the Soviet military, and we did not attempt to displace them, but set up our own control points wherever we felt it was necessary, a move which effectively duplicated control at the crossing-points. The arrangement must have seemed more symbolic than practical, but it served to emphasize our sovereignty, and we were careful to avoid confrontation with the Soviet guards. However, our efforts in this direction brought new dangers, as the OMON had discovered that our new customs posts were very easy targets. Most of our installations were wooden huts, often old railway wagons, and they provided little more than shelter from rain. They were easily burnt down, and were repeatedly attacked in incidents which were described as 'fighting the fascist separatists'. However, OMON was not only motivated by this high-sounding sentiment; they were already working in close contact with the murky economic forces which later emerged as the post-Soviet mafia. It was a development which was particularly dangerous for our guards, who were unarmed as a matter of policy, and some of them found the vulnerability of their situation intolerable. A few shotguns were taken privately into a number of the border posts as a result, but when Marijonas Misiukonis, our minister for internal affairs, discovered that this had happened, he gave instructions that such weapons must not be used against a direct attack. We knew that the outcome of any armed conflict would be exaggerated to show that Lithuania was sunk in uncontrollable conflict, that a firm stand was needed, and that this could easily have provided an excuse for sending in paratroopers and other forces. Our men were therefore ordered not to retaliate if they were attacked, even if the provocation was extreme, for example, when documents, or our nation's flag, were thrown about and burned. It was an increasingly intolerable situation for us, especially when our men pleaded to be armed. Of course we gave them every moral support, but they were nevertheless instructed to stick firmly to the agreed strategy. It was vitally important not to retreat from our declared position, whatever the pressure, so we did our best to hold the line by rebuilding the border posts as soon as they were destroyed in order that things could carry on. The policy was one of grim determination, and the border guards understood that they represented their country's will and could not allow themselves to be provoked into armed retaliation. We were acutely aware of our responsibilities and the pressures upon them, and many of our Supreme Council deputies went regularly to show personal support for this heroism throughout the months during which this situation lasted. That even this moral support was sometimes a risky business was discovered by our deputy, Rasa Rastauskienė, when she was ambushed and shot at by the OMON on just such a visit. She was ordered from her car and placed against a nearby wall with her hands up. She remained there with her husband also standing helplessly at her side while the staff of the post were savagely beaten. Shortly afterwards she was invited to Norway and was able to give a vivid first-hand account of the experience to a horrified audience. When she came back, she told us that people outside Lithuania had only a very vague understanding of the border conflict because foreign journalists and their cameras were not often to be found in the places where these things were going on. When the situation became known to people in the West, as it gradually did, public opinion changed unmistakably. Our forbearance cost us many painful casualties, but eventually this policy of patience meant that the Soviets lost credibility once again.

One incident on the Belarus border ended in bloodshed. A car had been waved down, and a man alighted who was dressed in civilian clothes, though it transpired that he was a militia officer in Belarus where he lived. He seems to have had a grievance against our guards since an earlier crossing, and was resentful of having been asked to stop. As he got out of his car, he pulled out a gun and started shooting. One of our guards then protected his colleagues by reaching for a rifle, which he fired. Heavy wounds were sustained by the aggressor, who subsequently died in a nearby hospital. Our prosecutor's office investigated immediately, and interrogated the guards, but before the investigation was complete the event acquired a new momentum when a carload of armed men arrived by night from Belarus. They seem to have toured several border posts looking for trouble and seeking the easiest target. Gintaras Žagunis was alone on duty at one of them, and they crept up and shot him. His was the first Lithuanian life to be lost in a border incident. He was wholly unconnected with the incident which his assailants were avenging, but nevertheless his children were orphaned in consequence. This death was swiftly followed by a second incident which occurred at Medininkai, not far away along the border, which was then our frontier with the Soviet Union. Reports of both incidents were distorted by our detractors to suggest some kind of conflict between the Lithuanian and Belarus governments. There were indeed some political problems which resulted from Žagunis's death. While the murder had taken place on Lithuanian soil, the perpetrators were caught in Belarus, where the authorities acknowledged the criminality of the act, but refused to extradite the men who had been responsible to Lithuania. They were given suspended sentences and released soon afterwards.

The fight over our borders continued despite the widespread concern over these incidents, and the Vilnius OMON was increasingly supported in its attacks on border posts by an even more aggressive unit of the same force based in Riga. Its members carried out attacks on posts along our frontier with Latvia, and along the Estonian border with Latvia, at random. However, unlike our border guards, the Estonians were well armed and fought the terrorists with considerable success. The news of their success in chasing them away, and the changes in our own situation, eventually encouraged us to change our policy. Of course, when we did this our opponents in Lithuania protested that this would provoke the Kremlin unnecessarily. They suggested that our change of mind would put lives in danger, but the real truth was that they did not want us to assert our sovereignty in any way because they saw no need to secure national boundaries. We countered their criticisms by saying that capitulation at this point would positively encourage the Soviets to continue their attacks, and similarly we dismissed the generous advice the leftist newspapers were giving us to disband the small garrison established by our Defence Department next to the Parliament building. We were determined to protect our parliamentarians and our borders from the violence which we felt had already gone too far, and we were unmoved by the arguments of the left because they were so obviously accompanied by attempts to divide us and by a constant barrage of agitation. Above all, it had become obvious to us that their demand that we should disarm our soldiers was definitely ill-advised. We had already had to face the difficult question of arming our customs officials and border guards for their own defence. Their ordinary duties on the boundary were already difficult and dangerous, and the pressures on them had been pushed to the extreme. To have stripped our own Parliament of its volunteer defenders at this point would have been to spurn their courageous support, and to have shown ourselves both naïve and foolish.

Soviet military action had not confined itself to attacking our border posts. Their forces were active in other ways, particularly in Vilnius, and they were adept at surprise tactics. In one such sudden move, the international telephone exchange in the capital was occupied with no previous warning. I have mentioned how I learned about this in Paris, at a meeting with high-ranking French officials. I was utterly shocked, and reacted with a torrent of bitter words, telling the minister for culture that his government and the western nations had observed our situation too long while doing nothing about it. I was outraged and pointed out that we had received no warning, and that Gorbachev had done nothing to restrain this vile action. Even during the attacks in January, when the full apparatus of military power had been brought into play, our telephones had not been cut off. We could still call Moscow, as well as appeal for international help. It was difficult to work out what lay behind their making this move so late in the game, but it boded ill for the future. It was clearly a move intended to intimidate us, to threaten us twice over: they could now strike hard, and at the same time we would be unable to tell our friends outside what was happening. In Paris my anger got the better of me for the first time, and I castigated the West's apparent acquiescence virulently. Then we learned just as abruptly that the Soviets had left the exchange only a few hours after entering it, and I was completely nonplussed. What were we to think now? The Soviets had announced that they had gone into the telephone exchange to find guns, but it was plain that they knew precisely where to look for them, while we had no inkling that weapons were stored there. The story told us nothing about why they had cut Lithuania off from the rest of the world, and it left us feeling apprehensive that this was a rehearsal for something worse. It was over almost as soon as it had begun and we were relieved and shaken at the same time, though we were certainly left wondering if we were to anticipate a more damaging blow in the near future.

Our tormentors had made a similar surprise move on 3 June when the army once again surrounded Parliament. Our intelligence staff suddenly informed us that military lorries and armoured vehicles were unloading troops near Parliament, and that soldiers were already marching towards the building. The soldiers then started controlling the traffic and questioning everyone leaving or approaching Parliament Square. We discovered that we were completely surrounded, and nobody was being allowed to proceed on their way. Later we learned that a study was being conducted to discover how to isolate Parliament from the people. It was a belated reaction to what had gone on in January, when our enemies had watched the people turning out to save their government and the independence of their country. Methods of preventing this courageous stand from being repeated were now being explored, so that the army's next foray against our constitutional authority would not meet with the same problem. The whole frightening rehearsal took place on the eve of my planned visit to Poland to meet Pope John Paul II, who had asked to come as close to the Lithuanian border as possible. His itinerary had been planned to include a visit to the cathedral town of Lomża, where the papal mass could easily be attended by Poles and Lithuanians from both countries. Large groups of Lithuanians had arranged to travel from the Seinai district, which is in Polish territory, but where their ancestors have lived since time immemorial. Lithuanian and Polish pilgrims were also there from Lithuania itself. My own invitation had arrived some months before from the bishop of Lomża and I had immediately agreed to travel with a delegation from the government. We had already invited the Pope to visit Lithuania just after the declaration of our independence in March 1990, and I wanted to renew the invitation, but I also wanted to meet him because of the great authority he carries, and his impressive personality. The Church authorities promised me a meeting with His Holiness, and time for conversation. This was very important to us politically because it would bring further attention to our country and the fact that we were suffering from Soviet terror and western prevarication in equal measure. It was at this moment that the Soviet military machine chose to surround Parliament, and I felt quite unable to leave. They made no declaration whatever of their intentions or purpose, and although it was a great disappointment to me I had to recognize that it was now my duty to withdraw from meeting the Pope, and I made a public statement saying just that. My move was widely observed and it served to provide the international community with yet another marker of the true character of our political problems. In some ways I was grateful for this because it threw further light on the dangers which surrounded us and the threats which they posed to our future.

My wife was on a concert tour in Poland at the time of the Holy Father's visit, and the politicians of the Solidarity movement ensured that she met the Pope and returned home bringing me his blessing. For what remained of that month and all through July our border posts continued to burn merrily, and threats to our security abounded, while the leftists were busily telling the world that we had lost the support of the people and accusing the Supreme Council of not living up to its responsibilities. Back in May the chairmen of a group of collective farms had arranged for their workers to be bused in from distant parts of the country to join in a demonstration outside Parliament arranged by a crowd of Yedinstvo supporters from the less friendly districts around Vilnius. They were protesting against the rising prices of fuel and agricultural machinery, though it had escaped them that policy on these matters was still very much dictated by the Soviet Union. The real agenda was of course to attack our land reforms and the organizers had come to see me beforehand, demanding that the position of the collective farms should be protected. Needless to say, this was a counsel which was not heeded, and on 18 June a law was passed requiring the return of the land which had been nationalized by the Soviets. This hugely important land reform was an established fact by 25 July, and at the end of that month two further events took place which marked a significant transition for us, affecting our relationships with Russia and the Soviet Union. The first was the bilateral agreement signed by Boris Yeltsin and me in Moscow on 29 July, under which Russia and Lithuania recognized each other's independence and sovereignty, and agreed a framework for regulating our future relationships. We had spent a whole year since the spring of 1990 preparing this protocol, and I had met Yeltsin both in Moscow and at Jūrmala, the seaside resort near Riga where all the Baltic presidents met their Russian counterpart to discuss matters affecting our three countries, and ways of regulating our relationship with Russia. We had taken the opportunity to announce the need for collective agreements, and work on these had begun immediately. The events of January had triggered considerable anxiety throughout the Baltic region, and the agreements between Latvia and Estonia and Russia were concluded in some haste. However, we Lithuanians were concerned that the process was being rushed because of this pressure, and believed the outcome was not as advantageous to Latvian and Estonian interests as it might have been. While we moved more slowly because of this, our eventual agreement was more comprehensive, and while the delegation which conducted our discussions had received terms of reference similar to those which governed our dealings with the Soviet Union, these talks with Russia were conducted in a wholly different and entirely constructive atmosphere. Both sides sought to formulate agreements which were mutually acceptable, and the Lithuanian contribution was energetically guided by Česlovas Stankevičius, my deputy as chairman of the Supreme Council. Our delegation was well qualified and did great work, completing its tasks early in July. After this I went to see Yeltsin personally to resolve a few problems about the preamble to the final agreement. This was because the way in which the peace agreements between Lithuania and Russia in 1920 and the Soviet Union's aggression against us in 1940 were to be mentioned, and whether the latter should be denounced in the final concord, was important to both of us, and the negotiators had agreed that these matters needed to be left until the final discussion.

The treaty with Russia was signed in Moscow on 29 July with all the publicity appropriate to an important international development. It is interesting to recall that George Bush was also in Moscow at the same time, involved in talks with Mikhail Gorbachev. We became aware of this when Yeltsin was invited to meet him at a gathering of the presidents of the Soviet republics, but he made the excuse that he was busy with me and did not attend. To this day I do not know whether it was by coincidence or by design that Yeltsin was meeting Landsbergis, the leader of Lithuania, in the capital of Russia on the very day that Gorbachev was meeting George Bush in the capital of the Soviet Union, but we certainly appreciated his priorities! Our entire delegation was present to conclude the agreement, and both sides made some concessions in the final sitting. During our personal discussion Yeltsin and I had agreed that the preamble would omit reference to the 1920 treaty (which had been signed between Lithuania and the *USSR* rather than with *Russia*), while he accepted in return that the annexation of 1940 would be denounced. But our final plenary meeting saw Anatoly Kozyrev and Ruslan Chasbulatov jumping angrily to their feet to hammer home an insistence that the text of the treaty should neither mention nor denounce the Soviet annexation. Yeltsin, however, kept his word to me on this matter at this awkward moment. When I had finished saying that if this was done we would insist that the treaty of 1920 was also mentioned, Yeltsin waved his hand and said firmly that he and I 'had agreed this matter already'. That was sufficient, the preamble remained as it was, the document was signed, and the whole treaty was ratified by the Russian Parliament later, after the Soviet Union collapsed. We can derive considerable satisfaction from the fact that Russia had so honourably refused to follow Gorbachev's hypocritical lead and dishonest insistence that Lithuania's entry into the Soviet Union had been voluntary. Under the agreement we had signed, both countries recognized each other as sovereign and independent states. Of course this declaration was obviously much more significant to Lithuania than to Russia, but we may note that this was the very first time that any international agreement had emphasized Russia's own independence since the Soviet Union had come into being. It is also worth pointing out that the Republic of Lithuania had signified that it respected the Russian interest, by confirming that civilian passengers and non-military goods might be transported to and from Kaliningrad over Lithuanian territory. Other advantages and privileges were also confirmed, not least that even those Russians who had become resident in Lithuania since 1990 were to be offered a choice of future citizenship, with the option to change their minds at a later date when Russia had finalized its discussion of its own citizenship laws. Thus our countries were committed to further co-operation, and Lithuania confirmed that relations between the two countries would be embodied in special agreements guaranteeing those Russian communities which had settled in Lithuania in earlier generations full rights of citizenship and cultural autonomy under our Lithuanian Citizenship and Minorities Law. Such guarantees were of course critical for Yeltsin's bargaining position, as Russia's nationalists had accused him earlier of not taking sufficient interest in the fate of Russians resident in the Baltic states. They were also important in finally laying to rest the Soviet accusation that our movement was hostile to the minority nationalities in Lithuania.

It is sad to record, however, that this achievement cost us dear. During the night of 31 July, not two full days after the agreement had been signed, seven of the eight border officials whom we employed at one of our crossing points into Belarus were brutally murdered. We learned about the crime from people crossing the border later that morning. All eight lay riddled with bullets inside the old railway carriage which served as our frontier post, but only two were still alive. Of these, one died on arrival at hospital; the other, by some miracle, survived. We were already accustomed to such atrocities in Lithuania, but the whole world seemed shocked by this new act of inhumanity. These men had not died in battle, but had been taken by surprise and slaughtered in cold blood. More to the point, they had adhered strictly to the instruction given by Marijonas Misiukonis, the minister responsible for their service, that they should not retaliate against uniformed Soviet military personnel. While they had clearly expected to receive the usual manhandling – a beating, verbal abuse and the confiscation of weapons – they had probably not been expecting to be murdered. But they had been forced to lie on the carriage floor in the foetal position. Then each one of them had been deliberately and systematically shot at close range with a bullet aimed at the head. It was an execution, no more, no less. When it was over and the news had spread, the journalists had rushed to the scene and filmed it. The resulting documentary was shown by the world's news services within hours. It showed that the campaign of terror against our nation had taken a new turn. It was plain that this was the reward for our success in Moscow. We could infer from it that such killings would be more frequent from now on. Officials would be murdered on duty at their posts, in their offices or in the streets. Nobody was safe. The deliberate aim was to destabilize Lithuanian society in the hope that the government could be split, or to provoke an armed confrontation with the Soviet military, which was still present on the streets of our capital and in the cities and towns of Lithuania. OMON was of course the primary instrument of this terror.

Few doubted that OMON had been deliberately charged with the appalling deed. They were already well known to us as the armed bandits who constantly stormed our border posts and beat our officials. The KGB quickly covered its tracks by planting rumours to suggest that 'the Lithuanians had fallen out among themselves', or that 'some other party' had perpetrated the massacre. Nevertheless, the act bore all the hallmarks of a KGB tradition going back to the days of the NKVD. The dead men had been dispatched according to the method of execution prescribed for political prisoners. They had used it in 1941 to dispatch the Polish officers interned at their infamous camp at Katyn, and it had become the practised trademark of their repression. The technique had been refined by the Nazis and the Soviets alike. We knew it well, too well, and having recognized it, we summoned our dignity once again to mourn our dead. The funerals, poignant though they were, were conducted with all the solemnity we could muster. Our Lithuanian soldiers and border guards stood as a guard of honour around their colleagues' lying in state, and each gave a silent promise to stand fast, and to remain faithful to his country.

After the funeral service at the cathedral, a vast crowd, not dissimilar to the one that had turned out in January, came together and then moved in silent procession to gather around the graves of Lithuania's defenders at the Antakalnis cemetery. This time there was foreign representation. Wolfgang von Stetten, a member of the German Bundestag, was among those who spoke there, and he expressed support for Lithuania on behalf of his country. An official representative of Russia had come, and his voice trembled with emotion. My own words were brief. I referred to the heartbroken mothers, wives and orphans, and asked: 'Can this continue for ever?' I answered my own question: 'Not any more. The future must be different!' I told the gathering that I had resolved that our border guards and officials would in future be provided with arms to resist our enemies. This painful issue had been long debated. The weapons were now available to us. I announced that OMON's existence would no longer be tolerated in Lithuania. 'Henceforth we shall have a simple message for them: "Omon-von! [Omon out! in Russian] Get out of Lithuania!"' These words became a slogan taken up enthusiastically by Sąjūdis, which immediately set to organizing massive protest rallies around the Vilnius Police Academy, where the OMON thugs were still in residence. People went there in droves with slogans on placards, shouting the same slogans, laying siege to the place and demanding that the occupiers should come out and be accountable for their crimes. Inside, the OMON force was armed to the teeth, while its members patrolled the perimeter and the rooftops. It was an ugly situation because they were now at bay. Some of them pushed the muzzles of their guns through the meshed fence and threatened to open fire. We recognized that the crowd's feelings needed to be controlled to prevent this situation exploding disastrously. Sajūdis was not experienced in controlling feelings such as these, but fortunately the right things were said, and by equal good fortune nothing serious occurred. The demonstration was shown on television outside Lithuania, where it had a very positive impact as it gave sound psychological and political evidence that the Lithuanians had reached a point where their toleration of the situation had run out.

Early that spring I had attempted to organize some action against OMON myself. This was just after the Soviet Union's referendum, which we boycotted, and which gave us many sleepless nights and increased tension. The Communist party had opposed us, and the pro-Moscow group, the so-called 'night-shift' led by Burokevičius, had gone ahead with the attempt to organize the Soviet referendum in Lithuania, making the most of the misunderstandings of some of the Russian- and Polish-speaking population. They had made little progress, but that increased their resentment towards us. On the night in question Audrius Butkevičius, the director of our Defence Department, was stopped and kidnapped by OMON as his car was passing Burokevičius's headquarters. He had Cabinet status, and the news reached me at the Supreme Council where I was spending most of my time. I reacted immediately by preparing an appeal to be broadcast to the public. I concluded by giving the address of the OMON office and asking people to gather there early the next morning to picket the place, to demand the immediate release of Audrius and the prompt departure of OMON from Lithuania. To my surprise, however, nothing happened the next morning, and when I asked what had gone on, I learned that that the second part of my speech (which had included the invitation to picket) had been omitted from the broadcast on the instructions of the deputy prime minister, Zigmas Vaišvila. He was in charge of all matters concerning the country's defence and state security and he had given these orders without any reference to me whatever. It appears that he had assumed this authority without consulting anyone else. He had deliberately disregarded both my supreme authority in matters of state and our normally good relations, and was wholly confident that I would not punish him. Of course I privately thought that he had overreached himself badly and got things wrong in making that decision, but I recognized that the stability of government was of more pressing interest than my anger. However, I was privately sorry that this opportunity for mass protest was missed. It is my opinion that if people had turned out in numbers to demand the release of the director at that juncture, and to emphasize their disapproval of OMON's continued presence in Lithuania, it is likely that the murders at Medininkai might have been avoided. Even though Butkevičius was released by OMON on their own initiative shortly afterward, this raised more questions than it resolved. As for his captors, they presented themselves as men who had 'challenged the head of the most important of the illegally armed organizations in Lithuania', attempting to disguise what was in effect a kidnapping.

It was now the beginning of August, and it had become clear that we would face further aggression for the foreseeable future if the Soviet Union did not remove OMON from Lithuania in accordance with our repeated demands. We knew that the real source of OMON's criminal activity lay in Moscow, and had noted that the outrage at Medininkai had coincided with an official visit to Moscow by the American president. Of course Soviet reasoning could be obscure, and the murders may have been planned at this particular time to take advantage of the fact that Bush would be prevented from denouncing the incident by a natural wish not to embarrass his hosts. To some extent this is what happened. A press conference was given by the two presidents in which the initiative in mentioning the massacre was taken by Gorbachev. The American president did not dissociate himself from Gorbachev's stance, and even seemed to give him some support, while Gorbachev took the opportunity to suggest that there were 'border conflicts between Belarus and Lithuania'. As he tried to wriggle out of his dilemma in this way, we could see that the old template was in use again. The allegation or provocation of conflicts between neighbours was once more being used to illustrate the lofty neutrality and essential fairness of the bandit state! But we also noticed that while the crafty Soviet politician was cleverly manipulating George Bush into being respectful to his host, his own tongue had slipped. His statement admitted that Lithuania did have a border! Thereafter, whenever a journalist might inquire about our 'border situation with Belarus', we would innocently correct them by asking: 'Do you mean the border between Lithuania and the Soviet Union?'

The Medininkai incident, however, did not pass unnoticed by the

Americans. They helped us in a humanitarian way by sending a specialist surgeon from one of their bases in Germany to save the life of Tomas Šernas, the eighth border official, whose skull had been penetrated by a bullet which had passed through his brain and come out on the other side. It was nothing less than a miracle that he survived both the wound and an operation by our most experienced surgeon, but the American surgeon had an advanced specialism in treating battle wounds, and when he arrived he reopened Šernas's skull to clear the bullet track of bone debris and blood clots. After that the patient improved, though only very gradually. Knowing that the perpetrators were not casual murderers but an efficient, professional and fearsome force that hated to leave witnesses alive, we were careful to put a tight security ring around him. However, the process which we had observed was not one-sided. As our sorely wounded patient improved, Russia's health deteriorated.

There are many other ups and downs in the sequel to the Medininkai story. When we saw Yeltsin in Moscow in January 1992 he assured us that he would extradite the criminal perpetrators of this massacre. However, nothing ever came of the promise and the case has dragged on, or rather petered out. An opportunity for justice was lost, and this was part of a wider pattern. We had signed a binding bilateral agreement with Russia and had promptly ratified it. Russia signed the same treaty, but then prolonged the process of ratification. The delay was beyond our comprehension, though ratification was eventually carried out. There was no good reason for the Russians not to co-operate straight away with criminal inquiries deriving from the Lithuanian justice system, but they never did in the Medininkai case, nor, I am sad to report, in the cases which arose from the events of 13 January 1991 which have run into a similar inertia. A number of the responsible criminals are known to be sheltering in Russia and Belarus, and several requests to have them brought to justice have not achieved any result. However, despite the passage of time, I have yet to lose my faith in justice.

The prison state in collapse

We have seen that there was a tendency in the West to view Lithuania's difficulties as 'a problem of the Soviet Union' rather than to consider the problems which we were having with the Soviet Union. We remember how, during the most difficult times in the nation's struggle for its separate identity, the Kremlin regularly claimed in broadcasts that our struggle for independence 'would cause great harm to our own people, to the future of the Union, and therefore the whole world'. The charges levelled against us at that time were endless – nationalism, separatism based on tribalism, ingratitude, disrespect for the constitution, subversion, rebellion, extremism, and no doubt very many other similarly objectionable tendencies. We offered, everyone was told, a bad example and many dangerous precedents for other countries in Europe, and the audience was reminded time and again of the dangers of the 'domino effect' within the Soviet Union. What would happen to the world if this masterpiece of socialist humanism should fragment into fifteen nations, all threatening each other, some with nuclear weapons?

These themes were popular in the western press, and were often repeated, even by prominent journalists and authors. We had few means to explain that the Baltic states had in reality none of the unpleasant inclinations which this insistent propaganda attributed to us, and that none of our nations anticipated having atomic weapons stationed on our soil once our independence had been achieved. Unfortunately the simplistic populist myth that it would be very bad for everyone if the Soviet Union disintegrated was very widespread. Of course it could only prevail as long as it remained an untested opinion, but the Soviets were absolutely resistant to the idea of allowing any experiments in the Baltic region. We countered the argument by pointing out that the United Nations had not decried the disintegration of colonial systems in Africa or Asia, and by asking pointedly why the Soviet empire and its colonial system should not be similarly encouraged to disintegrate in a natural and amicable manner. We pointed out to the West that there were only two choices: to support a system which was essentially unreformable, or to regard the Baltic states as a separate case. The issue which we represented was not the disintegration of a nation-state. Ours were occupied countries, and Lithuania and her two neighbours were quite sincere in wishing to free ourselves completely from the Soviet system. There were many, many occasions when I tried to tell western politicians that the Soviet Union was not fifteen constituent republics, as it claimed, but twelve at best because three of them had been independent before they were incorporated by force, an event which had occurred during my own lifetime. I argued that their recognition of the independence of Lithuania, Latvia and Estonia would actually help the Soviet Union to resolve its future in some alternative and better way, and that other nations within the Union would also aspire to freedom once the possibility had been established. I pleaded with western nations to give serious support to the process of peaceful decolonization which we were advocating by encouraging democratic evolution, especially in those republics which had neither a democratic past nor any previous experience of statehood. The contribution of such friendly support to world peace would be immense. At the very least, those republics which possessed a peaceful and democratic outlook, and which were capable of forming independent governments without being gripped by civil war or a bloody revolution, should be supported.

I cannot say that my words influenced the western leaders, and indeed their speeches often suggested to us that they were ignorant of political life within the Soviet Union. One example of this lack of awareness was the opinion given by George Bush during his visit to the Ukraine, when he advised the Ukrainian nation 'not to seek their independence'. It was an error which the State Department had to correct afterwards, but a couple of years were lost to the people of the Ukraine as a result of those few ill-chosen words. My own efforts to change attitudes involved joking with journalists about the alternatives which we faced, and I sometimes caricatured the situation in an attempt to get them to see things in a more flexible way. I went so far as to suggest that if the Soviets continued to deny the Baltic peoples their independence, and the West did not support us, we would be forced back into the Soviet prison. In that impasse, we should have no alternative between staying in the Soviet prison until doomsday, and attempting to blow it to smithereens. The point I was trying to make was simple enough: 'Help us *now* before events turn out in the very way which you most fear.' It was our misfortune that the free world was so caught up in its own preoccupations, and so fearful of the consequences of others gaining their freedom.

So we were left to fend for ourselves, and we did not do badly. After signing the treaty with Russia we signed another with Armenia, and began preparing an agreement with Moldova. Next, we were the first nation in Europe to recognize the independence of Slovenia and Croatia. I had begun to use the concept of an evolutionary and positive disintegration of the Soviet Union as a propaganda tool. In January, and later in the year, we distributed leaflets carrying this message to Soviet soldiers. In the summer of 1991, OMON intensified their activity, and the commanders of the Soviet forces began to make threatening statements and arranging troop movements throughout the country, claiming that they were 'on manœuvres'. We felt that matters were getting out of hand, and the Supreme Council decided to make a direct appeal to the soldiers. I therefore prepared the text of a leaflet, which was also published in the Russian-language newspapers, which took issue with what the soldiers had been told, namely that their military oath 'to defend the Soviet Union' meant they must obey orders to crush Lithuania's advance to freedom. This idea was being actively promoted by OMON, but we argued that the oath did not hold if that Union was not a voluntary association of nations, but rather a forced integration. It was less of a Union at present than a prison, and was currently beginning to break apart. I then pointed out that the Baltic states, together with Moldova and the countries of the Caucasus, were no longer Soviet republics, but were national republics which had declared themselves independent. They were being 'kept in the union' by the threat of arms. We did not regard the forced soldiers' oaths of loyalty to the Soviet Union as valid because that Union was imposed by imperialist force. It was the product of coercion. Of course, the Soviet commanders were infuriated by our advice and our actions.

A new momentum was emerging as this concept of progressive decolonization took root. After about 1988 it had been commonplace to joke that all the republics, including Russia itself, were 'colonies of the central bureaucracy'. The 'parade of sovereignties' which had begun in Estonia and Lithuania was initially a process of economic liberalization. Though its progress had been impeded, it was a very real process which had now reached an advanced stage, and it was the realization of this fact which had eventually spurred Gorbachev's staff to offer a 'new and improved' Union agreement. In discussion with foreign journalists, I commented on this project by drawing an ironic parallel. It was, I said, as if the Tsar had decided to offer a constitution to his vassal dukes at a time when they had effectively become sovereigns and were able to control their own finances. In such circumstances each would have to decide for himself on the advantages of retaining a central figure to co-ordinate their separate affairs! The various draft projects for their new constitution were all still being sent to me, as part of the pretence that Lithuania was still a Union state and that I was a Soviet deputy holding office in a republic within the Union. I read these papers, and I could see that the whole process being proposed was less than satisfactory in its concept and drafting. I was a natural critic of Soviet conventions and procedures, and I could see that, in virtually every case, the starting dates for the privileges and liberties which were being prescribed so vaguely were to be deferred until some unspecified or distant future date, while the dates by which others were being asked to give their written assent to the agreement were almost immediate! Naturally, we did not return any of these blank cheques, and at one point it even seemed that the Soviet system might 'let us go' by default, dropping us from the renewed union because we had not signed these quasi-contractual documents, but eventually the bureaucrats woke up to the fact that the three Baltic states were looking for a way of dropping out unnoticed, without conflict or negotiation. Once they had woken up to this possibility, they suddenly introduced the absurd concept of the 'two Soviet

Unions': that the 'new' Soviet Union could exist concurrently with the older constitutional arrangement. It was a proposal which would have dealt with our non-compliance by putting us into the slow stream, leaving us in a constitutional time-warp, still in the grip of the Soviet system but remaining under the provisions of its 'old' constitution for an undefined time. It was yet another message that we were not easily going to be allowed to escape.

The contradictions of the system were now apparent, and it was also at last becoming clear that its centre was less and less likely to hold. The eventual outcome was as we had anticipated, and though it did not come as peacefully as we would have liked, it came faster than we had dared to hope. Attempting to keep the Soviet Union together by force, Gorbachev fell into his own trap. His grandiose dreams were interrupted by the strange *putsch* which took place in Moscow in August. Its effect was dramatic: the essential issues and stark choices were thrown into sharp relief, and once the hour of greatest danger was over it became evident that Gorbachev's attempt to develop some alternative form of Soviet Union had failed. The whole system then collapsed, because it had been a house built on sand from the start. Once this fundamental truth became apparent, the liquidation of the Soviet empire proceeded at speed, and by the end of 1991 that empire was history. It was naturally a matter of great satisfaction to us to see that the prison walls had fallen, and while we know of some who dream of rebuilding the edifice, its demolition is really complete. We were proud that Lithuania was the agent which made the empire's eventual destruction certain. While we were certainly not alone in working towards this end, we were a crucial part of the process, and no one can deny the centrality of our contribution. Whether the part we played is worthy of praise or condemnation will depend on one's point of view – though the wider world certainly seemed to appreciate our efforts at the time the Soviet system crumbled. However, since then people have heard so much about the new and complex problems that face the nations that have emerged from Soviet domination, that these have tended to overshadow our achievements in the minds of some people. We have to remember that everything happened in the way it did because we were forced to find our own way out of an impasse. While we may have stumbled along the road, it really was the only one. Though we understood soon enough that the path ahead of us led through a danger zone, we also knew that other oppressed nations had travelled by the same route to freedom. Other nations will also have to face this truth, and they must not be overawed by the difficulties of the road to be travelled or by the realization that there will be worse problems for humanity if the issues of freedom and justice between nations which dominate our age are not attended to. These are issues for the whole planet, which will again be haunted by the threat of imperialist domination or everlasting nuclear confrontation if justice for suppressed nations is not integrated into the whole world order. These are the alternatives which lie along the road. Many nations and communities are confronted with a moral choice which must be faced up to. If the great western democracies do not give these matters their attention, then sooner rather than later they will find themselves confronted by forces which will be equivalent both politically and morally to the red totalitarianism which menaced them for so long.

I have no doubt that we accomplished a great and a good deed by following the Lithuanian road to freedom, and firmly believe we did not find that route for ourselves alone, but for all Europe and for humanity and the cause of freedom everywhere. It is important that this truth be fully recognized and again I stress, not by ourselves alone, because there are still political forces, especially in Russia, which regret the loss of the Soviet Union and will spare no effort to resurrect it or some comparable tyranny. In their eyes Lithuania is the worst culprit in recent history, and if ever they should succeed our country may expect them to take terrible revenge on us.

Recognition at last

Lithuania's progress in its first and formative year was decided by two processes. On the one hand there was the gathering momentum of official international recognition of our independence, expressed through international relationships, and on the other there was the continuing attempt to halt this process by forces inside Lithuania and throughout the Soviet Union. The forces of reaction had become more open in their aggression, and were increasingly emphatic in their intimidation and intolerance of anything which might weaken their empire, or reduce its territorial claims. They attempted to crush any idea of decolonization, of an association of sovereign states, or of total independence, wherever these ideas might appear. However, the particular strength of Lithuania's new position and her chance to consolidate it in the international field lay in the fact that most of the world (with the exception of Sweden and New Zealand, which had both made the mistake of recognizing Soviet rule in the Baltic countries at some time in the past) had never withdrawn their formal recognition of the pre-war Republic of Lithuania. While the newer states created after the Second World War, when the other colonial empires were dismantled, had no predetermined views about the changes which the war had brought about in eastern Europe, their interpretation of our position was largely dependent on the views held by the western states. In most of these countries some ghost of our former recognition remained, in a faded apparatus of embassies and consulates which had maintained itself for just over fifty years. It was therefore quite clear to everyone, whether in Lithuania, Moscow or the West, that the renewal of diplomatic relations was the all-important step in the restoration of normality, because the recognition of a state 'in principle' has to be complemented by working diplomatic relations between national governments if it is to be effective.

In our case the achievement of the active recognition which was so vital to our standing made erratic progress. The first move was made by Iceland when its Parliament, the Althing, voted that its original recognition of the Lithuanian Republic in 1922 was still valid and that it therefore wished to restore full diplomatic relations as soon as possible. This determination resulted from my visit to Reykjavik in October 1990 and the subsequent courageous visit made to Lithuania by their foreign minister in January 1991. Denmark then took note of Iceland's efforts and signed an agreement with us, which was followed by Estonia and Latvia making similar joint declarations that the relationships between our nations 'would be returned to where they were when our countries had achieved statehood some seventy years ago, as soon as the general situation permits'. These moves meant that we had several declarations of intent, though no date for actual recognition, an indeterminate situation which was not resolved until the government of Iceland moved forward. The Soviet Union protested strongly against these decisions, but both Iceland and Denmark responded calmly, with statements that they 'had never relinquished their recognition of Lithuania, nor the other Baltic states'. Indeed, the Icelanders were quick to point out that the recent visit to Lithuania by their foreign minister was itself an active statement of recognition. We derived much encouragement from these gestures, and made constant efforts to persuade our other friends to respond to us in the same way. Of all the Baltic states, Lithuania took the most initiative on the diplomatic front, and renewal of relationships with Iceland was our first reward. I was the first national leader to receive the text of Iceland's proposal for a joint declaration. The government and the Supreme Council gave approval shortly afterwards, but we were careful not to make this public because we wanted to avoid unnecessary problems and certainly did not wish to be cheated by last-minute difficulties. We knew that both parties intended to proceed, but we were also aware that the Soviets knew what was going on, and would be hoping to nip our enterprise in the bud. They did their best to delay our efforts, even planning military action inside all the Baltic countries in the hope that such activity would interfere with our project. A secret diplomatic race was on and the stakes were high. We knew many of the factors which would influence the thinking of other parties, but there were unknown factors at work which might affect both the intermediate decisions and the outcome. Not least among these was our relationship with Russia. This was good and even solid, because we had excellent contacts with the democratic forces there, to whom we had offered mutual assistance. Of course we knew we could be optimistic about a more secure future for Lithuania if Russia could make her own escape from the stranglehold of the Soviet octopus, which could scarcely survive without its core component. Russia too was dominated by the colonial colossus and I said this in many speeches around this time, declaring that the Russian people had been imposed upon, run down and exploited by the imperial structures of the Soviet Union, especially by its intelligence agency, the KGB, the State Planning Committee and the military-industrial complex. Each of these was a repressive structure, and the maintenance of these colonial systems was a constant drain on resources which prevented Russia from modernizing and liberalizing its government, industry and society. Our struggle for recognition on the diplomatic front had, however, illuminated an awakening understanding of what had been going on in the so-called autonomous republics that made up the Soviet Union, and perhaps most of all in Russia itself. A process had begun, and now many of the republics were starting to seek the right to control and exploit their own natural resources instead of sacrificing them to maintain the enormous and inefficient edifice which had controlled them for so long. Russia itself now wanted to control its own income and expenditure, a development which had come about sooner than I had dared to anticipate. Having noted this emerging trend, I was swift to speculate, publicly and at times not too politely, on the future of the Soviet president. I would ask mischievously whether *Russia* would consider employing him in the future: after all, the *basic assets* of the Soviet Union really belonged to Russia. Gorbachev was clearly one of them, as the Soviet Union had almost nothing else to recommend it!

In their attempts to recover control of a situation which was in fact rapidly slipping away from them, Gorbachev and his followers planned several new schemes to revive the old concept of the Soviet Union. They were increasingly active in their attempt to ensure that the republics were not persuaded to follow the natural interests of their own people, rather than remaining mesmerized by the Soviet Union's view of itself as the benefactor of the human race. In the process Gorbachev attempted to entice Russia and the other republics into signing a 'new agreement', presenting himself very flexibly in order to encounter the least resistance. He made definite promises to 'give more freedom to the republics', though he failed to spell out the details of what was actually implied. Gorbachev was a politician who always wanted to play safe, and Moscow prepared a whole series of 'new agreements', all of which safeguarded his position and the interests he most wanted to preserve. All of them were sent to me as if I were the head of a Soviet republic, despite my obvious attempt to divest myself and my country of this unwelcome standing, but I read them just the same, and I perceived them as full of devious traps. Of course we made it plain that we did not intend even to discuss any of them, let alone sign, because the process proposed was not a constructive one. However, even our marginal perspectives on what was going on sometimes allowed us a glimpse of the possibility of a real treaty emerging between nations which had once again been accorded the basic right to manage their own assets and sovereignty. Occasionally some of the more liberal of the Gorbachevists would begin to suggest that this was an unavoidable evolution and that some kind of 'common market' arrangement might emerge. However, the trend was noticed by the committed reactionaries in Moscow's central structures, and they consolidated their positions by forming a tight ring around their president. Soon it was hard to discern whether the man was being manipulated or whether he was in fact still manipulating the show. We can now see that the question was a 'chicken and egg' puzzle, and in the end they all went down the chute together!

Though Gorbachev's grandiose schemes were stealing the limelight, Boris Yeltsin was busy strengthening the basis of his country's sovereignty, and it was not for nothing that Gorbachev scornfully dubbed him a 'Russian separatist' in his memoirs. We were on good terms with Yeltsin, and our hopes for the future were naturally bound up with his. The propaganda machine which surrounded Gorbachev constantly belittled Yeltsin in the same way as it belittled me, and we were both frequently attacked for our efforts to develop co-operation. Those inside Lithuania who supported the Kremlin's views stoutly maintained that the West had no regard for Yeltsin and called him an adventurer without a future. They told us that we must align ourselves with Gorbachev because we would have no prospects without him, and a number of Lithuanian politicians joined in this sycophantic chorus, even after the January events. They, and many western politicians with them, were mesmerized by Gorbachev and could not see beyond him, and indeed even Boris Yeltsin had to face highly undignified meetings in Paris and Washington where these views had powerful supporters. However, he was firm in his belief that his chosen policies were right for Russia, and he persisted. We had a lot in common with him, but he faced enormous problems, and got too little help from potential allies. When a delegation of American congressmen led by Steny Hoyer visited Lithuania in the spring of 1991, we explained that our situation had developed since the events of January, and they naturally asked us why our negotiations with the Soviet Union seemed to be unproductive. We told them about the two-faced character of the Soviet government and how its delegation persistently used every pretext to postpone serious dialogue, while continuing to press the same unchanged demands. The delegation took great interest in what we said, and I sent messages back to George Bush who had used Senator Lantosz to convey his support. The visit was particularly useful because it opened a further channel of communication with the president and the Congress. When the visitors were about to leave us, I answered questions following an after-dinner speech. The last question put was: 'How can we help you?' It was direct enough, and my answer was short and to the point: 'Give your support to Yeltsin.' The surprise of the American visitors was obvious, and because such advice from me was unexpected, it clearly made an impression. They went home realizing that American policy had not yet moved forward because their government had still not made up its mind about whether to support Gorbachev or Yeltsin. It was in fact still supporting Gorbachev, but by default and through inertia. He was still their favourite eastern politician, but I think my advice that he should now be dropped in favour of Yeltsin did at least make some people sit up and notice that the balance of power was tilting.

At this time the Soviets were juggling with 'New Union' agreements, but constantly postponing the process of final endorsement in order to accommodate concessions to the republics, which had now begun to see the advantages of the arguments for sovereignty. Most significantly, democratic Russia was firmly developing its position. The stakes were rising, and so far as the Soviet Union was concerned, it was clear that a final agreement would have to be reached soon. The emerging situation was obviously not to the liking of the *apparatchiks,* who thought that things had already gone too far. A plot to disrupt the progress of the 'new constitution' began to be hatched in secret. It was intended to maintain the *status quo* and perhaps to return to the centrist and totalitarian system of the Stalinist past, whose aims, of course, could be achieved only with the support of the KGB and the armed forces. While the August *putsch* was the culmination of this activity, its tentacles embraced not just Moscow but the whole of the Soviet state, and the conspirators naturally treated the Baltic states as republics of the Soviet Union. Gorbachev had never written these conservatives out of his script, and when they attempted to overthrow him in their *putsch,* their imperialist ambitions were evident for the whole world to see. It is interesting to speculate what the actual relationship between Gorbachev and these conspirators was, but this could only be discovered by a commission of inquiry, which will never happen. However, some people have attempted to investigate what went on, and have reported suspicions that he was, at least at some stage, in league with the *putschists.* When the attempted *putsch* actually occurred, we were naturally rather less concerned with the inner workings of the cabal, and what lay behind it, than with its outcome. The big question was whether the known allies of these conspirators would try to annihilate us immediately, as they had probably intended had they been successful in January, or whether our demise would follow a little later, after democratic Russia had been systematically destroyed.

We had enough experience to realize that there was no doubt about the objectives of the *putsch.* Its aims were clear, but there was some uncertainty about the exact route they might take to arrive there. We gathered at the Supreme Council very early in the morning after the news came through, and set our defence arrangements in train, just as we had in January. Our civil defence was put on red alert, and civil servants were briefed once again on how to behave if the legal government of Lithuania fell and a puppet regime was installed. The allies of the potential quisling government which was waiting in the wings were still in control of the television tower and the radio station. They would sit pretty in Moscow, welcoming the first movements of the regime which would shortly be installed in Lithuania. In the mean time we made our own preparations, to ensure that those of us who survived could continue our work – underground if necessary. At around midnight I made out an order for half a million roubles in cash, which was passed to Birutė Nedzinskienė, a deputy from Kaunas where the prospects for secret work would be better than in Vilnius. We prepared instructions to be passed on to ordinary civilians too, and as we got on with these preparations we remembered that the barricades around the Parliament had remained in place since January. This was reassuring because we knew that they would be useful, if only as a symbol of our resistance to a military attack which again seemed all but inevitable.

Some of the western nations showed a vacillating and ambiguous attitude to the attempted *putsch* in Moscow. They would have come to terms with whoever came out on top, and have been prepared to co-operate with them. No one in the West seemed likely to be brave enough to take our part, and back us up. However, we believed that we had to get on with life, and the most important decision we were able to take at this point was the ratification of the agreement with Russia. We regarded it as a significant recognition of the validity of our Independence Act of 11 March 1990 which had reinstated the Lithuanian state, and was therefore one of our greatest achievements in the process of consolidating our independence. While I had persuaded Yeltsin to include a denunciation of the Soviet Union's aggression against Lithuania and its annexation in 1940 in the preamble, this boost to our pride needed to be ratified before it could take effect. We were now uncomfortably aware that our control of Vilnius was hanging in the balance, and indeed that in a matter of hours our very lives might come to an end. Although the outcome of the *putsch* in Moscow could not be predicted, we felt it necessary to finalize the agreement with Russia very quickly. It was an act which could only improve our morale, but before we could achieve this we needed to change the minds of a number of deputies who still considered the terms not entirely suited to Lithuania. They wanted to have it discussed in greater depth before proceeding with ratification, and might have attempted to postpone the debate if I had not pointed out that even if their doubts were taken into consideration, the agreement was virtually ready for acceptance and meanwhile the *putsch* had affected our bargaining position. There were greater risks to be incurred by not moving ahead. We simply could not afford to leave this business unfinished in the current situation! Eventually the decision was agreed, together with a second resolution declaring our support for Russia. I was then able to telephone Boris Yeltsin to wish him and his countrymen courage and every success in doing whatever was necessary to end the threat posed by the conspirators. We could do little more to help, but moral support did mean something. Late that day, still 21 August, the Supreme Council ratified the treaty and issued a decree to say that anyone found co-operating with the conspiracy to overthrow the legal government of Russia would be arrested and punished. When the Council finally rose late that evening, I prepared an appeal addressed to the world's governments and the United Nations Organization, referring to what was going on in Moscow, and asking them to give support to the government of Lithuania before it was too late. I pointed out that our government had been elected to bring justice and stability to our country, and pleaded that they should condemn the continuing and unacceptable Soviet military presence in Lithuania, which represented an anachronistic continuation of the Hitler–Stalin pact. I also said quite plainly: 'You must not allow the tragedies of Budapest and Prague to be repeated among the reborn nations on the shores of the Baltic.'

I told Yeltsin all this in a telephone conversation when I rang to say that we had ratified the agreement between our nations. I also asked him to ensure that his Supreme Council ratified our treaty, even though they had many pressing responsibilities in the current crisis. It was unfortunate from our viewpoint that these other considerations crowded in. Of course they came first, and it seemed to be a very long time before they got around to doing what was necessary. However, for our part, the fact that we had ratified the agreement on the very first day of the *putsch* seemed to be a real contribution to the historic struggle which was going on. It was at once an act of defiance and of consolidation, another means of showing our commitment to a decent future. But while it was another step to normalization, it did little of course to prevent the *coup* from having its impact upon Vilnius and the other towns of Lithuania. First the Soviet forces began to occupy our public buildings and communication centres. Next they began demanding that our defence forces should be disbanded, and I received a telephone call from Sajūdis in Kaunas, asking what line to take. Were Lithuanian patriots to resist or to obey? I advised that arms should *not* be surrendered, though armed confrontation should be avoided wherever possible. This was the line which we took everywhere, and the Sajūdis movement continued to put a lot of energy into planning a joint demonstration with the People's Fronts of the other Baltic countries to mark the anniversary of the Molotov–Ribbentrop Pact. The plan was to reproduce the huge demonstration held two years before, when a continuous chain of people had linked hands across our lands all the way from Vilnius to Tallinn. This year it was to be called 'Blazing the Baltic Way', and was to be accompanied by blazing bonfires along the hills between our three capital cities, as a reminder of a shared history and a common aim for the future. Beacons would be lit on the hilltops, each within sight of the next, to create a chain of fire stretching out across the three nations. Such chains of fiery beacons stretching from one hill fort to the next had alerted people to danger and called them to resistance throughout our common history. These fires have burned deep in the consciousness of all our Baltic peoples because we know that they were used by our forefathers to give warning of the arrival of their enemies and to call men to arms.

There was a strange correlation between the movement of the enemy into our streets and offices, disrupting our television service and cutting off transport links and telephone exchanges, and this powerful pageant which had been organized so successfully to demonstrate the free spirit of three nations. General Achalov, who had recently been sent to Vilnius by the leading figures of the *putsch*, issued an urgent order requiring us to call off our event. It was not to take place, his communiqué said, because clashes and casualties would be inevitable. Any such consequences would be our fault. Needless to say, I rejected his demand, but my reply also told him that our communications had been cut by his troops, so we had no way in which we could cancel well-understood arrangements! However, I reassured him that our people were responsible, well informed and peaceful, and would take no action against the military. I also warned him that if the Soviet military should attack unarmed people, as they had in January, they would again be seen as murderers. It was a sharp exchange, but as these messages were being passed backwards and forwards, the momentum of the *putsch* was beginning to fail. From 19 August onward we had all been glued to our television screens following developments in Moscow. I had an open telephone line to our representatives in the city, and was therefore well informed of what was happening around the Russian Parliament. The Muscovites had a keen appreciation of our earlier contribution to the drama now being played out in their city: 'We are copying Vilnius, they have taught us well, Lithuania has set us an example!', they cried, and emulated us by placing barricades around their Parliament, where crowds of determined people had gathered, ready to stand in front of the threatening tanks that tried to disperse them. Three defenders of Parliament had been crushed, but the Russian government did not waver. The well-prepared KGB forces stood by. They too observed, but they did not attack, and immediately after the *putsch* had collapsed we learned that their hand had been held as a result of what had happened in Vilnius. Our night of tragedy in January had taught the world that the KGB was a force which murdered unarmed people. Its leaders knew in advance that they would stand condemned if they took the same path again. They were therefore thwarted by what they knew about themselves, and what was now known about them. No one can deny that our experience in Lithuania, or to be more precise the events which had taken place in Vilnius in January, were a real inspiration to the people of Moscow and a powerful influence on the emergence of Russian democracy, and not only during the days of *putsch* there. Our experience had taught us, and others, that what was happening in Moscow was no new development but a further surfacing of the forces which had previously struck out at us. While the West perceived things differently, seeing what was happening in Moscow only in terms of a time frame extending from 19 to 21 August, our longer perspective told us that that the *putsch* had begun in January. The men behind what was now going on in Moscow had decided to organize terror all over the Baltic states. They feared that the flame of freedom which we had lit there might spread and engulf them. Vilnius had been the trial run for what was now taking place in Moscow, but the evil which was erupting there had been planned a year before in the autumn of 1990, and its seed might even have been planted on the very night when Gorbachev, probably obeying the order of someone unknown, abandoned his project to 'liberalize Soviet industry in five hundred days'.

The speed with which the *putsch* collapsed was surprising, even though the announcement of its end was not entirely unexpected in view of the sequence of events. We were both anxious and expectant as we waited for the end to come, and none of us had any idea how the drama between the military and Mikhail Gorbachev, semi-democrat and quasi-reformist that he was, would finally be played out. Once things were moving, however, we were able to apply educated guesswork as we attempted to discern who had a good hand to play, and who might have to resort to cheating and bluff in order to survive. Against this background I had a flash of clear insight when I saw the televised image of Gorbachev as he descended from the plane which brought him back to Moscow after the *coup* collapsed. It seemed to me that he had no inkling that he was returning to an entirely different state from the one he had so recently left behind, and his subsequent speeches revealed how consistently he failed to comprehend what had really transpired. He, the Soviet leader, had gone to the Crimea 'for a rest', and when he returned, it was to a Russia which had a new ruler! The whole process was deeply gratifying to view, especially when we learned that the leaders of the *coup* were on the run. It was seen as a victory both in Moscow and in Vilnius, indeed it was more than that, because it was a kind of salvation. Of course we had been able to do little to help, though I had issued one significant order. Our intelligence service had intercepted a secret message sent from Moscow's Vnukov airport to the Soviet military airport at Šiauliai in Lithuania. Permission was being sought to land a plane coming from Moscow, and it was immediately clear to me that the *putschists* were securing an air escape route through Lithuania, hoping perhaps to go on from there to the West. Realizing this, I immediately wrote out an order which was sent to all airports in Lithuania, including the Soviet military ones, stating that they were subject to the law of sovereign Lithuania and must not under any circumstances allow this plane to land within our territory. While I probably went beyond my proper authority in doing this, my move was a considered political response. In the event, the concern lasted only a few hours until we learned that the leaders of the *putsch* were flying, as might be expected, to the opposite side of the world. However, I later learned that the senior Soviet military personnel in Lithuania had panicked when they received my order, and had decided to obey it. Their preparedness to accept a decision by the president of the Lithuanian Supreme Council in these circumstances suggested to me that even they had at last realized that the Soviet system was falling apart, and that at the same time the last hope of a military take-over was passing out of their reach. For a brief moment they realized that they were in Lithuania, and that there was a Lithuanian government which they must obey. It was only a temporary break in the pattern of their ways and they later reverted to their old self-assured, cocky and difficult behaviour. It would still require a great deal of effort and time to get the Russian forces to accept that their presence and activities within Lithuania were now subject to constraints, but we knew at last that they had glimpsed what was previously unthinkable.

The days which followed the *coup* were full of decision, action and the happy recognition that our enemy, who had set themselves against the aspirations of so many nations and been so hostile to the spirit of democracy, had at last been overcome. On 23 August I made a speech at an international parliamentary conference in Vilnius on 'The Freedom of the Baltics and the New Europe'. I finished by appealing for an international tribunal on the lines of the Nuremberg Tribunal to deal with the crimes of the Soviet system, and added that I would ask Lithuania to initiate a legal process comparable with the denazification process in Germany forty-five years before, and invited the International Court to sit in Vilnius. Lithuania would be happy to provide the venue for this service to humanity. However, I was also aware that we had to be careful. A mortally wounded beast may still kill; the crazy men who ran the OMON might well go berserk, and the criminals in the Communist party might attempt to support them. However, the reality was that the latter were now exhausted and frightened, so found it more important to save their own skins. When they heard the news, the communists locked themselves in their Central Committee headquarters, guarded by Russian soldiers, and hurriedly burned their documents, knowing that we were planning to take over the premises. We put a ring of our soldiers around the building in order to prevent the reactionaries from escaping, but late that night a car left the building at great speed, turning towards Antakalnis. Before it had travelled far it was stopped by the security forces of the Supreme Council, who shot at its tyres. In the moments of silence which followed, a handful of soldiers got out; it then became apparent that the organizers of the January events at the television tower, and the other leaders of the Lithuanian Communist party, were still sweating it out in their building! They had sent out these envoys in the hope that the main Soviet military garrison stationed in Šiaurės Miestelis, the northern suburb of Vilnius, would come to their rescue. That this hope was not vain became apparent soon enough when an armed column made its appearance later that night. It moved into the inner yard of the buildings, and out again shortly after. We had no way of stopping them, short of attacking the Soviet forces, and so Burokevičius, Jarmalavičius, Naudžiūnas and a whole crowd of comparable or lesser traitors were snatched from justice. They spent a few days at the barracks, and then moved eastwards. This was probably the day after the end of the *putsch*, and the Russian military was already being shaken up by a series of sudden changes both to its senior staff and in the attitudes of its leaders. There was much for us to think about, but at this point we were distracted by the arrival of a welcome if unexpected guest in the person of Anders Bjorck, the Swedish current president of the Parliamentary Assembly of the Council of Europe. He had come to us straight from Finland, and had travelled from Tallinn by car without observing any of the usual diplomatic niceties. He arrived in Vilnius late that night, and came directly to Parliament, where he was warmly greeted before going on early in the morning to the guest house. We met him over coffee, told him about the events which had overtaken us and discussed their implications for the rest of the world. We also discussed the prospects for future co-operation now that the great threat which had hung over the Baltic nations for so much of our lives seemed at last to have ended. I put Lithuania's application to join the Council of Europe into his hands before he left us.

Anders Bjorck's visit was the first of many by foreign diplomats and leaders. A number of ceremonies giving diplomatic recognition to Lithuania now took place in rapid succession in several capital cities, almost as if there were a race among the other nations to be the first to exchange ambassadors with us! As our foreign minister was planning to fly to Iceland he received a message inviting him to go to Oslo first. This would have made Norway the first country of the western world formally to recognize the re-establishment of our independence, but we had to be correct in our dealings with Iceland, and said as much. The Norwegians were gracious enough to acknowledge that we could not have acted in any other way, so he travelled first to Reykjavik where he signed the treaty which we had prepared in the spring. After this he went on to Denmark, and then to Norway, which became the third country to make a formal agreement of recognition. Lennart Meri, then the Estonian foreign minister, told me years later how he and the other foreign ministers of the Baltic states had walked through the courtyards of Copenhagen's royal palace late at night, under the stars, escorted by a guard of honour, to meet the queen of Denmark, who was waiting to receive them. As he entered the palace he had remembered how he and the same companions had been turned away from the CSCE meeting in Paris only nine months before. He had been all but moved to tears at the suddenness of the change in the fortunes of his country, and it was indeed difficult not to feel overwhelmed with emotion as we contemplated the transformation which we were witnessing. Within days the representatives of the larger nations began to appear in our capitals. The first to arrive in Vilnius was Roland Dumas, the French foreign minister, and this visit more than made up for what had happened in the past. It was also far-sighted, and he made it plain that France was taking trouble to initiate friendly relationships and wanted to give us constructive help to re-establish ourselves. As he entered Parliament, Dumas stopped to gaze in amazement at the barricades and the sandbags which we had used in our protracted effort to protect our democracy, and we stood for a joint photograph against this background to celebrate the re-establishment of diplomatic relationships. (Dumas was also astounded, when he arrived at the airport, to find that a Russian soldier attempted to push aside a Lithuanian border guard in order to check his passport. We had not yet taken full control of our borders.) Hans Dietrich Genscher, the German foreign minister, followed him, and indeed dignitaries from abroad seemed to be presenting themselves almost on a daily basis and exchanging diplomatic credentials.

We naturally waited with some eagerness for the United States of America to take the same step, but it seemed that the president was in no hurry to move. Soon we had no alternative but to deduce that US policy was still tied up with their views of Moscow, and though I had no real information on the reasons for this prevarication I surmised that George Bush must have given Gorbachev assurances, perhaps on the eve of the Gulf War or when the two men had met in Malta. We sensed that he was still waiting for a word from the Soviets, though for us to expect any kind of recognition from that quarter seemed to be as hopeless as it had ever been. The Soviet Congress of Peoples' Deputies and its Supreme Council both still contained too many reactionaries and imperialists. Eventually the decision to recognize the independence of the three Baltic states was made by a Council of State called by President Gorbachev soon after his return to Moscow. The decision was preceded by an invitation from the Russian Democrats, asking the Lithuanian deputies of the Soviet Union to travel to Moscow for a discussion on the future of the Union and Mikhail Gorbachev's role during the *putsch*. I was one of those invited, though our former colleagues should have realized long before this that the status of deputies of the Soviet Union was one which we had relinquished for ever. Of course, we showed that we were not prepared to go to this meeting, but even now this stand was not clearly understood by everyone in Vilnius, and so the matter had to be discussed in our Supreme Council in the light of the new situation in Moscow.

There were some there who held the opinion that our presence would give the democratic forces extra voting strength, but I saw the matter quite differently. The Supreme Soviet's proposal to discuss Gorbachev's role and his responsibilities in relation to the *putsch* was a very necessary one, but any Lithuanian participation would have been an absolute error of legal judgement. Deputies might well be asked to vote on the independence of the Baltic states, and the mere fact of our being represented would have implied agreement that the conference had some authority over our independence, or could even deny it. While the conference was therefore not graced by our presence, the discussion did act as some sort of leverage on President Bush, to whom I then wrote a letter which suggested that Gorbachev might have had more influence on the *putsch* than had been made apparent. I advised him of the need for an early decision on Lithuania's independence. I was doubtful that my letter would make much difference to thinking in the White House when I sent it, but was happy enough when I was notified that President Bush would telephone me. It was in this conversation that he told me that he intended to make an official statement on Lithuania soon. Although I had been left to guess what he would say, I informed the foreign journalists in our capital that such a statement would be coming soon. They were keen to have some hint from me of what America's attitude would be, but I played safe and made it plain that we would not condemn America if it did not immediately give us what we wanted. We were, I said, entirely confident that the important step of recognition must come sooner or later, and that it might come in a matter of days rather than weeks. We waited patiently for further news from the USA, but it was Argentina which became the first state in the New World to recognize us, being the eighth country to do so.

The slow movement of the United States on this front was all the more frustrating because the majority of our Lithuanian exiles evidently believed that full recognition by the USA was the most important international recognition we could obtain. They were now impatient and George Bush was blamed for the delay. Eventually I wrote a letter, which was published in the American press, emphasizing the absurdity of procrastination. We were still waiting for the American statement when I received an invitation to go to Budapest to sign an agreement with Hungary. It was a visit which made a lasting impression. The Hungarian Parliament welcomed our delegation with a standing ovation, and we felt a profound solidarity as our colleagues spoke of their own bitter experience of the common enemy. We were still in Budapest when the news of the American recognition of Lithuania finally reached me. Two days later, Gorbachev and the State Council of the Soviet Union made a similar decision. This Soviet recognition was not accompanied by the same kind of agreement that we had signed with Russia and other countries, and it embodied little reference to the historic continuity of the Lithuanian state, but it was nevertheless a vitally important document which stated unequivocally that Lithuania was recognized as an independent state by the Soviet Union. Even then we had no idea that the institution which had so long resisted our freedom, and had agreed to the present statement only after prolonged resistance, had little future, but it was this announcement which finally eliminated the remaining hesitation among the western nations.

It was finished. The independence of the three Baltic states was now formally accomplished, and during the afternoon of 17 September 1991 the process reached its culmination when Lithuania was admitted as a full member of the United Nations. Before the ceremony, I flew to Washington with the leaders of the other Baltic states to meet President Bush at the White House. As we walked to the Rose Garden to meet the journalists assembled there, I informally asked the president if he would agree to my raising the status of Stasys Lozoraitis, independent Lithuania's *chargé d'affaires* in Washington, to that of ambassador. Later we left to travel back to New York, to do further business at the United Nations Assembly.

Our membership of the CSCE had by now established that any new aggression against Lithuania would automatically be referred to that international organization. That agreement conferred some status and security, but it was our admission to membership of the United Nations that was the really symbolic milestone. It was the culmination of our long struggle for independence, and I was well aware of the symbolism of my speech in the General Assembly. I made my speech in our native Lithuanian after beginning in English. This was the very first time that our language had been heard in the Assembly, and its use conveyed the symbolic message that our ancient nation now had its own voice in this great forum of the nations. When the sitting was over, many of the ambassadors accredited to the United Nations came to greet the Baltic leaders and shook our hands. Later, I visited the secretary-general and other high officials of the organization. We still had business to do, and our consistent theme was to urge the importance of removing foreign troops from our sovereign territories at the earliest moment. The acting president of the General Assembly was a Bulgarian who well understood this issue, and he expressed his support for our stand. As we left the building we looked up to see the flags of our nations being raised in front of the Assembly building. *Lithuania's was now there too*!

When I returned home I learned that the speech I had delivered at the United Nations had been broadcast in full. While most of our people were proud of the achievement, the transmission itself was something of a disgrace. We had long lacked finance for modern equipment and the television service was in the hands of people who had been appointed years before and whose long co-operation with our communist rulers had coloured their careers. All these factors had resulted in a recorded broadcast which was badly presented, and which went out during an interval in the transmission of a cheap erotic film. We believed that this was probably not an accident, and that the demeaning presentation was an indication that the *nomenklatura* were unhappy with the way things were now going. During my time in New York and Washington, and when I was in the other capitals on the journey home, I had begun to seek financial and economic support for Lithuania. We looked forward to faster economic development in an environment which we presumed would involve the politically unrestricted co-operation with the western economies. We also had the naïve illusion that everyone would be willing to help us, and that we would be able to reward their interest by showing our skills and capabilities in return. It seemed to us that Lithuania would quickly rise to the top by a programme of rapid modernization enabling our country to join fully in western structures. We also believed that we should in no time at all be able to remove the last sign of occupation by finally getting Soviet forces to leave Lithuania. In addressing the world's representatives at the United Nations I had required this of our oppressors, saying: 'We demand the removal of all foreign forces which are illegally stationed on our territory.' When journalists asked when and why this should be done, I would reply, 'Before the next *coup* in Moscow!'

I think that 17 September, the day when Lithuania was given membership of the United Nations, should be marked in our history as the real anniversary of our liberation. For me that day in 1991 marks the true end of the struggle to extricate ourselves from the Soviet Union's grip on the life of the nation. However, there were residual concerns, and new ones began to develop when we discovered that the shadow of the Soviet Union did not go away as we had expected. First there were offers of some kind of common economic arrangement, then suggestions that we should creep under the umbrella of their defence systems. Our stance was to avoid such ensnarement, but these and many other silly ideas were regularly presented to us, and I also began to receive phone calls from Yeltsin, and Shatalin, who had previously been one of Gorbachev's advisers, on these matters. While some people were still extremely anxious about what might follow from the Soviet Union's disintegration and feared chaos, Moscow's army of administrators was not unnaturally preoccupied with the attempt to retain influence in the countries which had been under Russian domination for so long. Although reason might suggest that new policies might be required towards the Baltic states, the old interests of Moscow were clearly still active. Naturally, we tried to resolve these matters in a friendly way, and Yeltsin eventually told me that he understood why we were suspicious of common economic and defence structures, but western journalists and politicians were often less ready to understand our caution. It was noticeable that they emphasized 6 September, the date when the Soviet Union recognized our independence, as the important date in Lithuania's passage to freedom. It was as though the rulers in Moscow had granted independence to a territory which had previously been a part of their state. To us this seemed odd. It did less than justice to what we had worked for and what we had achieved. *We* had gained our independence, it was done by the sovereign will of the Lithuanian nation, and had been declared definitively on 11 March 1990. The overwhelming recognition given to us when we were formally welcomed into the world's family of nations by the General Assembly on 17 September 1991 was accorded to a restored state which had begun the modern stage of its existence over seventy years before, a nation state which was already very old before Columbus discovered America. The political and legal fight for our country's independence now being concluded had continued for exactly a year and a half, and had ended in Lithuania's peaceful victory. For us this was its own justification. Others might not fully understand, but we knew that the sacrifices which we had faced, and the death of our martyrs, had not been in vain.

CHAPTER 18

1992: the burden of independence

Our international standing improved gradually. We became members of the CSCE; we signed the Helsinki final Act which set the agenda of collaboration and human rights between East and West; and we agreed the articles of the Paris Charter, another significant milestone on the path away from the Cold War. The Baltic states were already members of the United Nations when the Soviet Union finally collapsed. These developments encouraged us greatly and kept us on course with the resolution which the Council of the Baltic States had made at its meeting in Vilnius in October 1991, when it designated the general diplomatic recognition of our countries and the removal of the military forces which had been stationed on our territory since 1944 as the primary objectives of a common policy. That meeting of the Council had firmly requested the Soviet authorities to remove their troops before the end of 1991 even though this seemed to be something of a utopian hope at the time. A little after this I decided to play to the gallery of international opinion and demand that the forces in Lithuania should leave us 'within three weeks', and while I subsequently modified this to 'three months' I continued to point out that the original occupation of Lithuania had taken less than three days, suggesting that what had been done in that time could be undone in the same period! Of course, it was necessary to show that we were flexible, so I began to ask the Soviets to show us some goodwill by at least removing the troops from our capital cities, but though my point was well understood by other countries the Russians did not take it. When François Mitterrand came to Vilnius in the spring of 1992 he saw the armed foreign soldiers in the centre of the city, and I drew his attention to their sullen stares and he then observed that they were 'very obviously still in occupation'. Although their allegiance had been switched by force of circumstances, as the Soviet Union had now fallen away, and they were now 'Russian' troops, their character as the old Red Army was still unchanged. He knew my feelings from the experience of his own country when he was a younger man and responded sympathetically. Later that day he made a vigorous speech in which he denounced 'the foreign force which is stationed in Lithuania against her will'.

Winter

At the beginning of 1992 events seemed to be moving in the right direction. First, Russia declared herself to be the Soviet Union's legal heir. Next, when Russia took over the Soviet seat in the Security Council of the United Nations President Yeltsin announced that his country would accept full responsibility for the Soviet military forces, including those stationed in the Baltic countries. When we went to Moscow to begin negotiations early in January it was natural that questions about how and when the former Soviet forces would leave our territory should be at the head of our agenda. Attitudes were positive at this stage and we received an assurance that they would indeed be withdrawn, though no date was attached to this promise. Yet, almost immediately after this, progress began to slow down. The Russians seemed to have changed their minds, and then began pressing to stay on in Lithuania. They even attempted to persuade us that it was necessary to protect their position by according them some kind of legal status. It was mere filibuster, since we had clearly agreed in January the terms on which the army should *withdraw*. We successfully arranged to talk about many other issues which required discussion, such as trade, armaments, and access to the files which the KGB had held on our citizens. Our government also managed to sign a trade agreement, which was vital to us because it ensured our supplies of raw materials, especially of oil and other fuels, for the rest of the year.

While the representatives of the new Russia tried hard to attract us into some kind of economic association during these negotiations, we saw their arguments as being essentially the same as those Gorbachev had trotted out. While they talked broadly of introducing market arrangements we felt that these were euphemisms for what they were really working towards and we were adamant that our birthright was not going to be sold so soon after it had been regained. At one point I felt it necessary to remind Yeltsin of a telephone conversation back in September 1991 when I told him that Lithuania had no intention of joining in any wider economic arrangements, and said that we had not changed our minds. He then recognized my argument that Lithuania's people would not accept any arrangement which might restrict their government's freedom of action, but this did not make the negotiations any quicker. There were obvious difficulties, but in the end we came to an agreement with the Russians, though for a single year only. The terms were detailed enough, and all the necessary clauses about prices and the means of payment were in place, but the mood had changed by the time it was signed and our Russian neighbours now seemed somehow determined to make difficulties for us.

Eventually things deteriorated to the point that they made a unilateral decision to renege on our agreement. This was done quite deliberately after only six months, and seemed an obvious attempt to pull the carpet from beneath our feet. The move landed us in extreme difficulties in the second half of the year, but while the later part of the story did not turn out well for us these difficulties were not apparent at the beginning of 1992. The achievement of the agreement meant that the year seemed to begin well, and I was able to concentrate on other priorities, of which our national security was the chief. As president, my primary aim in this area was to hasten the withdrawal of Russian forces from Lithuanian soil, and my attention was now drawn to the fact that troops were being concentrated in growing numbers just over our border in the Kaliningrad area. I was also concerned at the continued presence of Soviet paratroops in Lithuania, as this presence in our country could be justified no longer if Russia's declaration of peaceable intentions was to be believed; their *raison d'être* was to be a strike force. Back in the autumn of 1991 I had requested the immediate withdrawal of the OMON and all the troops which were still stationed in Vilnius. I now repeated this request, combining it with a demand that the forces which were in place around our borders must also be removed to allow our Ministry of Defence to take control of Lithuania's frontiers. This demand gained a response, and the OMON left, much to our gratification.

At the beginning of 1992 our only controls on our western borders were the visa and luggage check points which we had established. We regarded border controls to be both a political and an economic necessity and took practical steps to secure them. I therefore advised our defence minister to establish a presence at the key border crossing points, in order to encourage the Russians to withdraw peacefully.

We desperately needed to improve our state security, and in the face of what often seemed to be a deliberate misunderstanding of our problems by the West we slowly acquired suitable arms for our defence forces. It was very important for us to establish contacts with NATO, and we were at last given associate membership of the North Atlantic Parliamentary Assembly. Toward the close of 1991 and early in 1992 we put a great deal of our effort into making applications for membership of the International Monetary Fund and the World Bank, and for assistance from the European Bank for Reconstruction and Development and the European Union. Our prospects of joining the IMF seemed good in 1992 because our reform of economic and governmental structures was already more advanced than that of the countries of the former Soviet Union. We felt that international experts would confirm that our privatization programme, and the other steps which we had taken to lay the foundations of a free market economy, had begun to work. Achieving membership of the IMF was an urgent matter because we planned to complete our reforms by floating the national currency, the *litas*, and needed the IMF's support to underpin its stability. We had carefully explained the need to implement this reform to western leaders and bankers, and had already asked Germany, France and the EFTA countries to support our application. Our arguments had seemed to be well received, and our prospects appeared fair. We then learned out of the blue that a decision had been taken to delay our entry into the inter-national financial and banking structures until all the other post-Soviet countries were also ready for admission. The decision was peremptory, final and brutally disappointing. We were to receive nothing before that goal had been achieved, however hard we might plead. From our end the decision appeared ill-considered and unfair, but there it was: we were to be treated as part of a batch despite our preparations. Such was the objective reality of our treatment by the West. We had lost six months of effort in what had now turned out to be a hopeless quest for support. This miscalculation had severe political repercussions.

Our application for membership of the Council of Europe developed on similar lines. The tendency to drag the process out and to defer real decisions to a later date was apparent, and our case was once again bundled with the problems of other countries. This time it was the allegation of shortcomings in Latvia and Estonia which provided the excuse; the issues of their treatment of national minorities, their slowness in arranging elections, and the delays in the finalization of their constitutional arrangements were all cited. We supplied documents to show that we had dealt with these matters and did so repeatedly though to little avail. We pointed out that fully democratic parliamentary elections had been held in Lithuania in 1990, with only the members of the occupying forces being excluded. We explained that our country had been governed under a provisional constitution since then, and we also told them that our Supreme Council had already enacted systematic legislation to protect our national minorities and had also offered Lithuanian citizenship to resident immigrants without imposing any restriction on them. It was unfortunate for us that the officials processing our application seemed uninclined to pay real attention to what we were saying. They had other preoccupations, other priorities, but we were suspicious about the delay and even began to wonder if there were socialists in the European Council who were deliberately delaying our entry because they were influenced by the old Soviet allegations that our Lithuanian national feeling was driven by xenophobia.

Despite these less than optimal conditions, we advanced our reforms on as wide a front as possible, notably by returning the country to the principle of private ownership. The programme for privatizing state assets began with the issue of 'investment vouchers' whose value was determined by estimating the global value of the assets which the state had acquired. Such vouchers were to be exchanged for state assets and could buy shareholdings in the larger companies being privatized, or be pooled to purchase control of smaller companies. As the scheme got under way some workers bought shares in the businesses in which they had been employed. Vouchers were also issued for the purchase of flats and houses which previously had belonged to the state, and this privatization was rapid. Almost all state-owned flats had passed to their occupants by the end of 1992. When the large industrial concerns were handed over, Gediminas Vagnorius, the prime minister, had announced that a third of the capital raised was to be earmarked to compensate people for the loss to their savings which had followed the currency reform. Simultaneously with these changes, which amounted to a social revolution, we also moved forward with the privatization of agricultural co-operatives, and the accompanying process of returning land to its legal owners. The Supreme Council had decided on taking this step very early on. It had caused vigorous debate but it was ruled that the wholesale expropriation of private ownership which had taken place under Soviet law had been illegal. Decisions were taken which ensured that the legitimate owners of the land, or their successors, should have their rights restored to them wherever possible, and a statute was passed to provide for compensation wherever the restoration of the actual title was not possible. This policy of restitution was defined clearly, but we found that there were enormous obstacles to be surmounted when we began to implement it, and these were most obvious when the transformation of agricultural collectives and state farms into share-holding companies began.

Conflicts of interest between the new companies and people who could prove ownership of land which they wanted to work independently were frequent, and the process met with fierce opposition, especially from the people who had practically controlled the collective farms in Soviet times. Until the recent past the life of the agricultural worker had often been dependent on the whims of the influential farm chairmen, party secretaries, and the team managers and other *nomenklatura* whose network of influence controlled virtually everything that happened in the countryside. These people were still in post, of course, deeply attached to their old ways and just as deeply resentful of the changes which were threatening their cosy lifestyles. They now showed their hand either by avoiding the implications of government decrees, or by applying their own dishonest interpretations to them. Many of them began to exploit the privatization process for personal gain, by means of illegal transfers, the appropriation of other people's rights, by corruption, or by manœuvring themselves into positions where they could acquire what was best and most profitable for themselves, leaving ordinary farm workers with the poorer fields, unhealthy livestock and broken-down tractors. We had wanted the processes of decollectivization and privatization to be rapid, but with the wisdom of hindsight it is clear that conflict was probably inevitable. Unfortunately, the worst offenders were often the local authorities who should have taken responsibility for the relevant administration. Under the former regime their members had been among the most privileged people in the land. They were determined to retain their privileges and used their considerable resources to ensure that blame for *anything* which went wrong was shifted onto the government. The prime minister, Gediminas Vagnorius, and I, the chairman of the Parliament, were their favourite scapegoats. By the spring of 1991, it had been established that a great deal of misappropriation of property by the communist *nomenklatura* had taken place, but there was much hesitation about taking steps against the culprits. When the government asked for extra powers to deal with the situation, this was refused and we realized that we did not command a majority in Parliament.

Communist functionaries had been so obviously incompetent as managers that the programme of agricultural privatization should have met with a great deal of goodwill. We had unexpected difficulties with the initial stages because the reforms proposed were radical, but we now faced a problem which was rooted in the structure of our government and administration. Where the Communist party had presided over an ideologically united system, there was now dual control. Sajūdis still had a slight majority in the Supreme Council though its control of government was weakened. However, the picture with regard to the regional, town and district councils was different; nearly everybody who held power in these local authorities had been placed in position by virtue of their membership of the Communist party. They were well used to working together, and now used their strength to resist a process of reform which they perceived as undermining their vested interests. The resulting tensions had become obvious and there was a determined call at the third Congress of Sajūdis to debate these problems, which were now coming to a head. Many of the contributors to this discussion saw a crisis impending, and demanded an overhaul of governmental structures at every level in order to resolve the difficulties. Among other things they called for the reinstitution of the Lithuanian presidency and said that the office should be vested with increased powers to regulate local government, since the existing constitutional arrangements seemed to make overhaul of the administrative law virtually impossible. The Congress acknowledged that the prime minister had already proposed something similar, and that his repeated requests for rational change had been consistently ignored. They asked why, and the debate showed that it was now painfully obvious that we could no longer count on the parliamentary majority which would be necessary to push such measures through. Contributors then discussed and condemned the attitudes of those members of the Sajūdis parliamentary group who had by now become supporters of the Lithuanian Democratic Labour party, as the Communist party had renamed itself, and strongly criticized those Social Democrats and the few Liberals who obviously shared their resistance to government reform. The old ideological loyalties were still lurking below the surface of our parliamentary politics, and it was clear that they were being fully exploited, but the exposure of this fact provoked the fiercest of reactions from the vested interests whose manipulations were now brought into the glare of publicity. Much of the press was in the hands of former communists, so the conclusions of the third Congress of Sajūdis were soon being attacked from this quarter and we were pungently described as 'extreme rightist' and as 'bad for the country'. The details of the machinery of local government had come under scrutiny only because so many of its officials had shown reluctance to implement the land reforms; the discussion revealed the extent to which our political differences were being polarized by the process of reform.

The Sajūdis organization now decided that it wanted to make its own contribution on the question of land reform, and a major conference was planned in co-operation with the Agricultural Workers' Movement. Officials from the Ministry of Agriculture and other government departments also participated. The intention was to review the progress of the land reform, and to identify the obstacles being encountered and what vested interests were delaying or frustrating the intentions of the legislation. It was urgently necessary to outwit the resistance to reform because a growing number of people who wanted to reclaim farms which they, their parents or grandparents had owned, were being prevented by the long delays from returning to farms which they wanted to cultivate. The law had been drafted to permit the return of property to the grandchildren of the dispossessed, and it was interesting to note the significant number of city-dwellers who were choosing to return to the land. When collectivization had taken place many farmers were deported and others were simply driven into the towns to start new lives. Even if they had avoided deportation in this way very few of them had returned home until now; many of their former homesteads and farm buildings had been demolished in the drive to enlarge the fields and create land drainage schemes when collectivization came. The process had changed the character of Lithuanian agriculture and the landscape, and the buildings which remained had been distributed to workers in the co-operative and state farms. The city-dwellers' wish to return to their farms therefore created a whole range of very specific problems on a case-by-case basis, and the opposition used the resulting resentments as a political tool. Provoking unrest wherever they could, they played those who were still living on the land off against those who had been driven away from it, saying: 'The city-dwellers will come. They will take your land and your jobs away', and encouraging rural people to be far from accommodating by adding: 'You will be left as an underclass, and as seasonal labourers.' To these threats was added an appeal to Lenin's dictum: 'the land belongs to those who work on it.' The dilemma was obvious, but there is no disguising the fact that this was a determined move to legalize the consequences of the Soviet occupation and their land nationalization. The fact that these holdings had originally belonged to someone else, and that the families who now wanted to return had been removed from their land and livelihood by force and by terror, was to be viewed as unimportant and something to be forgotten. All the victims of that former brutality were now to be disregarded, or written off in the Marxist cant as *'petit bourgeois'* just because suppression and coercion had driven them either to the gulags or to the towns. It was a confrontational line and it was pushed hard by the 'old guard' who took their arguments to the extreme. They made no attempt to look for possibilities of compromise or to accommodate special cases because the new order might affect their power base. It was a case of deploying every possible opportunity to destabilize the process of agricultural reform and to magnify social conflict. In matters of propaganda, the communists had long experience.

This was the general outlook at the beginning of 1992. By March the division in the Supreme Council on the question of land reform was very clear and was exacerbated by our disagreements over the procedures for unmasking KGB informers and their agents and collaborators which we had instituted following the failure of the Moscow *putsch* in the autumn of 1991. We had established a State Commission to investigate the KGB network in Lithuania and this Commission had just begun to issue reports. All too frequently the people implicated were deputies in the Supreme

Council. We were concerned at the scope of the evidence and had begun to discuss the possibility of a desovietization on the Czechoslovakian model. This attracted a great deal of attention but left us in bitter confrontation with the former communists and the groups under their influence. This political Left was now happy to call 'foul' at every turn, and we were told that such legislation would be an infringement of human rights. Apparently it would embody a principle of collective responsibility and this was unjust because individuals were responsible only for their own deeds. The thrust of the argument was that no one could be condemned for having belonged to the Communist party. This of course missed the point that, although it was no longer possible to deny the crimes which had been perpetrated by that party, our plans would not have affected every member of the former Communist party of the Soviet Union, nor were court proceedings envisaged. What we hoped was that the proposed law would debar from public office former high officials of the Communist party, proven collaborators with the KGB, and anyone who had misused an official position to infringe the legal or human rights of another person. While we believed that *not* to impose such relatively mild restrictions, at least for a period of a few years, would be a virtual indecency, there was no intention of extending such restrictions to the ordinary members of the party. However, the leaders of the Lithuanian Democratic Labour party tried to drum up support by exciting the fears of ordinary people and talked inconsolably about our 'planned retribution' and 'antidemocratic tendencies'. They also struck a 'dog in the manger' attitude to everybody and everything for the rest of the parliamentary session, until the elections held in October and November saved their bacon. Those elections were hurriedly arranged because of circumstances beyond our control, and their outcome was hard to believe. By an incredible political paradox, the men and women who had collaborated most closely with the illegal regime which had occupied our land for so long were returned to government as the legally elected rulers of free Lithuania.

Spring

Numerous attempts were made by members of Sajūdis to persuade members of the Supreme Council to give more support to our prime minister, and deputies were asked on several occasions to use any influence they might have with local authority officials and collective farm chairmen to speed up land privatization. When difficulties continued, the Supreme Council was asked to give the government authority to dismiss public servants because our programme was being undermined by blatantly slow administrative responses when property titles were sought by their rightful owners. Cruder methods of swindling claimants of their rightful inheritance were also being reported widely, and justice demanded that those responsible for this criminal behaviour be dealt with summarily. It was clear by now that our Privatization Act had not been thought out properly. Its reliance on local authorities as the agents of registration and redistribution had been too trusting; the government had ceded major responsibilities without retaining any role of inspection or arbitration. Corrupt officials had recognized that we could not easily interfere with them, and while the existing communist-inspired legislation allowed us to ask the Supreme Council to penalize offending civil servants, the procedure could only be invoked in the event of a gross miscarriage of justice. While the Council had a right to interfere under such circumstances, its prerogatives had seldom been exercised; the checks and balances were more symbolic than real, as the procedures were clumsy and impracticable in most cases. To add to all this, I knew that the Supreme Council as then constituted would have thrown out almost any proposal, however well founded, which emerged from the government. The situation was a strange one which drained our energies over a prolonged period. The increased opposition to the government was now obvious to everyone. Late in the spring of 1992 a small parliamentary faction calling itself Tautos Pažanga (National Progress), which had presented itself as being on the radical right, showed its true colours and moved to the left. This shift had the effect of changing the balance of power in Parliament. Faced with this reality, Gediminas Vagnorius told the Supreme Council that his government no longer commanded a majority.

As we have seen, some of the smaller political groups had now effectively aligned with the opposition in the Supreme Council. This meant that the Left, which was being cleverly controlled by the former Communist party, was in a majority. This occurred at a time when the government lacked support on vital matters, especially with regard to its attempt to curb local councils who refused to come to terms with the land reform programme. Our attempts to deal with bribery and corruption, and the illegal acquisition of privatized property, were also being blocked and we were hampered by the fact that there were both ministers and members of our legal services who were no less corrupt than the more difficult of the local authority leaders. We faced a situation which had become anarchic to the point that government ministers felt able to oppose or contradict the prime minister publicly on matters of policy without fear of dismissal. In these circumstances our progress was necessarily limited, so much of our thinking focused on the idea of reintroducing the office of president into our constitution and on how to conduct future presidential elections, because the restoration of that office seemed to hold the key to resolving the constitutional impasse which we were facing. Perhaps not surprisingly the Left in the Supreme Council reacted negatively to these ideas, and they passed a resolution that no reforms could be made which affected our internal national administration before all foreign forces had left our territory and a new constitution had been adopted. We had no means of overturning this decision, and the new majority in Parliament took its own initiative by preparing to draft a new constitution. They did this without reference to the group of Sajūdis members which had already been working on a draft. We were now in a minority, and were being actively ignored, but we were not without initiative and sought to recover our hope of introducing governmental reforms by deciding to seek a referendum. Sajūdis therefore intensified its efforts to reinstate a Lithuanian presidency and argued that presidential elections should take place *before* the next parliamentary elections in order that the new occupant of that office should be in position when the incoming government was elected. He would then be able to preside over the appointment of the government, and the allocation of ministers to their departments, while the relationship between the ministries and local councils could also be defined. We also pointed out that a president would have authority above that of the prime minister, and could therefore exercise powers which Parliament might not be keen to use itself, because of its political composition. In advising this we were, of course, openly critical of the way in which the Supreme Council had seemed to be allowing the misuse of authority by corrupt local councils at a time when the government lacked unity and effective executive authority. It was against this ambiguous political background that Sajūdis began to collect signatures for a referendum in April and May, making its appeal to the nation as a whole. This was a move to find a way out of our impasse, and was possible because we were able to take advantage of a law which ruled that a referendum must take place if there were sufficient signatures, whether Parliament approved or not.

The question which was to be resolved through the referendum was simple: we wanted amendments to the existing constitution, first to establish the presidential office and to define its authority, duties and relationship with the government and Parliament of Lithuania. The opposition protested that our proposals implied excessive presidential authority, and tried to mislead the people by claiming that as Lithuania had not yet devised its own constitution we could not have a president. Those who swallowed the line, or were puzzled about what was afoot, were advised that the proposed ballot was 'merely another device to promote Landsbergis' and the Social Democrats enjoyed themselves by recycling the old communist arguments. They even issued a leaflet which affirmed that Lithuania would lose her position among the democratic nations if Sąjūdis was successful in the referendum. Citizens would then find themselves out of jobs, would even be persecuted and, to rub it in, they would have to pay huge taxes to maintain the president in the state to which he would like to become accustomed! Their campaign was pursued with some venom, and we needed an affirmative vote from more than 50 per cent of the electorate before our proposals could pass into law. The provision for a referendum was inherited from Soviet times, and reflected the conditions of that period, requiring a majority vote of all the eligible electorate, rather than a simple majority of the votes cast. It was this requirement which caused our efforts to fail. Despite gaining a large majority of the votes cast (59 per cent), our vote was insufficient because it amounted to only 41 per cent of the votes eligible to be cast. It was a majority in favour, but it lacked the absolute majority necessary for the law on the presidency to be adopted. Of course, our opponents were quite delighted. They trumpeted it about that those who did not participate in the ballot were neither passive nor doubting, but rather united in purposeful opposition to the establishment of the presidency! They also claimed that the outcome meant that the majority of our citizens supported *their* constitutional project rather than ours. As we have already noted, there were two constitutional projects being drafted simultaneously. One involved a commission of deputies, and as it was sponsored by the new majority in the Supreme Council, it obviously reflected the interest of that group. It set out to leave the whole system in the hands of the parliamentary majority, with the presidential office introduced as a final decorative flourish. These plans dispensed with the idea that the constitution could be changed in future by a general referendum without the previous approval of Parliament. The second project was ours and this draft was being discussed by two groups, one of them made up of Sąjūdis deputies, the other a select group of lawyers, scientists and politicians. These proposals envisaged a more clearly defined and unifying presidential role which would create an overall balance between the president, the government and the future Seimas.

We submitted our finalized draft constitution to the Supreme Council when it had been completed to our satisfaction, but the Left majority not only refused to entertain our proposal, but also said that constitutional changes must be submitted to the people in another referendum. It was obvious that they planned to use their majority to move their own project forward, and did not want our proposals to compete. Sąjūdis, however, took its own initiative, and decided once again to use the provisions in the existing temporary constitution which allowed a referendum to be called on the basis of a petition. The required number of signatures was collected very soon afterwards, but the Supreme Council ignored this move. Their resistance was quite transparent and looked as if it would be permanent, but I used my authority as its chairman to intervene and the result was quite unexpectedly fruitful as a discussion took place which led to a joint proposal being accepted. The referendum was then arranged for 25 October and had a wonderfully successful outcome, with the Sąjūdis proposals being accepted by the country as a whole. Once again our opponents were not pleased with the outcome, and they used their well tried methods of distortion to claim that this outcome was not really a victory for Sąjūdis and Landsbergis because 'our' earlier referendum on 23 May had not succeeded. It made little real sense, and was nothing more than sour grapes, but they also demanded that the government, or the chairman of the Supreme Council, should now resign! I hit back with a statement which I made to the Council from the platform of its debating chamber in which I said that the communists and their 'creeping revolution' were not to be trusted, calling them a force which was 'detrimental to the Lithuanian state'. I underlined my point by quoting from a document which the Vilnius KGB had transmitted to Moscow in May 1990, which reported how Algirdas Brazauskas had secretly informed them that he was expecting the imminent collapse of Lithuania under the pressure of the blockade. I made quite sure that everyone understood exactly what I was doing, by reading the contents of this internal KGB communiqué twice in the original Russian, and once again in Lithuanian translation. It was my way of telling everyone present that we knew that Brazauskas had welcomed the idea of 'presidential rule' by Mikhail Gorbachev at the time of our nation's greatest vulnerability. My intervention naturally produced complete uproar, but it had the desired effect because, only a few days later, the Council promulgated a constitutional law to prevent any future Lithuanian government from joining any post-Soviet structure. As an after-effect it was interesting to notice that the constant niggling demands for my resignation also subsided for a while, not a murmur being heard for some weeks, where there had previously been a regular cacophony. However, some people are incorrigible. Soon enough one of my deputies, Kazimieras Motieka, turned on me, launching a bitter attack in the press when I was abroad. He was probably making the point that he would make a much better chairman than Landsbergis, while those who encouraged him knew that the appointment could be only a temporary one at best!

The Left was clearly planning to take over the government, and waiting only for the right moment. However, their way was blocked for the time being because I was involved in negotiations with the Russian president and planning for the Helsinki summit, while the referendum planned for 14 June, on troop withdrawals, was also drawing near. Another complicating factor was the discord between the government and the Central Bank of Lithuania. The Bank had taken a confrontational line and was refusing to settle inter-company accounts under arrangements which should have been imposed to limit the rapid growth of credit, which was threatening to get out of control. The root of the problem lay in bad practices inherited from the Soviet Central Bank, although it had been triggered by the dislocations of credit which had followed from the blockade and more recent disruptive activities deliberately engineered by Russian banks. Since then many financial settlements within Lithuania had remained unresolved. The Bank was either unable to make the necessary settlements, or was simply refusing to carry out its obligations because even those transactions which were being honoured were taking an impossibly long time and the whole banking system was in question as a result. Such a situation was clearly intolerable for any government, but it was strange to discover that our opponents in the Supreme Council were supporting the Bank and not the government. This was not our only problem with the Bank. There had been major printing and delivery difficulties affecting the introduction of our own currency. The new *litas* notes had arrived late and were disgracefully poor in quality when they came. The Bank had tried to cover up its errors, and its officials had avoided the government's call for talks until the prime minister lost patience and accused the Bank of incompetence. This confrontation between the Bank and the prime minister delayed the introduction of the *litas* further, and was highlighted in the press. The episode did Lithuania's prestige no good, and in late May or early June I came round to the view that the difficulties with the Bank were beyond ordinary methods of resolution. At this juncture I called the prime minister and the chairman of the Bank into my office for a joint meeting. We reviewed the situation and at the end of the meeting I found that there was no alternative but to ask the chairman of the board of the Bank of Lithuania to resign so that the relationships between the Bank and the government could be improved, and a coherent financial policy implemented. I knew this would provoke a crisis, but I did just that. Of course my constitutional authority was limited to the ability to make a formal request to a civil servant to resign. The chairman was accountable to the Supreme Council not to me, and he knew it. He bluntly refused my request, and took the matter to the Supreme Council, which then compounded the problem by not voting him out of office. The conflict remained unresolved because we were involved in a scenario which had been conceived in malice by our opponents, who were using their majority vote to advance the principle that the worse the situation became for the government, the better it was for them!

Summer

Even though my negotiations with President Yeltsin in January had resulted in an announcement that the withdrawal of Russian forces would begin in March, by the end of that month the sum total of progress had been the withdrawal of just eight soldiers from Kaunas though a further hundred had left Vilnius. An enormous propaganda harvest accompanied these minuscule manœuvres. Once again movement was being delayed, though there were pretexts and excuses in abundance. At first Russia's strategic interests were mentioned, then we heard that the delay was linked with some kind of global defence system which had been proposed to the United States. We were told that this meant that Russia would need to deploy its forces strategically to be available anywhere in the world, and Lithuania was clearly a convenient place to start! There were other mumblings, and, as we might have foreseen, many of the Russian forces actually *preferred* to remain in the Baltic states and were reluctant to move on. There was another objection, this time on social grounds: we learned that there was a shortage of accommodation in Russia, especially on the military bases. That vast country lacked sufficient living quarters for its troops at present. Next we were informed that the repatriation of such large numbers would create enormous internal tensions in the homeland and might upset the development of democracy in Russia, or even affect President Yeltsin's position! We were exasperated, but eventually stoical when we realized that an endless stream of arguments would be advanced. We then began to make our own suggestions and informed our neighbours that we would be very happy to help them out with the construction of accommodation if someone would pay for the project. If Russia could not finance the work itself, maybe they could obtain funds for building from the West and we would supply the materials and the labour. We did a lot of work on the problem, and the Scandinavian countries, with their experience of timber construction, came up with useful practical suggestions, because their interest in moving the Russian forces away from the Baltic region was almost as great as ours. Curiously, Russia seemed to lose interest when they came up with these proposals. Their long bluff was called. At last even these masters of procrastination understood that their arguments for delaying the withdrawal of their forces no longer held water.

Yet even this was not quite the end of the story. To our amazement we learned that the Russian forces based in the Baltic countries might themselves refuse to move, and that if they did, Russia would be powerless to move them on. We remembered that armed followers of General Bermont had stayed on in Latvia and Lithuania in just this way in 1919, and we were warned that the forces which remained in our countries might begin to operate independently in the same way and impose a 'local military rule'. The dangers to the people of our countries and the threat to our independence was manifest; the message we were being given was that an uninvited guest who had bullied the family and long overstayed his welcome had decided to stay even longer, and that we were quite powerless to proceed with his eviction. We received many threats from one Russian general after another, and when we asked why neither the president of Russia nor the general military headquarters in Moscow seemed able to control the language being used by these local commanders, whose lexicon suggested that they might turn their frustration into a brutal attack at almost any moment, we received no direct reply. The implications of this circus were that commanders of the forces could continue to threaten us with military take-over with impunity. We were weary of these pressures, and unimpressed by the excuses. The repertoire was endless, and before the end of the saga, they tried another tack: it was now discovered that the rights of Russian speakers in all the Baltic states would be threatened and undermined once the troops were withdrawn. Because of this peril it had been discovered that it might be a good idea for the foreign force to stay on for a while. It was the replay of an age-old practice. Had not the empires of the past found it necessary to defend something of their own in their neighbours' countries?

We now began to rethink our campaign to attract international support for our struggle to get the Russian forces removed from the Baltic states and responded to the prevailing political climate by framing our arguments in terms of European and international security rather than as a bilateral question or a local issue. The Russian military presence, we repeated on many occasions, affected the stability of the entire region, and added that the situation needed to be resolved urgently and unconditionally. We persisted, and in the end our argument won the day because it was accepted by all the European Community and the North Atlantic Treaty countries. This same standpoint was eventually reflected in the wording of the Helsinki Summit Declaration in July, and later the General Assembly of the United Nations took it up in the autumn of 1992. The slow process of persuasion was eventually rewarded by an agreement which was drafted and finally signed in Moscow on 8 September. The story behind this accord is of major importance because the process which led up to it had really begun on 14 June when our referendum was held. That ballot had put two questions to our people, first: 'Should Russian forces remove themselves from our country before the end of the year?', and second: 'Should the government of Lithuania seek reparations for the damage done during Soviet occupation?' The nation had answered affirmatively to both questions, and this 'double Yes' response obviously strengthened our position because international pressure for the withdrawal of foreign forces from all three Baltic states became much more obvious in the weeks which followed. However, the next really positive step forward came on 10 July at the CSCE Summit, when we finally achieved the precise formulation we required. The Final Act of the Helsinki summit spelled this out by imposing an obligation on all the parties concerned 'to negotiate an *early, orderly and complete* withdrawal of the foreign forces'. We also learned that Russia had agreed to it, and recognized that this was a very important achievement indeed. It was quickly followed by real negotiations. Up until then the discussion of the military question had been a purely verbal exchange, but the meeting spelled out Russia's obligations in detail. It then passed the final declaration which also bound Russia to the obligation of an 'early, orderly and complete withdrawal'. When this was done, I went to the dais and explained exactly how Lithuania understood those words, then walked back into the auditorium to sit next to Boris Yeltsin who murmured to me: 'We must conclude that agreement at last.' His concession was notable. Russia had not committed herself to anything like this previously. The Helsinki Conference had finally cut through this intransigence and once this had happened the process moved forward quickly.

The documentation for the agreement was completed in August. When it was signed we could feel some satisfaction, knowing just how persistent Lithuania had been in pursuing this initiative. We had proposed draft projects since the beginning of the year, and our positive offensive had continued unbroken right up to the time we met Yeltsin in Moscow to finalize the accord. When we got there we had been disappointed by the rigmarole which ensued. Seven heads of agreement had been proposed by us, and we were willing to go ahead on all of them. Yeltsin, however, was not satisfied with them and kept on suggesting alterations until the very last moment, refusing to sign several of the articles even at that late stage. The sense of frustration was enormous for us at this point, but three of the protocols had actually been signed, including the most important – the agreement to withdraw the Russian forces. Further, we now possessed a schedule and the date for the final withdrawal, and had seen the signing ceremony taking place in front of the television crews with both heads of state present. While we were delighted at this outcome, other people were not so pleased, and we observed afterward that the Russian diplomats were trying to diminish what we had achieved, 'because not all the agreements were signed'. A few were audacious enough to suggest that the three articles which were agreed had 'no effect because the others had been passed over'. The manœuvre brought them no respect at this stage, because international opinion had at last consolidated. We now had an effective clause confirming that all the troops would be away from Lithuania by an agreed date and without further delay. This arrangement had international approval. We made sure that the documents which confirmed all this were registered at the United Nations as swiftly as was possible, and when this was done we felt that the matter was concluded. We believed that Russia would have benefited considerably if its negotiators had accepted all seven of our (carefully drafted) proposals, but someone in their foreign ministry must have been too clever by half because the clauses which were rejected had conceded privileges to their officers and men, including the right to buy and sell the houses in which they lived. Because the other side had been inflexible we had only secured those clauses which affected Lithuania's essential rights, though, of course, these were the most important for us. Yet we could not help noticing their bullying approach, the veiled and actual threats and the bravado which they displayed while negotiating with us. If they had behaved more generously they would have gained more from us. Sadly this was the old, old story – their behaviour was a pretty close replay of what had gone on in Gorbachev's time.

The domestic reforms which were central to our strategy had not yet begun to yield the results we were hoping for. While the process of privatization was gathering speed, corruption was also growing as the shadowy forces of the Mafia improved their money-laundering skills. Much of their money was actually obtained from deals arranged through Communist party connections or criminal activity, and their criminal operations were expanding at a speed which suggested that they might soon be installing their own economic regime. Some liberal activists even tried to claim that there was nothing objectionable in all this, arguing that it was spearheading free market activity and that everything would even out after a while. 'After all, *non olet pecunia,* money does not smell', they said, but political, moral and social considerations made it quite impossible to agree. At this time I was spending a lot of time travelling to meetings around the country to talk with people in the rural areas as well as the towns, in order to find out what they felt. I had meetings with local authorities at which I urged them to tell me how they saw the progress of agricultural reform, always asking them whether they felt it should be speeded up or slowed down; to describe their experience of the procedures being used to confirm whose land was where; their views on the rights of the current occupants of properties which had been claimed and how they should be compensated, and so on. On almost every occasion they answered in unison that the sooner the reform was consolidated, the better. But it was also clear that the whole process needed clarification because it had been promised that people would return to the land by the previous autumn, and already a new spring had come. A large number of those concerned were again ready to move, many of them having already purchased animals and agricultural implements. Very many of them then seemed to be stuck in the queue to receive their land, and so the start of farming was being delayed. Naturally many of them had begun to worry that they might not be arriving in their fields in time to gather the hay crop. Such a delay would of course threaten the survival of their stock during the cold winter months. Meanwhile it was clear everywhere that the process of return to the land had already released great energies and one could find new buildings being constructed in many places. Such activities were often a sign of a new spirit as there was a sense of excitement abroad accompanying the mood of eagerness to get established. The joy of ownership was often infectious, and spirits had obviously been uplifted. New enterprises were begun in many places, and even in the great prairie-like expanses where the communist system had removed the fields and imposed unnatural drainage systems on the land by levelling the landscape and stripping the earth of its orchards and dwellings, one could see new foundations being laid and piles of bricks being stacked as families began to rebuild the old places which had been laid waste. Those who had reclaimed their soil were beginning to rebuild their homes, and this movement generated hope for the revitalization of the Lithuanian countryside and economy. However, the whole process was interwoven with a number of problems. Many of the country people were being cheated of their rightful shares in the collectives by self-interested and crooked officials. The *nomenklatura* always knew just how to help themselves to the best and the most, leaving those who did not have their inbuilt advantages with the leftovers, and many applicants had come face to face with bureaucratic condescension and contempt. Some had experienced vicious rejection by arrogant officials who often made things difficult for claimants by seeing to it that the processing of an application was long drawn out in the hope that people would give up. Officialdom was also adept in the art of one covering up for the other, and it was not only the returning town-dwellers who were the victims of their greed. Many cases came to our attention in which land-workers from the former collective farms had decided to stay on as shareholding employees of the new companies. Not infrequently these people found their interests were being marginalized by conspiracies against them; their experiences were often disheartening in the extreme. Many told us of their fear of being cheated which was a well justified fear: some had been encouraged to pass their investment vouchers over to clever confidence tricksters and had come out of the deals with nothing. Many of them then blamed the state for not having provided adequate instructions and advice, but the government had its own problems in this area. We had introduced the reforms in good faith, made the ground-rules clear enough, and asked the state television service to broadcast detailed programmes to help people understand their rights and what was going on. Unfortunately the administrators of the service refused to give more than five minutes a week to programmes to explaining the process. They remained obdurate even when faced with a strongly worded demand. It was plain that they had no wish to help the land reform programme in any way.

As these tensions were developing, the rapid rise in prices was becoming a political problem. The prices of agricultural produce were still partially subject to government control, but the costs of imported agricultural machinery and of fuel were rising very rapidly indeed. Our farmers were now complaining that it was no longer worth their while to rear livestock. It took a year to raise a bullock, they said, but its sale price was less than the cost of a fortnight's tractor fuel. It was a 'no-win' situation for everybody because farm production prices were depressed, while retail prices were unreasonably high in the towns. We tried to maintain an equilibrium between these important lobbies, and intervened to increase salaries and pensions some time before we floated the price of agricultural produce. This was a fortunate move which avoided conflict, and our pensioners subsequently looked back on the period in question as one of their better times. Unfortunately the respite it gave was too short as it was already summer. We were now halfway through the year and the tensions around us were building up rapidly as the Left majority intensified its opposition in Parliament. They were active in their attempts to dismiss the prime minister and matters were brought to a head when he made his attempt to remove the minister for energy and the chairman of the Central Bank of Lithuania. Gediminas Vagnorius had hoped to gain control over some aspects of an increasingly difficult situation by this move, and when he failed to get his way he tried to resign. At this point he proposed that his opponents should assume responsibility for the government, but though this was the obvious next move, the ballot which should have determined the issue resulted in the Left finding itself short of a single vote. It was a result which left the reluctant Vagnorius still in office, which was probably the worst possible outcome for him. Obviously the situation needed a great deal of reflection. Most of the Sąjūdis deputies believed that the overall situation would be more stable if Vagnorius stayed in the post for a while, but things could not continue as they were for much longer. This resolution was necessarily a temporary one and a general election must be held before long. Both Vagnorius and the Sąjūdis group were agreed that arrangements for the election should be set in motion as soon as possible, but we discovered that our opponents had another agenda and were not prepared to co-operate to bring this about as quickly as we hoped. They did not want to be hurried because they had other plans which needed more time to ripen. They were scheming to find a way of taking over the only large-circulation paper which supported Sąjūdis's viewpoint and to gain even more control of the television networks before entering on an election campaign. Additionally, they had found the reports of the commission we had established to investigate KGB activities much too embarrassing, and were looking for a way to disband or otherwise neutralize its work. They wanted to get rid of our government, but only at the moment best suited to their purposes. It all amounted to a plan for what I called the 'creeping take-over' and it was not really very difficult to discern what was going on. As the picture became clearer I informed Parliament that I would not stand idly by while these twilight activities went ahead in the effort to undermine us. Our opponents were playing a murky game, and as I was not willing to allow them time to gain the maximum advantage for themselves I decided to set the cat among the pigeons and told the Supreme Council plainly that the split in its ranks was now obvious. The conflicts of opinion were so deep that it was best to acknowledge them openly and admit that there were two sides, the Left and the Right, and that this could mean that a handful of floating voters could influence our country's fate. It was an intervention which seemed to clarify the deputies' minds and the two groups held separate meetings for a while.

We agreed in the end that there was only one way to settle our divisions; a general election should be held in the autumn. We got around the intransigence of the Left by turning once more to the constitutional provisions which allowed for the calling of a referendum. Sąjūdis set to work collecting 100,000 signatures more than the minimum requirement of 300,000 for its petition to allow a referendum on the question of holding early elections. We had hoped to arrange the contest for August or September so that the new government would be comfortably in place before winter set in with its accompanying problems, but procedural problems frustrated this hope. The electoral law which had operated in Lithuania until this time was based firmly on a 'first past the post' principle. There had been no provision for the outcome of an election to be adjusted to respond to the state of the parties across the country and there had already been discussion of reforming the electoral law to introduce the principle of proportional representation. When the Supreme Council debated the petition for the referendum, it did not fulfil its duty to decide upon the questions to be put before the electorate. As a result the parliamentary majority took the opportunity of including a question about the introduction of proportional representation and proposed a new arrangement which would introduce voting on party lists so that their overall performance across the country could be reflected in the eventual state of the parties in the legislature. We were initially opposed to this proposal, but were prepared to compromise even though the additional time involved in the discussion and establishment of the new system meant that the election was not held until October. The new electoral system was based on half the seats being distributed as before after the first ballot on a 'first past the post' principle, while the second half were to be allocated after a second ballot in proportion to the votes gained by each of the parties.

This whole debate about the general election and the introduction of proportional representation took place in the shadow of another national referendum. This had been arranged for 14 June, to measure the extent of the popular demand for the withdrawal of Russian forces from our national territory. Preparation for this event had naturally involved extensive political discussion, not least because there were many other urgent issues which had to be resolved if we were to get our house in order. When the Supreme Council examined the proposal early in May it was proposed that the opportunity should be taken to put *two* questions before the public on the day of the referendum, a question on the re-introduction of the Lithuanian presidency being added to that on the withdrawal of troops. While Sąjūdis deputies supported this motion, the majority of our opponents were adamantly against it, though they succeeded in winning their point only with the support of a handful of radicals from the parliamentary faction Tautos Pažanga. These demagogues had split from their former colleagues in Sąjūdis to join forces with the Leftists. Their argument was convoluted as they were actually against holding any plebiscite for the removal of foreign forces because they feared that people might not vote in large numbers for something on which the nation was agreed already. They said the Russians would then argue that a low vote meant that the people did not really want the troops to go, and even suggested that the demand for a referendum had been engineered by KGB agents! Their antics were noticed by only a few people, but this intervention ensured that the two questions were each put to the country in separate referenda.

It was agreed that these were to be held on two different days regardless of the increased costs, and while it was the Tautos Pažanga members who made the proposal, the allied forces from the Social Democrat, Liberal and Lithuanian Democratic Labour parties took full advantage of it. Their combined votes pushed the measure through, though the intention of the Left was to discourage the electorate from voting on the presidency question. They believed that this tactic would serve that objective, and the result of their posturing was that the vote on the presidency was held on Sunday 23 May, a date which happened to cause me some real personal annoyance because I had been invited by Yale University to receive an honorary doctorate on that day! The university authorities had told me that I could receive this signal honour only if I attended the ceremony in person. I now faced a dilemma! If I had gone to Yale and the referendum had failed, the resulting reproaches would never have ended. Of course I stayed in Lithuania, and the outcome was really heart-warming, both then and on 14 June because the people voted overwhelmingly both for the withdrawal of the Russian forces and for the institution of the presidency. The convincing political victory on both occasions was a result which did us no end of good on the international scene, and the second result seemed to break down a great deal of the longstanding western psychological resistance. I have already mentioned how it prepared the way for the call made at the Helsinki Summit for 'the removal of foreign forces'. Russia was not named in the statement, but the request for an 'early, orderly and complete' withdrawal from the Baltic states could only be delivered to one address! The clarity of the results obtained from these Lithuanian referenda was also a factor which influenced the agreement made in Moscow on 8 September, when the actual treaty for withdrawal of the Russian forces was finally signed.

We made other significant progress on the international front as well. I attended the World Environmental Summit at its meeting in Rio de Janeiro, and signed the resulting Charter on behalf of Lithuania. The opposing majority in the Supreme Council probably did not want me to travel there, but fortunately I was not beholden to them, as the Danish government was prepared to finance my flight! In the summer we were at last admitted to the International Monetary Fund, and early in the autumn we became members of the World Bank, which at last opened the doors for credit facilities and other economic support to Lithuania. Meanwhile our application for membership of the Council of Europe progressed, and we were granted special guest status in the autumn, though only after our government had changed. The Left, now ready to strike, finally voted to remove Vagnorius's government from office just *before* the elections. It was then my duty to propose another prime minister, so I called upon Aleksandras Abišala who had previously held the post of minister without portfolio. He then nominated as his deputy Bronius Lubys, an industrialist who had been close to the last Soviet government and was therefore in touch with the political and economic interests which had so successfully undermined Vagnorius. The Left would allow no other changes. Abišala's declared wish to make additional appointments was refused, so the rest of the government remained as it was. It was a deliberate ploy which meant that the friction continued inside the government because the new prime minister was forced into dealing with several ministers, and also a chairman of the Lithuanian Central Bank, with whom he would have been much happier not to work. It was a very difficult situation, an unpleasant compromise from which only the outcome of the general election could release us.

These tensions naturally affected my own position, but I had other important things on my plate. I did my best to deal with them, taking particular care to hold consultations on crime and the problems of business and industry. I also kept a watchful eye on the needs of the Jewish organizations which had come to me with complaints about our prosecutor's office and the problems they had when attempting to reclaim titles under the land reform programme. Such consultations usually took place in my office, and meetings on the agricultural reform brought representatives of the farmers, land workers and the Ministry of Agriculture together. I was, however, increasingly frustrated by the fact that the agreements made in these meetings were frequently not implemented. At one point we agreed that the Ministry of Agriculture would set up a land registration scheme to allow transactions to be monitored, and that the local agricultural service offices would display land reform schedules in places where they could easily be seen by members of the public. The ministry also agreed to accelerate the preparation of cover notes for applicants who had been unable to organize themselves in time for the agreed transfer of land titles in the autumn of 1991, or had as yet been unable to trace the records in the land registry or other archives. These developments should have been in place by August because we needed to ensure that claimants could begin to work the land in peace, knowing that they would receive the deeds to the properties sooner or later. We also believed that the public display of land reform plans would improve communication and reduce the possibility of unco-operative bureaucrats sabotaging the process, but we continued to receive a plethora of reports of the abuse, sarcasm and belittling comments which were being uttered by officials in local government and land service offices, and examples of persistent reluctance to conform with the directives. Yet while we tried to put a stop to these things, many who had been promised the return of their land by the autumn of 1991 were still without it in the spring of 1992. Even the promise of 'a definite completion by the following autumn' often failed to materialize and I was made aware that an impression was being freely conveyed in local government offices, and even in the Agricultural Reform Commission itself, that the prospect of a different government being elected meant that the process of returning land to its proper owners would soon come to an end. It was a deliberate and perverse invitation to procrastination. When I also became aware that my efforts to reduce the difficulties in this area were being largely ignored, I could not help feeling that there was a conspiracy to deal unjustly with these people and that it had a consistent political motive.

Autumn

We did not retain the authority of government in our hands for much longer, even in the fragile condition to which it had descended. However, before we left office we were able to pass a Mortgages Act. Its terms should have been incorporated into the earlier Land Reform Act to complement the provisions of that Act, but the necessary experience had not been to hand when the statute was drafted. The external pressure on the country and the great demands of other areas on our legislative programmes had delayed this measure along with several other important projects for more than a year, and while I saw the need for a law to provide for co-operative enterprises like those which had existed in pre-war Lithuania, the opportunity to pass such a law did not present itself. It was now obvious that many of our laws and decrees needed radical improvement, for example the legislation which prevented landowners from renting fields to other farmers – a complete anomaly in a situation where private farming was being restored. Many such anomalies remained because we were being forced to make endless compromises with the socialist dogma which was deeply engrained in the country's statutory framework, even while we were busy reintroducing the concept of land ownership. It had been relatively simple for those who already lived in the countryside and were able to start farming immediately to return to the land, but there were often major problems for those who lived in towns. They might hold an entitlement, but many of them were unable to afford to start farming until the Mortgages Act was passed. While the application of this law relieved many such

331

problems, there were yet other kinds of hardship which remained in the queue for legislative consideration.

The autumn witnessed the privatization programme in turmoil. We heard of many cases where assets were effectively looted from their owners, and the incompetence of the police and the justice system to uphold the law was apparent. Everywhere there was dissatisfaction, which was often expressed in public protests. We had endless problems with our prosecutors and with the courts themselves, and I often issued formal admonitions, which were just as frequently disregarded. There was plenty of evidence of identifiable abuses by local government officials, which included theft, corruption and the stripping of state assets. However, even when relevant information was supplied to our law officers, noticeably few cases were called to court. We knew of hundreds of criminal cases which could have been brought, but only a handful of these cases reached the courts. Quite simply, the evidence told us that the efforts of honest officials were being blocked, sometimes because their seniors were unwilling to become involved in conflict, but more often because the old *nomenklatura* ties amounted to a national protection racket. The closeness of this group was itself an obstacle to change, a relic of the Soviet regime when local government officials, councillors, police, law officers and justices, and Communist party officials had all worked closely together. They had all been friends, a privileged and close class, hunting together, taking saunas together, wining and dining together. By now, their ties had developed over a lifetime, and against this background it was naturally rather difficult for any one of them to take action against another, because there was a whole nexus of mutual obligation to be overcome and it proved an obstacle which we were unable to surmount. Our only hope lay in the gradual recruitment of new judges and prosecutors, new civil servants and new ideas. For the present we were almost helpless, but the people were angry and aggrieved to see so much blatant contravention of the law, and of course nothing was more natural than for them to blame the government. These feelings were expressed clearly and openly in the autumn elections. It was the only way in which the people could register their discontent and disappointment at our lack of success.

Our parliamentary elections were held in October and November. These were months in which events seemed to conspire to add to the misfortunes of Sajūdis and the democratic movement. Even the weather did not help. First we had suffered a drought when the driest summer for many a long year had devastated the crops. Then, as October came, drastic sudden frosts came with it. As we started feeling the cold we learned to our dismay that Russia had decided unilaterally to break the terms of our reciprocal accord on the supply of fuel. Our oil supply was therefore suddenly discontinued, though we were offered reconnection if we paid tariffs which were well beyond our capacity to pay. So, just weeks before an election, we found ourselves facing a stark situation, with no alternative but to introduce the harshest imaginable controls in order to conserve the tiny supplies of fuel which remained for use during the rest of the winter. It meant taking drastically unpopular decisions, which brought sharp questions, even from our friends. 'Was it necessary to do this?', we were asked. We were also advised that politicians normally deal with their electorate rather cautiously in the run-up to an election. 'Perhaps the government believes that economic considerations are more important than the minimal comforts of the people?', commented our critics. 'Perhaps the obvious internal conflict in the government has led someone to decide it is better for Sajūdis not to win in the forthcoming elections?', was another wisecrack. We were not complete fools, of course, but we were trapped by circumstances and so the questions went on being asked and remaining essentially unanswered, and in the mean time we were unable to find any way out of the impasse in which we found ourselves. Quite simply, Russia's abrogation of the agreements for 1992 had thrown us into a real crisis, and moreover that country was in no hurry whatever to prepare new agreements for 1993.

We were facing these difficulties because Russia was the monopoly supplier of our oil and gas and we were hostages of fortune because we had not found an alternative supplier during the previous two and a half years. It had been suggested that an attempt should be made to crack this problem by constructing an oil terminal on our Baltic coast, but progress on this project was slow. We had planned that we would bring oil in from the West, to be refined at Mažeikiai, with the surplus being sold on, but the project fell foul of various intrigues and our energy people had seemed essentially uninterested in the project's progress. We had even tried to outflank them by making a feasibility study of other possibilities, and after that idea had gained support from the European Union several international banks had offered credit, as had the governments of Japan and other nations. Altogether half a billion US dollars would become available as a result. All these things might have seemed to put things on a firm foundation, but this help had in fact come a little too late for us to gain any immediate advantage. It was the new government which inherited these credits, because, by the time they arrived, we had been voted out of office and the former Communist party had marched in to rule what was ostensibly 'post-Communist' Lithuania.

The election results shocked the world when they came through. The independence movement Sajūdis had been rejected; the Communists had won the election! Yet though this outcome seemed wholly topsy-turvy it was explicable as the natural and even democratic expression of a deeply dissatisfied people. They imagined that a new government would be more capable and competent than ours, and indeed they expected instant improvement. The former Communists, who naturally claimed to be the only experts in ruling the country, contrasted themselves with our performance by telling everyone that we were 'clumsy amateurs' and hinting that their long experience made them the 'natural party of government', which was all proven by the way in which we had shown ourselves to be quite incompetent to govern! This very active propaganda, coming together with the real difficulties of reforming the economy, had influenced the population. While the reasons for our difficulties were well known, political propaganda cannot be expected to be objective, and in the end the election really hinged on a single issue – the alleged incompetence of our government. It must, however, be said that the Lithuanian Democratic Labour party, as the former Communists now called themselves, had worked unsparingly to secure victory in this election. Their campaign was thorough and calculating. Their time had come.

In the last days before the poll there was still one major item of our programme which remained to be completed: the introduction of the *litas*, the national currency. The *Litas* Committee had been established over a year before and comprised three of the most senior members of the government, who were authorized to make wholly confidential decisions. The committee met in my office, but all its resolutions had to be agreed and signed unanimously by all three of us. We had already ordered the suspension of the rouble, the common currency of the former Soviet Union, and now of the Russian state, and had introduced a temporary currency, the *talonas*, during the summer. It was of course a decision which made it plain that we had definitely left the 'rouble zone'. (Strangely enough, the International Monetary Fund had, before we were admitted to membership, suggested that we should stay within it.) The *Litas* Committee held a final meeting on 30 October and agreed the first stage in the creation of a stable financial system. This decision separated Lithuania from the rouble zone, a step which was designed to protect the economy against inflation and the outflow of funds. We also insisted on controlling the money supply. These developments effectively took account of Russia's move to raise the prices of fuel supplies and her refusal to pay for Lithuanian goods, and the fact that we had been advised by the IMF that the *talonas* had stabilized sufficiently. We recorded this information and bequeathed the task of implementation to the new government. Incredibly, they took no action for a further six months.

The major historical contribution made before we left office was the adoption of the new Lithuanian constitution. I have already mentioned how two different drafts had been proposed. We had planned to settle which of these would be adopted by calling a referendum to give the nation an open choice between the two sets of proposals which had emerged, but the parliamentary situation eventually meant that we did not have that option open to us. Though this should have been obvious to everyone it caused some discord and eventually I called both constitutional working groups into my office, where I insisted on a joint discussion. It must have responded to an instinctive need, because these meetings continued into the long cold nights of our fuel crisis, and indeed it is possible that the deepening cold may even have helped differences to be resolved, because both sets of commissioners finally agreed, and the Supreme Council was then able to move the adoption of the new constitution, by putting the matter before the public in a referendum on 25 October. It is interesting that this formal parliamentary agreement did not prevent a faceless campaign for the rejection of the new constitution after the referendum was announced. In a remarkable display of energy these opponents of the proposed constitution had posters placed everywhere in the country, denouncing the 'unsuitable and unworthy proposal which was being offered'. Fortunately, even though the election and this referendum were held on the same day, the nation was not conned on this score. When the result was announced the people of Lithuania had voted, quite definitely in each case, to put the ex-Communists in power but under the constitution which *we* had proposed! It was an ironic outcome but was in fact just another turn in the long series of strange twists of fate which dogged Lithuanian politics throughout 1992.

The infighting among the members of our Parliament, or Supreme Council, intensified as the year wore on. I knew that many people outside the building did not understand this constant bickering. It was endlessly tiresome, but it was symptomatic of disagreements which were much more profound than the usual 'tit-for-tat' which is the essence of every parliament's business. What outsiders could not see, of course, was the sinister influence of the KGB which permeated everything which went on. They had their agents in the government, as well as elsewhere in the Supreme Council. We wanted to put an end to this, but unfortunately our attempts to exclude people who had belonged to, or were still collaborating with, the KGB from participation in future governments only exacerbated the problems which we experienced from this quarter. When it became known that there were parliamentarians among the informers, and while proceedings were actually begun against some of these people, it was all too obvious that many other Lithuanians had collaborated at some time or another. A commission was set up to investigate the organization's activities, and under its terms of reference KGB informers who confessed past involvement and discontinued further contact with the organization would not be prosecuted, but most of the informers made a definite effort to remain anonymous and their defensiveness created nasty undercurrents and unhealthy collusion. While those who had reported themselves to the commission found that their confidence was maintained, the Democratic Labour party now proposed a policy of burning the commission's archives, 'so that a new start could be made by everyone'. It was a concept which clearly had attractions, but no one doubted that this stand was dictated by pure self-interest. This was made plain when one of our newspapers ran a story about a figure named Kliugeris who was one of the KGB's agents. His minder's file, which had come into the hands of the editor, identified him unmistakably as an undercover agent who had long worked inside various Lithuanian exile organizations. It showed that he had then become a Democratic Labour party activist and had advanced to become a member of the party's central committee, where he was still one of the power brokers. It was unfortunate that stories of this kind were not able to persuade the party to drop those of its members who had this kind of history, even when we were able to demonstrate that the KGB associations were still active. Worse, however, from our point of view, was the widespread failure of the community at large to understand the implications of this scenario for public life and the future of the country. We learned to our cost when the general election came that the electorate seemed unable to recognize even the visible corruption of the Communist party, whether past or present. Incredibly, they were still prepared to vote for Kliugeris's party, and from our point of view this was the strangest kind of psychological phenomenon, because it meant that they were often choosing to vote for candidates who were actually known to have misused their positions for their personal benefit, or had stolen property which belonged to the state. It was puzzling, but is perhaps best explained as a phenomenon comparable with that of the victim who invites bullying, or the vassals who return to the service of a feudal lord even when they know that the price they will be required to pay for his protection will be their freedom!

When we took stock after the election of the new Seimas we saw that we were facing an entirely new situation; we wondered what was to become of the Lithuanian state and how its social and political structure would now develop, and whether the new government would play the game. Perhaps we would experience some kind of 'national Communism', essentially patterned on what we had experienced up to

1988, but with the country enjoying more autonomy than we had as a Soviet republic. It was also possible that we might continue to be some kind of Russian satellite without any real freedoms, or perhaps our new government would feel it had more in common with the socialists in Europe and might then try to creep into Europe under those colours, presenting its case as some kind of new socialist party. We wondered how the other socialist organizations would respond to such a move, not least because the real problem in our country was the absence of a developed democratic tradition and the traditions of tolerant statesmanship which naturally accompany it. However, the behaviour of the Lithuanian Democratic Labour party's activists did not encourage us to believe that they really wanted to go far in that direction. Perhaps they were most influenced by the fact that they had achieved an absolute majority in the Seimas. Once they had formed the government they announced that they would continue to affirm Lithuanian independence and that they would commit themselves to all the reforms necessary to maintain this position, but the government's decrees as it settled into office reflected their long-established self-interest rather than the real needs of the nation, and they developed their policies in much the way that their behaviour before the election might have made one expect. They were systematic in their approach: first, the privatization processes were delayed, or their effect was blunted. Next, we heard that the planned public flotation of state companies had been replaced by a ruling which provided for ministerial discretion in the privatization of state assets. Each of these changes was deplorable because they all offered new possibilities for corruption.

The new Parliament included a powerful group of former chairmen of state and collective farms, all of whom were manifestly unhappy with the course our agricultural privatization had taken. This clique now came up with the Bolshevik argument that there was 'no need to return the land to town-dwellers', and announced that ownership would be transferred *only* to people who were currently living on the land, a policy which implied a clear subversion of the process which we had set in train and which would have probably have meant a return to a collective system in the end, managed, of course, by the interests that they represented! Their language in describing their plans was interesting, as they called the people who had been thrown off their farms by the Soviet Union and deported to Siberia 'deserters', and the collective farms 'the owners'; they also set about reversing the provision which we had made to help families who wished to take their share of land, livestock and equipment, and leave the collective farms. This meant that many people who had begun the process of applying to leave in good faith, but had not yet received their share or begun to work the land which they had been given a right to claim, were deliberately frustrated. The new government's intention was to preserve the collective system, and to stop privatization in its tracks by preventing the development of a small farmer class. Considerable effort was put into the policy. It was dressed up as being a 'new deal', but it was in fact a return to the structures of the Soviet Socialist system.

The first place in which democratic principles were put to the test was in the relationship between the Democratic Labour party government and the opposition members in the Supreme Council. The latter now comprised the Sajūdis coalition together with the Christian Democrat deputies who, in all, constituted a block of fifty-two members, an alliance which we called Tēvynēs Santara, or 'Homeland Accord'. My status as the former chairman of the Supreme Council led to my election as leader, but then the Seimas majority tried to prevent our organization of a formal parliamentary opposition, telling us that any arrangements we made would have to be debated and our proposals approved. Of course they had no experience at all of the structures of opposition which are normal in democratic countries, nor had those structures been able to emerge properly in the lifetime of the Parliament which had recently ended, so it was clear from their remonstrance that no such approval would be forthcoming. So we carried on regardless, without reference to them and without a debate, to organize the Opposition on our own terms. The situation was far from satisfactory: we had no recognition and no budget, but nevertheless we opened an office, appointed press representatives, called meetings and issued briefings. We had a fight on our hands for the right of access to public opinion right from the start. Access to the facilities of state-sponsored television was refused to us, and the few independent private studios which now existed were warned not to help us. However, the very fact that we *insisted* on existing as a parliamentary Opposition was a determined statement about democracy and a contribution to its establishment, so we struggled hard to consolidate our position in the Seimas. It was evident, however, from every move they made, that our post-Communist majority had not reconstructed its attitudes in any way. Their behaviour also made it apparent that key government figures had little competence and none of the necessary imagination to deal with the implications of the new national and parliamentary situation. They clearly intended to stay in power for a long time, however, and quickly set about strengthening their position in anticipation of the forthcoming presidential election which our constitutional arrangements had kept separate from the elections to the Seimas. Wanting to make the most of their recent victory and perhaps build on it, they decided to call this election as soon as possible. There was a definite impropriety in this as the ground rules of the electoral process had yet to be agreed, and had not even been discussed, so when they announced that the presidential election would be held almost immediately, that is in January 1993, we naturally kicked up a fuss. The disagreement did not do much for us, but in the event it purchased a tiny delay, as the date of 14 February was subsequently adopted. An electoral law for the election of a president was then cobbled together by the Democratic Labour party's inner caucus, designed, naturally, with their own interest alone in mind, and certainly without reference to the Opposition. Again we resisted these autocratic procedures very vigorously, the disagreement being focused on their proposals to establish an electoral commission to supervise this election. We had already established such a commission which had worked effectively in the recent referenda, parliamentary elections, and in the local government elections which had been held in November. It had been designed to supervise *all* elections in Lithuania, but it was now seen as having the defect of not being controlled by the ruling Democratic Labour party! It must have been a rather sudden recognition on their part, because they held a rushed discussion and invented the device of a special 'presidential electoral commission' at rather short notice. Needless to say, it was designed specially to respond to their wishes, with the majority of its members 'from the Left' and many of its key members from the judiciary, a body which had always been carefully vetted under Communist rule, with no one entering who was not nominated to the position by the party. As the members of this new commission were nominated, their connections with the Labour party became more and more obvious. Intriguingly the whole process took place at a time when the question of political connections, especially in the legal profession, was being highlighted for other reasons. We had noticed a tendency for legal officers to call off corruption trials wherever possible. The question had already been aired before the general election when our press had reported that a number of leading advocates had pleaded 'difficulties of proof' in a series of cases, none of which had been taken to court. It seemed to have occurred so often that the suspicion of complicity, or even a broader conspiracy to disrupt the course of justice, was a natural conclusion. Now we saw the control of the whole machinery of the presidential election being put in the hands of dedicated nominees of the ruling party, and the underlying script became apparent. The state was clearly not neutral in these matters! To rub the point in, the new electoral law, which they now passed to establish the commission, empowered it to make its own decisions on amendments proposed while the elections were taking place, and allowed Parliament to confirm such changes immediately, even during the election period. It was only too obvious that these conventions would be extremely convenient to the puppet masters of the system. When the time came to sort things out, their Democratic Labour supporters would cheerfully follow the well-

339

known conventions established under Soviet rule and follow the Party recommendations.

Naturally, we argued that this law was unconstitutional, and I used this viewpoint as the explanation of my decision not to stand in the elections, though there were other reasons for this calculation. I had already been the butt of a rising and vicious campaign of slander and libel for over three years. This nasty propaganda had reached the point where it was harmful not just to me but to the whole country, because it had generated an atmosphere of hatred in which I was ruthlessly blamed for anything and everything which went wrong, being castigated for every last flaw in the system, right down to the mismanagement and thefts by chairmen of collective farms! So, as the new year 1993 dawned, I thought seriously about my future and the future of democracy in Lithuania. I understood deeply that democracy itself was becoming problematic in the strange circumstances which prevailed, but I was even more concerned for the link between democracy and the independence of our country. I did not want to see Lithuania becoming some kind of eastern European 'puppet republic', in a state of dependency, her policies dictated from elsewhere. To be legally independent, yet under the control of a post-Communist oligarchy which would be concerned to run the state and the economy only to suit itself, was a profoundly unattractive prospect. I was despondent, and wondered how we had come to travel so far yet achieve so little. We were now faced with a real possibility that the *nomenklatura,* dominated by the idea of gain, would use its current advantage to perpetuate the corrupt style of government which was its native habitat, while becoming seriously reliant on the Mafia that was already emerging fast in Lithuania. The people who currently held the reins of power had long condemned and disdained the ideal of independence, so it was unlikely that a concept which they had long despised as being 'naïve and unrealistic', would become their guiding principle in the difficult economic circumstances which our nation faced. I was fearful that my country would find herself being sold down the river, and decided that I would dedicate myself to writing and speaking, and arguing that to avoid this fate Sąjūdis and its allies must work together as a wholehearted, continuous and intelligent Opposition. The real task of the Opposition would simply be to manifest itself. Its active existence would itself be a primary condition of openness and freedom of expression in the whole community of Lithuania, and it was now our solemn duty to popularize these values. We would only succeed by *living* these qualities and it was necessary to show that this could be done!

The main issue which now troubled us was the realization that the Communists would be happy to undermine the very act which had re-established our independence, because they needed to diminish the achievement which flowed from it. It was now possible that much of what we had accomplished in the two and a half years which had gone by since the Act of Independence was passed on 11 March 1990 would be dissipated. The Democratic Labour party might be happy to erase what we had achieved, but we were not prepared to think of the independence period as an aberration which had taken place only because the 'wrong' government had been elected at the time. We noticed that their press favoured articles which claimed that 'historic errors' had been made while independence was being re-established in Lithuania. Because of this we were not surprised to observe the monuments of our struggle being removed as they returned to power. The concrete barricades around our Parliament with their patriotic decorations and slogans of resistance were the first to go, being taken away literally within hours of the change of government. It was an act of deliberate disrespect, with no regard for the feelings of the people; clearly this symbolic gesture was one of their priorities, but it was received with wide misgiving by the greater part of the public, and was perhaps seen as a portent of things to come. We had noticed other odd signs, which included an attempt to describe the newly elected parliament as the '*Fourth* Lithuanian Seimas'. This shift in nomenclature also carried a political message and embodied a deliberate disregard for the history of our country, ignoring the memory that no fewer than *five* parliaments had served Lithuania between the years 1920 and 1940.

We spoke out against this manipulation of history, saying it was only now, now that the Republic of Lithuania was reborn, and our country had become an independent nation once again with its independent parliament and constitution, and with the means of electing her own president, that we could say that we had a *Seimas* in Lithuania. The word itself asserted the sovereignty of its debates, and that of the nation which the Seimas serves. Lithuania had regained her independence in 1990, but had been governed until recently by a Supreme Council. An attempt was made to show that such a gathering had a lesser status than the Seimas because its existence was purely expedient. It had begun its career as a Soviet device, and had been retained as a transitional device. We had given it a provisional status, only to prepare the way for the reinstatement of our own constitution and Parliament, and that status was entirely evident from the moment that a temporary constitution was enacted on 11 March 1990. We were now in a different situation and had, at last, our own Lithuanian Seimas once again, the very name being an expression of our nation's freedom and of the national spirit. We were saddened that this moment of triumph, at the beginning of 1993, could be sullied by a cast of mind which reeked of Soviet habits, as so many of its members clung tightly to the sentimental relics of their own political past.

The Orwellian propaganda of the ex-Communists, always self-justifying and self-satisfied, now began to offer a convenient new explanation of our history. We learned that it was the Lithuanian *Communist* party which had freed us from Soviet occupation, and that they had saved democracy. This was very instructive, and entirely novel for some of us, not least those who had studied these matters closely! The more sceptical among us had already noticed the capacity for self-delusion which affected the tellers of the story and its comparability with a similar fairy tale related to members of the Supreme Council in 1990 after members of Sąjūdis had presented a document with details of the Soviet aggression and annexation of Lithuania earlier in the century. On that occasion ideologists from the Lithuanian Communist party had provided their own 'scientific version' of Lithuania's recent history, telling us how democracy in Lithuania had really ended in 1926. The Soviet arrival had only displaced an authoritarian Lithuanian government and was at worst a case of the 'summary replacement of one barely legal regime with another'. It was a confabulation designed to suggest that the Soviets had merely rescued us from ourselves, and that it had been the ruling nationalists who had led Lithuania to its downfall, just as we were now alleged to be doing. It also played down the Communists' part in the betrayal of their country and exonerated Stalin, who was not presented as the wrecker of Lithuanian independence but as an actor playing his role in a complicated set of circumstances! Of course the Lithuanian Democratic Labour party was supported in its historical revisionism by the politicians of the new Russia who also wanted to blur the facts about the invasion of 1940 and the crimes which followed it. According to them, Lithuania, like the 'other republics', had joined the Soviet Union voluntarily, and Russia was innocent of any wrongdoing. There never was any real problem as far as they were concerned; they believed that the difficulty was entirely one of our imagination, and anyway the Soviet Union which would have been responsible for any grievance had vanished from the scene of history. Now no one had any legal responsibility, and any problems which survived were certainly not theirs!

When I look back over this period I feel that I did well when I decided to stand aside and devote myself to ensuring that the process of restoring normality to the Lithuanian state did not become fatally entangled with the posturing of the new government. Our struggle to preserve a truthful explanation of the events which took place on 15 June 1940 and

11 March 1990 was aimed at maintaining the essential landmarks of the fight for decency and democracy in our nation. These dates are haunted symbols which must remain forever inviolate as immovable signposts of the drama of Lithuanian history, standing as an unsullied reminder of how a people's rights were taken away, and how they were regained. We must also ensure that the events associated with them are not confused with such matters as the *coup d'état* which took place in Lithuania in December 1926, or those which occurred in Moscow in September 1991 and in October 1992, important though they may be. As I make this point, it is worth drawing attention to two documents which speak volumes in their own right. The first is a statement prepared in Moscow in January 1991, just before the bloody attacks in Vilnius, and afterwards in Riga. It was circulated among the Soviet government ministries, having been drafted as a response to the freedoms which the peoples of the Baltic countries were claiming as their human rights, and described methods of controlling them. It was published in a Latvian newspaper six months after it was first circulated, but I doubt if the rest of the world paid much attention then. Its text is chilling and reflects the cold indifference of its authors to questions of freedom and justice. It said:

> We have powerful weapons at our disposal, unrestrained and clever propaganda, patience, the ability to adapt to circumstances, rapid reaction, and determination. No fighter for truth has ever managed to make better use of these factors. We have great experience in manipulating large crowds and removing unwanted persons from the scene, without taking the lead obviously. The academician Sakharov is one of the better examples of what we can do. We have finished him off just as we planned to do. The same scenario can be applied to the overthrow of other leaders, and this is only the beginning.

The second was a speech made by Vaclav Havel in which he referred to Samuel Beckett's drama *Waiting for Godot*. He spoke of 'waiting for Godot after Communism', and described a state in which people were left hanging around, having lost their sense of direction and purpose, in which responsibilities were being postponed. He then reminded his hearers that history moves slowly. However much one may resent this, or the slow response of one's fellow human beings, history cannot be speeded up! There is much truth in these words. However, when Vaclav Havel became president of the Czech Republic, I congratulated him – *as a man who had quickened the pace of history*.

CHAPTER 19

Epilogue, but not the end!

When Lithuanian voters returned the Communists (or the 'Lithuanian Democratic Labour party' as they now called themselves) to power, the western world was astonished, and even poked fun at us. A cartoon in a German newspaper showed a crowd of Lithuanians behind the national flag. They were marching through a broken prison wall towards a voting booth, but those who had voted were marching straight back into the prison! While the image has stuck in my mind, we were not really returning to a situation exactly like that before the election. Things had changed and changed decisively, if only because the Soviet Union was no more. The party now in power may have wanted to rearrange things to suit itself, but it was going to take some time even in Lithuania to turn the clock back that far. Though we reacted to the election result with some shock, we were soon determined that we must do what we could to slow down the regression. While Europe might well raise its eyes in astonishment at Lithuania's about-turn, the hard truth for us was that we had come full circle. The fantastic efforts of our long march to independence had brought us back to a situation in which the Communists were returned to power *by an election*, a result which at first appeared almost to be perverse. We began to wonder if there was some deep fault in our nature, but when the Estonian municipal elections, and the election of the Polish Seijm and Russian Duma brought similar results, people stopped wondering about what had happened to us. They no longer felt we were freaks, and started thinking of Lithuania as a trend-setter! After all we had been the first to take determined action on our independence and events had later made it clear that there was a common effort to break out of the Soviet prison state as other nations followed us in the same struggle. Now at the end of 1992 Lithuania was a political barometer again, even though alarm bells had been set ringing all around the continent by what had happened. Inside the country even the victors were taken by surprise, but those who had been deeply involved in Sajūdis were not entirely taken aback, because we had noted a strong undercurrent in people's attitudes which had been evident for several months. We had noticed reduced support for our members in public positions, and a greater inclination in the community to believe those who brought accusations against us. Political memory is short, even in the great democracies, and we had noticed that confidence in the new order was increasingly disappearing from public life. The fact was that standards of living had dropped sharply, and our explanations were not being accepted as they had been in the past. As a result we felt the ground disappearing from under our feet, and I shall never forget the feeling.

Once the 1992 election was over there was little time for the post-mortem. To analyse the mass psychology of the former communist countries could lead to endless speculation, and we had little time to spend on that luxury. Our immediate object was to adjust ourselves to a new style of political action which would defend and maintain our real independence. The democratic parties had gone into the election on three separate though co-ordinated lists because they were not yet ready to form a real coalition. However, we made what agreements we could, and soon the alliance which we called Tėvynės Santara (For a Democratic Lithuania) emerged to include more than a third of the members in the new Seimas. We were then able to use this combined strength as the basis for a proposal to establish a majority voting system based on the concept of an official Opposition, the idea being to follow the common practice of the English-speaking countries where the Opposition has a formal status, with democratic co-operation on parliamentary committees and elsewhere. However the Democratic Labour party majority refused to debate this proposal which was not even allowed a place on the parliamentary agenda. It was clear that the government did not recognize a place for group or proportional rights. We were to be treated as the 'out-party', an 'enemy in the class struggle', whose politicians deserved only limited opportunities and were to be belittled and rejected whenever the opportunity offered.

Although there was no formal agreement of the type which applied in the case of the government's opponents, the Lithuanian Democratic Labour party was aided in the Seimas by the Social Democrat party and the group of Polish deputies. This support meant that the Democratic Labour party was quite secure in its majority, and a product of this security was its deliberate slowness in setting up a constitutional court. This was a provision which had been clearly indicated as a necessary safeguard in the preconditions of the 1992 referendum on the constitution, and the cynical failure to implement this aspect of proposals which had been accepted by the nation at that time affected the integrity of the procedure followed when a newly elected president was to be sworn into office. Three months had already passed since the elections, and a single judge was selected to perform the required duty. The person taking this role should of course have been selected by the Constitutional Court, but the government had postponed the process of appointing the judges. We asked questions about what was happening, and were told that the delay was due to shortage of suitable nominees. While it really should not have been difficult to assemble a list of candidates, this communication made it crystal clear that it suited the government's purposes much better not to continue with the establishment of the Court. Again it was not hard to work out why. Democracy is a system of checks and balances, and the absence of a Constitutional Court meant that the government majority in the Seimas was not subject to the process of surveillance which was the very reason for the institution of the Constitutional Court. The government would therefore remain quite free to implement resolutions of doubtful legality, knowing that they could not be effectively challenged: the Opposition had not been granted the necessary status and was without recourse to the very court which could act as a check and balance. As long as the Court was inoperative we were helpless to deal with the many constitutional transgressions which came to our attention, and our rituals of protest when we asked that difficult issues should be referred to the Court were blithely ignored.

The situation was obviously unsatisfactory, but it dragged on. When the president was elected, a judge was found to administer the oath, but no attempt was made to find premises for the Constitutional Court or to enrol its members. In this ambiguous situation we were unable to enter a legal protest against acts which violated the constitution. The issue which concerned me most was the newly established presidential election commission. As we have seen, the new Lithuanian constitution made provision for a single election commission which had been intended to hold final authority over the organization of *all* elections and referenda. This commission had already organized both the first elections to the Seimas, and the referendum on the constitution and we argued that the creation of a further electoral commission without reference to this final authority was very clearly unconstitutional, and had been set up to avoid having the process of electing the president scrutinized by a body which was not entirely controlled by the dominant party. My refusal to stand as a candidate for the presidency had been intended to make my views of the whole situation crystal clear, and when election time came I urged every voter who was opposed to the Labour party candidate to unite in support of Stasys Lozoraitis, the Lithuanian ambassador to the United States, who was presented as a common anti-Communist candidate.

I had another equally important reason for refusing to stand for the presidency. My opponents had used every nasty device available, and stories were being put around by the media and by word of mouth to say that I had misused government funds to build a villa for myself in Switzerland. This horrible slander campaign went on for more than a year, and another such rumour said that I was not really a Lithuanian but rather a foreign (Soviet!) agent who had deliberately contrived the land reform policy to damage our agriculture. As I was no more responsible for these things than for the summer drought or the autumn frost, I believed that I could do nothing to prevent such virulent stories from circulating as they had nothing to do with anything which I could control. The Democratic Labour party itself began to attack me person-ally with an offensive poster campaign which was often promoted by local government employees. It was based on the slogan 'Go and see Landsbergis!', and copies were placed in state shops, post offices and banks. They presented me as the man who was responsible for every shortcoming in public life in the entire land, and as a result I received daily evidence of the dark and irrational hatred which had been engen-dered. I knew of only one way to dispose of this ugliness, and did it by getting out of the race, hoping that 'the Party' would not have enough time to launch a similar campaign against Lozoraitis. I said that in public, but my enemies had no compunction, and it was not long before their press had turned its hand to a bombardment of his reputation too. As ambassador he had fought long and diligently for Lithuanian indepen-dence, but this was now forgotten and we were told variously that he or his Italian wife were 'of Jewish extraction', in what was just about the first public manifestation of anti-Semitism in Lithuania. He was also alleged to have embezzled Lithuanian gold deposits, and was described floridly as 'a stranger', a 'foreigner', 'badly educated', and 'not needed by Lithuania', gibes which were naturally designed to compare him unfavourably with 'the home candidate', the leader of the heroic Communist party of Lithuania (I nearly forgot ... I mean the *Democratic Labour party* of Lithuania!), the expert in economics, our own, our very own, Algirdas Brazauskas!

The Labour majority in the Seimas had voted to hold the presidential elections as soon as it possibly could, presumably so that the voters would have as little time as possible to work out exactly what was going on. Although our candidate Lozoraitis was virtually unknown in the country, his popularity grew with surprising rapidity. After only one month of campaigning, some 40 per cent of the electors voted for him. Unfortunately the government gained even larger backing, and so Algirdas Brazauskas gained the presidency in Febuary 1993, a result which confirmed my task as leader of the Opposition. This was an unde-fined function, with no legal status, but the press and the people soon became accustomed to talking about it and perhaps began to learn to value it. Yet though the election was over, the smear campaign was not, and we noticed how the tide of criticism would rise and then subside, as if someone was regulating it. By now, however, we had learned to live with it and stopped reacting to stories about how the leader of the Opposition had, for example, stolen the reserve supplies of Lithuania's Decoration of Honour 'for resale', or had purloined a certain gold sword with a diamond-studded handle, the property of the state. Of course, the sword did not and never had existed, and the stories were a malicious fabrication. Sometimes, I could still get annoyed about them, but when this happened I would tell myself that the Soviet system was totalitarian and rooted in lies and theft. We had disengaged our nation from its mainstream politics, but it was now obvious that we had a long way to go before the turgid atmosphere of moral degradation and mutual suspicion which it bred could finally be left behind.

As an Opposition we conceived it our duty to resist every tendency to revive Soviet traditions and methods of government. Our chief desire was to defend our country's independence and encourage its reorientation to the West, so we redoubled our efforts in that direction whenever we saw the ruling party claiming 'to have improved relations with Moscow' or promising to 'to draw Lithuania closer to Russia again'. Their election programme had included some paragraphs confirming Lithuania's neutrality, but their subsequent postures suggested that Lithuania might be moving back into the Russian sphere. Fortunately, however, our policy in respect of the *litas*, our national currency, had moved so far that the momentum was continued after an initial delay, and the agreements on the withdrawal of Russian forces were at last being honoured. As both changes implied a greater autonomy and a decline in Russian influence we took care to keep these issues in high profile as the government would have been pleased to say one thing and do another. As time moved on it became more obvious that the Democratic Labour party had acquired no vision and had assimilated no new thinking, though it was of course hard to imagine how it could when its entire historical experience had been shaped by totalitarian rule and the wealth and privilege which this had offered to its self-selected ruling class. We noticed how its officials remained curiously unbending despite the setbacks the party had experienced in recent years. It had survived and been returned to power but its atmosphere and conventions were strangely unrelated to the new constitutional atmosphere, and citizens who found something to complain about would find themselves being told that 'the government has a four-year mandate', the message being that they could govern as they liked in the mean time. It was clear that the sense of having to be attentive to an electorate had not really dawned on them. The attitude of party members seemed to have changed little since Soviet times when the government had always behaved as if it was there for eternity, and was accountable to none. As time went by ordinary people became frustrated with this attitude and the inertia which ran through the system. The government was 'waiting for Godot', and people often did not know where to turn for advice and help and were even uncertain as to whether they could protest because they had *elected* this government after all! For a while inertia ruled but gradually resentment began to build up and to be directed to the right place. The government's policies were then increasingly recognized as lacking in imagination, and implemented erratically, the fact being that many of their strategies were essentially unsuitable for the transition to the new market economy. It was a time when earnings had decreased and savings were dwindling, and this fact was painfully obvious as the majority of people were becoming poorer, though oddly enough the *nomenklatura* were shielded from this aspect of the economy, and many of its members were increasing their wealth in a rather obvious way. They had, of course, acquired lucrative interests in the privatization of the state assets, and this did not pass unnoticed!

Despite these setbacks Lithuania managed to continue to improve its international standing. In retrospect we can now see that the momentum in this field was unstoppable. In the spring of 1993 our country became a full member of the Council of Europe, and by the autumn the Russian forces had finally withdrawn from our soil. Once this happened the government found itself in full control of Lithuania's eastern borders at last, and decided to introduce visa controls on journeys to and from the Russian Federation and the other CIS countries in a move designed to parallel the policies already followed by Estonia and Latvia, so that Lithuania was not out of step with its neighbours. Early in 1994 Lithuania announced it wished to join NATO, a further move which implied that Lithuania had stopped looking eastwards to Moscow, contrary to earlier signs. The government was of course being carried along by a tide of history, but our work as a parliamentary Opposition has contributed to these realignments. We developed a policy of endless lobbying and persistent demands for full explanation, and were always insistent that our enquiries received attention. Gradually we won some recognition despite the fact that the system set out to be unresponsive; the government was being moved along in spite of its prejudices. The struggle may have been an uphill one, but changes were taking place which indicated a new situation, and this also affected the Opposition. As time moved on, the framework Sąjūdis provided seemed less capable of maintaining the broad alliance which had underlain its successes, and when this was brought home to me I joined up with people of like mind to found a new party which was established on 1 May 1993. I was asked to become its first chairman and we named it Tėvynės Sąjunga (the Homeland Union), and I suppose we are the Conservative party in Lithuania, if one uses western terms. Though we have chosen to build a separate identity we made an early decision to retain our close contact with the Christian Democrats. The government ignored us, as it ignored the formation of other opposition parties, but while we were excluded from making a contribution to the formulation of national policies, we committed ourselves firmly to building an alternative consensus in association with our allies, and in maintaining a vigilant collective stance as an Opposition.

After the unsuccessful elections in 1992 I had a personal dilemma to sort out. At that point I might well have considered that my contribution to the fight for Lithuanian independence was complete. This might have been a time to announce my resignation from active political life. It would have been deeply attractive to me to pursue my musical interests and write a few books. I could perhaps have slipped into the slow lane, where it is more peaceful, even though I might be needed in some national crises or called to fight another election. Such a decision would have made those whom I had never had any particular wish to please very happy indeed, and would certainly have pleased Gražina, my dear wife, whose life has never been easy since I became a politician. However, as I contemplated this, I saw the work for the renewal of Lithuania unfinished around me, and contemplated the weight of corruption and the other dark forces which still throw their shadows across our hopes for democracy and prosperity. I then sensed the longing of my colleagues for the full restoration of these values. I know their hopes, and I look back across our common efforts and achievements throughout the journey which we have travelled together. It would not have been right for me to turn aside from the task which my country still faces, nor to choose personal comfort while her difficulties remain. I am still a politician!

Editor's Postscript (Easter 2000)

In the spring of 1995 the parties of the Centre Right won the municipal elections throughout Lithuania. Later, the parliamentary elections held in October and November 1996 resulted in victory for Tėvynės Sąjunga, which took half the seats in the new Parliament, and went on to strengthen its majority in coalition with the Christian Democrats. Vytautas Landsbergis was elected to the chair of the Seimas, the Parliament of Lithuania, and he currently still holds this post.

Notes

¹ The title 'Supreme Council of Lithuania' was the term used to describe the nation's Parliament under the provisional constitution which was passed into law on 11 March 1990. The assumption of this title reflected the repudiation of the Soviet constitution, and so the title 'Supreme Council of the Lithuanian Soviet Republic', by which the assembly had been known since the Soviet occupation began, was abolished at the same time. The use of the term 'Supreme Council of Lithuania' reflected the transitional character of the provisional constitution. The restoration of the historic term 'Seimas' was then reserved for the time when the new Lithuanian constitution had been agreed and implemented.

It should be noticed, however, that the term 'Supreme Council' is often used interchangeably in this text to describe both the 'Soviet' body and the 'independence legislature'. This is an obvious convenience, but it should be remembered that the legality of this transitional arrangement had been established by briefly reinstating Lithuania's pre-war constitution. This procedure was also enacted on 11 March 1990, and ensured that the elected representatives of the Lithuanian people were acting with full legality under the terms of the country's own constitution. However, as it was not written to deal with the situation which the country was facing in the early 1990s, that constitution was immediately suspended and a 'provisional and temporary constitution' introduced. This temporary arrangement naturally retained many of the Soviet conventions, although the Supreme Council was now charged with irrevocable sovereign authority. Thus, the term 'Parliament' is used interchangeably with the term 'Supreme Council' to describe the nation's legislature after that date.

The new constitution of Lithuania came into effect in 1992. From this date the Lithuanian term 'Seimas' is used in the text again interchangeably with the term 'Parliament'. Readers are also asked to notice that the former Supreme Council was (like the present Seimas) a unicameral or single-chamber legislature. Thus, when the term 'the government' is used it refers to the prime minister's administration and the Cabinet. Recalling these facts will clarify the reasons why Professor Landsbergis, when he was president of the Supreme Council of Lithuania, did not always enjoy the full support of the government. It should also be remembered that, in the proto-democratic situation of those times, the Sajūdis movement included members of the Communist party, many of whom were (to say the least) ambivalent in their support for him. This situation did not resolve itself easily, and much of the interest of the present narrative is sustained around the implied ambiguities.

² Mamutė is the affectionate diminutive for mother, Tėtė is for father.

³ The later Sajūdis movement, to which Professor Landsbergis has made so

important a contribution, began in 1988. Its full title, at first, was Persitvarkymo Sąjūdis which means 'the movement for Perestroika' or 'Lithuanian reform movement'.

⁴ This is an opportunity to explain the Lithuanian system of personal nomenclature. The suffixes -*as*, -*is*, -*us* (and occasionally -*a*, and –*ė*) in a family name always denote a male person, while the suffixes -*ienė* -*aitė*, and -*ytė* and -*iūtė*, denote a married woman and an unmarried woman respectively.

There is, therefore, when using a surname in the Lithuanian language, an instant recognition of the gender status of its bearer which is the equivalent of our 'Mr' (*ponas*), 'Mrs' (*ponia*) or 'Miss' (*panelė*). As these attributions of gender status are made so explicit in the form of the surname, gendered titles are used only in formal situations, though Vanda Zaborskaitė would have been called *Miss* Vanda Zaborskaitė if she had travelled to the English-speaking world at that time.

⁵ The order was founded in 1202 as the German Order of the Brothers of the Sword. Later it became the Livonian Order, a branch of the Teutonic Knights. The movement began in a tent hospital established by pilgrims from Bremen and Lubeck at the seige of Acre in 1189, its rule being modelled on that of the Knights of St John. The order later came under Templar influence, and added the 'conquest of infidels' to its nursing activities. After the fall of Acre its members returned home, to become active in Livonia (a region which could be broadly described as 'the territories of Riga'), early in the thirteenth century. They justified their crusade because these territories were among the last in Europe to retain the ancient pagan beliefs.

⁶ The letter č in Lithuanian is pronounced 'Ch', as in 'Cheshire'.

⁷ The translation here includes a certain licence, and should read 'like a brown dog'. In the Lithuanian idiom a brown dog is not to be trusted. The wording used here is meant to imply that this creature was unpleasant, to say the least!

⁸ Sąjūdis (są = self, or common, jūdis = movement) means 'common activity', but can be translated simply as 'the movement'.

⁹ The name 'Antis' means 'the duck', but carries a deliberate *double entendre* as it also means 'anti' in Lithuanian in exactly the same sense as in English.

¹⁰ It was a common practice throughout the whole Soviet Union and other countries in the Eastern bloc for entire suburbs to be supplied with central heating and hot water from a single district central-heating station. The decision referred to here meant that the urban population faced the onset of the central European winter with no heating whatever in the home or in the workplace for the remainder of the cold season.

APPENDIX

A brief history of Lithuania

ANTHONY PACKER and DARIUS FURMONAVICIUS

The Vytis

These memoirs are a major contribution to the understanding of a critical period in Lithuania's history. As that history is a long one, and accounts of it may not be easy to come by, an outline is offered here to give further insight into the character and determination of the nation whose struggle for independence is so vigorously reflected in Vytautas Landsbergis's text.

Introduction

At the time when the second Soviet occupation of the Baltic States was beginning in 1944, a British diplomat observed: 'Lithuania is not a new state of Europe, either politically or culturally, she is as old as most of the other European nations and possesses a striking history with dramatic vicissitudes.'[1] Indeed the origins of this nation are as old as, or older even than European civilization, while the beginnings of the Lithuanian state reach back over more than 700 years. Long before Columbus sailed to America, Lithuania's rulers commanded an empire which included all the territories that lie between the Baltic and the Black Seas, and it endured for several centuries, playing a major role in the continent's history.

That Lithuanian state first emerged during the twelfth century. Its formation was intimately connected with the struggle of the Baltic peoples to protect themselves against the eastward movement of German-speaking people who were seeking to colonize the territories in which the Balts lived, and where they settled perhaps 3,000 years earlier. This Germanic migration was spearheaded by crusading monks, the knights of the Teutonic Order. Though they spoke of converting these pagan nations to the Christian faith – by the sword if other means failed – their real motive was exposed when their attempts at territorial aggrandizement continued for centuries after Lithuania had joined the community of

353

Catholic nations. It is one of the paradoxes of history that the nation was curiously strengthened by this experience of perennial warfare, which made it a formidable military power and one of the more powerful states of medieval Europe. Fate then placed Lithuania in the path of a new invasion, this time by the Tartars whose expansionist ambition had originated in Mongolia, but had become fired more recently by the idea of placing Europe under the domination of Islam. So the struggle continued. The Lithuanian people turned to defend their country, and indeed the whole of Catholic Europe, from these ruthless horsemen who swept in time and time again from the east, posing what seemed to be an apocalyptic threat. Though many have forgotten it, Europe long felt indebted to Lithuania for repulsing their incursions. If the Tartar objective had been achieved, the whole history of the West would have assumed a quite different direction and character.

In later times Lithuania was again the first bulwark of western culture against eastern invaders on many occasions. In the seventeenth and eighteenth centuries, her resistance to the emerging Russian state's attempt to make the Baltic her own was of huge importance. More recently she made vital, even catalytic, contributions, to the events which brought the Soviet dominance of eastern Europe and the global ambition of its ideology to an abrupt and welcome end. These matters are well reflected in this book, but it is not unrealistic to suggest that, if he had understood Lithuania's history better, Gorbachev would have foreseen that his attempt to keep this country inside the Soviet Union (into which it had been illegally incorporated in defiance of the essential principles of international law) was unlikely to succeed. We could also say that a fuller realization of what that history implied would have made him more realistic about the problems he was making for himself. The demands of the Sajūdis movement during the final years of the Soviet occupation of Lithuania were clearly formulated, mildly stated, and often repeated to him. Had he taken notice he might well have avoided the débâcle he finally faced. Russia has occupied Lithuania on four occasions, in 1655–60, 1795–1914, 1940–1 and 1944–90. Each of these intrusions was accompanied by heavy brutality, and they all met with persistent resistance, but whatever levels of 'russification', oppression or terror were applied, the Lithuanians still rebelled against them. The same response occurred in generation after generation. There were revolts in 1794–5, 1812, 1831, 1863–4, 1905, 1918–20 and 1941, and the armed resistance of the 1944–56 period is notable as the longest partisan war of modern European history. Lithuania's patriots returned to the theme again in 1987–90. If the breakthrough had not occurred then, it is certain that their heroism would have been repeated.

The determination of the Lithuanian people not to live willingly under the yoke of any foreign power goes far back in time. A pattern can be seen to run through the nation's history. When, for example, the consequences of Grand Duke Algirdas's victory, at the Battle of the Blue Waters (near the Black Sea coast and over a thousand miles south-east of his capital city, Vilnius) in the fourteenth century are compared with the outcome of Vytautas Landsbergis's declaration of national independence in the twentieth, we can glimpse its implications. That distant battle in 1363 released the entire territories of Kiev and Podol (the modern Ukraine and Belarus) from Tartar domination. Six centuries later an identical national stubbornness, once more against odds which others deemed overwhelming, again contributed to the release of those territories from another heavy-handed, ruthless and brutal oppressor. As with the Mongols in 1363, so with the Soviet Union in 1991. If every strategy of medieval warfare had been deployed against the fourteenth-century enemy, the twentieth-century tyranny was faced instead with peaceful demonstrations and moral exposure. The methods were different because the age was different, but the risk, the application, the calculation and the bravery were the same. The engagement in Vilnius in 1991 lay between unarmed people and the tanks of the Soviet army, but the savagery confronted was no different from the earlier occasion, and both situations reflected a concern which belonged to Europe as a whole, rather than to Lithuania alone. The strategic response was, however, quite different this second time, Lithuania's recent revolution having been *entirely peaceful* despite the Soviet savagery. It is important that the radical implication of this principled stance is firmly emphasized, because it was exactly this peaceful strategy which brought the nuclear empire of the Soviet Union to its abrupt end. If other tactics had been deployed at that juncture, that demise could well have been delayed. The Soviet system might have lingered, and even been strengthened by the stimulus of counter-violence. The effect of such determined but non-violent resistance in undermining its hardened stances was therefore quite dramatic. The outcome was remarkable, and the path which led to that achievement has clear implications for the future of civilization. We might wryly add that those implications have an economic as well as a moral measure. Vytautas Landsbergis (who as leader of Sajūdis and chairman of Lithuania's Parliament was responsible for many of the key decisions taken as the struggle unfolded), recently found it necessary to inform a major conference on Lithuania's reintegration into the West: 'We have contributed to your security, we are saying to the West, and you were able to save billions, hundreds of billions. Yet when we are asking for security for our small state, we find ourselves speaking to a brick wall.'[2]

Early history

The precise origin of the Baltic nations has been long debated, but the Lithuanians are neither German nor Slavic in origin. Little is known of their early movements, but archaeological evidence shows them already settled in the territories east of the Vistula, particularly along the Nemunas and Dauguva rivers, in the second millennium before Christ. Their languages (Lithuanian and Latvian are the most prominent survivors) were quite closely related to Sanskrit, the classical language of India, and from this it has been surmised that the Indo-European peoples had a common origin in the Eurasian steppes more than five millennia ago.[3] While the secluded character of the regions in which the Lithuanians settled enabled the archaic forms of their ancient language to be preserved, it also left them remote from the main currents of European history. As a result they were particularly late to convert to Christianity. While eastern Slavic territories were evangelized by the Orthodox church from the tenth century onward, the impetus for converting the Baltic lands came from Catholic Europe. It was inseparable from the wish to conquer and exploit these territories, but it led to the creation of the first Lithuanian state.

The archaeological record links many of the older settlements near the Baltic shores with Byzantine, Viking and even earlier interest in the amber trade, which is still important in these regions. While the nineteenth-century polymath George Borrow, in his classic work *Wild Wales* (1862) intriguingly suggested that the Welsh name for Brittany (*Llydaw*) derived from the memory of Roman deployment of Lithuanian mercenaries in defence of the Armorican peninsula in the last stage of their occupation of Gaul,[4] the earliest documentary mention of the Lithuanian nation dates from 1009. Found in the annals of a German monastery, this eleventh-century description of an imperial campaign is an early account of a struggle which was later taken up by military orders dedicated to the subjection of the Baltic peoples as a religious duty.[5] The Teutonic Order and the Livonian Order ('the Knights of the Sword'), which later merged, applied patterns of warfare first devised in the Crusades against the Arabs to the contest for these northern regions.[6] Their efforts provoked a fiercely defensive reaction over three centuries. During this time most of the Baltic peoples were conquered or assimilated, the Lithuanians alone being successful in the creation of an independent state at that stage of their history.

King Mindaugas and the founding of Lithuania

In the thirteenth century Grand Duke Mindaugas, who has been described as a 'modernizing autocrat,[7] unified the emerging Lithuanian state. Its beginnings were already found in the regions of Aukstaitija and Kernave, and around Vilnius and nearby Trakai, but by 1248 he had brought the people of these areas together in defensive alliance against the Teutonic Knights. In 1250, he achieved a spectacular victory against this formidable enemy at the Battle of Durbe, in the north of the country near the modern town of Siauliai, where he destroyed a whole army. He then found his eastern borders being threatened by the disintegration of the Kievan principality of Rus, and the consequent campaigns saw the expansion of his domain into the territories of the eastern Slavs.

An astute ruler, Mindaugas attempted to remove the ostensible reason for the continuing military threat from the Germans by conversion to Christianity in 1251. The manœuvre enabled his achievements to be consolidated, because the resulting papal recognition was followed by the establishment of a diocese in Lithuania, a development which permitted Mindaugas to be crowned by its founding bishop. This coronation took place on 6 July 1253. The sacral act conferred public recognition of his kingly rights by the sovereigns of catholic Europe, and also implied the investiture of the Lithuanian state with full sovereign recognition. It was an achievement of the utmost significance for the country's legal and international standing, both then and in our own time, and its anniversary is observed as a national holiday in modern Lithuania for this reason. Yet though his conversion and coronation implied a rapprochement between the king and his external enemies, many of his countrymen saw the religious difference which now lay between them and their king as a betrayal. The attachment to their ancient religion was strong enough for them to force his abdication in 1261, which allowed the pagan creed to remain a public faith in Lithuania longer than elsewhere in Europe. Its endurance had implications which have affected the country's character and culture ever since, in a way which is reflected in a comment made at the end of the nineteenth century, in an article in *Cassell's Encyclopaedia*, which observed that 'the names of the old gods are still familiar to all classes there', and noted 'a rich unwritten literature and abundance of songs, idyllic and lyrical poetry, inspired by tender sentiment and love of nature which derives from this source'.[8]

Grand Duke Gediminas

Mindaugas must be considered the founder of the Lithuanian state, though it was Grand Duke Gediminas (*c*. 1275–1341), the founder of a dynasty which ruled Lithuania and Poland until 1572, who placed Lithuania on the way to becoming a great power. He also established the city of Vilnius, which became his capital, in 1323, and began to pave the way for the great state which would emerge under his successors by arranging the marriages of his seven sons in a way which gave him control over Vitebsk and other western principalities of Russia. He encouraged merchants and artisans to settle in Lithuanian towns to develop trading links. The policy stimulated the development of a prosperous domestic economy, but the tensions which had affected the last years of his predecessor's reign continued to haunt him. The Lithuanian nobility's refusal to accept Christianity had led to Mindaugas's deposition, and their continued reluctance to do so brought constant military pressure from the Teutonic Knights. Gediminas considered conversion as a way of warding off their intrusion and corresponded with Pope John XXII on the matter. His letters protesting that his enemies had a greater interest in gaining land than in winning souls survive, and he remained a pagan, though he was tolerant even to the extent of employing Christian monks in his Chancery. As his conquests reached deeper into the Slavic lands, this disposition brought big improvements in the quality of urban life everywhere in his domains, as merchants, doctors, monks and nuns, and others from the Catholic countries came to settle in the cities under his policy of persuasion. To encourage them to make the maximum contribution to economic development he granted them the rights their class enjoyed in their native places. These free citizens contributed enormously to the Grand Duchy's prosperity, and the army and administration were progressively europeanized under the influence of this migrant class, whose activities led to extended contact with western Europe, and attracted broader diplomatic interest in the affairs of the Grand Duchy.[9]

Among Gediminas's successors, two brothers, Grand Duke Kestutis (1345–82) and Grand Duke Algirdas (1345–77), are the figures to whom European civilization recalls a debt for the resistance they offered to the Tartar armies. Algirdas's generalship protected the whole continent from their domination. They had already subdued much of Russia, and if the Lithuanian victory at the 'Battle of the Blue Waters' in 1363 had been less decisive, our civilization would have pursued a different course. The same battle added the territories of Kiev to those of Lithuania, a notable gain because these lands included the modern Ukraine, and more.

Vytautas Magnus and Jogaila

The Grand Duke Vytautas Magnus (who ruled 1392–1430), stands out as the most important ruler of medieval Lithuania. Though born the eldest son of a reigning grand duke, Kestutis, he found his own path to that position fraught with struggle and intrigue. It seems very likely that it was his cousin Jogaila, Algirdas's son and future king of Poland, who murdered Kestutis in 1382. Certainly he imprisoned Vytautas in the castle of Kreve immediately afterward, and took the grand ducal title himself. Vytautas, fearing for his life, then engineered an escape and fled to seek protection from the knights of the Teutonic Order. He was baptized in 1383 while staying with them, and later accepted their military help in his campaigns against the opportunist Jogaila. However he clearly nurtured ambitions far beyond being a pawn in the hands of his nation's great enemies. Eventually he broke free from them, having found an opportunity to reclaim the leadership of Lithuania on his own terms.

Vytautas's fortunes changed dramatically in 1385. In that year Jogaila became king of Poland under the treaty known as the Union of Kreve, by marrying Jadvyga, the ten-year-old queen of Poland, whose hand the Polish nobility had offered in order to draw Lithuania into an alliance. His acceptance of the offer linked the Polish crown with his grand ducal title. The resulting arrangement was to continue for some centuries, though it is important to notice that this union was legally invested in the *person* who held these offices, and did not affect Lithuania's *statehood* in any way. The Lithuanian nobles remained deeply mistrustful of Polish manipulation, and revolted against Jogaila under Vytautas's leadership. He soon won a decisive victory, and it was not long before Jogaila found it necessary to acknowledge his cousin's military strength by negotiating with him. The outcome of this diplomacy was reconciliation between the cousins, and Vytautas was acknowledged as the sole ruler in Lithuania. The agreement was one of convenience, but provided the basis of Lithuania's great medieval achievements, as Vytautas was now free to pay full attention to defending Lithuania against the Tartar threat. He pursued this objective vigorously, and the Grand Duchy's boundaries moved even further eastward in the process.

Early in the 1390s Vytautas Magnus arranged the marriage of his daughter Sophia to Grand Prince Vasili I of Moscow, acquiring Smolensk as part of a deal which greatly strengthened his campaigns in the eastern regions. The action against the Tartars continued successfully, adding greatly to his domain, until the enemy reversed a whole decade of defeat by gaining a spectacular victory at the Battle of

Vorksala in 1399. Vytautas was then pushed back into Lithuania itself, but was not easily dissuaded and fought relentlessly to recover the lost territories. It was a slow struggle. Nearly a decade passed before he had recovered what had been lost, and his relationships with Muscovy were soured on the way. This was the beginning of a tension which became a serious threat in later centuries, but was not then sufficient to prevent him turning away from the eastern front to settle some long neglected scores. In 1398 he had conceded the western province of Samogitia to the Teutonic Order in order to square up to the Tartars. Now in 1409, its people rebelled against their new rulers, and appealed for his support. He responded with a joint Lithuanian and Polish campaign, which led to a decisive victory at the Battle of Zalgiris, or Tannenberg, on 15 July 1410.[10] It is recalled as one of the great battles of European history, and led eventually to the Treaty of Melno, which defined the Lithuanian-Prussian border for the next five centuries.

Lithuania had reached the height of its territorial expansion and influence at this point in Vytautas Magnus's reign. However, though his rule in the Grand Duchy was wholly independent of the Polish crown, he had been granted only the governorship of Lithuania under his first agreement with Jogaila. As time passed, his military position became pre-eminent, and this arrangement seemed increasingly unsatisfactory. Eventually Jogaila, as ruler of Poland in his own right following Queen Jadvyga's death, fully acknowledged Vytautas's position and conceded the grand ducal title to him in the agreement known as the Act of Radom. The position was, however, granted only during Vytautas's lifetime. It was a limitation with which he could scarcely contain his impatience, and he moved deliberatively to make arrangements for his own coronation, knowing that this investiture would secure a more favourable implication for his dynastic succession. However, Jogaila, having gained information about what was planned, opposed his scheme and intervened crudely to prevent the planned ceremony from taking place, even stealing the crown which had been sent by the emperor for the occasion. The infuriated Vytautas made plans for a new ceremony, but his death intervened before the situation could be repaired. After this event it is apparent that something had happened in the balance between the two communities. From this time onward the influence of Polish culture and language was more apparent among the powerful noble families of the country, although they continued to show a marked independence of the political pressures on them to conform with Polish interests.

Casimir

This consistently independent national expression is exemplified by the events which followed the assassination of Grand Duke Sigismund Kestutaitis in 1440, in retaliation for his attempt to expand the Lithuanian nobility by admitting some more prosperous subjects to that class, although they had no hereditary titles. Sigismund's son Mykolas was the natural successor as grand duke, but the powerful Lithuanian magnates overlooked him, and nominated his cousin Casimir to the position. He was a mere thirteen years old, and younger brother to Wladyslaw III, the king. The Polish nobility agreed to his accession, but only as a *viceroy* of the Polish king. Not unnaturally, the Lithuanians repudiated a restriction which would have reduced the standing of the Grand Duchy to that of an appanage of the Polish crown. They therefore proceeded with Casimir's coronation as Grand Duke without further reference to Polish interests. The resulting dispute was acrimonious, and indeed embittered relationships for decades, though when Wladyslaw III died suddenly only two years later in 1442, the Poles accepted the Lithuanian coronation as a *fait accompli*, and even proposed Casimir as king. They probably assumed that the centrifugal tendencies implied by the earlier Lithuanian stand would be overtaken by this elevation to the throne, but Lithuania's nobility were acutely aware of potential threats to their interests. They insisted that the sovereignty and the territorial integrity of the Grand Duchy must be formally guaranteed, and only when this was agreed were they prepared to lend the constitutional support necessary for Casimir's election as king to be finally confirmed.

There were many other disputes between Lithuania and Poland at this time, not only about the implications of the dynastic alliance for the two countries, but over the control of the Ukrainian provinces. Despite this bickering Casimir's rule was essentially untroubled on the internal front. His external dealings, however, brought him into conflict with the growing power of Muscovy, which was now ruled by Ivan III (known to history as the 'Great'). Ivan was already strong enough to deal with the Tartars himself, but had started picking away at the Grand Duchy's eastern provinces, a process that would continue into the future. Casimir dealt with this provocation as it arose, but was secure enough to be able to turn his attention towards his western neighbours with whom he enjoyed better success in his dealings, using diplomacy and dynastic marriage with great effect to improve his position. In 1456 he married the Hapsburg Princess Elizabeth of Austria, daughter of the future Holy Roman Emperor, Ferdinand I. Later in his reign his eldest son Wladislaw was elected king of Bohemia (1471–1516) and afterward of

Hungary (1490–1516). After 1470 Casimir was the most influential ruler in central Europe, and his accomplishments marked the beginning of a dynastic dominance which continued until the sixteenth century. Lithuania's orientation toward Catholic Europe was now fully established. Within a century of her conversion bonds had been established which would endure, to ensure that her imagination was irrevocably linked with the tidal flows of western European civilization.

The two Sigismunds

In 1506 Casimir's son, Sigismund I (b. 1467–d. 1548), succeeded an elder brother as grand duke of Lithuania and king of Poland. In 1529 he gave Lithuania what was effectively its first constitution, by codifying the country's laws in what is known as the 'First Lithuanian Statute'. This new code outlined the rights and duties of the grand duke, and the privileges of the nobles. It also modernized the administrative laws of the country. It is notable that this fundamental constitutional document included no reference to the dynastic tie with Poland, and firmly excluded foreigners from holding any public office in Lithuania. Indeed its whole tenor implies that the relationship between Poland and Lithuania was legally based, not in a shared crown but rather in an *alliance*. As a constitutional statement it still has considerable interest because it established humanistic relationships and religious tolerance in a manner which was not achieved elsewhere until much later. The divisions of the Reformation were already eroding long-standing bonds in European society, though its turbulent spirit had also stimulated interest in science and manufacturing. Sigismund's tolerance allowed freedom of worship and entrepreneurial advance, and he made no attempt to prevent Protestants from settling in Lithuania; there was therefore little conflict about its principles. In the end Protestantism had little success there, though the first printed book in Lithuanian was a Lutheran catechism written by Martynas Mazvydas, a clergyman living in Prussia, which Sigismund I had incorporated into his realm only a few years earlier.

In 1530 the elder Sigismund (sometimes known as Sigismund the Old) arranged the coronation of his ten-year-old son, Sigismund Augustus (b. 1520–d. 1572), as grand duke of Lithuania and king of Poland, to hold the titles conjointly with himself. Known as Grand Duke Sigismund II (and the last ruler of Lithuania to be born in Gediminas's palace in Vilnius), the younger man took control of Lithuania in 1544, though he did not rule in Poland until his father's death. He was very active in bringing the ideas of the Renaissance into the country, and encouraged the new fashions in architecture to which he gave notable expression in the construction of the Lower Castle in the centre of Vilnius. Although a prolonged invasion of Livonia by Ivan IV (the 'Terrible') resulted in significant setbacks to the domestic prosperity of Lithuania in the early years of his reign, his policies of support for manufacture and trade were eventually enormously successful, and yielded manifest prosperity throughout his dominions. He married Barbora Radvilaite, the daughter of a powerful Lithuanian family, a year before his father's death. Like his first wife, she died without giving him an heir, and in 1553 he married Catherine of Hapsburg. Again the marriage was without issue, and his later years were overshadowed by the dilemma of the succession. It was clear that the dynasty founded by Jogaila was coming to an end. Toward the close of his reign, in 1566, Sigismund II ratified the second Lithuanian Statute, an enlightened measure which clearly emphasized Lithuania's distinct identity by defining the Seimas as the nation's supreme legislative body and initiating a major reform of the legal system. The judicial system thus instituted is regarded as having been the most advanced in the central European area, its courts being mandated to deal distinctively but fairly with the often widely differing interests of the different social classes.[11]

Union with Poland

After clarifying Lithuania's legal position in this way Sigismund II and his advisers moved to prepare new constitutional arrangements for the kingdom as a whole. These issues were confirmed in 1569 by the agreement known as the Union of Lublin, a statute which initiated the 'Commonwealth' of the Grand Duchy of Lithuania and the Kingdom of Poland, in a union which was called a Republic. The measure reflected the realization that the dynastic succession had come to an end, and involved a closer political union than previously. Yet while as much as a third of the former territory of the Grand Duchy was transferred to Poland, the rearrangement preserved Lithuania's independent identity. Significantly, the Grand Duchy's army, Treasury and distinctive legal system continued to exist separately. Over time, however, the new arrangements had the effect of accelerating the trend of cultural assimilation ('polonization') which had already begun – to the degree that Lithuanians now regard the treaty as a national tragedy, not least because it failed in the long term to stem the political and military decline of the united kingdom.

In 1572, only three years after the Union of Lublin, Sigismund II died.

His selected successor, as king and grand duke, was Henry of Valois, the younger brother of the French king, who stayed only two years before returning to rule France. The next elected king was the Hungarian Stefan Batory, whose reign saw the founding of Vilnius University by the Jesuits in 1579. It was the first university in the Baltic region, and its establishment brought the culture of the Counter-Reformation to Lithuania, though without the turmoil which accompanied its progress elsewhere. The urgent issue of his reign was to ward off the developing Russian determination to dominate the Baltic Sea, and he worked with considerable success to contain the expansionist policies of Ivan the Terrible. He was followed as king by the Swedish monarch Sigismund III (Vasa), who sought the position to give his own country an advantage in this context. He too was successful in restraining the Russian bear, and the Lithuanian and Polish armies even occupied Moscow briefly under his command. However his gains were short-lived because the dynamic policy followed by the Romanov dynasty, which had arrived on the Russian throne in 1613, was already changing the regional balance of power. Unfortunately, as Russian power increased, so did her resentment of Lithuania's opposition. The tension was destined to accumulate, and was eventually catastrophic for Lithuania.

The decline of the united kingdom

This changing power balance was a portent of other troubles. The Swedish entanglement in Lithuanian and Polish affairs involved both states in the early dislocations of the Thirty Years War, and a relentless Russian campaign ended in Cossack troops occupying and sacking Vilnius in 1655. They were soon ejected, but the campaign was so ferocious that it persuaded the Ukrainians, whose link with Lithuania had been loosened as a result of earlier Russian activity, to renew the political union with Lithuania. It was a development which intensified Russian fury and a renewed attack followed. It was repulsed, but with difficulty, and the episode was followed by famine and an outbreak of plague. These combined misfortunes resulted in a million deaths, and the sequence of military and natural disaster left the Lithuanian state at an extremely low ebb. Worse, the difficulties were destined to accumulate because the realpolitik of the 'Commonwealth' did not allow the country to relinquish involvements which were progressively reducing its capacity to respond effectively to the growing eastern frontier problem. When Turkish armies rampaged across central Europe in 1683, the Polish King John Sobieski organized their expulsion. He was widely praised, but the kingdom was already manifesting fatal weaknesses, had lost more resources, and was not surrounded by friends after his death.

These complex circumstances left the cultured classes of Lithuania perpetually engaged with concerns broader than those of their own Grand Duchy. At the same time many of them were increasingly alienated from the peasant people by intermarriage with Polish families of comparable status. It was a process which progressively affected family interest and culture on a broad scale, and one effect was the tendency increasingly to use the Polish language rather than Lithuanian. In parallel with these social shifts, the politics of the elective kingship of the Commonwealth were weakening the very foundation of the state. The fact that the lower nobility possessed majority voting rights had been manipulated to the point where higher noble titles had been abolished, and the king's role reduced. Unfortunately the state was surrounded by autocratic powers who were on the one hand fearful of the effect that this democratic approach to government could have on their own educated classes, and prepared on the other to offer bribes to subvert what they did not like. The state was thus dangerously open to manipulation from outside, and this malign influence extended even to the matter of the royal election. Successive rulers were therefore heavily influenced by their covert connections with Sweden, Russia or Prussia, and these perverse developments were particularly disadvantageous to Lithuania, whose historic strength was progressively eroded by her continuing attachment to an arrangement which had originally served the needs of a now defunct dynasty. While the modern reader can observe the historical rationale of the union of Lithuania's crown with that of Poland, it is very hard to see that it brought any real benefits to either country at this stage of their history.

Constitutional change and reaction

The foreign powers were determined to profit from the difficulties of a state whose constitution had evolved to the point where its king was only the lifetime president of an Assembly whose members could veto his every decision. Despite having a crowned head, the state was a republic, in name and in fact. However admirable these arrangements by the standards of a later time, this quality of democracy prevented effective executive action in the contemporary political context in which the country was surrounded by well-armed and hostile autocracies. In 1764 Stanislaus II determined to end the now pernicious practice of *liberum veto* (free voting), with its ultimate nightmare possibility that a single disgruntled nobleman might effectively block even a widely approved measure. To his great misfortune this modest reform came to the attention of, and enraged, the Russian Empress Catherine. The supreme autocrat of the age, and perhaps the most unscrupulous of her ilk, she wanted to keep the Republic weak, lest it should encourage political ambitions in her own country. Her attitude was fully shared by the Prussian king and they actively colluded to destabilize Stanislaus's government. When this had been done the Prussian ruler first announced that Stanislaus's kingdom was no longer viable, and then cut a cynical deal with Austria and Russia to invade territories which all three powers had long since envied, and to share them out. This 'first partition', completed in 1772, reduced the kingdom to a third of its former area, and regions that Lithuania had ruled for centuries were lost to the Grand Duchy. The province of Courland passed to Prussia, while Latgale, Polotsk, Vitebsk and most of Minsk now came under Russia's domination.

Continued pressure and assimilation

Despite these savage losses, the process of dismantling the kingdom was not yet ended. When the process was recommenced some twenty-one years after that first division, its momentum reflected the reaction of the great autocratic powers to the implications of the eighteenth-century enlightenment on political life. Interest in democracy was lively at this time in all the cities of Lithuania and Poland and had royal approval. The fashion was fuelled by reports from the fledgeling United States of America. It became something of a passion and resulted in the adoption of a modern constitution, the first of its kind in any European state, in May 1791. Its provisions made the government answerable to Parliament, and gave the urban bourgeoisie the right to vote; this was a significant achievement which was consciously emulated by the National Assembly of revolutionary France two years later. It is perhaps not surprising that the autocrats in Russia and Prussia again reacted negatively and sent armies in 1793 to support opponents of the new constitution. The ageing Empress Catherine cynically claimed that her own government was threatened, and arranged a treaty with Prussia which first curtailed the constitution and then reduced the Republic's remaining territories by half.

In this renewed assault Russia took the city of Minsk, and all of what is now Belarus away from Lithuania. However the humiliation of these setbacks, and general anger at being robbed of the new constitutional freedoms, provoked a popular uprising. A revolutionary fervour swept the streets of both Vilnius and Warsaw, and would have been successful, had the Russians and the Prussians not responded with a crushing campaign which continued until 1794, and ended only when Catherine called a conference to dismantle what survived of the Republic. The outcome was a decision to allow Russia to grab all the Lithuanian lands east of the River Nemunas, while Prussia and Austria divided the rest of the kingdom between them. The Hapsburgs took large tracts of southern Poland, including Krakow, while Prussia seized central Poland and the regions adjacent to East Prussia which included the ethnic Lithuanian lands to the south and west of the River Nemunas. Thus most of Lithuania was incorporated by Russia, while the remainder passed into Prussian hands. Finally, the last ruler of the Commonwealth, Stanislaus Augustus Poniatowski, was forced to abdicate in November 1795 under the Treaty of Partition which was signed in St Petersburg in January 1797. Lithuania and Poland then disappeared from the political map for more than a century.

Resistance to the Russian occupation

Thus Lithuania entered the nineteenth century as part of the Russian empire. The oppressive rule now imposed provoked a series of popular risings, of which there were five in Tsarist times. One of these, in 1830–1, was followed by the closure of Vilnius University, while another in 1863 was followed by even more severe repression. Throughout this era, policing was intense, and russifying policies were enforced strictly, including even the prohibition of all publications which did not use the Cyrillic alphabet. Such intellectual restrictions affected the middle classes deeply, but the common people were even more harshly oppressed by the extension of serfdom. This continued until 1861, when the regime initiated a degree of liberalization which included its abolition. The essentially autocratic style of government continued uninterrupted, but these changes reflected the development of the Russian economy in the later nineteenth century, which had enabled a growth of cultural expression as the middle classes in the cities of the empire increased in numbers. This new atmosphere, and a sudden inter-est by scholars from other parts of Europe and from America, encouraged a heightened awareness of the linguistic distinctiveness of the Lithuanian language. A new cultural self-consciousness appeared which fused itself with the widespread resentment of Russian rule to create the conditions in which national movements led by Vincas Kudirka and

Jonas Basanavičius emerged. Their appeal was limited at first, but the cultural sensitivities they nurtured were spurred by the ideas of liberal democracy which had lingered and were again becoming popular among the educated classes. A vigorous national consciousness was awakening, and the trends were greatly strengthened by the heroic work of the *knyg-nesai*, or 'book-carriers', who regularly risked exile in Siberia by smuggling books and newspapers printed in Lithuanian. These had been printed in the German-ruled, but Lithuanian-speaking, region of Lithuania Minor around the East Prussian university city of Königsberg. These activities contributed to a linguistic renaissance, and a determined drive to widen the use of the nation's language among the educated urban classes which had earlier assimilated to Polish influences.

The ban on the Lithuanian press was finally lifted only in 1904, and the relative relaxation of the Tsarist regime in the following decade created conditions which gave further impetus to the patriotic revival and the accompanying movement to repossess and standardize the ancient language of Lithuania, and to record a cultural inheritance which had earlier been perceived as backward and rural. It is interesting to note that those who were most active in this process of reclamation were the very intelligentsia whose education had been designed to alienate them from this background. Their commitment to the struggle for national identity was made more intense by a personal effort to repossess the language lost by an earlier generation which had regarded it as having little social status or economic worth. It was to this generation that Vytautas Landsbergis's grandparents belonged.

After the First World War: renewed independence

The German army occupied Lithuania in 1915, and in September 1917 its military administration permitted a conference to be held in Vilnius in which the historic resolution was made to restore the Lithuanian state. A National Council chaired by Antanas Smetona was established and began to prepare for independence. On 16 February 1918 the Declaration of the Nation's Independence was proclaimed by the members of Lithuania's National Council in its capital city, Vilnius. Its text was published on the front page of *Lietuvos Aidas*, the country's most prominent daily newspaper. It announced the restoration of Lithuania's statehood as based on the right to national self-determination, and proclaimed its fulfilment in the democratic rule of a constitutionally elected government. Yet despite this hopeful beginning, these goals were not fully realized without a war of independence in which the principal opponent was the Bolshevik provisional government of Russia, which took its orders from Lenin. The struggle at this stage was complicated by the presence of undisbanded units of both the German and Tsarist armies, and the Polish claim to Vilnius and its surrounding region. A series of Lithuanian victories however created a situation in which Lenin was prepared to relinquish the Russian claim, and then proceeded to agree the Moscow Treaty on 12 July 1920, under which the independence of Lithuania 'for all future ages' was guaranteed. This announcement brought widespread international recognition of the country, but sadly it did not resolve the general problems of the region. In October of the same year, Poland precipitately occupied Vilnius, disguising this crude territorial aggression by suggesting the restoration of the former union of the two countries. This action seriously complicated the relationship of the two countries until the Second World War.

The first Lithuanian Republic

Despite these troubles, the first Seimas (Parliament) of the new Republic began its work on 15 May 1920. The nation's constitution, finally agreed on 1 August 1922, named Kaunas as the temporary capital of Lithuania because of the recent Polish occupation of Vilnius. The government was faced with critical tasks in building an economy and a new educational system. For the first time Lithuanian became the language of administration and the normal language of schooling. A national press emerged, and literature, music, theatre and other arts flourished. The Vytautas Magnus University was founded in Kaunas. However this state-building process was increasingly interrupted by the activities of extremists both of the left and of the right. The outcome was a military coup which took place on 17 December 1926, and Antanas Smetona, leader of the Tautininku (National) party, became president of the Republic. While the resulting government was undoubtedly authoritarian it was not totalitarian, although the black propaganda of the Soviet period would have it otherwise. The view taken of it must now be considered, not with reference to that distorted vision, but to the extreme pressures on the infant democracy which were the result of the inexorable development of Stalinism in Russia, the uneasy relationship with Poland and the rise of Nazism. It has been accused of being extremely right-wing, but it is important to recall how it put a number of Nazi extremists from the Klaipėda region on trial in 1935, in the first case of its kind in Europe. The outcome was the banning of fascist organizations everywhere in Lithuania. There were complex issues to resolve internally, and the government also faced the general deterioration of international trade and the collapse of confidence in currencies. Standing as it did 'between the devil and the deep' it was soon overwhelmed by a disaster not of its own making. Yet when the course of those brief years of independence is compared with the country's bitter experience under the three uninvited foreign occupations which followed, those years of independent government are justifiably felt to have been something of a golden age. It is also useful to remember that the diplomatic corps appointed at that time continued to serve the interests of its homeland throughout all the periods of occupation. This was possible only because neither the British nor the United States governments had acknowledged the incorporation of Lithuania and the other Baltic States into the USSR. That historic continuity of diplomatic representation, which many deemed to be a token defiance of Stalin's incorporation of the Baltic states, was destined to fade away as its representatives grew older, but eventually became an asset of huge value. It was an important legitimizing factor when the time finally came for the restoration of Lithuania's independence.

The Molotov–Ribbentrop Pact, and the first Soviet occupation

On 23 August 1939 the Soviet Union made the notorious agreement with Nazi Germany known as the Molotov–Ribbentrop Pact. Under its terms Lithuania was assigned to the German interest. However, on 28 September, just after the war began, Lithuania was passed back to the Soviet interest in an equally arbitrary fashion. On 10 October, secure in their knowledge of this secret arrangement, the Soviet authorities forced Lithuania to 'accommodate' some 20,000 military personnel, literally overnight. It was an abrogation of the rights and privileges of an independent nation, but this bullying manœuvre was accompanied by the paradoxical news that Vilnius and its region, taken over only days previously by the Red Army, was to be returned to Lithuania. Other and less welcome arbitrary decisions followed. On 14 June 1940 Moscow demanded the formation of a new government, sending a further 100,000 Soviet troops into the country to reinforce the order. The country was now under alien occupation, and a 'People's Seimas' led by the journalist Justas Paleckis, a communist collaborator with the occupying power, was convened. Its first resolution, passed on 21 July, declared Lithuania a 'Soviet Socialist Republic'. It was then announced that the country had applied for membership of the Soviet Union. Needless to say this application was granted and the reply came instantly, with Stalin's congratulations of course. The collaborationist assembly which had assisted these disgraceful arrangements then redesignated itself as the 'Supreme Council of the Lithuanian Soviet Republic'. As soon as these predictable formalities had been implemented, the inevitable totalitarian structures were installed. The sovietization of the culture and the economy began in earnest, and the apparatus of intimidation was unfolded. It involved the immediate imprisonment of 19,600 people, and the deportation of a further 34,260 to Siberia, without warning, and also without trial.

The German invasion and Nazi occupation

Against the brutal background of this summary incorporation, it is not surprising that the Lithuanian reaction to the outbreak of war between the Soviet Union and Nazi Germany on 22 June 1941 was an immediate uprising against Soviet occupation. Radio Kaunas broadcast a new Declaration of Independence at 3.00 p.m. on the same day, and a Provisional Government was then formed under Lithuania's own national constitution. However it was able to exercise authority only until 5 August, when it was summarily displaced by the incoming Nazis, who arbitrarily imposed a 'General District' administration on the country without delay. Under this regime the native Lithuanian population was heavily repressed. The first manifestation of the harshness of the new regime was the seizure of a huge number of citizens for forced labour within days of the invasion. Despite the dire circumstances a resistance movement sprang into being, which had some success in disrupting the recruitment of young men into the army, most notably in preventing the occupiers' plan to establish a Lithuanian corps of the SS. Nevertheless, over 160,000 Lithuanian Jews and 45,000 Lithuanians were massacred by the Nazi occupation. The rich Jewish life of Vilnius and Kaunas, both long renowned as important centres of Jewish scholarship, was abruptly and unforgivably terminated as a result of this raw barbarism.

The second Soviet occupation

The return of the Soviet order in 1944 was followed immediately by new programmes of repression. A mass deportation of Lithuanian citizens was planned by Stalin in revenge on the nation for its Declaration of Independence in 1941, which he called 'collaboration with the Nazis'. Naturally the Communist party took charge of the programme, but as its Lithuanian membership was tiny its headquarters was filled up with staff from other parts of the Soviet Union. These *apparatchiks* eventually dispatched 442,060 men, women and children, packed into cattle trucks, to the *gulags* in eleven campaigns of mass exile. The extent of this genocidal attack on the nation remained hidden until independence was achieved, but the number of the victims is now established. Even the official Soviet statistics acknowledged that 120,000 people were deported between 1945 and 1953, but the actual number was far greater. It is a sobering thought that between 1940 and 1959, Lithuania lost nearly 33 per cent of her pre-war population of 3,081,239 (the figure is adjusted to include the population of the 'then occupied' territories of Vilnius and Klaipėda). Over a million people (1,003,185), were the victims of a series of deadly attacks on the nation's dignity. The Nazi occupiers killed some 210,000 people in random executions and the holocaust, but the number victimized under the Soviet occupation was much higher. Its eventual total was 592,660. A high proportion of those who were exiled under Stalin's savage policies did not live to return home to Lithuania. The mortality of the Soviet tyranny, including deaths in exile, was 473,185 persons, but we must also remember the 320,000 people who fled at the time of the invasions. Some of these were foreigners returning home, but most were refugees who felt compelled to move westward when the second Soviet occupation began.[12]

While these atrocities were being perpetrated there was little recourse for the victims other than to be mild before their oppressors, but the resentment at the renewed occupation and the enforced collectivization of land which followed was natural and deep. These feelings gave birth to the resistance movement, Lietuvos Laisves Kovos Sąjūdis, which recruited thousands of members, and sustained an active partisan war in Lithuania which continued until 1953. Despite vicious reprisals against its members and against whole communities if they were suspected of being in sympathy with its work, the movement did not finally fade away until 1965. Authoritative writers estimate that 1 per cent of the native population was active in guerrilla activity at the peak of the campaign, and that around 50,000 of the 100,000 who became involved in partisan activities were killed in action. Their activities were significant for the first nine years of the movement. After that the programmes of rural collectivization had so transformed life in the countryside that the conditions for guerrilla activity no longer existed and the movement, but not its spirit, faded away.

The passions that had driven the guerrilla movement still burned and by the later 1960s new types of dissident movement had begun to form. They have been classified in three groups: those concerned with the rights of the Catholic Church and other believers; those advocating national rights and self-determination; and those working for the advancement of human rights or monitoring their violation by the regime.[13] It is important to note that these Lithuanian underground movements attracted a balanced representation of intellectuals, workers and peasants. This even-handed appeal was again reflected in the composition of Sąjūdis when it finally emerged as a broadly based social movement. The dissidents also received valuable moral support from the Lithuanian radio broadcasts transmitted from the West, which often gave them valuable information and fresh ideas, and eventually publicized their activities when the time was right.[14] Recent comparison of the Lithuanian dissident movements with similar developments in other countries shows that activity in occupied Lithuania was significantly more intense than in other regions of the Soviet Union. While her population was a mere 1.3 per cent of that of the Soviet Union, approximately 10 per cent of all the protests and demonstrations that took place between 1965 and 1978 in all that vast territory took place in Lithuania. The country also had the greatest number of underground periodicals, of which the most famous was the *Chronicle of the Lithuanian Catholic Church* which the KGB failed to suppress throughout the eighteen years of its publication before the declaration of independence in 1990.

The emergence of Sąjūdis: the call for independence

Lithuanian resistance to the Soviet system was consistent. Its development can be outlined in three phases: first, the national revolt in 1941; next, the partisan war between 1944 and 1953; and lastly, the underground dissident activity between 1953 and 1987. There was a continuous and active rejection of the Soviet regime throughout the occupation. Its persistent character makes it plain that the successive waves of occupation, russification and terror failed to destroy the nation's longing for independence and a democratic government, and shows that there were dedicated Lithuanians who were busily exploring every opportunity for resistance with the goal of restoring the nation's independence even in the worst times. The campaign continued for fifty years, throughout the whole period of occupation, and the experience of this long-enduring, patient and principled resistance itself gave the Lithuanian people a certain wisdom in its dealings with the Soviet system. When they needed help in exploiting the weaknesses of the regime which oppressed them, they would often look into their own history. They learned there that the communist ideology was quite alien to Lithuania's Christian and European inheritance, and found that it was never lacking in inspiration for their current struggle against the Soviet system. By these means occupied Lithuania found subtle ways of emphasizing her western longing and democratic identity, and eventually in the late 1980s, she found peaceful and parliamentary methods of liberating herself.

Gorbachev's reforms were first proposed in 1987. They were a manifesto to save communism rather than a proposal to create an open society, but they offered a recognizable hope for an improvement in the conditions of public life and received a broad welcome on those terms. The Lithuanian national liberation movement Sąjūdis, founded in 1988 under the leadership of prominent intellectuals, recognized this potential and offered itself as an exploratory response to those opportunities. It then worked diligently to expand the stated political and social objectives of *glasnost*, and its first conference called for the restitution of democratic and national rights. The movement declared, from its inception, that it would use 'all constitutional means' to restore Lithuania's sovereignty 'through peaceful and non-violent means'. The need to end the humiliating limitations which had been imposed on public life since the Soviet invasion was discussed, and an unambiguous call for the restoration of an independent Lithuania was eventually made in public. The large-scale demonstrations of support which followed led to an increasingly tense relationship with the Kremlin, and it was in this atmosphere that Sąjūdis eventually determined to contest elections to the Supreme Soviet of the Soviet Union in 1989. It was a brave and a shrewd move. The movement's candidates were marvellously successful in the resulting contest and eventually won 36 of the 41 seats available for Lithuania. Subsequently Lithuania's representatives in Moscow were able to exercise considerable influence in the Lithuanian Supreme Council. In due course they tabled constitutional amendments there which were designed to overturn the decision taken in 1940 to make the country a Soviet Republic, by declaring the supremacy of Lithuanian laws over Soviet legislation. Meanwhile, Sąjūdis's representatives at the Supreme Soviet demanded, in sessions held within the precinct of the Kremlin itself, that the fundamental illegality of the Molotov–Ribbentrop Pact must now be acknowledged before the whole world. They also asserted that the incorporation of the Baltic states into the USSR, an outcome of that dark agreement, should also be acknowledged to have been a flagrant breach of the conventions of international law.

When Sąjūdis proposed the separation of the Lithuanian Communist party from Moscow, an Extraordinary Congress of the Communist party of Lithuania was called. When it met, the vote for independence was overwhelming. This development effectively split the party into the 'Lithuanian Independent Communist Party' and a smaller pro-Kremlin group. This separation of the majority of the Lithuanian communists from Moscow, with their consequent affirmation of the supremacy of Lithuanian laws, was a huge achievement which made it clear that Sąjūdis had succeeded in removing the last major internal barrier to the restoration of national independence. The final outcome of its campaign was then simply a matter of time. In 1990 the movement contested the first general election fought under democratic rules for more than half a century. As a result of its huge success in that election Professor Vytautas Landsbergis was elected to become the chairman of the Supreme Council of the Lithuanian Soviet Republic. That body then moved swiftly under his energetic leadership to take a series of decisions to end the indignities under which the nation had laboured since the time the Soviet system had first marched into Lithuania. The country's standing as a Soviet republic was repudiated on 11 March 1990, and the sovereignty of the Republic of Lithuania was restored by reinstating the nation's pre-war constitution in assertion of the fact that its legality had never been surrendered. The Supreme Council then agreed, for practical reasons, to carry on with its business under a temporary constitution, in order to allow time for a new independence constitution suited to modern conditions to be drafted. When this was completed in 1992, the ancient and honourable title of Seimas – the Parliament of Lithuania – was revived, with much joy and satisfaction.

It is significant that the Act which accomplished this historic restoration of Lithuanian independence incorporated the essence of the two constitutional acts which had restored the Lithuanian state and the nation's international standing on the occasion when the nation's independence had previously been reasserted, earlier in the century. These were the Declaration of Independence of 16 February 1918, and the Parliament Act of 15 May 1920, which declared Lithuania's adherence to democracy and 'to the universally recognized principles of international law'. To these solemn foundation statements the 1990 Act added 'the principle of inviolability of borders, as formulated in the Final Act of the Conference on Security and Co-operation in Europe in Helsinki in 1975', and gave a formal guarantee that 'human, civil and ethnic community rights' were essential to its understanding of the future of civil society in Lithuania.[15] Despite the nobility of these declarations, and the long struggle which had brought Lithuania's people to this proud moment, the response of the Soviet authorities was to make concerted attempts to deny, and then to undermine, what had been done. First, they attempted to organize civil tension inside the country, then they mounted an extensive international campaign of vilification outside its borders. When the outcome of these subversions proved unsatisfactory, they imposed a severe (though finally unsuccessful) economic blockade. Finally they unleashed the bloody events of 12–13 January 1991. It was a matter of pride for the people of Lithuania to realize their sacrifices had not been in vain, and that the reaction to this atrocity was a clear watershed in international attitudes to what had been happening in their homeland and the other Baltic countries. It can now be seen that the defeat of the attempted *coup d'état* which overwhelmed the Kremlin itself in August 1991, when the hardest of the communists desperately attempted to regain control just as it slipped beyond their grasp, was another consequence of the reaction to that outrage.

These events finally led to a cascade of international recognition for Lithuania's regained independence, and the formal ending of the Soviet regime. As a result of these changes, Lithuania became a member of the United Nations in 1991, and a member of the Conference for Security and Co-operation in Europe in the same year. In 1993 the Russian army finally left Lithuania, a whole year before its withdrawal from either Poland or East Germany. The country is now a member of the Council of Europe and of the North Atlantic Co-operation Council, and a candidate for membership of NATO. She is also an associate member of the European Union, and it is anticipated that full membership will be the outcome of the process of application that has now begun. These developments signal the full return of Lithuania to the western family of nations.

Darius Furmonavicius (MA in International Relations, University of Nottingham) is completing his doctorate as a member of the Baltic Research Unit, Department of European Studies, University of Bradford.

Notes

[1] E. J. Harrison (then British vice-consul in Kaunas and Vilnius), *Lithuania's Fight for Freedom* (London, Federation of Lithuanian Societies in Great Britain, 1944), p. 3.

[2] Vytautas Landsbergis's speech, delivered at the International Conference 'Euro-Atlantic Integration as a Key Aspect of Stability', held in Vilnius, Lithuania, 3–4 September 1998.

[3] Marija Gimbutas, *The Balts* (London: Thames and Hudson, 1963), p. 43.

[4] George Borrow, *Wild Wales: Its People, Language and Scenery* (first publ. 1862; republ. Oxford: Oxford University Press, 1946), chap. xix, p. 171.

[5] The *Annales Quedlingburgenses* were the chronicle of the Benedictine abbey

founded in 963 by the Emperor Otto I at Quedlinburg, a small town in Thuringia, in the northern foothills of the Harz mountains near Magdeburg, which was a favourite residence of the Saxon emperors. The significance of this account in Lithuania's preparation for the nation's millennium (to be celebrated in 2009), is discussed in *Lithuania at the Turn of the Centuries* (Vilnius: Algimantas, 2000), p. 21.

[6]   See end note 5 to the main text.

[7]   John Hiden and Patrick Salmon, *The Baltic Nations and Europe* (London: Longman, 1994), p. 12.

[8]   See entry on Lithuanians, *Cassell's Encyclopaedia of General Information*, vol. 6 (London: Cassell, *c.*1900), p. 217.

[9]   S. C. Rowell has observed: 'We should do well to remember that when Lithuania emerges as a regular player in the affairs of Christendom in the 1320s, her ruler employs the latest (Franco-German) political clichés, seeks the latest (German) technology, and is taken seriously as a useful piece in the international great game between Pope and Emperor, Teuton and Slav, Catholic and Orthodox' (*Lithuania Ascending: A Pagan Empire within East-Central Europe, 1295-1345* (Cambridge University Press, 1994), p. 304).

[10]   It is also sometimes known as the Battle of Grünwald. The battle took place between the villages of Tannenberg and Grünwald. As the Lithuanian and Polish armies encroached on the stronghold of Marienberg, the knights moved forward in pre-emptive action. A complex engagement followed, the allied armies fighting around the two villages separately for tactical reasons. This explains the dual nomenclature.

[11]   Edvardas Gudavicius, *Lietuvos Istorija* (Vilnius: Lietuvos Rasytoju Sajungos Leidykla, 1999).

[12]   See Adolfas Damusis, *Lithuania against Soviet and Nazi Aggression* (Chicago: American Foundation for Lithuanian Research, 1998), pp. 266–83.

[13]   V. Stanley Vardys and Judith Sedaitis, *Lithuania: The Rebel Nation* (Oxford: Westview Press, 1997), pp. 84–5.

[14]   It is proper to recall the important contribution of the BBC, Radio Free Europe and Radio Liberty (both the latter were based in Munich and financed by the United States Congress), and the Voice of America which also broadcast in Lithuanian. The partisans had hoped for direct military aid, but this was as far as the United States would go. For many years these broadcasts were the only counterpoint to the Soviet censorship and monopoly of information.

[15]   Quotations from the Act for the Re-establishment of the State of Lithuania (cited by Vytautas Landsbergis in *Laisves Byla* (Vilnius: Lietuvos Aidas, 1991), p. 18).

Index

INDEX